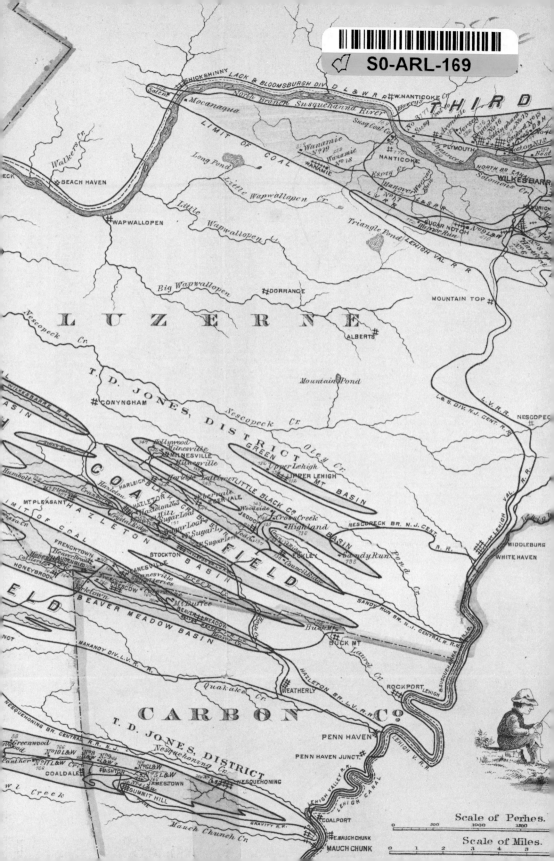

The Anthracite Aristocracy

The Anthracite Aristocracy

Leadership and Social Change in the
Hard Coal Regions of Northeastern
Pennsylvania, 1800–1930

Edward J. Davies II

Northern Illinois University Press
DeKalb, Illinois · 1985

Library of Congress Cataloging in Publication Data
Davies, Edward J., 1947–
    The anthracite aristocracy.
    Bibliography: p.
    Includes index.
    1. Elite (Social sciences)—Pennsylvania—Wilkes-Barre
—History—19th century.   2. Elite (Social sciences)—
Pennsylvania—Pottsville—History—19th century.
3. Coal mines and mining—Pennsylvania—Wilkes-Barre
Region—History.   4. Coal mines and mining—Pennsylvania
—Pottsville Region—History.   5. Elite (Social sciences)
—Pennsylvania—Wilkes-Barre—History—20th century.
6. Elite (Social sciences)—Pennsylvania—Pottsville—
History—20th century.   I. Title.
HN90.E4D38   1985   305.5'2'0974833   85-2947
ISBN 0-87580-107-2

For My Mother and Father
and
For Marilyn

Contents

Tables

Illustrations and Maps

Acknowledgments

URING THE RESEARCH and writing of this book, I have incurred numerous debts to persons who willingly gave me their assistance. As an undergraduate, I first encountered Harold E. Cox, professor of history, Wilkes College, who stimulated my interest in history and continued to be of great help in the preparation of this book. Without his prodding and support, I would never have reached this point in my career. Fellow graduate student Burton W. Folsom and I spent years discussing our related research topics. His humor, as well as his critical abilities, helped countless times early in the life of this project. Samuel P. Hays, of the University of Pittsburgh, gave me the skills and direction that made this book possible. His perception of history and the rigorous analytical training his students go through have greatly rewarded all who have worked with him. I am no exception. Robert Doherty and Julius Rubin, also of the University of Pittsburgh, and John Ingham of the University of Toronto, took time from their busy schedules to read through this book in early stages and offered valuable criticism of the work. H. Benjamin Powell, professor of history at Bloomsburg State College, Pennsylvania, also read through the manuscript some years ago and spent hours discussing my ideas and research with me. His vast research experience with the Wyoming Valley and the southern anthracite region were of enormous help to me. Paul Kleppner went through the manuscript at virtually every stage before the editorial process. His faith in the work kept me going through some difficult moments.

In the later stages of the manuscript, Edward G. Hartmann, professor emeritus of Suffolk University, Boston, provided invaluable assistance. A native of the Wyoming Valley and a talented researcher on its ethnic groups, Professor Hartmann generously offered me his time and aid in reviewing the manuscript. I would like to thank him for his suggestions, which have greatly improved the book.

Outside the academic community, I owe my greatest debt to the late Ralph

Hazeltine, past curator of the Wyoming Historical and Geological Society. Mr. Hazeltine, himself a skilled observer of the Wyoming Valley, proved a constant source of inspiration on the project, as well as a font of knowledge of the Valley's history. His passing greatly saddened me, and I dearly regret that he is not here to see the completion of a book to which he contributed so much. Margaret Craft, research librarian at the Wyoming Valley Historical and Geological Society, spent considerable time helping me locate sources, accommodating my outrageous photocopying requests and providing space for me to work. I would like to thank her for her patience and help. Carol Leavesly, librarian of the *Wilkes-Barre Times-Leader*, also provided space and time for me to read through microfilm of the city's newspapers. Finally, William L. Conyngham, a descendant of the Valley's oldest and most prestigious family and a prominent business and community leader in Wilkes-Barre, found time in the midst of an extraordinarily busy schedule to read through the first half of the manuscript and offer me his comments and observations. I sincerely appreciated his effort.

I would like to thank the editors of the *Journal of Social History* for permission to reprint substantial portions of an article which appeared in the *Journal* ("Regional Networks and Social Change: The Evolution of Urban Leadership in the Northern Anthracite Coal Region, 1840–1880," *Journal of Social History* [1982]: 47–73). I would also like to thank the *Public Historian* and its editor as well as the *Journal of Urban History*, its editor; and Sage Publications for permission to reprint material which appeared in these journals.

Judith W. Rock typed the entire book not once but several times. Her tolerance of my continued changes and revisions was almost saintly. Without Mrs. Rock's skills and patience, the book would never have been finished.

Marilyn, my wife, contributed her editorial skills as well as emotional support throughout the long years of research. While pursuing her own career in business, she always found time to read through draft after draft, as well as put up with every changing temper. I am not sure how she coped, but without Marilyn's presence, I know I could not have persevered to the end.

Last, I would like to express my gratitude and appreciation to my parents, who have been a constant source of support in both my academic and personal life.

Salt Lake City
September 1984

The Anthracite Aristocracy

CHAPTER I

A Comparative Analysis of Urban Leadership

RBAN LEADERS in nineteenth- and early twentieth-century Wilkes-Barre and Pottsville, Pennsylvania, played a key role in transforming agricultural-commercial or near-subsistence communities into thriving industrial centers. Men such as Mathias and George Hollenback in Wilkes-Barre built trading networks, explored for anthracite coal and promoted banking ventures. Jacob Huntzinger and Charles Atkins, their Pottsville counterparts, developed iron and steel operations, established flourishing insurance and banking companies and successfully sought out new markets for their manufactured and hard coal products. In the process, leaders such as Hollenback and Atkins built prosperous regional economies which helped support the entire northeast with one of its main sources of energy, anthracite coal. Located in the hard coal fields of northeastern Pennsylvania, these men represented enormous power and wealth. Their decisions on the allocation of capital and the expansion of coal production touched many of the country's prime industries and affected the lives of thousands of workers and their families. At the same time, their influence reached beyond the region itself to the state capital in Harrisburg and even to Washington, D.C.[1]

The impact of leadership groups in these cities and others in shaping the character of industrial America has provided scholars with a rich field of research. Historians have been particularly interested in the connection between urban entrepreneurial leaders and urban development. Julius Rubin, Arthur Cole, Blake McKelvey, and others have exhaustively studied the impact of entrepreneurial decisions on large and small cities from New York to Baltimore. Their works have unequivocally shown the vital role urban leaders have played in community development. These leaders' entrepreneurial initiative and ventures into industry, commerce, and finance were essential in the growth, decline, or stagnation of the city or town. They developed new forms of production, exploited natural resources, created new markets and built transportation lines, all of which substantially contributed to urban industrial growth during the nineteenth and early twentieth centuries.[2]

Scholars have exhaustively studied leadership within the context of the community. Issues such as social mobility, economic and political power, and the persistence of prominent families have commanded the attention of historians and social scientists for decades. With the wealth of information acquired from this scholarship, it is now possible to move beyond the community to the region as a broader setting for the analysis of urban leadership.[3]

Scholars in a variety of disciplines have explored the dynamics of regional development from southeastern Pennsylvania to upstate New York. Historians and geographers alike have examined in great detail population shifts within the region, trade flows between regions, and the distribution of industry among communities in the region. Scholars have yet to combine this approach with the existing knowledge on urban leadership to study the persistence and decline of the community's most powerful men.[4]

The focus of my work is the formation and evolution of urban leadership in the context of region. I have two particular concerns: the relationships of the northeastern Pennsylvania upper strata in Wilkes-Barre and Pottsville with other leadership groups in these two regions and with entrepreneurial leaders of Philadelphia and New York City from 1800 through 1930. Scholars have used the community as a context for studying the upper strata and related power issues and have clearly examined the region; but this study looks at urban leadership within the region and, therefore, unites the two traditions.

The first community, Wilkes-Barre, is located at the center of the northern anthracite region, where it is the largest among a number of communities. In the nineteenth century, the region consisted of the Wyoming Valley, about the size of Manhattan Island, which was situated in Luzerne County and bisected by the Susquehanna River, with mountain barriers on each side. The region originally encompassed Wilkes-Barre's hinterland, which stretched from upstate New York to nearby Columbia County and included the northeast corner of the state. The rise of Scranton during the 1850s and 1860s undermined Wilkes-Barre's pull in the northeastern section, and Scranton even began to compete for resources in the towns along the Susquehanna. Wilkes-Barre did retain its hold on the towns bordering the river, including communities such as Braintrim and Wyalusing. The Wyoming Valley and the hinterland along the Susquehanna River provided Wilkes-Barre's leadership with the boundaries for most of its entrepreneurial and social activities.

The second community, Pottsville, was situated in the southern anthracite region, which included the coalfields of Schuylkill and Northumberland counties, adjacent or near to Luzerne County. Until the late 1800s, Pottsville was the largest community in the region and, economically, it had the strongest leadership of any of the urban upper strata in these coalfields. The region and its cities and towns were oriented toward Philadelphia, relying on transportation lines and markets there to distribute local leaders' coal and other products.

Map 1. The Anthracite Coal Fields and Their Outlets to Market

Philadelphia's leaders, in fact, would play a major role in the fortunes of Potts-ville's upper strata, as well as the fate of all leadership groups in the southern coalfields.

The upper strata in Wilkes-Barre and Pottsville are ideally suited for a comparative analysis. Outwardly, they are similar in many ways. Their entrepreneurs had tied their fortunes to anthracite mining and its related industries and services. These men sold their primary export, coal, in similar or identical markets. The two leadership groups lived in adjacent, extractive-based regions and in communities dependent on coal for their survival. In fact, by 1870, both Wilkes-Barre and Pottsville were roughly the same size, between 10,000 and 13,000. The two groups of leaders began their development at about the same time, the 1840s being a rough beginning date. Yet Wilkes-Barre's leadership persisted almost intact into the 1920s, while Pottsville's upper stratum had almost entirely disappeared by that decade. Despite superficial similarities, the two groups were profoundly dissimilar.

My analysis will show that fundamental differences in the formation and evolution of these two leadership groups explains the persistence of Wilkes-Barre's upper stratum and the breakdown of Pottsville's. These differences accounted for the dissimilar capacity of each group to exploit the other leadership groups of the region and to build and maintain strong local economies. The contrasting patterns of extralocal relationships and the entrepreneurial strength of the Wilkes-Barre and Pottsville upper strata were the keys in understanding the fortunes of the leadership in these communities.

In these extractive-based regions, the strength of the local economy and the pattern of extralocal relationships were inextricably linked. The prosperity of the local economy and, therefore, of its leaders demanded intense entrepreneurial involvement beyond the community. The key resource and the origin of most profits for Wilkes-Barre and Pottsville leaders—anthracite coal—was widely scattered over large portions of both coalfields. Entrepreneurs from the two communities had no choice but to pursue their economic interests wherever the coal was discovered. In fact, this was true for all urban leaders in both regions. As a result, the main industrial operations and, therefore, the largest investments of Wilkes-Barre and Pottsville leaders were not centralized but rather to be found in all sections of their regions. To sustain these mining collieries, leaders in the two cities had to run provision, equipment, and general stores near their mines; they also had to guarantee railroad spur lines to ship out coal and bring in supplies. Land also attracted those leaders from Wilkes-Barre and Pottsville who saw land ownership as a way of controlling the key resource, hard coal, and, therefore, the anthracite industry.

As a result, entrepreneurs in the upper strata of both cities were extremely active throughout their regions. Of course, profits from their operations sustained the entrepreneurial activities of leaders within their own communities; and these activities were the heart of the local economics in Wilkes-Barre and Pottsville. But the relationship between activities beyond the community and those within the city was a reciprocal one; for ventures in the community, such as banks, financial houses, and services, helped sustain mining collieries, provisioning stores, and manufacturing operations beyond the community. In this sense, the urban leaders and their operations within the city, whether Wilkes-Barre or Pottsville, were highly interdependent with their entrepreneurial activities outside the community. This extralocal dimension is crucial in understanding the dynamics of economic development of the community and the entrepreneurial prosperity of urban leadership in Wilkes-Barre and Pottsville.

The economic and entrepreneurial activities of the upper strata in the two communities is only the first part of the investigation. The second deals with a social analysis of the two leadership groups. This section of the study includes a description of social traits from ethnicity to religion, to social activities and residential choice, to blood and marriage ties, and to occupational patterns and entrepreneurial careers. In the last part, the focus shifts to the network of extralocal ties that the leadership in Wilkes-Barre and Pottsville fashioned with other leadership groups in their respective regions. This involvement beyond the community derives in part from the leaders' attempts to exploit coal reserves and to maintain their widely dispersed mining operations. Naturally, these men encountered entrepreneurial members of other urban leadership groups in this endeavor who shared their interests in mining, land speculation, and other related activities. Often, they competed for resources; sometimes they joined in common ventures.

Entrepreneurship was only one dimension to these extralocal relationships, albeit an important one. Familial, social, cultural, and other noneconomic ties were also vital parts of these networks. Their presence could reinforce the entrepreneurial links and work to the advantage of the leadership fashioning the network. These relationships were crucial in the persistence or dispersal of the upper strata in Wilkes-Barre and Pottsville. The evolution of urban leadership groups within the community, then, is only part of their story. Their relationships and competition with groups outside their communities is the other, and unresearched, side. Yet it was those ties that were ultimately critical to the fate of the upper strata in the two cities.

The formation and evolution of Wilkes-Barre's leadership reflected this dualistic approach of developing the local economy while exploiting dispersed coal reserves. Since the early nineteenth century, members of Wilkes-Barre's upper stratum had dedicated their efforts to creating a viable anthracite industry. These men realized the vast potential of hard coal and saw their prosperity tied to its development. By the 1850s, the fulfillment of these efforts had begun to transform Wilkes-Barre's local economy from one dependent on agriculture and commerce to one built on the profits from the dispersed coal-mining industry. At the same time, entrepreneurs in the community's upper stratum created coal-related industries and services to sustain their operations throughout the northern coalfields and the city's rapidly growing population. By the 1870s, members of Wilkes-Barre's leadership had established the most diversified and powerful local economy in the region. As a result, Wilkes-Barre had also become the largest community in the region, a fact that only increased its attractiveness for other entrepreneurs in the neighboring communities. In the process of building their thriving economy, Wilkes-Barre's leaders had taken at least partial, and sometimes complete, control of the majority of the mining and anthracite-related operations over the entire region, and their power stretched from one end of the northern coalfields to the other.

The common entrepreneurial objectives of the city's upper stratum derived, in part, from that group's cohesiveness. This rested on a similar and, often, an identical set of social characteristics, including ethnic ties, religious and church affiliations, and club associations, shared by almost all members of the upper strata. Common ancestral origins, reinforced by rearing and socializing in small, confined, and exclusive neighborhoods, further solidified this cohesiveness. This pattern is similar to those upon which the Philadelphia Main Line and the Boston Brahmins were based. Like the families in those groups, the families in Wilkes-Barre's upper stratum frequently intermarried; a great many of the members shared blood or marital ties. Unified through culture and kinship, neighbors and entrepreneurial allies, the members of the community's leadership were able to maintain their unity and their economic objectives regarding the city and the coal industry.[5]

The overwhelming majority of urban leaders throughout the northern coal region shared the social characteristics and familial ties which joined the members of Wilkes-Barre's upper stratum. This commonality constituted an important part of the network of extralocal ties that Wilkes-Barre's leaders slowly but steadily built over the first seven decades of the nineteenth century. The social, cultural, familial, and economic institutions of the city's leadership were the basis of the network. These were, by far, the most stable and well developed in the region. The institutions increasingly drew participation from urban leaders outside Wilkes-Barre as early as 1800. Over the next seventy or eighty years, the ties sustained through the upper stratum's institutions reoriented the other leadership groups in the region toward Wilkes-Barre and its upper stratum. By the 1870s and 1880s, the city had become the center of social and cultural life for the upper levels of urban society throughout the region. These associations strengthened and even promoted the growing entrepreneurial and other economic ties between Wilkes-Barre's leaders and those elsewhere in the Wyoming Valley. Through this multiplicity of extralocal ties, entrepreneurs from Wilkes-Barre's upper stratum penetrated the local economies of the other communities in the valley and began to take control of key industrial and financial activities.

During these same years, leaders and their families from the Valley communities began to move into Wilkes-Barre. Their loyalty to their native cities and towns sapped by participation in the institutions of Wilkes-Barre's upper stratum, these men both emotionally and physically abandoned their communities for the economically more prosperous and socially more appealing Wilkes-Barre.

Steady before 1850, this migration intensified after that decade and persisted into the twentieth century. This movement enabled Wilkes-Barre's leadership to expand and survive at the expense of the upper strata in communities over the region. These urban centers were left with their leadership ranks disrupted, their industry and capital controlled by Wilkes-Barre's leaders, and their autonomy irrevocably undermined. By consolidating the resources and talent of the region's nineteenth-century leadership, Wilkes-Barre's expanding upper stratum was able to deal on a reciprocal basis with New York City entrepreneurs who also sought to exploit the coal deposits in the Wyoming Valley.

The emergence of Pottsville's leadership was also based on its efforts to exploit resources and other leadership groups in the southern anthracite region. Fundamentally unlike Wilkes-Barre's upper stratum, Pottsville's leadership relied almost entirely on economic, occupational, and entrepreneurial ties which reflected its own makeup during the nineteenth century. By 1870 a community barely forty years old, Pottsville had an upper stratum whose members had acquired their wealth and power in the post-1830 coal boom, which sparked urban growth throughout the southern anthracite fields. These men largely came from outside the newly developing region and from diverse ethnic and social backgrounds. They shared little by the way of culture, social characteristics, or family experiences. They did share similar entrepreneurial concerns, occupational experiences, and economic interests; and these served as the basis for their rather new and heterogeneous leadership. This group would not, however, develop a social basis comparable to that of Wilkes-Barre's upper stratum; and Pottsville's leadership would remain vastly different in composition and values from its counterpart in Luzerne County.

In pursuing profitable operations over the southern coalfields, Pottsville's leaders capitalized on their own entrepreneurial base. They, of course, established mining collieries, small-scale iron foundries, machine shops, real estate ventures, and commercial activities both within the town and throughout the region. The share of the wealth held by these men was substantially larger than the proportion controlled by other leadership groups in the region. At the same time, the Pottsville economy surpassed all others in diversity, power, and influence. The other leadership groups in the region were identical to Pottsville's in their varied social and ancestral origins; and they, too, relied on common economic interests, entrepreneurial, and occupational experiences to sustain their cohesiveness. Blocked by none of the normal social barriers typical of established leadership groups, Pottsville's leaders had begun to fashion numerous ties with the urban leaders in communities elsewhere in the region based on their similarities. Banking, commercial, manufacturing, mining, and speculative land and other entrepreneurial ties enabled Pottsville's leaders to begin to exploit the other local economies and upper strata in the Schuylkill-Northumberland coalfields.

While Pottsville's leadership group was the most prosperous and powerful in the region, its numbers had not increased at the expense of other such groups in the southern coalfields, for those groups had developed at roughly the same time as Pottsville's. The city's leaders had begun to attract capital from these groups through control of key economic activities such as iron and steel operations and partnerships in land, coal, and other ventures. Leaders from other communities had even begun to relocate their operations to Pottsville by the 1870s. However, a series of economic reverses during the seventies and early eighties would irrevocably alter the evolution of Pottsville's leadership. These reverses would undermine its incipient network of ties and remove the possibility of drawing in talent from other communities in the region and, ultimately, lead to the dispersal of Pottsville's leadership.

First, Pottsville's upper stratum faced its stiffest competition not from other leadership groups in the region but from Philadelphia's leadership, whose entrepreneurs vied for control of the southern anthracite region's key resource—hard coal. Entrepreneurial leaders from the Pennsylvania port and, to a lesser extent, from other large urban centers such as New York City and Boston, had been active in the region since its inception. By the 1850s and 1860s, these men had begun to build a network of extraregional ties with the urban leadership throughout the southern coalfields, including Pottsville's upper stratum. In fact, the vast anthracite holdings of these outside interests actually overshadowed Pottsville's coal-mining operations, although the latter remained the largest among the regional leadership groups. Beginning in the 1870s, corporate leaders in Philadelphia decided to consolidate control of all mining operations, coal-related industries, and landholdings in the southern coalfields. Compelled by a chronically overproductive coal industry and increasing competition from entrepreneurs from New York City, Boston, and other outside urban centers, Philadelphia leaders believed they had no other choice if their operations in the region, and even the anthracite industry itself, were to remain viable.

The execution of this decision crippled Pottsville's network of extralocal ties as well as its local economy and, therefore, the interests of its urban leaders. At the same time, other entrepreneurs from Philadelphia's leadership moved into the noncoal sectors, such as transit and utilities, further eroding the economic strength of Pottsville's upper stratum and, therefore, its stability. Along with these reverses, the city's leadership had to cope with the effects of the depression of the 1870s. The resulting business failures and company closings, as well as personal bankruptcies, further undermined the stability of Pottsville's leadership. Cut off from its extralocal ties and with its own entrepreneurial activities in disarray, the city's upper stratum no longer exercised regionwide influence by the end of the 1880s.

The decision of Philadelphia's corporate leaders was not an inevitable one, given the proximity of Pottsville to the metropolitan center. The anthracite-based city had flourished for most of the decades before the 1870s, and its leadership had been the most powerful in the region until the late nineteenth century. Only market pressures and the economic downturn of the 1870s led to the decision by Philadelphia leaders and the decline of Pottsville's leadership.

Communities much closer to Philadelphia managed to maintain their independence at least until the early 1900s or later, and almost all these cities equalled or surpassed Wilkes-Barre's population by the 1920s or before. Reading, to the south of Pottsville along the Schuylkill River, and its leadership prospered well into the early 1900s. So, too, did Norristown, Bethlehem, and their entrepreneurial leadership groups. Wilmington, buttressed by the wealth and power of the DuPont family, remained free of Philadelphia's control until the present day. Geography alone was not sufficient to explain why Philadelphia leaders chose to consolidate control of the anthracite industry in the southern coal region.[6]

One last problem facing Pottsville's leadership as it coped with the strains of the late nineteenth century was the rise of a series of anthracite-based communities in the undeveloped northern rim of the southern region. This development intensified the downward spiral of Pottsville's leadership. Financed largely by Philadelphia capital, these communities actually drew money and talent away from Pottsville. By the 1920s, Pottsville leaders and/or their sons had left the community almost entirely. Pressed by bankruptcies and company closings, Pottsville's remaining leaders confronted decreasing opportunities within their community and the region. Many chose to leave. Among those who remained, few sustained their families into the twentieth century, as sons chose to seek careers in other communities.

The economic fortunes of the upper strata in Wilkes-Barre and Pottsville affected all the leadership groups in their respective regions. Wilkes-Barre's leadership had co-opted the members of these competing groups via its network of extralocal ties. Increasing participation in the institutions of Wilkes-Barre's upper stratum eventually undermined the institutions of the other leadership groups in the region. Destabilized, these groups slowly but steadily dissolved, as their members and families moved into Wilkes-Barre, whose upper stratum quickly assimilated them.

Wilkes-Barre's leadership steadily expanded as these other groups shrank. This movement into Wilkes-Barre further strengthened the grip Wilkes-Barre's upper stratum exercised over the cities, towns, and villages of the northern coal region. As a result, the leadership in Wilkes-Barre persisted almost intact into the 1920s.

The move of Philadelphia's leadership into the southern region also affected the urban upper strata throughout the coalfields in Schuylkill and Northumberland counties. Pottsville's leadership, with the greatest assets in the regional economy at stake, experienced the greatest distress; but other leadership groups tied to Pottsville's upper stratum also felt the impact of the takeover by Philadelphia's leaders and the destabilizing of Pottsville's leadership. Cut off from both key resources in the region and access to Pottsville's capital, urban leaders elsewhere in the coalfields faced shrinking opportunities, business failures, and bankruptcies. Few of these men or their sons remained in the southern coalfields by the 1920s.

This broader context of extralocal ties within a region is essential for understanding the evolution of upper strata in Wilkes-Barre or Pottsville. The network that originated with the leadership groups in these communities spanned the entire region and were key in the health of the local economy and, therefore, the prosperity and the persistence or dispersal of the leadership in each community. At the same time, these networks enabled the upper strata in Wilkes-Barre and Pottsville to exploit the other leadership groups and their communities in the two regions. Without considering the regional dimension, virtually any analysis of these two leadership groups would be incomplete.

THE UPPER CLASS AND THE ELITE

The general terms *leadership* and *upper stratum* are used interchangeably in this book, simply to denote the upper levels of urban communities. Their subcategories, elite and upper class, have more precise, technical meanings. I have used the term *upper class* to refer to a social group whose members participate in the same institutions, are frequently related through blood and marriage, and are involved in the same social and cultural activities. They often share some commonality of ancestry and will nearly always locate themselves in common residential areas (and, frequently, styles of housing therein). They are at the top of the local status hierarchy. Most important, the institutions and families of the upper class persist for generations and become sharply identified with the community in an historical sense. The upper class includes both the men in this high-status group and their families. In this study, the upper class both persists and exercises power. Of all those included in the study, Wilkes-Barre is the only community in which an upper class developed. In Wilkes-Barre, those who dominated the major spheres of economic and political life in the city were also those who were members of the upper class.[7]

I have used the term *elite* in a more restrictive, and contrasting, sense. An elite is, in this study, those individuals who occupied the positions of economic and political power in the community. Members of an elite are, therefore, only loosely organized in a social or familial sense. They inevitably form associations and establish institutions that reflect the degree of heterogeneity of the leadership. Elites lack cohesiveness and often do not persist within a generation or between generations.[8]

All leadership groups in this study except the upper class are classified as elites. Pottsville's upper stratum demonstrates the characteristics of an elite. It was heterogeneous in makeup; it also failed to develop one set of institutions that encompassed all members and their families. Most importantly, it did not persist. Pottsville's leadership was unlike the familiar heterogeneous upper strata of Charleston[9] and New York City,[10] from which persistent and viable social and cultural institutions did develop and in which frequent intermarriage occurred among the leading families.

Pottsville, unlike New York and Charleston, had no leadership prior to the 1820s and the coal boom. The city had no dominant group comparable to the

English of Charleston before rapid growth began in the post-1830 decades. As the city rapidly grew, an upper stratum began to emerge, based largely on the flourishing anthracite trade and coal-related industries. Yet the opportunities inherent in this growth came to an abrupt end in the late nineteenth century. These conditions differed markedly from those of stagnating Charleston or explosive New York City. Pottsville also differed from Charleston and New York City in that the leadership in those metropolitan centers developed over a considerably longer period of time, and its development was not hindered by any powerful neighbor.

In addition to Pottsville's leadership group, elites existed throughout both regions. By the 1920s, an elite comprised of men whose social characteristics differed from those of the upper class and who operated in the secondary levels of the local economy emerged in Wilkes-Barre. These men had neither the wealth nor the power of their upper-class counterparts and were unable to penetrate the coal companies and major commercial banks. Leadership elsewhere in the region during the 1920s demonstrated the same social and economic characteristics as the Wilkes-Barre elite during the 1920s; these leaders are also classified as elites. In the nineteenth century, leadership groups in communities other than Wilkes-Barre were unable to build enduring institutions or persist intact into the twentieth century and, accordingly, are treated in this study as elites. Last, leadership groups outside Pottsville in the southern anthracite region demonstrated virtually all the qualities of an elite. These groups had few and comparatively weak institutions, exhibited diverse social characteristics, and showed a high turnover. Few, if any, of their members or their sons persisted, except in the literal sense, into the twentieth century.

THE REGIONAL CENTER

The term *regional center* is used often in this study and requires a precise definition. It is applied to a particular type of city, the largest community and the economic hub of the region. Urban leaders are critical to the transformation of a city into a regional center. These men centralize and maintain ownership and control of the region's main economic activity. Through this control of the primary export (i.e., main industry), the city's leadership exerts influence over all the other cities, towns, and villages. Because the community's leaders consolidate regional transportation and communication, the city becomes the nexus for the emerging urban industrial centers in the region. In addition, members of the community's leadership also concentrate the main financial, administrative, and service activities of the region in their city, making it the true hub of the developing regional economy and urban centers. As a result of the leadership's entrepreneurial activity, the regional center has a considerably more diverse economic structure, a stronger capital base, and a larger and more rapidly growing population. All of these assets rest on the social, economic, and cultural institutions of the city's upper strata.[11]

In terms of size, the regional center during the late nineteenth century ranged upward from 10,000, at least by 1870. The other cities in the region varied between 10,000 as the upper limit and 3,000 as the lower limit. The towns and villages are the smallest communities in the region, their populations extending from 3,000 to 1,500 for the town and 1,500 to 500 for the village. During the years of the study, only the leadership in Wilkes-Barre transformed their community into a regional center. The dispersal of Pottsville's leadership derailed that city's emergence as a regional center.

METHODOLOGY AND CHRONOLOGY

The chief method of identifying persons in leadership groups is the positional. I selected this technique since it is best suited to pinpointing the intersections of spheres of influence among men who exercised power both within their own communities and between communities. Simple and direct, the method has the advantage of establishing the parameters of urban leadership. Accordingly, individuals with economic power are defined as those who held a directorship or an officer's position and/or served as a charter member in an incorporated company. In addition, those individuals who held $30,000 or more according to the manuscript census or who were rated by R. G. Dun and Company as having $30,000 in assets were ranked as exercising economic power. Political power is defined by the holding of public and/or party office.

This study employs three characteristics to define high social status. First is membership in the community's leading social clubs, lodges, or other societies. Scholars such as Ingham, Baltzell, and Jaher have concurred that exclusive organizations reserved for members of the upper stratum are excellent indicators of high social status. These organizations separated leaders from the rest of the population and marked their social prominence in the community. Admission to such clubs and societies was usually based on the recommendation of members and then a vote by the majority of the group, a procedure that effectively screened out those not wanted. Organizations such as the Westmoreland Club and the Malt Club in Wilkes-Barre during the twentieth and nineteenth centuries, respectively, as well as the Fishing Party in Pottsville, were exclusive, confined to the top levels of local society.[12]

Participation in two or more cultural institutions of the upper stratum was another sign of high social status. Membership in churches which drew their congregations from the top levels of society is one example. In such churches as St. Stephen's Episcopal in Wilkes-Barre, pews were sold to parish members for sums as high as $500, an amount that certainly excluded those of modest circumstances. Last, descendants from First Families in communities whose history stretched back to the Revolutionary or Colonial periods were considered to have high social status. Members of these families combined distinguished lineage with ancestral ties to the community's founders. This rare combination of colonial ancestry with direct ties to the community's First Families was an important indicator of high status, especially when the leadership stressed its eighteenth-century origins.[13]

Although the positional method leads thus to definitions of social status, it is only one means of identifying leaders. Reputational and decision-making methods can also be used. The reputational method, pioneered by Floyd Hunter in his study of Atlanta, depends on interviewing persons selected from the population to learn their ideas on the identity of the most powerful figures in the community. While modified since its inception, the reputational method has relied on the interview procedure and does not serve well in an historical study, even one stretching into the twentieth century, given the precariousness of memory.[14]

The decisional method approaches the issue from a different perspective. Scholars who have relied on this technique identify two things: the key issues and decisions during a given time span and those men who had major decision-making roles. This method has been effectively used in Whitman Ridgway's study of political leadership in Maryland from the late eighteenth roughly through the mid-nineteenth centuries. Ridgway pinpointed key political issues such as the nominating debates and which men ultimately decided the final outcome. Decision making in the economic realm is far less visible, since it is not a formal process open to public scrutiny. Whereas positional analysis allows a researcher to establish the parameters of all leaders who potentially could exercise power, decision making, given the availability of sources, is a far less effective method to accomplish this end. It is also difficult to establish which were major or minor decisions, presuming one has a clear idea of all possible decisions. Yet the decisional method is effective and certainly not to be discounted. The present study includes numerous decisions within the community and the region. The leaders identified through the positional method were involved in decisions to incorporate companies, allocate capital, lend money (either as individuals or as bank officers), open up new coal veins, suspend pay to miners, close down or expand operations of coal and other companies, buy out companies controlled by outsiders, relocate companies from other communities and numerous other economic decisions. Decision making, then, is used to complement the positional method.[15]

This study covers the years 1800 through 1930. The beginning and ending dates correspond approximately to the first efforts of entrepreneurs to exploit anthracite coal and to develop a thriving market for their product and to the last decade when anthracite coal flourished, effectively unchallenged by oil. That decade, the 1920s, also marked the last period when the urban leaders who relied on hard coal as a main source of profit enjoyed relative prosperity. The depression of the 1930s and the emergence of oil as America's main source of energy signalled the end of anthracite as a prosperous industry.

CHAPTER II

Consolidating the Regional Economy

 HE MEMBERS of Wilkes-Barre's upper class built a thriving local economy dependent, in large part, on the leaders' entrepreneurial activities throughout the region during the nineteenth century. Wilkes-Barre's upper class established mining operations, provisioning and general stores, urban transit, and other entrepreneurial activities which touched every leadership group and community in the northern coalfields. Through these enterprises, members of the upper class exercised increasing power over the affairs of competing urban leadership groups and their communities in the Wyoming Valley and hinterland along the Susquehanna River. The associations generated by these activities developed slowly, almost imperceptibly, over the course of decades. Yet these ties were the basis of entrepreneurial efforts of Wilkes-Barre's upper class and essential for their survival. It was these relationships that constituted the foundation of the upper-class regional networks, which were essential in controlling the economy of the northern coal region and in transforming Wilkes-Barre itself into the regional center for the anthracite fields.

The upper class was in a unique position to develop this network and to promote the economic growth of the city, more so than any other socioeconomic group in the community. First, these men had access to the capital and credit necessary to support the expanding industrial base of the city and the region. Next, upper-class leaders had already ventured out into the markets beyond the community and the Wyoming Valley to sell their own commercial goods. These operations gave the leaders valuable experience not possessed by other groups in the community. These experiences also increased their recognition of the need for adequate transportation to develop anthracite coal as a marketable commodity. Last, these men controlled large amounts of coal lands in the anthracite fields and had the greatest vested interest in promoting the anthracite industry.

Certainly no one could have predicted in the early 1800s that Wilkes-Barre's leaders would build this network of extralocal ties and transform their small commercial community of a few hundred people into a prosperous industrial center with a population in excess of 20,000 by the 1880s. In the first decade of the nineteenth century, Wilkes-Barre leaders confronted the formidable challenges of securing capital for their risky ventures and of overcoming natural obstacles that blocked access to coastal and other urban markets. As late as the 1840s, the nascent coal industry continued to lag behind all other anthracite-producing regions, including the nearby Lackawanna Valley, the economy of which would eventually rely on steel.

This chapter will first describe the efforts of the upper class to meet these challenges and to create a viable coal industry with easy access to the thriving eastern markets. The remaining portions will focus on the efforts of the upper class to secure a hold on all the main economic activities of the region, at the same time expanding Wilkes-Barre's economic base. In part, these objectives involved a consistent strategy among upper-class entrepreneurs to establish a series of major economic institutions, ranging from large-scale coal companies to profitable manufacturing and banking operations whose influence stretched over the entire region.

EARLY HISTORY

At the start of the nineteenth century, prominent men from Wilkes-Barre were beginning to recognize the tremendous potential of anthracite coal as a base for economic development. In the early 1810s, two leading and wealthy Wilkes-Barreans, Jacob Cist and Robert Miner, were actively promoting the development of the industry. The two men argued that a link with the seemingly prosperous and growing Philadelphia would stimulate growth of the industry, the city, and the region. Cist and several of his colleagues began mining in nearby Summit Hill (Carbon County), in the middle anthracite fields, and shipped coal down the Lehigh River to Philadelphia via the Delaware River. While these efforts were largely unsuccessful, they prompted men back in Wilkes-Barre—George Hollenback and John L. Butler, for example—to start their own primitive mining operations during subsequent decades. These small-scale operations produced as little as a ton of coal a month. Undaunted, the early coal entrepreneurs persisted in shipping the coal by flatboat along the Susquehanna River.[1]

The high costs of transportation impeded any real progress toward full-scale economic growth. Costs for lumber to build the wagons and the highly vulnerable arks were prohibitive. In addition, the absence of any direct route to Philadelphia or New York City made the hauling of coal even more expensive. Hemmed in by mountains and rough terrain and lacking easy access to the newly emerging markets, Wilkes-Barre's leaders remained rooted in commercial and agricultural activities confined largely to northeastern Pennsylvania. Coal mining remained secondary throughout the early nineteenth century.[2]

Leaders in Wilkes-Barre and throughout the Wyoming Valley recognized the need for cheap, reliable transportation in order to develop the anthracite industry and saw their answer in the phenomenal success of the Erie Canal, which sparked a rash of canal building during the mid-1820s. In exchange for backing the Pennsylvania Main Line Canal, advocated by representatives in the Philadelphia area, political leaders from northeastern Pennsylvania won legislative support for the proposed North Branch Canal. Headed by state representatives Garrick Mallary and George Denison, both of Wilkes-Barre, the northeastern group gained a strong voice on the state canal commission and eventually won long-term state funding for the construction and maintenance of the North Branch Canal. The waterway was designed to connect northeastern Pennsylvania with the New York Canal System at Elmira and to join up with the West Branch Canal at Northumberland, near Sunbury, and flow south to the Juniata division of the Main Line Canal north of Harrisburg. To the entrepreneurs in Wilkes-Barre, the North Branch Canal, built along the Susquehanna River, supplied the easy access to markets in eastern and central Pennsylvania. Agricultural interests in the hinterland would also benefit from the increased range of new markets. By the early 1830s, the Wyoming Branch, from Northumberland on the Susquehanna River to Pittston and Nanticoke, was completed.[3]

Unfortunately, the completion of the canal to Northumberland did not materially improve the fledgling anthracite industry in the Wyoming Valley. Leaders in Wilkes-Barre and elsewhere were unable to capitalize on the North Branch Canal to transform the northern anthracite region into a serious competitor with other hard coal–producing fields. While anthracite was shipped to markets in the south and along the West Branch Canal, the journey to Philadelphia from the Wyoming Valley was still long and tortuous; moreover, the canal could not generally operate during the winter months. Competition, insufficient demand, and poor transportation seriously impeded any major increases in coal production by Wilkes-Barre's entrepreneurs. For example, coal output by mine operators in the Wyoming Valley in 1841 and 1842 constituted only 4 percent and 5 percent, respectively, of all anthracite mined in eastern Pennsylvania. Coal entrepreneurs in the Wyoming Valley lagged significantly behind those in neighboring districts, both in sheer tonnage and in percentage of total output. The entrepreneurs of the competing Hazelton district, in the middle anthracite fields, produced two to four times as much coal as those in the Wyoming Valley. The center of the coal industry at this time was clearly the southern region, where mining entrepreneurs produced over 60 percent of all hard coal in the United States.[4]

In the mid-1840s, urban leaders in the Lehigh Valley and along the Schuylkill and the central Susquehanna rivers began to develop iron and steel operations. Wilkes-Barre entrepreneurs next turned to the railroad in order to tap these markets. As early as 1833, members of the upper class, such as Charles Miner,

Ziba Bennet, and Andrew Beaumont, had advocated the construction of a rail line. In 1846, Charles Parrish and Alexander Farnham, in conjunction with several Philadelphia capitalists, sponsored the Lehigh and Susquehanna Railroad. This line ran from the Wyoming Valley to White Haven on the Lehigh River, where it joined the Lehigh Canal south to the newly developing iron and steel towns of the Lehigh Valley. In 1852, local leaders helped to finance the Lackawanna and Bloomsburg Railroad, which connected the Wyoming Valley with the iron and steel communities of Danville, Bloomsburg, and Sunbury to the west. By 1860, the railroads were carrying more than 70 percent of all anthracite coal produced in the Wyoming Valley. To strengthen these vital transportation links, upper-class leaders, in combination with New York and Philadelphia capitalists, built telegraph lines between the Wyoming Valley and the seaport centers. These gave local entrepreneurs rapid communication with businessmen and markets in the New York City and Philadelphia areas.[5]

Next, corporate executives of major rail lines ordered spur lines built into the Wyoming Valley during the late 1850s and early 1860s. Most of these companies had their main terminus in Wilkes-Barre. The first of the lines completed was the Delaware, Lackawanna and Western Railroad, which extended rails to the Wyoming Valley coalfields in the very late 1850s. It actually ran down the west side of the river from Scranton and through Kingston. During the next ten years, the Lehigh Valley Railroad, the Delaware and Hudson Canal Company, the Lehigh Coal and Navigation Company, and the Central Railroad Corporation of New Jersey followed suit by constructing major rail networks in the Wyoming Valley. These rail lines connected Wilkes-Barre and the Valley to the markets in New York City and New England, as well as those in Philadelphia, further increasing demand for anthracite coal. The Delaware and Hudson and the Central Rail lines joined Wilkes-Barre and the region with the New York City area. The newly built rails also joined the northern anthracite fields with Buffalo and the Great Lakes regions, further expanding the scope of the new markets.[6]

WILKES-BARRE'S UPPER CLASS AND THE RISE OF THE ANTHRACITE INDUSTRY

The decision of the Wilkes-Barre upper class to tap the rapidly growing markets of the East Coast and Great Lakes led to a basic change in the organization of the anthracite industry. The upper class hit upon the device of the incorporated company, which thereafter rapidly displaced the small-scale and less technologically sophisticated family-controlled operations that had dominated coal production in the Wyoming Valley since the early 1800s. Incorporation encouraged larger capital investment and a wider scope of operations and thus made possible a consolidation of smaller-sized producing units into larger and more productive ones. By the 1870s and 1880s, incorporated companies dominated the northern coalfields and accounted for the greatest increase in anthracite production.[7]

The producers displaced by the incorporated company—the individual families—had dominated coal mining since the industry's inception. These entrepreneurial families operated out of a dozen small towns and villages, from West Nanticoke to Plainsville, and covered the entire Wyoming Valley. For example, Washington Lee and his nephews ran mining operations in Nanticoke, Hanover Township, and Newport Township from the 1820s through the 1860s. Calvin Parsons of Plainsville owned coal mines in Plains Township and Georgetown, while John Shonk ran anthracite-mining operations in his native Plymouth and Plymouth Township. Often, these early mining activities began by accident, with the discovery of coal on family-owned farmland. The Harveys of Plymouth—Jameson, William J., and Henry—began their first coal-mining efforts in this way. Branches of the family began coal mining on grazing and planting land in West Nanticoke and Plymouth Township during the 1820s. After exchanging their coal landholdings for shares in the Susquehanna Coal Company (headquartered in Wilkes-Barre), the members of the Harvey family began moving to Wilkes-Barre in 1860, where they invested their money in locally based enterprises. Most family coal operators followed the pattern of the Harveys.[8]

The movement to Wilkes-Barre was gradual and at times imperceptible. It took years for members of families in these urban elites to sever ties with their original resident communities. The migration of the Harvey family occurred over eleven years, from 1860 through 1871; the Wadhams, another family whose members belonged to Plymouth's elite, moved to the city over the course of twenty years. These spans were not uncommon among the leaders who journeyed to Wilkes-Barre. Abandoning family, home, and enterprise was an imposing task, particularly since many of the men belonged to First Families. Once in Wilkes-Barre, members of these entrepreneurial families invested in locally based industrial and service activities and further strengthened the city's economy.

With the gradual disappearance of the family-controlled operations, the incorporated company came to dominate the landscape of the Wyoming Valley. Prior to this time, the city's upper class had directed its efforts toward acquiring mining technology, establishing adequate transportation, finding new markets, and encouraging coal-mining activity. After the early 1850s, Wilkes-Barre's upper class began to establish chartered companies that would centralize regionally owned mining operations in Wilkes-Barre. After a modest beginning, these companies eventually grew to encompass mining operations throughout the entire region, with capital assets often exceeding $1,000,000. Most important, they facilitated a large measure of control over the anthracite industry by the Wilkes-Barre upper class.

The men in the upper class kept control of these vital operations within their grasp. This control was especially crucial because it insured input by Wilkes-Barre's upper-class leaders in the development of the anthracite industry and in

Table 2-1. Executives, Directors, Incorporators, and Partners in Local Companies under the Control of Members of the Wilkes-Barre Upper Class and Other Groups, 1850–1885*

| | Company Positions | |
Residence and Economic Position	Executive Posts	Directorships and Partnerships
Wilkes-Barre: Upper class	95%	76%
Wilkes-Barre: Non–upper class	2	1
Communities in Wyoming Valley:		
Urban leaders†	0	10
Philadelphia and New York City:		
Investors	3	13
Total	100%	100%
	(65)	(232)
n = 297		

*Some examples of these companies are Dundee Coal Co., Hollenback Coal Co., Hillman Vein Coal Co., Parrish Coal Co., Wyoming Transportation and Coal Company, Warrior Run Coal Co., Hanover Coal Co., Landmesser Coal Co., Washington Lee and Co., and Forty-Fort Coal Co. See also Edward J. Davies, "The Urbanizing Region: Leadership and Urban Growth in the Anthracite Regions, 1830–1885" (Ph.D. diss., University of Pittsburgh, 1977), p. 94, Table III-3, chap. 3; see also Table III-3 for sources.

The dates chosen reflect the fact that before the 1850s, few incorporated companies existed in the city. Accordingly, I chose companies' officeholders from these years.

†Refers to community leaders in the Wyoming Valley who invested their money in Wilkes-Barre-controlled companies, but only those who persisted in their native communities.

the use of profits generated by coal mining.[9] At the same time, the entrepreneurs from within the region, but outside the upper class, constituted only a small group among the directors and officers of these upper-class-controlled coal companies. These non-upper-class men constituted only 10 percent of the directors or partners and just 2 percent of the executives in the more than thirty coal companies active in the region, while members of the upper class comprised 76 percent and 95 percent, respectively, of these positions (see Table 2–1). In only one case, the Kingston Coal Company, which had its operations in Edwardsville, Pringle, and Larksville and which was under the control of Welsh immigrants, did entrepreneurs outside the upper class actually control the operation. The average capitalization figure of these companies—more than $500,000— and the total amount invested in these operations—$17,000,000—demonstrates the commitment of the upper class to sustain power in the anthracite industry.[10]

As a result of the efforts of Wilkes-Barre's upper class, coal mining had spread to virtually every community in the region by the 1880s. Many of the locally sponsored mining operations, in fact, formed the basis for most of the towns incorporated after 1850. While the anthracite collieries covered the entire region, the financial and administrative ends of the business were located in Wilkes-Barre. The city had become the headquarters for most major coal companies in the region. The control and power arising from this centralization constituted the foundation of Wilkes-Barre as a regional center. As important, the upper-class leaders also invested considerable time and money in landholdings, which gave them control of a large portion of coal lands in Wilkes-Barre and the region. Men such as Charles Parrish, Hendrick B. Wright, Edmund Dana, and John Swoyer, among others, exploited and parlayed their landholdings into substantial profits. These lands often enabled the leadership to benefit from mining operations not locally controlled. Entrepreneurs from New York, Philadelphia, and elsewhere had no choice but to lease mining rights from Wilkes-Barre's upper-class leaders.[11] An examination of the main coal companies and leading entrepreneurs shows the influence of Wilkes-Barre's upper class in the coal industry and the region after 1850.

The Wilkes-Barre Coal Company was one of the earliest and most prominent. In 1849, leaders from the Bennett, Conyngham, and Bedford families, as well as other wealthy members of the upper class, established the Wilkes-Barre Coal Company, which initially capitalized at $200,000 and increased to $300,000 within a year. Headquartered in the city's emerging central business district, this company became one of the leading independent coal producers in the northern anthracite region over the next thirty years. During those decades, major coal entrepreneurs such as Charles Parrish and John Phelps became directors and officers of the company. Under their leadership, the Wilkes-Barre-based company constantly expanded its mining operations. By 1900, these operations spread from the east bank of the Susquehanna River near Wilkes-Barre to as far south as the Schuylkill coalfields.[12]

One of the most important operations in the northern coal regions in the post-1850 years was the Wyoming Coal and Transportation Company. Founded in 1864, it incorporated at $500,000. At first, the company's directors concentrated their efforts on the west side in Forty-Fort and Swoyersville, the site of rich anthracite beds. By the 1870s, operations had spread to the northeastern perimeter of Wilkes-Barre, where eight new collieries were built in Hudson and Plainsville. With the backing of such powerful men as John Swoyer, its main organizer; John Phelps, president of the company; and Charles Parrish, a major financial supporter, the Wyoming Coal and Transportation Company maintained these operations for more than fifty years and survived as an independent and locally owned operation until the early 1900s. At that point, the Temple Coal Company, a subsidiary of a New York–based rail company, absorbed the Wilkes-Barre-based coal operation as part of an industry-wide consolidation movement. However, two members of the city's upper class served as directors of the Temple Coal Company and maintained some measure of local influence.[13]

The Wilkes-Barre Coal and Iron Company, separate from the Wilkes-Barre Coal Company, was the second-largest mining operation in the northern coal region until the 1860s. Charles Parrish, a leading member of the upper class, was the key man in securing the capital for this company and in setting up its operation. Backed by the Lehigh Coal and Navigation Company, where he was a major stockholder and director, Parrish became the first and only president of the company. Other members of the upper class joined Parrish in this venture by serving as incorporators, directors, and officers of the newly formed coal company. Their presence insured local input into the company's operations and policy decisions. The stock and directorships controlled by members of the upper class insured a large measure of local control over company affairs. Parrish, in fact, was probably the most experienced coal entrepreneur in the northern coalfields and the main person in running the company. Within a few years of its founding, the company's securities were increased to $4,000,000, making it the largest coal company in the region at that time. This rise in capitalization reflected a tremendous increase in production and expansion of existing facilities. Before its merger with the Lehigh and Wilkes-Barre Coal Company in the late 1860s, the coal and iron operation exceeded $20,000,000 in assets and employed thousands of workers. By this time, the Wilkes-Barre Coal and Iron Company operated mining collieries scattered over five towns—Plymouth, Sugar Notch, Ashley, Wilkes-Barre, and Plains.[14]

Following his success with the Wilkes-Barre Coal and Iron Company, Parrish formed the Lehigh and Wilkes-Barre Coal Company in 1869. Backed by the Central Railroad of New Jersey, Parrish was able to absorb the Honeybrook Coal Company, a major anthracite operation centered in the Hazleton area, and his Wilkes-Barre Coal and Iron Company. Parrish's position as director and a major stockholder in the Central Railroad of New Jersey facilitated the company's financial support of the Lehigh and Wilkes-Barre operation. Parrish then expended over $2,000,000 to acquire Hendrick B. Wright's coal lands in Newport Township, the Hollenback coal lands in Hanover Township, and old Lehigh Coal Company's operations in the Hazleton area. Parrish's company also built or acquired mining collieries in Plymouth, Ashley, Sugar Notch, Wanamie, and Wilkes-Barre, bringing the total number of breakers up in excess of twelve by the mid-1870s. With this strong economic base, the company was able to produce more than 2,000,000 tons of coal per year and employ large numbers of men and boys. By 1929, the worth of the Lehigh and Wilkes-Barre Coal Company would climb to near $90,000,000. These extensive and powerful operations remained largely under the management of upper-class leaders, at least until the 1890s. Parrish, in fact, held the presidency until his death in 1896.[15] The extent of Parrish's influence in the coal industry cannot be fully appreciated without a close examination of his career and of the careers of his kinsmen.

Parrish was deeply involved in pioneering and developing the anthracite industry. His accomplishments contributed greatly to centralizing the industry in Wilkes-Barre and maintaining considerable local control over the lucrative and widely sought-after mining operations. Parrish served as president of the Kimberton Coal Company, the Parrish Coal Company, the Wilkes-Barre Coal and Iron Company, the Annora Coal Company, and the Lehigh and Wilkes-Barre Coal Company. Parrish's influence extended beyond the Wyoming Valley through his directorships on the powerful Pennsylvania Railroad, the Central

Railroad of New Jersey, and the Lehigh Coal and Navigation Company. He was also president of the First National Bank of Wilkes-Barre, which handled most of the financial transactions for the anthracite coal companies.[16]

Parrish further extended his influence through his relatives, all in the upper class. These kinsmen were active in mining operations, merchandising of coal, supplying necessities for the "patch towns" that sprang up around mining collieries, and providing materials and equipment for mining. Parrish's in-laws and blood relatives held more than fifteen directorships, three executive posts, and two high-level managerial positions on major coal companies, such as the Wilkes-Barre Coal and Iron Company; the Red Ash Coal Company; the Parrish Coal Company; and the West End Coal Company. These companies operated mining collieries throughout the entire region, accounted for a sizable percentage of total production and together employed some 8,000 men. In addition, the Conyngham family operated a series of company stores located at Parrish mining collieries. These mercantile concerns provided foodstuffs, clothes, tools, and all the necessities of life required by the miners and their families.[17]

The activities of the coal entrepreneurs penetrated every dimension of the industry. Charles Parrish Hunt and Charles M. Conyngham formed the concern of Parrish, Phillips and Company, in conjunction with a New York City entrepreneur. The company was a sales agency that marketed anthracite coal to buyers from New York and New England. William Lord Conyngham, a brother-in-law, also owned and managed a merchandising agency with branches in New York City, Chicago, St. Louis, and other big cities.[18]

Parrish's kin were also active in coal-related industries. Gould Phinney Parrish, Charles's brother, ran a powder mine at Wapwollopen Mills in Hollenback Township and made the explosives required for blasting coal. Charles's in-laws served as directors and officers in manufacturing companies, such as the Hazard Wire Rope Company and the Vulcan Iron Works Machine Tool Company, which produced materials and machines used in collieries. During the 1880s, the Conynghams established the Eastern Pennsylvania Supply Company, located in Wilkes-Barre. This operation became the largest supplier of mining equipment in the northeastern part of the state. These coal-related operations added greatly to the local economy, created jobs and new capital, and significantly strengthened Wilkes-Barre's hold on the industry. The extent of the Parrish family's involvement in the industry can be seen in Table 2–2. Parrish and his relatives had established a vertically integrated system that supplied virtually everything from the raw materials and manufactured goods needed to extract coal to the final sales and distribution. The degree of this participation in all dimensions of the anthracite industry by the Parrish group was typical of many entrepreneurial families in the upper class.[19]

While active in the Wyoming Valley, upper-class entrepreneurs were also deeply involved in the hinterland. There, the activities of the upper class did not encourage development as much as they exploited the resources of the land necessary to sustain the rapid growth in the anthracite coalfields. The quarry in

Table 2-2. Selected Coal and Coal-Related Companies Based in Wilkes-Barre and Controlled by the Parrish Family Network, 1850–1885 [*]

Economic Activity	Company	Area of Operation
Backward linkage: Commerce	Conyngham Stores Swoyer & Stoddard Stores	East Side[†] West Side
Backward linkage: Manufacturing	Hazard Wire Rope Company Hunt Lumber Company	Region[‡] Region (Hinterland)
Backward linkage:[§] Finance	First National Bank Second National Bank	Region Region
Main export: Anthracite coal	Lehigh and Wilkes-Barre Coal Company[‖] Parrish Coal Company West End Coal Company Wyoming Valley Coal Company	Region West Side West Side East Side
Forward linkage: Transportation	Central Railroad of New Jersey[#] North West Branch, Pennsylvania Railroad	New York City to Buffalo[**] Pennsylvania
Forward linkage: Sales and distribution	Parrish, Phillips & Company Conyngham, Hill & Company	New York City Baltimore

[*]The companies are listed by name of company and area of operation within the region and the nearby metropolitan centers.

[†]Refers to the east or west side of the Wyoming Valley and the communities in each section.

[‡]The company sold to collieries throughout the region, as well as to Parrish companies.

[§]Backward linkage necessary to produce item, forward linkage necessary for marketing of product.

[‖]This is only a partial listing of the fifty companies the members of the Parrish family network were involved in.

[#]The railroads were under the control of New York C.ty leadership.

[**]Connected with Buffalo via the Lehigh Valley Railroad at Scranton.

Meshoppen, the lumber mill in Mehoopany, and the grist mills in Wyalusing, all in the upper Susquehanna River area, north of the Valley, were just a few of the operations initiated and financed by the members of the upper class. The economic institutions of the upper class spanned the entire region, thus creating and maintaining the vertical links that enabled Wilkes-Barre's upper-class leaders to subordinate the economies of other cities and towns in the region.[20]

This control would be challenged, particularly after 1869. In that year, the Pennsylvania State Legislature passed an act that enabled the railroads to purchase stock in iron and coal companies. The anthracite railroads soon began to compete aggressively with local leadership groups for control of the anthracite industry throughout the region. While the railroads succeeded in establishing themselves in the Lackawanna Valley and in colonizing the Schuylkill-Northumberland regions, they failed to monopolize coal production in the Wyoming Valley.[21]

Entrepreneurs from outside the region had always been a factor in the northern coalfields. As early as the mid-1850s, local mining operators formed the Wyoming Valley Operators Association to protect the interests of mining entrepreneurs within the region. Headed by Colonel John L. Butler, a prominent member of Wilkes-Barre's nascent upper class, the group met in the house of another upper-class leader, Colonel H. B. Hillman, where the participants apparently discussed issues ranging from overproduction in the anthracite industry to the presence of outside-based capitalists. While short-lived, the association demonstrated an awareness on the part of the local entrepreneurs, including those in the upper class, of capitalists from outside the region whose aims in the coal industry diverged sharply from their own.[22]

Leaders from Wilkes-Barre's upper class exercised considerable leverage with the major outside interests in the region—the anthracite railroads. Stationed in New York City or Philadelphia, the leaders of these corporations saw anthracite coal as an important energy source and, therefore, as a source of profits. Wilkes-Barre upper-class leaders often sat on the boards of these large-scale companies, as the Parrish case indicates. Parrish served as director on the Lehigh Coal and Navigation Company for more than thirty years and was a close associate of the company's managing personnel. He also owned over $1 million in stock of the Central Railroad of New Jersey, where he sat on the board of directors. Parrish was not the exception. Other leaders in the upper class also held directors' seats on the Lehigh Valley Railroad; its subsidiary, the Lehigh Valley Coal Company; the Pennsylvania Railroad; and the Delaware, Lackawanna and Western Railroad. In fact, members of the Harvey and Hillard families of Wilkes-Barre's upper class, among others, owned large amounts of stock in the Lehigh Valley rail system and the Delaware, Lackawanna and Western Railroad.[23]

While Parrish and others did rely on outside investors, they borrowed primarily from entrepreneurs in Wilkes-Barre's upper class and from upper-class-controlled financial institutions in that city. Parrish, in particular, owed substantial sums to relatives, friends, and creditors in the upper class whose money sustained his many diverse operations. In-laws of the Conyngham family held $80,000 of Parrish's Lehigh and Wilkes-Barre commercial paper as a security for supplies provided to the company's employees. Business ally Herbert Ashley also held thousands of dollars in commercial paper (notes based on collateral offered to the bidder with the lowest interest—matured in ninety days or less) from the Lehigh and Wilkes-Barre Company for which Parrish was responsible. Similarly, his nephew, Charles Parrish Hunt, lent Parrish substantial capital to help sustain him through the difficult times of the 1870s depression. Parrish even borrowed in excess of $100,000 from the Second National Bank of Wilkes-Barre, an important financial agency of the upper class, where he served as director. This money was needed to maintain his sagging Hazard Wire Rope Company, which was suffering from the effects of the depression of the seventies. Parrish also set up a separate company, Charles Parrish & Company, to mine coal lands of the floundering Lehigh and Wilkes-Barre Coal Company during the seventies downturn. Parrish ultimately recovered and by 1880 was once again doing an extremely profitable business. [24]

Parrish is not a unique example. Local upper-class creditors sustained other coal operators, among whom the most prominent was John H. Swoyer, one of the more successful members of the upper class. In order to obtain working capital for his numerous operations, Swoyer secured $300,000 in loans from the local banking house of Bennett, Phelps & Company in exchange for his commercial paper. The families who owned this banking house were long-standing members of the upper class and associates of Swoyer. Swoyer also relied on loans from the Miners' Savings Bank and the Second National Bank, both controlled by the upper class. (Swoyer, in fact, served on the board of the Second National Bank.) Swoyer was probably the second most important coal operator, behind Parrish, who was related to Swoyer through marriage. Swoyer owned hundreds of acres of coal lands in Kingston, Pittston, Spring Brook Township, Wilkes-Barre, and Plains Township, as well as mining operations in and around these places. [25]

Entrepreneurs in the upper class obtained most of the capital for operating expenses, for company securities, for acquisition of land, and for other expenditures from business associates within the upper class and/or from its financial institutions. These transactions kept vital resources and key companies within the grasp of the upper class, whose members insured their autonomy through this strategy. For example, the men in this group owned the stock in all but a few of the coal companies operating within the region. They also served as directors, officers, and incorporators on all these companies, thus giving the members of the upper class control from start to finish. Charles Parrish and his relatives and business allies in the upper class controlled the stock in the Red Ash Coal Company, the Parrish & Company, and the Leavenworth & Company operations. John Swoyer and fellow entrepreneurs in the upper class owned the stock shares in the Riverside Coal Company, the Forty-Fort Coal Company, and the Wyoming Valley Coal Company. Members of the upper class also controlled the shares in the Warrior Run Coal Company, the Wilkes-Barre Coal Company, and the Hanover Coal Company, to name just a few of these operations. As a result of its economic power, the upper class was in a position to deal on a reciprocal basis with investors and corporate executives from the metropolitan centers of New York and Philadelphia.[26]

The energies of Wilkes-Barre coal entrepreneurs thrust the Wyoming Valley and the Luzerne coalfields into the lead as the major producer of anthracite coal. The mining operations of the locally based companies produced several hundred thousand tons of coal annually, employed thousands of men, helped spark tremendous population growth, and created a strong capital base. The first expansion of coal output occurred in the 1830s, when the southern extension of the North Branch Canal was opened. The biggest percentage increase, 562 percent, came in the 1840s, when new markets began emerging and the construction of the rail net was started. The dramatic rise in absolute numbers occurred in the decades after 1850, when incorporated companies were replacing the family-dominated operations. On the average, production grew at the rate of 5,476,724 tons per decade from 1830 through 1880, with the largest single increase—17,830,796 tons—occurring in the 1870 to 1880 period. By the late 1870s, entrepreneurs in the northern coal region were mining almost half of the total output of anthracite coal in the United States.[27]

The economic influence of the upper class created by these coal companies encompassed the entire region. These operations were organized and sustained largely by the money and effort of the "Coal Barons" in Wilkes-Barre, whose economic power stretched from Hazleton, Summit Hill, and Eckley in the middle anthracite fields to Nanticoke, Plymouth, and Pittston in the north. The geographic range of these companies insured Wilkes-Barre's status as a regional center and guaranteed local input into the direction of the coal industry's development. Companies such as the Lehigh and Wilkes-Barre Coal Company, the Red Ash Coal Company, and the Parrish Coal Company, which operated numerous mining collieries, constituted the foundation of both Wilkes-Barre's and the region's economic growth.[28]

Wilkes-Barre upper-class leaders dominated the anthracite industry within the region. During the years 1850 through 1885, almost all anthracite operations in the Wyoming Valley had placed their company offices in Wilkes-Barre. With all the major coal exchanges in the region, capital-rich banks, and regular lines of communication with developing markets, the city offered advantages found in no other community in the region. In fact, only two cities in the valley—Kingston and Plymouth—served as headquarters for regional coal companies. With only one company each, Plymouth and Kingston hardly posed a challenge to Wilkes-Barre.

Through its operations, Wilkes-Barre's upper class exercised partial and, in some instances, almost complete control of the main export of virtually every city, town, and village in the region. Many of these communities, such as Sugar Notch, Alden, Wanamie, and Warrior Run, sprang up around upper-

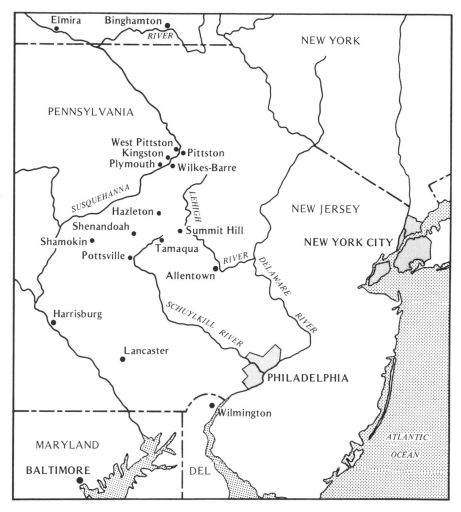

Map 2.   Principal Cities and Towns of the Wyoming Valley

class-owned mining collieries and depended solely on them to survive, with the Welsh-dominated Kingston Coal Company of Edwardsville the exception. This dependency only increased the towns' subordination to Wilkes-Barre, at the same time increasing the power of its upper class. Moreover, the major coal companies in the regional center weakened the capital base of many older communities, such as Kingston and Plymouth. Investors and entrepreneurs in the nearby communities often backed a coal company controlled by the upper class. For example, Samuel Hoyt, Abram Nesbitt, and William Loveland, all among the top wealth holders in Kingston, were incorporators in mining operations such as the Wilkes-Barre Coal and Iron Company and the Wyoming Valley Coal Company. While undermining their own capital base, these leaders only strengthened Wilkes-Barre's money reserves.[29] As important, the flourishing anthracite industry tied the upper class to Wilkes-Barre and the region, in this way sustaining their fortunes and insuring their future prosperity.

The fulfillment of their entrepreneurial aspirations created a sound economic base for the upper class as a whole. Key in the effort was the network of extralocal economic ties which strengthened and helped to diversify Wilkes-Barre's local economy and increased its influence over the northern anthracite region. The power and wealth generated by these activities within and outside the community secured a long-term commitment of resources and capital to the city, as well as cementing the loyalty of the next generation of upper-class leaders. Their fortunes and power were equally tied to the continued exploitation of anthracite and the regional economy in general. Last, the power and wealth of the upper class in the late nineteenth century also acted as a powerful attraction for leaders from other communities scattered over the region who saw in the upper class and the city opportunities not available elsewhere in the northern coalfields. This recognition was an important factor in drawing talent and capital into Wilkes-Barre and further augmented the power of the upper class.

WILKES-BARRE'S UPPER CLASS AND THE DIVERSIFICATION OF THE CITY'S ECONOMIC BASE

The Wilkes-Barre leaders recognized the need for local investment to strengthen their city's economy and diversify its industrial base. While most of the capital went back into anthracite coal production, the upper class made serious attempts to build up manufacturing, banking, and other service activities. Through the efforts of leaders in the upper class, Wilkes-Barre ranked first of all the communities in the Valley in terms of capital invested in these activities and in numbers of incorporated companies engaged in manufacturing, banking, and other operations by the late nineteenth century. For example, the city's financial institutions, controlled by the upper class, accounted for 66 percent of the more than $4.4 million of capital stock in banking found throughout the region, while the upper-class-owned transit companies constituted 69 percent of the $970,000 in the valley-wide traction industry. Of the total invested by entrepreneurial leaders in all these activities, from manufacturing to services, the sum invested by Wilkes-Barre's upper class was three times greater than the combined capital invested in these operations by urban leadership groups in other communities in the region. The comparatively large amount of capital in the hands of city leaders translated into a greater volume of economic activity in Wilkes-Barre than could be found elsewhere in the northern coalfields. In addition, members of the upper class extended their influence by supplying capital or serving as directors for companies and banks scattered over the cities and towns of the Wyoming Valley and hinterland.

Always a wealthy group, Wilkes-Barre's leadership increased its share of asset worth in the region from 1850 through 1870, according to the manuscript census. At mid-century, members of the upper class accounted for 49 percent of the personal wealth ($3,677,000) among leading entrepreneurs (assets greater than $8,000) in the region. The nearest competitor, the Pittston elite, held only 9 percent of the total. By 1870, the upper-class share had jumped to 56 percent of the more than 21 million dollars held by entrepreneurs with assets greater than $30,000. In contrast, the share controlled by leaders in the smaller communities (i.e., those which did not reach 10,000 by 1900) shrank from 23 percent in 1850 to just 1 percent in 1870, as capital and talent moved out of these towns into Wilkes-Barre. At the same time, the capital held by Wilkes-Barre's upper class in 1870 was almost five times as great as its then-closest rival, the Hazleton elite.

With this wealth and power, it is not surprising that Wilkes-Barre itself grew rapidly after 1850. In that year, its residents comprised only 27 percent of the urban population among communities that reached 10,000 by 1900. By 1880, Wilkes-Barre's share had risen to 48 percent. By virtually every measure, the upper class and Wilkes-Barre had become the dominant power in the region.

After Wilkes-Barre's upper class, the elite with the most substantial manufacturing base was in Pittston. Unlike Wilkes-Barre, however, Pittston's companies were largely outside controlled. Members of the Scranton elite, for example, dominated the Pittston Stove Company, one of the largest concerns in the community. Similarly, Wilkes-Barre's leaders bought out the Pittston Machine Tool Works in the 1880s, thereby removing all local influence over this company. Unable to pursue coal mining because of penetration by entrepreneurs from Wilkes-Barre and New York, the local elite had few options remaining. As a result, those in the business elite turned to industries where they had the least competition. They established several local textile plants and a small iron foundry and used their remaining capital to maintain community services. In nearby Wyoming, a similar situation developed. The community had only one factory, a shovel and tool plant, that satisfied the needs of many of the mining collieries on the west side of the Wyoming Valley. A local entrepreneur, Payne Pettebone, had initially put up the capital for this operation and guided the company through its first years. Eventually, his son William, by then a member of the Wilkes-Barre upper class, took over partial control of the operation.[30]

With equal frustration, the elite in Plymouth tried to develop a manufacturing base. Burdened with scarce capital and the early lead of Wilkes-Barre's upper class in this area, local leaders started two unincorporated iron works. One closed the same year it began production. The other, the Wren Iron Works, barely survived into the mid-eighties. Owned by former Mahanoy City iron producers George and Thomas Wren, the iron works provided mining machinery for the anthracite collieries surrounding Plymouth. Competition from Wilkes-Barre and excessive borrowing eventually closed the plant. The other two manufacturing concerns were the Howells-Mining Drill Company and the Plymouth Planing Mill, a lumber company partly owned by the Harvey family in Wilkes-Barre. Neither of these companies capitalized over $35,000, a small sum compared with the money poured into similar operations in Wilkes-Barre by the upper class.[31]

Upper-class leaders in Wilkes-Barre also built a more widely diversified economic base than did leadership groups in other communities. Leaders from the upper class built strong lumber, iron and steel, and textile industries, thus providing sources of employment and profit and stimulating population growth. Lumber, used for construction of the anthracite breakers and deep coal bed tunnels, thrived on the steady increase in coal production, the expansion of new mining collieries, and the rapid growth in housing. Similarly, owners of the local iron companies prospered with an expanding coal industry by producing machine tools for the collieries. Unlike lumber entrepreneurs, whose market was largely confined to northeastern Pennsylvania, the iron manufacturers eventually tapped into the national market. This same pattern also characterized the local textile producers, who moved quickly from a regional to a country-wide market.

The lumber operations began to flourish as coal mining developed in the 1850s and 1860s. During those decades and before, George Hollenback, Jameson Harvey, Robert Ricketts, and others began buying timberlands, constructing lumber mills, and combining these operations with coal production. Ricketts was among the most aggressive of the lumber manufacturers. Recognizing the potential in lumber, he acquired vast tracts of timberland in Luzerne, Sullivan, and Wyoming counties, either through purchase or inheritance. By 1870, Ricketts had amassed a small fortune and ranked among Wilkes-Barre's top wealth holders. Hollenback and Jameson Harvey, whose economic interests were solidly committed to coal, supplied the new anthracite companies with more than 2,000,000 feet of lumber annually. In a similar fashion, Conrad Lee, William and Henry Harvey, Theodore Ryman, Samuel Sturdevant, William Goff, and other members of the upper class built up thriving lumber mills, which fed both the coal mines and the rapidly growing construction industry. These men developed a lumber industry ranging from Bear Creek Township, south of the city, to Wayne County in the northeast corner of the state.[32]

Iron manufacturing also began with the emergence of anthracite. The first manufacturers, August C. Laning and Samuel Marshall, produced machine tools for the anthracite collieries and built steam packet boats for the North Branch Canal. Badly managed and poorly funded, the operation failed to survive the 1860s. Similarly, the Vulcan Iron Works, also established during these years, floundered and was in danger of closing when members of the upper class took over complete control in 1866. These men immediately incorporated and pumped $200,000 into the Iron Works. Now on a firm footing, the Vulcan Iron Works began to expand. In the late 1880s, the directors bought the competing Wyoming Valley Manufacturing Company and the Pittston Engine and Machine

Company of West Pittston. Ten years later, the Vulcan Iron Company purchased the Carter and Allen Company of Tamaqua. By the 1900s, the capital had been increased sixfold, and the annual value of its products reached $4,000,000.[33]

As the Carter and Allen case suggests, members of the upper class did not limit themselves to the region in their search for new manufacturing. Charles Parrish bought the Hazard Wire Rope Company in Mauch Chunk along the Lehigh River in Carbon County. Undercapitalized and poorly managed, the company seemed destined for closure. Sensing the operation's potential, Parrish moved its facilities to Wilkes-Barre in 1868, the year of purchase. Parrish, along with other local leaders, poured $300,000 into the company and, within a few years, the company was prospering. By 1880, Parrish and his associates were successfully marketing the company's products over most of the eastern United States; and by the 1890s, the Hazard operation had established thirty-five branch offices throughout the country. Also in the 1890s, Wilkes-Barre ranked second behind Scranton as the largest producer of iron and steel products in the anthracite coalfields from Pottsville to Carbondale.[34]

Parrish's efforts to build up the manufacturing base of Wilkes-Barre included the Manufacturer's Aid Association, which he and other members of the upper class established in 1879. With this organization, Parrish and his fellow entrepreneurs hoped to create an economic and tax environment favorable to manufacturers. With the assistance of local banks, the association made considerable sums of capital available for expansion of existing facilities or to prospective manufacturers interested in moving to Wilkes-Barre. Short-lived, the association was succeeded by the Board of Trade in 1884. Formed by many of the same leaders, the board continued the policy of promoting diversification of the city's economy. In the same year of its founding, members of the Board of Trade persuaded the Sheldon Axle Works to relocate to Wilkes-Barre from upstate New York, a stated objective of the Manufacturer's Aid Association. Within a year, members of the upper class had pumped over a quarter of a million dollars into the operation and had taken control of the company. These developments showed the Wilkes-Barre upper class to be an aggressive and unified group, whose efforts made Wilkes-Barre the only city in the region with successful iron and steel companies.[35]

The upper class also attempted to create secondary industries unrelated to anthracite coal. Members of the upper class incorporated the Wilkes-Barre Lace Company in 1885 and the Wyoming Valley Lace Company in 1891. The abundance of a largely unemployed female work force, the wives and daughters of the region's coal miners, greatly facilitated this decision. Supported by capital from powerful members of the upper class such as John W. Hollenback and Lazrus D. Shoemaker, the Wilkes-Barre Lace Company quickly became a major operation and an important source of employment, using the labor of 1,400 local men and women. In an effort to secure this growing textile base and complement the female workers, men in the upper class imported several hundred Nottingham weavers from Great Britain during the late nineteenth century to man the Wyoming Valley Lace Company. With an abundance of ready available capital, a skilled labor force, and a surplus pool of female workers, the plant rapidly became a major component of the local economy.[36]

Entrepreneurs in Wilkes-Barre successfully promoted two breweries, which remained an important part of the local and regional economies well into the twentieth century. Together, these establishments provided jobs and salaries for more than 800 men, women, and children, whose efforts supplied rapidly expanding local and regional markets. The older, the Reichard Brewery, was the creation of John Reichard, who had turned it into a very profitable operation by mid-century. The brewery produced 150,000 barrels a day and employed some 200 men. Later, George and Henry Reichard, in cooperation with George P. Weaver, would continue the operation. Quick to realize the potential of the regional market, the founders of the second company, the Stegmaier Brewery, set up outlets in neighboring Pittston, Plymouth, and Nanticoke, the largest communities in the Wyoming Valley outside Wilkes-Barre and Kingston by the early 1900s. Later, this brewery's owners expanded their markets beyond the Valley into the hinterland along the Susquehanna River in towns such as Towanda and Bloomsburg. By the early twentieth century, these entrepreneurs had even moved their branches into the nearby Lackawanna Valley, long the preserve of the members of the Scranton elite, whose city served as the economic and administrative center for that area.[37]

The extent to which the members of the upper class dominated the city's manufacturing industry can be seen in Table 2–3. Wilkes-Barre's upper-class leaders controlled 87 percent of the board positions on all companies. They also owned the stock in these companies. For example, Charles Parrish owned almost all the shares in the Hazard Wire Rope Company. His fellow leader, John S. Wood, controlled the stock in the Wilkes-Barre Paper Manufacturing Company, while other local prominent men held the securities of the Vulcan Iron Works Company, the Wyoming Valley Manufacturing Company, the Sheldon Axle Company, and the Wyoming Valley Ice Company. Only leaders from nearby communities in the Valley showed any noticeable representation in Wilkes-Barre manufacturing operations. Virtually all of these men had immediate relatives among the city's upper class and usually counted cousins and sons-in-law among their fellow board members.[38]

The rapidly growing population of Wilkes-Barre and the region, as well as the pace of economic development, created an acute need for transit and utility services. Members of the upper class naturally became the major entrepreneurs in these industries, particularly since they were essential in sustaining the workers and their families who were employed in coal mining and manufacturing. The city's upper class chartered nine trolley, turnpike, and bridge companies, all headquartered in Wilkes-Barre. These operations joined Wilkes-Barre with every urban community in the region and made the city the transportation hub of the Wyoming Valley.

The transit industry developed late. As of 1880, only two lines were in

Table 2-3. Proportion of Executive Posts, Directorships, Ownerships and Incorporators in Local Industry under the Control of Members of Wilkes-Barre's Upper Class and Other Groups, 1350–1885*

Residence and Economic Position	Positions in Local Industry			
	Manufacturing (%)	Banking (%)	Transportation (%)	Utilities/Services (%)
Wilkes-Barre: Upper class	87%	83%	75%	85%
Wilkes-Barre: Non-upper class	1	6	0	1
Communities in Wyoming Valley: Urban leaders	10	11	21	14
Philadelphia and New York City: Investors	2	0	4	0
Total	100%	100%	100%	100%
	(126)	(232)	(155)	(150)

n = 663

*The economic positions were collected primarily from the biographies located in the local histories, the *Laws* of Pennsylvania, company and bank histories, and the R. G. Dun and Company Collection. These were counterchecked against newspapers, which listed the annual election of company positions, as well as ownerships of local companies, if unincorporated.

operation. By 1890, a dozen new companies had blanketed the Wyoming Valley with their lines. They provided transportation to the constantly growing work force, which often relied on these lines to reach the dispersed mining collieries. This system extended from Nanticoke to Pittston and Dallas to Ashley, with all lines running through Wilkes-Barre, which served as the main terminus for the transit net. In constructing this net, local leadership invested $660,000 in capital. Wilkes-Barre leaders were unique in their efforts to create a regional transit network. At most, leaders in other communities merely joined Wilkes-Barre's leaders in financing a line to their city from the emergent regional center. The transit system complemented the economic ties growing out of the anthracite industry and reflected Wilkes-Barre's dominant position in the region.[39]

Upper-class leaders also took the initiative in organizing region-wide utility operations. At first, the upper class confined its activities to forming local gas and water companies. In 1866, Charles Parrish; L. D. Shoemaker; Washington Lee, Jr.; and other prominent Wilkes-Barreans incorporated the Crystal Spring Water Company, which eventually supplied water to communities in the southeastern part of the region. Several years later, Wilkes-Barre's upper class broadened its base of operations by chartering the Wyoming Valley Gas and Water Company, which provided services to Kingston, Plymouth, Forty-Fort, and Pittston. Members of the upper class established the company in conjunction with leaders from other communities, but it was clearly dominated by those from Wilkes-Barre's upper class, who constituted eleven of the fifteen incorporators. No more than two leaders from any other community served as directors. Members of Wilkes-Barre's upper class were also involved in chartering the Plymouth Water, Plymouth Gas, and the Plymouth Light, Heat and Power companies in the period of the 1870s through the mid-1880s. In subsequent years, local notables such as John Swoyer, Charles Parrish Hunt, and John W. Hollenback joined in founding the Spring Brook Water Company and the Wilkes-Barre Electric Light Company. These two operations eventually absorbed a majority of all local utility companies. Owners of the Wilkes-Barre Electric Light, at this time, had absorbed the Wilkes-Barre Gas and the Plymouth Gas companies. These mergers were a prelude to the massive consolidations at the turn of the century. The upper class complemented these efforts with the incorporation of two telephone companies, which provided almost instant communication among the communities in the region.[40]

BANKING AND THE UPPER CLASS

The expanding local industry and wide-ranging investments of the upper class required a sound financial base to support the volume of economic activity. Long-term capital was needed to finance coal, manufacturing, and other types of companies. At the same time, short-term capital was necessary to support upper-class real estate and property investments and to participate in the speculative anthracite market. Upper-class leaders frequently financed local enterprise through borrowed capital, generally accessible only through publicly chartered or private banks. Members of the upper class moved energetically to control these institutions in order to insure a steady flow of capital for the growing local and regional economies.[41]

During the late nineteenth century, finance was in a state of transition. By the mid-1860s, three types of banks were operating within the regional and national economy. The most common were the private banking houses. These performed all the functions of a state or federally chartered institution, except that they could not issue bank notes. Instead, private bankers relied on deposit banking and checking to create capital for entrepreneurial ventures. Federally sponsored commercial banks appeared with the passage of the National Currency acts of 1863 (also commonly called the National Banking Act) and 1864. Their dual purpose was to create a market for government bonds issued during the Civil War and to establish a uniform currency to replace the mixture of private and state bank notes in circulation. The third type of bank was the state bank. Unlike the national banks, those chartered by the state were only banks of deposit, not issue. State banks were also not limited in the amount of money they could lend to entrepreneurs, nor were they blocked from freely participating in the real estate market. This gave the state banks tremendous advantage over the federal institutions, given the high level of investment in mortgages and property by members of the upper class.[42]

The same pattern of local control characteristic of manufacturing and coal companies was also true of the local financial institutions. Upper-class leaders constituted 83 percent of all directors and officers (see Table 2–2) in city banks, while members of elites in the Wyoming Valley, again, ranked as a distant second in the number of positions held. The efforts of upper-class leaders transformed Wilkes-Barre into the financial hub of the Wyoming Valley. These men chartered nine national and state banks and operated eight private banking houses and two insurance companies, both of which performed most financial functions. No other leadership group in the region matched this combined total of thirteen institutions. Leaders in the upper class also invested $2,870,000 in financial institutions, a sum four times greater than the capital put into banking by the elite in the next largest city, Pittston. Members of the upper class dominated not only Wilkes-Barre banks but finance throughout the region. The city's prominent men frequently presided over banks in other regional cities and towns, such as Pittston, Plymouth, and Ashley, or drew in investors from these communities.[43]

An examination of Pittston, Plymouth, and Ashley, the only other cities in the Valley with chartered banks, clearly shows this influence. During the years from 1850 through the 1870s, members of the Wilkes-Barre upper class held sixteen directorships and four executive positions and counted twenty relatives among the bank directors native to these cities. The Pittston Bank, the first one incorporated in the town, numbered two prominent Wilkes-Barreans among its major investors. These two men became officers of that institution and occupied these positions until the bank's merger with the First National Bank of Pittston. Wilkes-Barre leaders and their relatives elsewhere in the region were also active in the First National Bank. Ziba Bennett and his distant relations, Payne Pettebone and William Swetland, were incorporators and directors of the bank. Moreover, ten of the fifteen board members of the First National Bank were close kinsmen of the upper-class leaders. In addition to their involvement in Pittston's financial circles, upper-class leaders such as Bennett were important members of the banking community in Wilkes-Barre, where they held a total of eight directorships and four executive offices.[44]

Members of the upper class were also active in the Plymouth banking community. William J. Harvey, H. Harrison Harvey, and John Lee served as directors on the First National Bank of Plymouth. Four of the remaining seven board members were related through blood or marriage to the upper class. Similarly, Elijah Wadhams, also a member of the upper class, was among the incorporators of the Plymouth Savings Bank, while fellow incorporator Joshua P. Reynolds was related to William C. Reynolds and the Reynolds family of Wilkes-Barre's upper class. In Ashley, members of the Wilkes-Barre upper class clearly dominated the board of directors. Charles Parrish, Charles M. Conyngham, Peter Pursel, and Henry Palmer, wealthy and established leaders in Wilkes-Barre, occupied more than half the directors' seats and filled all the officers' posts. They also provided the greater part of the capital.[45]

The upper class relied heavily on this dominance of regional and local finance to shape its own future. Control by members of the upper class of the majority of bank boards in Wilkes-Barre and the Wyoming Valley insured a single voice in the financial affairs of the city and the region and, most important, reinforced decisions made, often by these same men, in industry. Entrepreneurs active in coal mining, manufacturing, and other activities were often the same people who ran the banks. For example, Charles Parrish was the leading coal entrepreneur among the members of the upper class and, at the same time, president of the First National Bank. Similarly, Lazrus D. Shoemaker was heavily involved in the anthracite and iron industries while board member and president of the Second National Bank. These men were best able to decide how the available capital should be allocated in a capital-hungry economy. Entrepreneurs such as Parrish often needed short-term capital to purchase new coal lands or improve their own holdings. Frequently, they required large conventional loans to maintain existing operations, expand their facilities, or move into new markets. Members of the upper class familiar with the economic affairs of their fellow entrepreneurs guaranteed that capital would be used in the best interests of their class. At the same time, upper-class entrepreneurs who encountered financial and other economic difficulties, as often happened in the late nineteenth century, were able to use personal contacts among upper-class colleagues in the banking community to borrow money they needed to stay afloat.[46]

This control of finance in the region gave the upper class the ability to screen entrepreneurs elsewhere in the Wyoming Valley and hinterland. As the main sources of capital in the region, upper-class bankers could be ruthlessly discriminating in lending money or vetoing projects deemed too risky. In effect, this power could be ruinous to entrepreneurs outside the realm of upper-class life. Usually, money was lent to relatives, close friends, and business associates, a practice which insured more than a passing familiarity with the borrower. It also guaranteed that local capital would be available only to select and mutually compatible groups of entrepreneurs.[47]

CHAPTER III

Wilkes-Barre's Upper Class and Regional Society

ILKES-BARRE'S UPPER CLASS was both a prosperous entrepreneurial and a tightly knit social group. This combination was responsible, in large part, for the leaders' persistence throughout the nineteenth century. The members of the upper class and their families took their places in a number of exclusive social and cultural institutions which screened out the vast majority of Wilkes-Barre's growing and increasingly foreign-born population. Participation in these institutions was a sign of high social standing in the community and a badge of membership in the upper class. Few could meet the social, genealogical, and educational qualifications those in the upper class generally demanded of new members. Leaders in this group cemented these strong social and cultural bonds through a network of kinship ties that buttressed entrepreneurial alliances and perpetuated the power of the upper class.

Men reared in small, socially confined neighborhoods and educated in exclusive local academies developed their friendships, business partnerships, and entrepreneurial alliances with colleagues who shared the same environment. These early associations eventually led to affiliations in the same churches, social clubs, and philanthropic agencies and intensified the commitment of leaders in the upper class to their primary social group and to Wilkes-Barre. Inevitably, these ties facilitated intermarriage among the families in the upper class; and by the mid- and late nineteenth century, almost all the leaders in the upper class had been joined together through some form of blood and/or marriage ties. Ultimately, this constellation of formal and intimate ties among the members of the upper class sustained the amazing cohesiveness of the group and reinforced the long-term commitment of its members to the city and the region. In economic affairs, the upper class presented a united front that grew out of the social interaction facilitated by these institutions and kinship ties. Entrepreneurial decision making among these men represented not only similar economic interests but also shared cultural values, family bonds, and social characteristics. The conjunction of economic and noneconomic similarities was the key to the long-term persistence and the strength of Wilkes-Barre's upper class.[1]

The following social analysis of Wilkes-Barre's upper class will examine the social characteristics and institutions of that group during the years 1848 to 1856 and 1870 to 1885. The first period corresponds to the shift in Wilkes-Barre's economy from a commercial-agricultural base to an industrial one. The second period opens at about the time of the incorporation of Wilkes-Barre (actually 1871) as the only third-class city (i.e., population over 10,000) in the Wyoming Valley and concludes as the region was slowly being integrated into New York City's orbit. The time span in both instances allows an analysis of the broader patterns of leadership, rather than focusing solely on one year. These two periods also make possible a comparison of the social profile of the upper class in order to demonstrate the continuity in makeup, despite the intense social and economic transformation of these years. The fourteen-year span between the last date of the first period—1856—and the beginning of the next—1870—may seem slight; but in thirty-seven years between 1848 and 1885 Wilkes-Barre's population and economy changed dramatically in size and composition. The opportunities created by this industrial growth and the length of time were both sufficient to produce a variegated leadership that was quite unlike the upper class.[2]

Expanding opportunities in other communities which experienced similar transformations often did produce urban leaders of vastly different social and economic backgrounds. In nearby Scranton, the industrial leadership that developed during the 1850 through 1870 boom years and the birth of the city was largely imported and often of immigrant origins. These men were remarkably unlike the agricultural-commercial leaders who inhabited Slocum Hollow (i.e., the future Scranton). Similarly, industrial growth in Bethlehem, to the south of Wilkes-Barre, beginning in the 1850s, produced two vastly different leadership groups within the fifteen years: one Yankee, entrepreneurial, and tied to the steel and rail industries; the other Moravian, traditional, and committed to a commercial-agricultural-based economy. These changes in urban leadership were not exceptional. In Poughkeepsie, New York, on the Hudson River, the upper stratum underwent a fairly rapid turnover in its ranks during a period of intense industrial and population growth in the city during thirteen years of the mid- and late nineteenth century (1857 to 1870). Instability also plagued the entrepreneurial class in Hamilton, Canada, which, except during the depression of 1857, sustained a high turnover of members during the relatively prosperous 1850s and early 1860s.[3]

WILKES-BARRE'S UPPER CLASS AT MID-CENTURY

First settled by Connecticut Yankees in 1769, Wilkes-Barre was almost a hundred years old by the mid-nineteenth century. During the community's early years, prominent men in Wilkes-Barre slowly began to build a series of institutions that would help sustain the upper class into the twentieth century. Many of these—church, lodge, family, and religion—apparently derived from the settlers' New England heritage. Dissenters in a Congregationalist world, the pioneers of the Wyoming Valley brought with them the notion that religious and church affiliation were closely tied to socioeconomic status. Similarly, the importance of education and family, particularly as the basis for economic endeavor, grew out of the upper class's New England tradition. The crucial role of inheritance in sustaining position in the community also persisted, especially as the members of the upper class began to accumulate substantial fortunes and the contacts necessary to a successful career. Sons and daughters came to depend on these, in addition to the social importance of their New England ancestry, for a start in life.[4] By the 1850s, Wilkes-Barre's upper class had developed into a cohesive and class-conscious group whose members shared many characteristics and were largely natives of the burgeoning town or the Wyoming Valley (Table 3-1). Almost all of Connecticut Yankee stock, these families belonged to Episcopal or Presbyterian churches and were well educated; the men generally pursued law as a career. The city's upper class socialized at meetings of the Masonic Lodge 61 F&AM and the Wyoming Athaeneum, and upper-class families met at informal gatherings in their River Street homes.

As community leaders, the men built Wilkes-Barre's first library and headed the Triton Fire Company, the first in the city. These men were also visible to the community at large through the annual celebrations, such as Independence Day, which they directed and funded. The nascent upper class established exclusive organizations, including the local private academy and the debating society, which separated the members of their own class from the laborers, miners, and foreign-born, who increasingly formed the larger part of the population.[5] These men, or their fathers and relatives, usually had occupied positions of power and status in Wilkes-Barre over the previous decades. George M. Hollenback and Andrew Beaumont were typical of this group. Beaumont, who pursued law early in life, had been a leading political figure in Wilkes-Barre for years. At various times during the years 1814 through 1851, he held the posts of prothonatary and clerk of courts, state representative, postmaster, and collector of revenue. He also belonged to the Masonic Lodge 61 F&AM (1816), the St. Stephen's Episcopal Church (vestryman), and the Triton Fire Company. Educated at the Wilkes-Barre Academy, Beaumont was related to the prestigious Butler family, among others, through marriage.[6]

Both Hollenback and his father, Mathias, had long been prominent figures in Wilkes-Barre, his father from the 1790s into the first decades of the nineteenth century and George from the late 1820s onward. The older Hollenback had built a small fortune on commercial activities that stretched north along the Susquehanna River to Elmira, New York, and south toward Harrisburg and Philadelphia. He had been a major figure in the efforts of Wilkes-Barre's early leaders to promote the community's growth. A resident since the 1770s, Mathias

Table 3-1.   Social Characteristics of Members of Wilkes-Barre's Upper Class, 1848–1856 and 1870–1885 *

Social Characteristics		1848–1856	1870–1885
Lineage	Connecticut Yankee and First Family	70%	75%
	Colonial stock	15	12
	Non–colonial stock	15	8
	Unknown	0	5
		100%	100%
Ethnicity	British	90%	69%
	Scotch-Irish	5	13
	German	2	16
	Other	3	2
		100%	100%
Religion	Episcopalian	62%	49%
	Presbyterian	20	29
	Methodist	11	14
	Other	1	6
	Unknown	6	2
		100%	100%
Education	None	4%	1%
	Common and high school	12	13
	Academy	22	29
	College	25	40
	Unknown	37	17
		100%	100%
Occupation	Lawyer	43%	38%
	Merchant	25	15
	Coal operator	12	15
	Banker	2	11
	Manufacturer	7	7
	Professional	5	11
	Other	6	3
		100%	100%
Birthplace	Wilkes-Barre	42%	20%
	Wyoming Valley	14	23
	Hinterland	15	25
	Areas outside region	21	23
	Foreign-born	8	9
		100%	100%
		(81)	(236)

* In this and subsequent tables, percentages are rounded to 100%.

Sources: See Appendix, Note on Table Sources.

Hollenback had served in local and county offices during the late eighteenth and early nineteenth centuries. The younger Hollenback inherited this wealth and power. One of the first directors of the Wyoming Bank (later to be the Wyoming National Bank), George Hollenback continued to serve in that capacity for years. Active outside his thriving commercial network, Hollenback branched out into mining, transportation, and services, areas where he held numerous directorships and other positions. Like Beaumont, Hollenback was related to the Butler family, among other clans in the upper class (Figure 1). Educated at the Wilkes-Barre Academy, Hollenback spent his entire life in the upper-class residential district, where he eventually built a mansion on South River Street. Active in the Wyoming Valley Historical and Geological Society after its formation in the late 1850s, Hollenback was a prominent citizen of long standing in Wilkes-Barre. His example was by no means unique among the members of Wilkes-Barre's mid-century upper class. Those in the Miner, Ross, Conyngham, and Mallery families, to name a few, matched the careers of Beaumont and Mathias and George M. Hollenback.[7]

Hollenback's family origins (i.e., his father as a prosperous merchant) were typical of Wilkes-Barre's mid-century upper class (Table 3-2). More than 40 percent of its members came from families in which the father had been either a merchant or a lawyer. Few started life in artisanal or farming families (2 percent and 9 percent, respectively); and none came from laboring families.

The practice of marrying into other upper-class families in Wilkes-Barre, as Beaumont and Hollenback did, was also typical of the city's upper-class leadership. Encouraged by the intense social interaction, this custom promoted a high degree of intermarriage among the members of the upper class. By the 1850s, more than 75 percent of these families were joined through various forms of kinship. Figure 1 identifies thirty-six of these families, related through blood and/or marriage. This group, including relatives not shown in the figure, represents a large portion of Wilkes-Barre's leadership at mid-century.

The men who monopolized high social positions in Wilkes-Barre also dominated its political and economic life at mid-century, as Hollenback and Beaumont demonstrated. These men controlled virtually all the wealth and owned the vast majority of the real estate and coal lands in and around the city. Their money and visibility were also dependent on their mercantile operations, which extended from Binghamton and Elmira, New York, in the north to Philadelphia in the south. In addition, upper-class leaders engaged in a variety of entrepreneurial activities, which ranged from banking to coal mining. The overlapping nature of this power and high social position is shown in Table 3-3. Clearly, the members of the nascent upper class dominated all facets of the community. Thirty years later, Wilkes-Barre's upper class still constituted a ruling class. Its hold on community power had hardly lessened. In fact, 92 percent of the 236 leaders identified for the years 1870 to 1885 held some combination of social position and economic power or political authority.[8] In both periods, these men constituted less than 3 percent of the city's population (2.9 percent in 1850; 2 percent in 1870; and 1 percent in 1880).

WILKES-BARRE'S UPPER CLASS IN THE LATE NINETEENTH CENTURY

The upper class expanded dramatically after the late 1840s, largely in response to the rapid growth of Wilkes-Barre's economy and population. The creation of

Figure 1. Kinship Ties among Select Families in Wilkes-Barre's Upper Class, 1848–1856[*]

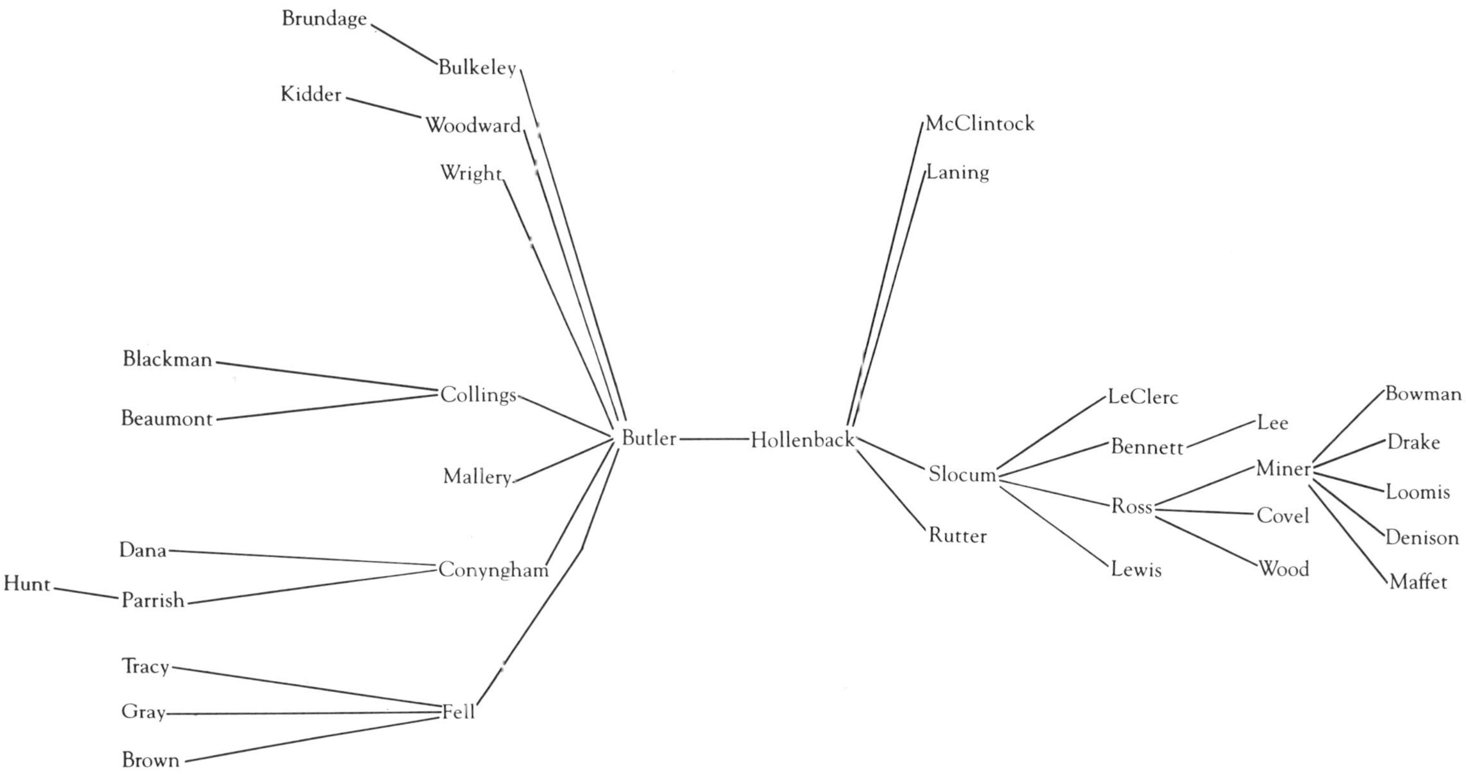

[*]The ties include only first cousins or immediate relatives, not remote connections, such as third or fourth cousins.

Table 3-2. Occupations of Fathers of Members of Wilkes-Barre's Upper Class, 1848–1856 and 1870–1885

Occupation	1848–1856	1870–1885
Merchant	22%	16%
Lawyer	19	17
Coal operator	6	14
Farmer	9	6
Professional	6	6
Manufacturer	2	12
Artisan	2	3
Banker	0	1
Unknown	33	26
Total	100%	100%
	(81)	(236)

Table 3-3. Overlapping Dimensions of Power: Political Authority, Economic Power, and High Social Status among Members of Wilkes-Barre's Upper Class, 1848–1856 and 1870–1885

Dimensions of Power	1848–1856	1870–1885
Political authority, economic power, and high social status	74%	53%
Political authority and high social status	15	11
Economic power and high social status	10	28
High social status	1	8
Total	100%	100%
	(81)	(236)
N = 317		

new companies, the incorporation of more banks, and the increase in political offices rapidly enlarged the number of leadership positions. These created an intense demand for entrepreneurial talent and capital, both from within the region and from the outside. Wilkes-Barre's success in recruitment can be seen in the large number of leaders born in communities other than Wilkes-Barre (Table 3-4). Yet, the preponderance of these migrants came from cities and towns in the region, and all had long-established ties with members of Wilkes-Barre's upper class. Joint participation in the regional network centered in Wilkes-Barre promoted this migration, while common cultural background facilitated assimilation into the city's upper class. In fact, this shared background was still the outstanding characteristic of the upper class and was even common among those from outside the region (Table 3-2).[9]

The members of Wilkes-Barre's upper class continued to demonstrate the same similarity in social characteristics apparent in the forties and fifties (Tables 2-2, 3-3). Regardless of birthplace, the city's leaders were overwhelmingly British by descent and Episcopalian or Presbyterian. Those men who possessed none

Table 3-4. Social Characteristics of Members of Wilkes-Barre's Upper Class by Birthplace, 1870–1885

Social Characteristics		Wilkes-Barre	Wyoming Valley Hinterland	Outside Region	Foreign-Born
Ethnicity	British	76%	75%	67%	26%
	Scotch-Irish	10	9	15	35
	German	8	13	16	39
	Other	6	3	2	0
		100%	100%	100%	100%
Religion	Episcopalian	70	46	49	17
	Presbyterian	13	32	35	35
	Methodist	15	18	9	9
	Other	2	2	4	39
	Unknown	0	2	3	0
		100%	100%	100%	100%
Education	No education	0	0	4	4
	Common school	0	9	9	13
	Public high school	0	1	7	26
	Academy	30	36	22	13
	College	61	41	33	9
	Unknown	9	13	25	35
		100%	100%	100%	100%
Occupation	Lawyer	46	43	38	9
	Coal operator	6	13	18	30
	Banker	9	8	16	13
	Merchant	13	15	15	22
	Professional	20	9	9	9
	Manufacturer	2	9	4	13
	Other	4	3	0	4
		100%	100%	100%	100%
		(46)	(112)	(55)	(23)

n = 236

of these traits were foreign-born and constituted a small percentage of the city's upper class (Table 3-4).

Like those in the upper class at mid-century, these men came from prosperous families (Table 3-2). Of the 236 upper-class leaders, 47 percent had fathers who were merchants, lawyers, or coal operators. Again, few were from artisanal or agrarian families, short on resources and contacts; none traced their origins to working-class families (Table 3-2). Typical was Walter G. Sterling of Braintrim, in Wyoming County. His career benefitted greatly from his father's business allies. Daniel Sterling had been a part of Hollenback's extensive commercial network. Sterling supplemented his commercial venture with timberlands and gristmills, the products of which he undoubtedly traded with Hollenback. This set of contacts facilitated the younger Sterling's entry into Hollenback's Wilkes-Barre operation as a clerk, the beginning of a successful career. Backed by Hollenback money, Sterling eventually set up his own banking house. By the 1870s, based on the fortune and power acquired through his banking operation, Sterling had become a leader in Wilkes-Barre's financial community.[10]

Robert Ricketts, too, was able to rely on a prosperous and well-situated family to ease his start in life. His father and uncle were the top wealth holders in Orange Township, Columbia County, where they ran a lumber and commercial business. A graduate of an upper-class academy, Ricketts eventually inherited or purchased vast timber holdings in Luzerne, Sullivan, and Wyoming counties. Ricketts buttressed his entrepreneurial success by marrying into the Reynolds family, whose members also belonged to the Wilkes-Barre upper class. Like Ricketts, John Laning, too, depended on his father's entrepreneurial success and position in the upper class. The father, Augustus, had been a longtime resident of Wilkes-Barre and a wealthy entrepreneur in his own right. Long a member of the upper class, the older Laning prepared for John Laning's future by enrolling him first at the Wilkes-Barre Academy and later, upon completion of his secondary curriculum, at Lafayette College in Easton. The son completed his education at Union College in Schenectady, New York. Augustus Laning willed his son $50,000, an amount that guaranteed John Laning's security and position in the community. Such stories were very common among members of the upper class. Rags to riches certainly was not characteristic of these men.[11]

As suggested by John Laning's early years, members of the city's upper class were exceptionally well educated (Table 3-4). All those born in the city attended private academies and/or colleges. Their native-born counterparts were equally well trained—77 percent of those from the region and 55 percent of the leaders born outside the coalfields had comparable educational backgrounds. Almost a fourth of the foreign-born enrolled in private academies or matriculated at a university. In an era when few Americans completed common school, the high percentage of college and academy graduates clearly separated the members of Wilkes-Barre's upper class from the general population.

Many of the upper-class leaders had attended the same colleges. Almost half of these men graduated from Yale, Princeton, or Harvard, as was also typical of upper-class groups elsewhere in the Northeast. In many families, this practice was a tradition extending back to the school's founding. Members of the Reynolds family, for example, had been enrolling at the Presbyterian-dominated College of New Jersey (i.e., Princeton) since the eighteenth century. This tradition existed even among leaders from outside the region. Garrick Mallery, a native of Connecticut, completed his education at Yale, as his father, grandfather, and great-grandfather had done. A number of upper-class leaders also attended Amherst, Wesleyan, Union, and Williams colleges, institutions that had long been popular with urban leadership groups in New England and the Middle Atlantic states.[12]

A commonality in lineage and family status further reinforced this cultural homogeneity (Table 3-5). No less than 91 percent of the local-born upper class were members of colonial-stock families, most of whom traced their origins to New England settlers, particularly those from Connecticut. Almost all of the men and women native to Wilkes-Barre and the Wyoming Valley, in fact, were descended from Connecticut Yankee families who had pioneered the Valley, and northeast Pennsylvania in general, during the late eighteenth century. Most of the great-grandparents of these men were members of the founding families in their native communities. In addition, more than half of the foreign-born married into these families and, in that sense, shared in this cultural tradition. This same pattern was true for the families of these men. With few exceptions, the upper-class leaders had been born into prominent families, whose members exercised considerable economic and political power in their communities.[13]

The institutions of church, private school, and social club were important in defining the parameters of interaction among the members of the upper class during the 1870s and 1880s. In the process, they continued to act as barriers to other socioeconomic groups in the city. In their New England tradition, Wilkes-Barre leaders maintained the St. Stephen's Episcopal and First Presbyterian churches. Leading members of the community had founded both churches in the early 1800s. Both institutions, as expected, drew their congregations almost exclusively from the First Families and the wealthier residents of the community. (The fact that pews sold for no less than $100 and as much as $500 confirms this conclusion.) The class origins of the individuals who directly controlled these organizations—the vestrymen, the trustees, and the directors—further demonstrate the exclusivity of these churches. All were members of the city's upper class and usually descended from colonial-stock families. The president of the board of trustees of St. Stephen's during these years, Lazrus Shoemaker, belonged to one of the Valley's First Families and married into another. He was a member of all the leading social clubs and served as officer or director on several major companies. The vestrymen and trustees for St. Stephen's and the First Presbyterian differed little from the Shoemaker example. Almost 60 percent of the upper class attended one of these two churches, with an additional 11 percent affiliated with the First Methodist Church. These institutions served a social, as well as religious, role. To a large extent, church membership, along

Table 3-5. Lineage, Family Status, and Kinship of Members of Wilkes-Barre's Upper Class by Birthplace, 1870–1885

Lineage, Family Status, and Kinship		Wilkes-Barre	Wyoming Valley Hinterland	Outside Region	Foreign-Born
Lineage	Colonial Stock First Family	95%	83%	51%	52%*
	Colonial Stock	2.5	11	29	0
	Non-colonial stock	2.5	1	9	48
	Unknown	0	5	11	0
		100%	100%	100%	100%
Family status	Member of Wilkes-Barre Leadership	100	10	11	78
	Member of leadership in community of origin	0	81	65	4
	Non-leadership status	0	1	6	0
	Unknown	0	8	18	18
		100%	100%	100%	100%
Kinship	Related through blood or marriage to other members of Wilkes-Barre leadership	98	90	87	57
	Unrelated to other members of Wilkes-Barre leadership	2	10	13	43
		100%	100%	100%	100%
N = 236		(46)	(112)	(55)	(23)

*Indicates the percentage of foreign-born leaders who married women descended from colonial-stock families who pioneered the Wyoming Valley in the 1770s.

with religious denomination, provided a quasi-ethnic character to the city's upper class by reinforcing the exclusivity of the "Old Americans."[14]

The social functions of the local educational institutions were as important to the upper-class leaders as their churches. The academies isolated the offspring of local prominent families from the class heterogeneity of the public schools and, at the same time, socialized the young for life in the upper class. The schools also prepared the young men for the rigors of college. Because of their numerous functions, the Wilkes-Barre Academy and the Wyoming Seminary played a critical role in helping to perpetuate family status and insure the success of the successive generations. More than half of the men from the region and outside attended one of the local schools. In the process of educating, these schools also created the basis for lifelong associations among the successive generations of the upper class, including young men from communities other than Wilkes-Barre. The local academies both helped integrate the newcomer into local leadership and reinforced the sense of class consciousness among the sons of Wilkes-Barre's upper class. Nor did the upper class ignore their daughters' educational needs: members maintained a finishing school, the Wilkes-Barre Female Institute, for the daughters of upper-class families. This institution performed virtually the same function for the young women in the upper class as did the male academies for the young men.[15]

Upper-class leaders also participated in a rich associational life. Clubs and organizations such as the Malt Club, Wyoming Monument Association, the Wyoming Historical and Geological Society, and the Cheese and Crackers Club, which were open only to members of this upper class, provided regular channels of communication among Wilkes-Barre's leaders. Several of these organizations, particularly the Wyoming Monument Association and the Historical Society, stressed the New England origins of the upper class through genealogies and accounts of the Valley's pioneering days. In contrast, men's clubs in the metropolitan centers probably inspired other organizations, most notably the short-lived Cheese and Crackers Club and the longer-lived Malt Club. These institutions touched the historical and literary dimensions of life for the community leaders and involved them in common activities not available to the local society at large. Consequently, a high proportion of Wilkes-Barre's upper class, 82 percent of the total and 87 percent of the native-born, belonged to at least one, and usually two or more, of these groups.[16]

Law was the most popular occupational choice among the upper-class leaders, for both community and business reasons (Table 3-4). First, the vast majority of men in the upper class who pursued law acquired their skills under the direction of attorneys who themselves belonged to the upper class. These legal apprenticeships, the chief means of training lawyers in the nineteenth century, lasted three to four years and were crucial in facilitating contacts within a wide circle of Wilkes-Barre's leadership. The lawyers worked closely with their apprentices, directing their reading and conducting weekly question-and-answer sessions. The apprentices accompanied their mentors to court and often socialized with them. In the process, they established close bonds with their mentors and other locally prominent families. These ties usually led to marriage into one of the genteel families and entry into the leading clubs and churches. In this sense, law performed an integrative function. Second, Wilkes-Barre was the county seat and had been since Luzerne County's formation in the late eighteenth century. As the political, judicial, and administrative hub, as well as the center for all major economic activity in the region, Wilkes-Barre offered ample opportunity for a young lawyer.[17]

Skills in business and law had become vital for the successful entrepreneur by the seventies and eighties. Since the 1830s, businessmen and lawyers had been deeply involved in rationalizing the legal system as it related to government and business. In some areas, this alliance produced modern forms of contract, property, and corporate law, particularly as they related to new types of economic activity. In others, members of both groups had successfully pushed for measures in state government designed to create standardized legal procedure as it concerned business. For instance, lawyers and businessmen were the chief agents in securing state general incorporation laws and in establishing standard negotiable instruments, such as bills of exchange. These and similar measures helped realize the lawyers' objective, a more rational legal system. They also aided the businessmen, for example, by providing for standard means of debt payment, capital transfer, and the installation of new companies without legislative interference, as so often happened with special, rather than general, incorporation laws. These associations also meant that skills in law and business were increasingly overlapping and interconnected.[18]

Since it offered both political and economic rewards, law was probably the most important of all the occupational pursuits among the members of the upper class. Lawyers from this group were almost always successful entrepreneurs, illustrating the alliance between the two professions. The training acquired while reading law also served as an effective preparation for business. Through his work, the apprentice or young lawyer generated numerous contacts with the leading entrepreneurs in the city and the region. These associations were crucial in securing loans, forming partnerships, chartering companies, and carrying out other entrepreneurial activity. From the 1830s through the end of the century, this pattern remained unchanged.[19]

Wilkes-Barre's upper class had, in fact, dominated the legal profession from the beginning of the nineteenth century, and the years 1870 through 1885 were no exception. During this time, members of the upper class constituted 88 percent to 92 percent of all lawyers in the city and 80 percent of those in the county. This preponderance placed members of Wilkes-Barre's upper class in an ideal position to regulate access to the profession and, ultimately, to political power. By sheer numbers, they controlled the chief means of training new lawyers—the legal apprenticeship. They also monopolized the county bar and, therefore, the examining committees that admitted new members to it. Last, the upper-class lawyers founded and dominated the Wilkes-Barre Law and Library Association, whose regular meetings provided a means of socializing for those in the city's legal profession.[20]

The visibility of the upper class was nowhere more apparent than in its exclusive residential district. During the 1840s, Wilkes-Barre's upper class families had lived along River Street. Over the next thirty years, the upper class expanded its residential quarters to accommodate the growing number of families in the city's leadership. By the 1870s and 1880s, an overwhelming proportion of the upper class, 92 percent, lived in an area bounded by Main Street and the Susquehanna River on the east and west, respectively, and confined between Ross and North streets. Almost all the social, religious, and educational institutions of the upper class were located within this district. St. Stephen's Episcopal, the First Presbyterian Church, the Wyoming Historical and Geological Society, and the Wilkes-Barre Law and Library Association were all on the same block of South Franklin Street, between Northampton and West Market streets, almost directly in the center of the upper-class residential area.[21]

During the post-1850 decades, when Wilkes-Barre began to experience its rapid growth, the central business district, which included the county courthouse, emerged immediately adjacent to the upper-class residential district. This location placed all the economic and political institutions of the city's upper class within a five-minute walking distance of its members. The presence of these institutions helped preserve the upper-class character of the area and to reinforce its attractiveness for future members of that group.

Within this district, the upper class carried out a variety of social activities. The diary of George Wright, whose father, Hendrick, had been prominent in city affairs since the 1840s, describes a constant and intense interaction among members of the upper class. He recorded numerous visits with these men and their families, including social calls with local notables such as Samuel Turner, George Bedford, and J. Pryor Williamson and dinner invitations from the Wadhams, the Hillards, and the Loops—all families in the upper class. Wright also regularly joined in election-eve gatherings with other prominent community figures. This interaction indicated considerable intimacy among those in the upper class and their families.[22]

This intimacy was apparent even during the funerals of leaders in the upper class. The men who eulogized Andrew T. McClintock, longtime community leader, all close friends and business associates, were among the most prominent men in the city. The pallbearers were men of comparable rank. Many were close relatives, such as John W. Hollenback and Augustus Laning, both first cousins of McClintock. McClintock, like most members of the upper class, was buried in the Hollenback Cemetery at the far end of River Street. The pattern of close associations persisted even through death.[23]

The upper class asserted its position in the local community through a variety of volunteer organizations. These groups provided medical care, cultural activities, youth recreation, and other service functions. The Young Men's Christian Association, the Home for Friendless Children, and the Osterhout Free Library were all located on the streets where the upper class lived. Only the General Hospital, at the northern end of River Street, was outside the upper-class district. The founders of these organizations were all members of the upper class who believed that these welfare institutions were in the best interests of the community. The Home for Friendless Children provides a case in point. Powerful leaders, among them Ziba Bennett, Lazrus Shoemaker, and John W. Hollenback, established the home to take care of the orphans of coal miners who were left without families. These men served as directors and supplied the funds needed to run the home. Their wives took care of the children by providing them with food, clothes, shelter, and education. The absence of any other social group with the capability of supporting such agencies meant that the upper class bore sole responsibility for establishing and supporting most welfare associations.[24]

Marriage and kinship were as important as the formal institutions in maintaining the cohesiveness of the upper class, particularly during the years of its growth after the 1840s. Regardless of birthplace, almost all of the upper-class leaders and their families were interrelated through blood and/or marriage (Table 3-5 and Figure 1). The practice of intermarriage had actually begun in the late eighteenth century, when northeastern Pennsylvania was still comparatively isolated, and was well established by the 1840s. During the subsequent thirty years, this practice had expanded to include the large number of successful newcomers with cultural and economic backgrounds similar to those in the upper class.[25]

Figure 2 shows the extent to which the Butlers and the Hollenbacks were related to other families in the upper class; it illustrates other kinship ties as well. Descended from the community's founder, the Butlers were the most prominent family in Wilkes-Barre, both in terms of social status and lineage; the Hollenbacks, meanwhile, had been one of the most powerful commercial and landowning families since the 1790s. The two families had been connected by marriage in the early 1800s, when Chester Butler married a Hollenback. During the nineteenth century, Butler men married into the Slocum, Bulkeley, and Mallery families. Similarly, their daughters and granddaughters chose husbands from upper-class families, such as the Wrights, Conynghams, and Woodwards. In the same fashion, Hollenback women married into the Rutter, Darling, and McClintock families. Members of the Reichard, Fuller, and Hunt families were tied through kinship to the Parrish family, while those in the Morgan, Stark, and Ketcham families were related to the Sturdevants. As these cases suggest, members of the upper class did more than simply marry members of the Butler and Hollenback families and their descendants. Kinship ties among the Dorrances and Farnhams, Wadhams and Shoemakers, and Reynoldses and Fullers give just a few examples of the interrelationships among the upper-class families. This description only hints at the density of marital and blood relations, often stretching back into the 1790s and extending forward into the 1900s, among these families and their members.[26]

Figure 2. Kinship Ties among Select Families in Wilkes-Barre's Upper Class, 1870–1885

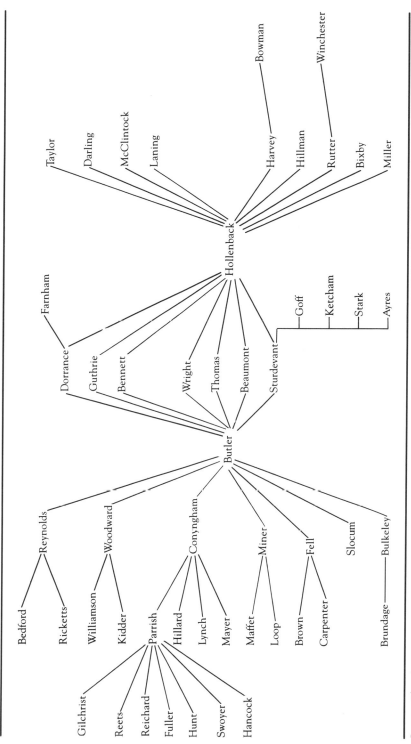

Source: The chart was adapted from Roger M. Haigh, *Martin Guermes—Tyrant or Tool?* (Fort Worth, Texas: Texas Christian University Press, 1968), 58, 60.

On one hand, these ties maintained the cohesiveness of the older families of the upper class. On the other, they quickly and effectively promoted the assimilation of newer families who arrived in large numbers after the late 1840s. A brief history of the McLean family demonstrates this pattern of assimilation through kinship and institutional ties. In 1840, Alexander McLean migrated from Northern Ireland to Mauch Chunk, a coal town at the eastern edge of the Lehigh coalfields. After eight years as a successful coal operator, McLean moved to Wilkes-Barre and settled on the southwestern end of the upper-class residential district. There, he and his sons later built an opulent mansion, comparable to other homes in the area. Once in the city, he invested his money in real estate and land. By the 1860s, he had become a major stockholder and a director of the First National Bank and the Wyoming Valley Coal Company, both controlled by members of the upper class. He also joined the First Presbyterian Church and later became president of the Central Poor Board, headed by leading residents of the Wyoming Valley. McLean's wealth and his investments ranked him among the top twenty-five wealth holders in Wilkes-Barre in the years after 1850. During the next few years, he acquired all the attributes of a full-fledged member of the upper class, except familial ties.[27]

He acquired these with the second generation. William, Alexander's son, attended one of the local upper-class academies and subsequently graduated from Lafayette College in Easton, Pennsylvania, where Wilkes-Barre's wealthy often sent their sons. Upon returning to the city in 1865, he began a legal apprenticeship under George Nicholson, a longtime member of the upper class and prominent figure in the local bar and the Wilkes-Barre Law and Library Association. Using his family's position and these skills, William made a successful career in banking, coal, and politics. These assets also paved the way for his entry into the exclusive Malt Club and the First Presbyterian Church and, in the 1890s, made him one of the founding members of the Westmoreland Club, which became one of the premier social organizations in northeast Pennsylvania. The marriage of his sister into the Ricketts family, one of the most prestigious in the city, further strengthened these institutional and social ties. Two of his younger sisters also married board members of the First National Bank, where all the male members of the McLean family had been directors or officers since its founding.[28]

Underlying the majority of such economic relationships among the members of the upper class were a strong set of kinship ties. The data in Table 3-6 demonstrate the overlapping character of familial and entrepreneurial relationships. The table examines the board composition of ten selected companies and banks, showing the distribution of directorships among six particular families in the upper-class kinship network; other members of the upper class who were a part of the kinship network; and members who were not a part of the kinship system.

An examination of two of the companies and one of the banks listed in Table 3-6 demonstrates the extent to which economic and kinship ties were inter-

Table 3-6. Upper-Class Family Concentration of Directorships in Selected Companies and Banks of Wilkes-Barre, 1870–1885

Selected Companies	Number of Directorships Held by Upper-Class Family							
	Parrish	Hollenback	Bennett	Shoemaker	Reynolds	Loveland	Other	Unrelated
Parrish/Wilkes-Barre Coal Companies	10	2	4	1	0	0	0	0
Vulcan Iron/Hazard Rope Companies	5	3	4	5	0	5	2	2
First/Second National Banks	2	3	0	10	3	5	5	6
Wilkes-Barre Gas/Crystal Springs Companies	3	3	5	3	5	0	1	0
Wyoming Valley Gravity/Wilkes-Barre Ashley Pass. Companies	2	4	5	3	1	3	2	4
Total	22	15	18	22	9	13	10	12

$\overline{x}$ = Number of directorships per family, 16.5.

twined. The Parrish Coal Company provides the most conspicuous example of a family-oriented business operation. Charles Parrish served as president and director. His brothers, nephews, and in-laws held six of the eight directorships in the company and filled all the executive posts. Along with the Conynghams and Hunts, the Parrish family also ran coal sales agencies in New York City and Philadelphia, a powder mill, numerous company stores, and several other anthracite companies.

Similar patterns of kinship ties appear among company directors for the Hazard Wire Rope Company and local financial institutions. Charles Parrish, John N. Conyngham, and George and John Reichard of the Hazard Rope Company were closely interrelated through marriage. Conyngham had married a daughter of the prestigious Butler family. John W. Hollenback, vice-president of the Hazard Company, was related to the Bennett and Thomas families through the nieces of his adoptive father, George Hollenback. Among the directors of the Miners' Savings Bank, later to become the largest financial institution in the city, John Laning, John W. Hollenback, Nathaniel Rutter, Edward Darling, and Andrew T. McClintock were all related, either through blood and/or marriage. Similarly, Andrew T. McClintock, Charles A. Miner, John P. Williamson, and J. F. Lee, directors of the Wyoming National Bank, the oldest in the Valley, were all kinsmen, distant and close. These familial and marital ties promoted cohesiveness among the upper class and formed the backbone of the members' economic relationships.[29]

The strength of these overlapping ties was vital for the economic survival of the entrepreneurs in the upper class. At no time was the importance of these ties more apparent than in the depression of the mid- and late seventies. The depression crippled the economic fortunes of Charles Parrish, the leading entrepreneur in Wilkes-Barre, through his L&WBCC. Parrish depended heavily on loans from relatives, who owned the Bennett, Phelps & Co. Banking House, to maintain his mining operations. The collapse of the L&WBCC threatened his entire future, particularly if the Bennett and Phelps called in his debts. However, his repayment was deferred until he had restored his own financial losses. Loans from other relatives and local entrepreneurs against his stock in the Hazard Wire Rope Company enabled Parrish to reopen the company's mining collieries in 1881 and guaranteed his economic survival. Similarly, Bennett and Phelps (in-laws themselves) were forced to suspend their own operations in the late seventies because of reverses such as Parrish's.[30]

The efforts of Bennett and Phelps to sustain Parrish also extended to distant kinsman John Swoyer, the second leading coal entrepreneur in the Wyoming Valley. By the end of the 1870s, Swoyer was in desperate straits. The depression had forced him to suspend the operations of his five coal and land companies, which covered the entire region. The willingness of Bennett and Phelps to carry his substantial loan was a major factor enabling him to avoid complete bankruptcy. Swoyer's troubles also severely worsened the financial fortunes of John and George Reichard, his father-in-law and brother-in-law, respectively. They, too, had purchased or endorsed large amounts of his paper, which became almost worthless during the depression. The Reichards apparently brought no pressure upon Swoyer, a fact which also helped keep him afloat during the rough times of the late 1870s. Recognizing the dangers, Swoyer also took drastic measures on his own. He sold $250,000 in Hillside Coal & Iron Company stock and $125,000 in real estate to meet his mounting debts. Ultimately, the aid provided by other members of the upper class saved Swoyer from financial ruin. By the mid-1880s, he had recovered and was again mining coal on many of the 1,000 acres of land he owned in Kingston, Pittston, Plains Township, Wilkes-Barre, and elsewhere.[31]

THE INSTITUTIONS AND KINSHIP SYSTEM OF THE UPPER CLASS AND REGIONAL SOCIETY IN THE MID- AND LATE NINETEENTH CENTURY

Critical in sustaining the upper class within the community, the kinship system and institutions reached out beyond Wilkes-Barre to integrate the urban elites in the region into the social world of the city's upper class. The extralocal ties that irrevocably bound these leadership groups to Wilkes-Barre's upper class reinforced its economic hold on the other communities and linked the entrepreneurial fortunes of their elites to the upper class. Increasingly, these assocations reduced the autonomy of leadership groups in their own cities and redirected their efforts toward promoting the objectives of the Wilkes-Barre upper class. The institutions and kinship system both recruited and assimilated leaders and their families from throughout the region. As a result, no competing groups with economic power emerged outside the ranks of the upper class. The recruitment of these men also enabled the upper class to expand in order to meet the demands of a growing economy.[37]

Prior to the 1840s, the elites in the other communities of the Wyoming Valley were deeply involved in promoting the coal industry and other economic activities. Generally, these men doubled as merchants and landowners in order to support their ventures in mining. In fact, many of them thought of themselves as merchants first and coal enterpreneurs second. Members of the elite in Plymouth, for example, had been engaged in commercial activities since the late eighteenth century and in mining and shipping of anthracite only since the 1820s. Henderson Gaylord typified the early entrepreneurs in Plymouth. Born into a family of farmers and merchants, he started his career shipping farm products to communities along the Susquehanna River. In the early 1820s, he began to diversify his operations from commerce to mining. By 1830, he was shipping anthracite, as well as grains and timber, to urban markets as far south as Harrisburg. He also maintained general stores in and around Plymouth to sell goods obtained in Philadelphia and Baltimore. In nearby Kingston, the community leaders were commercial farmers and major landowners; they capitalized on local coal deposits to make their fortunes. These men also trafficked goods up and down the Susquehanna River to other communities in the Wyoming Valley and beyond. The activities of these elites differed little from those of their counterparts in Wilkes-Barre.[33]

The elites in these communities demonstrated social characteristics and ancestry identical to those in the Wilkes-Barre upper class (Tables 3-7 and 3-8). The greatest proportion of leaders in the other communities of the Valley were of British descent, usually Episcopalian or Presbyterian and, in most cases, from families with considerable status and economic power (see the family status data in Table 3-8). In Plymouth, for example, 74 percent of the members of the elite were British, and 45 percent participated in the Episcopal or Presbyterian denominations.

The vast majority of these men traced their ancestry to the Connecticut Yankee settlers or colonial pioneers in southeastern Pennsylvania and elsewhere. Pittston was an exception, but other Valley communities illustrated these characteristics, with more than 72 percent of the elites from Plymouth, Kingston, Wyoming and other communities descended from old-line families. These similarities made possible the participation in the institutional structure and kinship system of Wilkes-Barre's upper class. Seventy-five percent of Plymouth's leadership and 77 percent of the elites in Wyoming and other communities were related to families in the Wilkes-Barrean upper class through blood or marriage (Table 3-8). After 1840, the members of these elites began to participate in the social and economic world of Wilkes-Barre's upper class.

Participation in Wilkes-Barre's upper-class institutions often began early in life for leaders from communities in the region. School was generally the first opportunity to associate with the members of Wilkes-Barre's upper class. By the 1850s, the city's academies had become the chief training ground for the upper levels of regional society. As a result, prominent families in these communities, such as the Tompkinses in Pittston and the Paynes in Kingston, frequently sent their children to Wilkes-Barre schools.[34]

Next, young men from local elites in nearby communities who pursued law as a career usually spent their two-year apprenticeship in Wilkes-Barre. During these apprenticeships, the aspiring lawyers usually boarded with upper-class families. Similarly, sons of entrepreneurs from towns in the region who came to Wilkes-Barre to acquire skills and experience in company operations also spent their business apprenticeships living with prominent families. Inevitably, these young men, whether in law or business, studied under the direction of an attorney or entrepreneur who was a member of the upper class. Lawyer Elisha Harvey of Plymouth trained under and boarded with Frisbie Hansen, a prominent Wilkes-Barre lawyer. Dunning Sturdevant came from Braintrim, in Wilkes-Barre's hinterland, to learn the skills of commission merchantry from his relative, Warren F. Goff, who ran a successful mercantile business in the city. As a member of the upper class, Goff also offered the young Sturdevant numerous business contacts which would later advance Sturdevant's career.[35]

Table 3-7. Birthplace and Social Characteristics of Leaders in Communities of the Wyoming Valley, 1870*

Birthplace and Social Characteristics		Plymouth	Kingston	West Pittston and Pittston	Wyoming and Other Communities
Birthplace	Resident community[†]	53%	44%	18%	35%
	Hinterland	10	8	11	9
	Wyoming Valley	8	28	14	18
	Outside region	21	17	26	29
	Foreign-born	8	3	31	9
		100%	100%	100%	100%
Ethnicity	British	74	75	56	65
	Scotch-Irish	6	5	19	3
	German	16	15	11	29
	Other	1	5	14	3
	Unknown	3	0	0	0
		100%	100%	100%	100%
Religion	Episcopalian	19	17	20	24
	Presbyterian	26	47	38	32
	Methodist	32	25	11	29
	Other	13	3	11	6
	Unknown	10	8	20	9
		100%	100%	100%	100%
		(68)	(36)	(92)[‡]	(34)
N = 230					

*These elites begin to break up during the 1870s and 1380s. Their members actually begin moving to Wilkes-Barre prior to 1870 and after 1880. The date 1870 represents a midway point in an ongoing process that spanned several decades.

[†] Born in community heading column.

[‡] On occasion, percentages were rounded up so that total would be 100 percent.

Table 3-8. Lineage, Family Status, Kinship, and Persistence Rates of Leaders in Communities of the Wyoming Valley, 1870

	Plymouth	Kingston	West Pittston and Pittston	Wyoming and Other Communities
Lineage				
Colonial stock and First Family	62%	64%	16%	32%
Colonial stock	10	11	28	44
Non-colonial stock	25	19	45	12
Unknown	3	6	11	12
	100%	100%	100%	100%
Family status				
High SES*	69	83	60	59
Non-high SES	19	3	17	26
Unknown	12	14	23	15
	100%	100%	100%	100%
Kinship				
Related to Wilkes-Barre upper class	75	92	47	77
Unrelated to Wilkes-Barre upper class	25	8	53	23
	100%	100%	100%	100%
Persistence rate				
Family persisted	12	17	33	21
Leaders to Wilkes-Barre	29	36	13	41
Family members to Wilkes-Barre; family gone by 1920	43	33	35	35
Family disappeared	16	14	19	3
	100%	100%	100%	100%
	(68)	(36)	(92)	(34)

n = 230

*Socioeconomic status.

Associations with Wilkes-Barre's upper class persisted through the next stage of the young man's life cycle. Marriage into a prominent Wilkes-Barre family helped strengthen earlier ties or create new ones with the city's leadership. Such leading families as the Wadhams, the Dorrances, the Starks, and the Laws had close familial ties—in Plymouth, Kingston, Plains, and Pittston, respectively—with members of the upper class, often extending back to the late eighteenth century. Once established in their own communities, these leaders often affiliated with Wilkes-Barre clubs, churches, and lodges. The men also joined in economic ventures, such as the incorporation of mining, traction, and manufacturing companies.[36]

An examination of the career of Charles Dorrance of Kingston illustrates clearly how this variety of ties affected leaders in other communities. Dorrance was descended from a Connecticut Yankee family that had maintained wealth and position throughout the nineteenth century. Given the advantages of birth, Dorrance was able to enroll at the Wilkes-Barre Academy and begin the socialization process into the upper class. Building on family ties and connections in Wilkes-Barre, Dorrance successfully pursued an entrepreneurial career in the city, where he served as director of several companies and banks. Dorrance also joined Wilkes-Barre's First Presbyterian Church, where his brother was minister, and belonged to Lodge 61 and the Historical Society. His assimilation into the upper class was completed by the marriage of his daughter into one of the city's leading families. While Dorrance remained in Kingston, his power and visible social position were derived from his participation in Wilkes-Barre's upper-class institutions.[37] Even in death, these associations persisted. As among their own members, upper-class leaders read eulogies and served as pallbearers at the funerals of leaders from other communities. Similarly, urban leaders outside Wilkes-Barre joined the upper class in burying their colleagues (i.e., of the elites) and relatives in the Hollenback Cemetery.

Another indicator of the close association between leaders in other communities and the upper class occurred in the naming of children. On occasion, members of elite families would incorporate the full name of an upper-class leader who was a friend and business associate. For example, Edwin Davenport, a member of one of Plymouth's oldest and most powerful families, named his first son after Stanley Woodward, a well-known Wilkes-Barre judge, entrepreneur and business partner. George Hollenback Flanagan took his first two names from another of Wilkes-Barre's most outstanding merchants and coal operators.[38]

Obviously, the institutions and kinship system of Wilkes-Barre's upper class were able to influence individual leaders throughout the critical stages of their lives. This pattern of participation extended beyond the individual, however, and included most of the members of all the urban elites in the Wyoming Valley. The data in Table 3-9 demonstrate the frequency and duration of the familial, institutional, and economic relationships between Wilkes-Barre's upper class and the elites in the region. The upper class had developed its closest relation-

Table 3-9. Proportion of Familial, Institutional, and Economic Ties between the Upper Class in Wilkes-Barre and Elites and Communities in the Region, 1850–1880*

Ties between Upper Class and Elites and Communities in Region	Plymouth	Kingston	West Pittston and Pittston	Wyoming and Other Communities in Wyoming Valley†	Communities in Hinterland‡
Kinship: Leaders in Wilkes-Barre and other communities interrelated	35%	33%	38%	28%	41%
Institutional: Ties held by leaders elsewhere in region	20	25	23	11	21
Economic: Directorships and partnerships held in economic institutions§	35	31	26	17	13
Economic/Subordinate: Economic activities controlled by Wilkes-Barre Upper Class‖	10	11	13	44	25
n = 1473	100% (343)	100% (342)	100% (239)	100% (265)	100% (284)

* The time span made it possible to establish the pattern of relationships. These ties generally existed before the 1870s and persisted after that decade. Kinship ties, for example, were often initiated in the 1850s and 1860s.

† Refers to Ashley, Plains, Hanover, Forty-Fort, Schickshinny, and Nanticoke.

‡ Refers to Wyalusing, Athens, Braintrim, Meshoppen, Tunkhannock, Orangeville, Mehoppany, and Elmira (New York).

§ Refers to economic institutions in both Wilkes-Barre and other communities.

‖ Includes Sugar Notch, Wanamie, Alden, Lee Park, Wilkes-Barre Township, Warrior Run, Mill Creek, and Yatesville. All of these were mining patch towns only a few years old by the 1880s. There is no degree of equality between economic/subordinate ties. In one case, a member of Wilkes-Barre's upper class might own a provisioning store for miners in another community and a second member of the upper class might own and operate a coal breaker. The ties have been merely tabulated.

Sources: See Appendix, Note on Table Sources.

ships with the leadership groups of Kingston and Plymouth, partly because these shared almost identical cultural backgrounds, social characteristics, and Connecticut Yankee origins. These leaders and their family members had been intermarrying with members of the Wilkes-Barre upper class since the 1840s and, in some cases, had participated in its institutions since that decade.[39]

These extralocal ties had important long-term implications for the entire basis of regional leadership. The facts that Wilkes-Barre achieved regional hegemony and that its upper class was the only leadership group in the urban system to preserve itself through the twentieth century was no coincidence. These two developments were very much a product of the ability of the city's upper class to sustain the broader regional networks. Associations generated by Lodge 61 F&AM, St. Stephen's Church, or marriages into Wilkes-Barre's upper class created channels of communication among all leadership groups. Leaders in smaller communities, of course, participated in their own institutions; but these ties were increasingly undermined by the growing attachments to Wilkes-Barre. In the subordinate communities, institutions such as the academy and the social club failed to survive the late nineteenth century; nor, in fact, did a large percentage of these communities' leading families persist beyond the early 1900s. The numerous familial ties with Wilkes-Barre's upper class drew a greater and greater proportion of leadership in all communities into the kinship system and, in turn, into the formal society of Wilkes-Barre's upper class.[40]

The evolution of Plymouth's elite demonstrates the consequences of its relationship with the Wilkes-Barre upper class. By the 1850s, the community's elite had developed a number of social and cultural institutions that formed the basis for interaction among its members. These included a local academy, an Episcopal and a Methodist church, and several social organizations. Yet none of these survived the 1880s as elite institutions, nor was their holding power considerable. The Plymouth Academy, which had trained a generation of leaders in the 1830s and 1840s, closed in the early 1870s, victim of its intense competition from the Wilkes-Barre private schools. From the 1850s, and even before, Wilkes-Barre schools attracted a growing share of the sons and daughters of Plymouth's elite.[41] The religious and social institutions of elites from Plymouth experienced the same gradual erosion of membership base. Founded through the auspices of St. Stephen's Church in Wilkes-Barre, St. Peter's Church in Plymouth proved unable to sustain its role as a mainstay of local leadership or to hold the loyalty of its members. By the 1860s, all of its incorporators had migrated to Wilkes-Barre or, in a few instances, left the Wyoming Valley. Families such as the Turners and Pattens, prime movers in establishing the Plymouth church, had become integral parts of the Wilkes-Barre upper class by the end of the decade. Relatives in both families had joined St. Stephen's Church there, along with the other institutions of Wilkes-Barre's leadership. Similarly, the core of the membership of the Plymouth Methodist-Episcopal Church (nineteen of twenty-five families) had also moved to Wilkes-Barre and transferred affiliation to the

First Methodist-Episcopal Church or, in some cases, had become members of St. Stephen's. By the 1890s, St. Peter's Church had lost its reputation as an elite institution. During the next ten years, the new leaders, who began replacing the Old Stock Protestants, came mostly from Irish Catholic families and immigrant Welsh households.[42]

Plymouth's social organizations were also disrupted as a result of interaction with Wilkes-Barre's leadership. The Shawnee Cemetery Association, a bastion of the local elite, saw its ranks disrupted in the 1870s because the majority of its members had moved to Wilkes-Barre or joined the Hollenback Cemetery Association, an upper-class group of the city. Whether they moved or merely transferred memberships, the leaders ended their ties with the Plymouth organization. Elite associations with the Wilkes-Barre upper class also intruded on the informal social world of Plymouth's leaders. Members of both leadership groups met frequently at dinner parties, weekly visits, and informal gatherings. Upper-class leaders attended funerals of members of Plymouth's top families, most of whom were relatives. Informal associations with Wilkes-Barre's upper class, combined with formal ones, contributed to the decline of Plymouth's elite lodges and the changing social basis of the Shawnee Club's membership. By the 1900s, leaders from foreign-born families or immigrants themselves, including those from Eastern Europe, had replaced the majority of the colonial-stock leaders who once dominated the community's social life.[43]

Kinship was another key factor in the configuration of Plymouth's elite (see the kinship data in Table 3-8; see also Table 3-10). A large proportion of Plymouth's top families were related through blood or marriage. Yet this familial system was disrupted as a result of the elite's interaction with Wilkes-Barre's upper class, a connection that actually contributed to the instability of the Plymouth elite. By the 1870s, 75 percent of the community's leadership had multiple kinship ties with the upper-class families in the regional center. These associations, plus the numerous institutional ties among the town's leading families, helped fuse the two groups, as more and more leaders and their relatives from Plymouth married into the upper class. By the 1860s, at least one member of most of the elite families had achieved upper-class status in Wilkes-Barre. Continued migration from Plymouth to Wilkes-Barre and intermarriage with members of the upper class over the next two decades further reinforced these ties. These familial and social ties oriented leaders in other communities toward Wilkes-Barre's growing economy and its dynamic upper class. The men in these smaller cities and towns increasingly saw their fortunes tied, not to their own leadership group, but to Wilkes-Barre's upper class. Kinship was crucial in developing this perception, since it brought leaders in other communities into close contact and long-term association with families in Wilkes-Barre's upper class. Kinship, to a great extent, undermined the integrity of Plymouth's elite; what happened here was unlike events in Wilkes-Barre, where kinship strengthened the upper class.

A brief examination of the Wadhams family demonstrates the gradual erosion

Table 3-10.   Familial Relationships between Selected Elite Families in Plymouth and Kingston and Upper-Class Families in Wilkes-Barre during the Late Nineteenth Century*

Plymouth's Elite Families	Relationships	Wilkes-Barre's Upper-Class Families	Relationships	Kingston's Elite Families
Lance (Oscar)	FaWi†	Hancock	FaBo	Dorrance (Charles)
Lee (John R.)	FaBo	Lee	FaSiHu	Denison (Hiram)
Turner (Sam.)	FaDaHu	Conyngham	FaSo	Shoemaker (Elijah)
Dietrick (W. W.)	FaDaHu	Turner	FaWi	Lewis (Thomas)
Gaylord (Hend.)	FaDaHu	Harvey	FaBo	Loveland (Wm.)
Reynolds (Abram)	FaWi	Hoyt	FaMo	Nesbitt (Abram)
Davenport (Edwin)	FaDaHu	Blair	FaSoWi	Payne (Hubbard)
DeWitte (Asa)	FaDaHu	Harvey	FaSiDaHu	Pringle (Alex.)
Creveling (Darly)	FaMoSiHu	LaPort	FaWi	Shoemaker (Geo.)
French (Sam.)	FaDaHu	Loop	FaDaHu	VanScoy (Henry)
Shupp (Andrew)	FaWiBoSi	Sturdevant	FaDaHu	Dorrance (John)
Harvey (Wm. J.)	FaWi	Laning	FaDaHu	Perkins (James)

*Familial ties are determined by kin relationship to head of elite families in Plymouth and Kingston in 1870. These ties persisted well beyond 1870 and generally existed for a decade or two prior to that date. The year 1870 represents a midway point.

†Abbreviations are as follows: Fa(ther), Mo(ther), Bro(ther), Si(ster), Hu(sband), Wi(fe), So(n), and Da(ughter).

Sources: Notations for familial ties were drawn from Bernard Barber, *Guardians of Virtue: Salem Families in 1800* (New York: Basic Books, 1972), 80–89; David M. Schneider and George C. Homans, "Kinship Terminology and the American Kinship System," *American Anthropologist* 57 (1958): 1194–1209.

of local identification with Plymouth. The first member of the family to move to Wilkes-Barre was Esther, whose father, Samuel, headed the family for most of the nineteenth century. She married into the Shoemaker family in Wilkes-Barre and moved there in 1848. In 1855, her brother, Calvin, moved to Wilkes-Barre in order to study law under Lazrus Shoemaker, Esther's husband. After completing his training, Calvin Wadhams remained in Wilkes-Barre, where he became a member of Wilkes-Barre's growing upper-class leadership. Both he and Shoemaker quickly became powerful landowners and entrepreneurs, as well as successful politicians. During the 1860s, another of Esther's brothers, Elijah, began investing his money in Wilkes-Barre banks. In that same decade, he sent his sons to one of the upper-class academies and, in 1873, moved his residence to the city. Elijah Wadhams did maintain his commercial and shipping operations in Plymouth but ran them from Wilkes-Barre. He also remained as director of several Plymouth companies and banks. His father, Samuel, continued to be a source of capital for Elijah and ultimately passed a significant portion of his coal land in the Plymouth area to this son.[44]

The ubiquitous presence of Wilkes-Barre's upper class was also apparent in Plymouth's economic institutions. By the 1870s, the community had no locally controlled coal companies. The city's entrepreneurs had actually been prime movers in the early coal industry during the 1830s through the 1850s, and most of the prominent families still owned considerable coal lands two decades later. These lands, however, were leased out to Wilkes-Barre-based coal companies operated by relatives of the Plymouth leaders. Often, the coal properties were in the possession of former Plymouth leaders who had become resident in Wilkes-Barre, as in the case of the Wadhams family. Members of the Plymouth elite were unable to develop and sustain major economic institutions outside the service and linkage sectors; and even in these areas, control was often shared with members of the upper class in Wilkes-Barre. Almost all those men in Plymouth who held local directorships or officer's posts were related to those in the upper class or were onetime residents of Plymouth who had moved to the regional center and had been assimilated by the upper class. The incorporators and board members of the Plymouth Savings Bank and the First National Bank of Plymouth were all relatives of members of Wilkes-Barre's upper class.[45]

The elite in nearby Kingston not only lacked economic institutions but also social and cultural institutions as well; and by the end of the nineteenth century, this elite had become a mere extension of the upper class in Wilkes-Barre. Roughly 91 percent of the leading families had married into upper-class Wilkes-Barre families or had relatives otherwise assimilated by that group. The leaders in Kingston participated in the institutions of the upper class, regardless of type. The extent of this participation undermined the development of any comparable institutions among members of the elite, which consisted of two churches attended by only a small portion of the top families. Members of the upper class dominated the local academy, where their sons matriculated in large numbers throughout the nineteenth century. In contrast, a sizable proportion of the sons of Kingston's elite attended Wilkes-Barre academies. For example, members of the Payne family graduated from the Wilkes-Barre Academy. They also belonged to the Historical Society, Lodge 61, and the First Presbyterian or St. Stephen's Episcopal churches. Hubbard Payne had served his legal apprenticeship under a Wilkes-Barre attorney and subsequently joined a law firm headed by a member of the upper class. He also acted as trustee for the Osterhout Free Library in Wilkes-Barre and was tied into the kinship system through his daughter and children. Such relationships, repeated many times over, undermined the integrity and the stability of Kingston's elite, whose members looked to Wilkes-Barre for their institutional basis and economic well-being.[46]

The character of Pittston's elite differed to a certain degree from the leadership in Plymouth and Kingston. The early history of the city and its position between the Lackawanna Valley, dominated by Scranton's elite, and the Wyoming Valley, controlled by Wilkes-Barre's upper class, changed the dynamics of the community's leadership. First, this elite was by far the most heterogeneous of all those in the Valley; it included both a greater proportion of foreign-born and leaders from outside the Valley. Next, the leaders of Scottish birth were oriented toward the Lackawanna Valley and Scranton, where the local elite had major investments in Pittston. Last, the area's rich coal reserves had attracted the attention of New York railroad executives, whose Pennsylvania Coal Company operated numerous collieries in the Pittston district.[47]

The first settlers came to the Pittston area long before coal mining actively began in 1849. The pioneering families in this section arrived with the Connecticut Yankees in the late eighteenth century. These families were generally of New England ancestry and colonial-stock lineage, characteristics which facilitated growing ties with leaders in Wilkes-Barre. By the late nineteenth century, members of the Pittston elite who were of English descent, Episcopalian or Presbyterian, and colonial stock had come within the orbit of the Wilkes-Barre upper class. In this sense, Pittston's emerging leadership differed little from elites elsewhere in the region. The rich coal deposits, in fact, inspired upper-class leaders from Wilkes-Barre's Butler, Conyngham, Mallery, and Miner families to open up mining operations in the Pittston area during the mid-nineteenth century, a move that further strengthened the growing ties between the Pittston leaders of English descent and the members of the upper class in Wilkes-Barre.[48]

By 1849, the Pennsylvania Coal Company, under William Griffith, had begun to mine the coal veins in and around the emerging community. Entrepreneurs, usually of Scottish origin and frequently from Carbondale, north of Scranton, followed the company into the Wyoming Valley. Welsh and Irish coal miners and their families soon joined this migration to Pittston, thereby completing the constellation of ethnic groups that constituted the city's burgeoning population and its leadership ranks.[49]

The first group of leaders—those of English and colonial-stock origin—had developed close ties with the upper class in Wilkes-Barre by the late nineteenth century. These men were primarily merchants, lawyers, and independent coal operators whose interests centered on the First National Bank and the People's Savings Bank, both of Pittston, the Pittston Ferry Bridge Company, the Pittston Knitting Mill Company, and local mining collieries. Sharing similar occupational and entrepreneurial concerns, these men became involved in a series of economic relationships with the members of the upper class, as their counterparts elsewhere in the Valley had done. At the same time, similar cultural and social characteristics encouraged numerous noneconomic ties and familial bonds.[50]

For example, Theodore Strong, president of the Pittston Ferry Bridge Company and the First National Bank, was Presbyterian, academy educated, and English. He was a brother-in-law to the Loveland family, whose members belonged to the Kingston and Pittston elites and the Wilkes-Barre upper class. Strong was also related, through his mother, Priscilla Lee Mallery Strong, to the Butler and Mallery families in Wilkes-Barre's upper class. In fact, early in his career, he worked for the Butler Coal Company as head of its mercantile department. Last, Strong also owned 2,000 acres of coal lands in West Pittston, Pleasant Valley, and elsewhere in the Pittston district. Similarly, Cornelius Stark, of the People's Savings Bank, was a lawyer, merchant, and timberlands owner. Affiliated with the St. James Episcopal Church in Pittston, Stark traced his roots back to a Connecticut Yankee family. Related to members of the upper class, he followed his son to Wilkes-Barre during the mid-seventies.[51] Fellow bank-board member John Richards was even more closely tied to Wilkes-Barre's upper class. Son of a Yale-educated father, Richards was related to the prestigious Butler family in Wilkes-Barre through his aunt, who married John L. Butler. A Dartmouth graduate himself, the younger Richards studied law under Andrew T. McClintock of the Wilkes-Barre upper class and worked for his uncle in the Butler Coal Company operations near Pittston. During the Civil War, Richards joined the volunteer company of Stanley Woodward, the latter a member of a noted upper-class family.[52]

Not only were Pittston leaders related to families in Wilkes-Barre's upper class, they also participated in its institutions. Ralph Lacoe, an officer in the Miners' Savings Bank and a manufacturer, joined the Wyoming Historical and Geological Society. A trustee from 1882 through 1889, he became a life member by the end of the eighties. Lacoe also belonged to Masonic Lodge 61 F&AM and was later buried in the Hollenback Cemetery, where his elaborate gravestone now stands. This multiplicity of ties was characteristic of the colonial-stock members of the Pittston elite.[53]

As a result, Pittston's leadership had to cope with its own internal divisions (i.e., ethnic and religious diversity) and the rule of Wilkes-Barre's upper class, both of which undermined the cohesiveness of Pittston's elite. It lacked the strong economic and cultural institutions to make this possible. The group of English and colonial-stock descent was centered around the St. James Episcopal Church, a distinct set of banks and entrepreneurial institutions, and Wilkes-Barre's upper class. Among the leaders of Scottish descent, all were Presbyterian and members of the First Presbyterian Church of Pittston. The Pennsylvania Coal Company employed most of these men, who were interrelated through blood and/or marriage. They differed markedly from their English-stock counterparts. A third group of leaders, descended from Welsh families, were merchants, wholesalers, coal operators, and generally born outside the United States. They, too, had little in common with the leaders of English and colonial-stock ancestry or those in the Wilkes-Barre upper class. [54]

Given this diversity of economic and cultural interests, it is also not surprising that the Pittston elite never developed a common entrepreneurial strategy that could have been shared by most members of the elite. In some cases, notably the water company, several local banks, and a few other activities, local Pittston leaders remained in control. These, however, were the exception. Entrepreneurs from New York and, to a lesser extent, Wilkes-Barre, ran most of the local mining operations. John H. Swoyer of Wilkes-Barre, for instance, owned $350,000 worth of coal lands in the Pittston district. He also controlled provisioning and general stores to serve the coal miners and their families in the area. Upper-class leaders in Wilkes-Barre also owned the Pittston Arms Company, the Pittston Engine and Machine Company, and the Pittston Mill. By the late nineteenth century, Scranton's elite to the north had taken over the Pittston Stove Company, a major concern in the sector of the local economy that did not depend on coal. Even the Pittston Knitting Mill, controlled by the English-stock leaders, eventually passed into outside hands by the early 1880s, when entrepreneurs from New York and Scranton bought the company out. Realizing the growing power of Wilkes-Barre's upper class and Scranton's elite, local merchants promoted an annexation campaign during the 1880s in an effort to recover Pittston's lost ground. While never successful, the drive indicated an awareness on the part of the Pittston leaders that local autonomy was a thing of the past. Without a strong economic base and lacking powerful social and cultural institutions, the Pittston elite could not sustain its ranks in great num-bers into the twentieth century. [55]

The weakening of elite institutions in these communities that resulted from these associations with the upper class was critical in precipitating a change in the social basis of leadership. By the twentieth century, the elites in Plymouth, Pittston, Wyoming, and other cities and towns were no longer composed primarily of colonial-stock families with their Episcopal churches, Masonic lodges, and private academies. Their departure made possible the rise of a new group of leaders from ethnic and religious groups relatively new to the Wyoming Valley. Except in Pittston, no more than 21 percent of the nineteenth-century urban elite families persisted through 1920 (see persistence data, Table 3-8). Most of the nineteenth-century elite families, again excepting the non–English stock in Pittston, moved to Wilkes-Barre, where they formally joined the upper class. In contrast, the majority of the leading families in Wilkes-Barre remained in the city and continued to hold upper-class status through the 1920s. The continuity in Wilkes-Barre's leadership was a direct consequence of its institutions and kinship system, while the change in the basis of leadership elsewhere in the region resulted from interaction with members of the upper class of Wilkes-Barre, facilitated by the institutions and family ties of the city. The social change occurred over the course of six decades, often imperceptible but surely inexorable.[56]

The change in the basis of leadership in the smaller communities of the Wyoming Valley was intimately tied to the participation of their elites in the regional networks centered in Wilkes-Barre. The long-term stability of these elites was clearly disrupted as a result of the intrusion of the upper class of Wilkes-Barre into the social and familial world of leaders in other communities of the Wyoming Valley. To a great extent, the institutions and kinship system of the upper class shaped a myriad of decisions concerning marriage, investments, church affiliation, club membership, and business partnerships. These irrevocably tied the regional elites to Wilkes-Barre's upper class and ultimately undermined the elite institutions and cohesiveness. The locally oriented institutions of the elites in the smaller communities collapsed under pressure from the regional institutions and kinship system of Wilkes-Barre's upper class. Only at this point were men from other social and economic backgrounds able to assume elite status and take control of the older institutions or develop new ones within these communities.

Similarly, the continuity of Wilkes-Barre's upper class was also a product of participation in the regional networks. On first sight, Wilkes-Barre's upper class appears to resemble the traditional leadership which preserved the sense of community and stability in a rapidly changing economic world. New England in origin, Episcopal or Presbyterian in religious affiliation, and bound by the ties of family, Wilkes-Barre's upper class certainly raises almost stereotypical images of the proper upper class. Yet the images are deceiving. The upper class was at the center of a series of dynamic social, familial, and economic networks that triggered and sustained economic growth, long-term social change, and an integrated urban system. Participation in these networks encouraged migration to Wilkes-Barre and facilitated assimilation into the upper class but at the same time preserved its ethnic and cultural character. Newcomers from communities in the region or even from outside failed to compete as power groups or to disrupt the equilibrium because of Wilkes-Barre's control of the broader regional networks and the Wilkes-Barreans' ability to recruit selectively.[57]

CHAPTER IV

Urban Elites and the Wilkes-Barre Upper Class in the Twentieth Century

Y THE 1920s, leadership in the city and throughout the region had become far more complex than in the nineteenth century. Two very different types of leadership had evolved in Wilkes-Barre—the upper class and the elite. Each had their institutions, patterns of social interaction, and configuration of extralocal and extraregional ties. The elite was far less cohesive than the upper class and lacked the power and contacts that grew out of the upper-class association with New York City and Philadelphia. The intrusion of large-scale systems had reoriented the upper class toward the metropolitan centers and away from the region, in contrast to the elite, whose members remained tied to the Wyoming Valley. The tension in the twentieth century was no longer between the locally oriented institutions in the smaller communities and the regional ones in Wilkes-Barre, as it had been during the 1800s. Instead, new tension was developing between Wilkes-Barre's upper-class institutions and the economic and social institutions in New York and Philadelphia. The economic power of the elites in the metropolitan centers and the strength of the large-scale systems they controlled intruded dramatically on leadership groups in the regional economies of the interior. While in Wilkes-Barre, the institutions of the nineteenth century did persist through the 1920s, Wilkes-Barre's leaders were also beginning to participate in leadership groups outside the region. The new associational ties, coupled with economic orientation, were clearly beginning to draw the members of the upper class toward the metropolitan centers. In a sense, the relationship between Wilkes-Barre and the other communities in the nineteenth century was being replicated, now between Wilkes-Barre and the metropolitan centers.

At the same time, members of the emerging elite of the 1920s had begun to develop a series of complex relationships with one another and with members of newer elites in the region. The activities of the elite overlapped with those of the upper class in only a few areas. Meetings of the Chamber of Commerce and the professional associations were among the few occasions where the members of the two groups rubbed shoulders. Otherwise, they remained distinct in their patterns of interaction.

While the upper class increasingly saw its fortunes tied to the metropolitan centers and their large-scale systems, the elite was far less cosmopolitan and was oriented more toward the region. The emergence of the elite underscores the process of social change. Both mobility and economic growth produced this group. Its ties, forged among other elites in the region and with organizations beyond the region, resulted from technology, the intrusion of the larger society, and Wilkes-Barre's position as the regional center. In the last instance, the upper class had created the conditions necessary for the development of the elite. The two remained interdependent, one meeting the service demands of the regional economy, the other sustaining that economy by its activities in the broader market.

Economic growth and mobility also precipitated the rise of new elites in the other cities and towns of the region. The breakup of the nineteenth-century elites, as their families joined the Wilkes-Barre upper class, opened up the leadership ranks in the smaller communities of the Wyoming Valley. Men of vastly different social and class backgrounds, who capitalized on the continued economic growth, began to move into these leadership positions after 1900. Eventually, they formed the basis for the new elites of the twentieth century. By the 1920s, these men had developed their own institutions and social ties, a process that distinguished them from the members of the nineteenth-century elite who remained in the community. By that decade, the descendants of the older elites had largely become extensions of Wilkes-Barre's upper class. Their institutional ties, social relationships, and economic investments were irrevocably linked to the upper class in Wilkes-Barre. Wilkes-Barre's dual structure of leadership could be found in other communities throughout the region.

The incipient networks of the Wilkes-Barre elite had begun to join these new elites scattered over the northern anthracite coalfields. While these groups remained rather separate, unlike the upper class and the descendants of the nineteenth-century elites, their members were still fixed on Wilkes-Barre. Its importance as the center of regional society was no less for the new elites than it had been for the leadership groups in the last century. Mobility, economic and population growth, and the presence of large-scale systems were all decisive in transforming the character of leadership in the northern anthracite region. For the upper class, the external and vertical relationships with the metropolitan centers and their leadership groups overrode the horizontal ties that bound their members to Wilkes-Barre and the region. For the elite in Wilkes-Barre and the newer elites elsewhere, the growth and the growing extralocal ties among their members had created a niche for these leaders that tied them to the Wyoming Valley.

SOCIAL ANALYSIS OF WILKES-BARRE'S UPPER CLASS IN
THE TWENTIETH CENTURY

Despite these profound changes, the social and institutional profile of the upper class persisted almost intact into the twentieth century. The business enterprises, philanthropic agencies, and historical associations of the 1800s remained an important, if not integral, part of upper-class life during the 1920s. Its members participated in coal and coal-related companies, the First National and Wyoming National banks, the Orphan's Home and the Wyoming Historical and Geological and Wyoming Commemorative societies, which had sustained the upper class in the nineteenth century.

At the same time, families from the 1870s and 1880s counted numerous relatives among their twentieth-century counterparts, from sons and daughters to nephews, nieces, and in-laws. A sprinkling of men and women from the upper class of the last century also survived into the 1920s and even the 1930s. More than anything, these persons symbolized the link between the two groups. Given the diversity of ties and the persistence of those from the nineteenth-century upper class, it is not surprising that almost all the upper-class families from the 1800s were still represented in the city's leadership during the 1920s. The new additions to Wilkes-Barre's upper class were leaders from other communities or their sons who had migrated to the city after the 1800s or managers transferred into the region by corporations based in New York City, Philadelphia, and Chicago.[1]

As in earlier times, the majority of the city's leaders had inherited their positions of power and status within the community. Birth, rather than achievement, was the primary determinant of inclusion in Wilkes-Barre's upper class. The members of the upper class continued to come from families in which the fathers held white-collar, prestigious jobs (Table 4-1). As in the nineteenth century, the great number of fathers of these men were lawyers and other professionals, coal company executives, manufacturers, and merchants. In most cases, the fathers were able to provide quality education through college, pass on wealth and contacts, and insure the beginnings of profitable careers. Generally members of the upper class, the fathers were also able to guarantee high social status for their sons.[2]

Similarly, the wives of these men came from upper-class or prominent families in other communities. Upper-class women were, obviously, crucial in sustaining the network of kinship ties among the families during the nineteenth and twentieth centuries. In the nineteenth century, women in Wilkes-Barre's upper-class families provided the links among these families and became the foundation of the kinship system. They and their daughters also ran several philanthropic organizations. An equally important duty was the rearing of the children in such a way as to pass on family traditions and class values essential for the leadership. In the twentieth century, upper-class women continued to

Table 4-1.   Occupations of Fathers of Members of the Upper Class, 1920–1930[*]

Occupation	%	N
Professional[†]	27	78
Coal mining	16	45
Manufacturing	12	34
Commerce	17	49
Real estate/Insurance	1	3
Finance	4	12
Utility	0	0
Contracting	1	3
Small business	0	0
Artisanal	2	6
Unskilled blue collar	1	2
Unknown	19	55
	100%	287

[*] The sources for this table are described in the appendix note on table sources.

[†] Includes lawyers, doctors, and one architect.

perform these functions. They also planned and presided over parties and other social events of note, oversaw weddings, and participated in new organizations, such as the Daughters of the American Revolution. These women had even begun to hold positions of political power after the passage of the women's suffrage amendment and, through inheritance, took control of considerable economic resources. They were vital in maintaining the cohesiveness of the upper class in both centuries.[3]

As suggested by this description of upper-class women, kinship was still an important aspect of life among Wilkes-Barre's upper-class leadership. More than 70 percent of the leading families were still interrelated through blood or marriage (Table 4-2). Again, members of the upper class married into the Butler and Hollenback families and a myriad of others of the class (Figure 3). It is not surprising that upper-class leaders experienced a sense of tradition and historical continuity that dated back to the eighteenth century.[4]

With few exceptions, the upper-class leaders in the 1920s carried on many of their fathers' ways. Still of British ancestry, maintaining the churches of that stock, they also continued to pursue excellent educations (Table 4-3). The majority of upper-class leaders also maintained the nineteenth-century tradition of attending one of the two local upper-class academies.[5] A surprising 63 percent of this group completed college, a figure comparable with those of leadership groups in Philadelphia or Pittsburgh. Members of old upper-class families continued a tradition extending back for generations and matriculated at Harvard, Yale, or Princeton, the chief universities for the urban upper classes of the northeast. A sizable number of upper-class families sent their sons to Amherst, Wesleyan, or the University of Virginia, which ranked just behind the three Ivy League schools in popularity among the upper classes.

Church affiliation was another important self-defining characteristic of the

Table 4-2. Birthplace, Lineage, and Familial Ties of Wilkes-Barre's Upper Class, *
1920–1930

		%	N
Birthplace	Wilkes-Barre	50	144
	Wyoming Valley	13	38
	Hinterland	18	50
	Outside region	19	55
		100%	287
Family Lineage	Colonial Stock	56	161
	Pre-1880	20	58
	Post-1880†	21	60
	Unknown	3	8
		100%	287
Familial Ties	Proportion related through blood and/or marriage	73	209
	Proportion unrelated to other members of Wilkes-Barre leadership	27	78
		100%	287

* I included several women in this analysis. This reflects their political and economic position, discussed in the first part of the chapter.
† This category includes leaders as well as families.

city's leadership, with the Episcopalian and Presbyterian traditions of the upper class remaining strong. Roughly 60 percent of the 1920 upper class belonged to either St. Stephen's Episcopal or the First Presbyterian Church. These churches remained strongholds of the upper class through the 1920s.[6]

The members of Wilkes-Barre's twentieth-century upper class continued to occupy the old residential district, in contrast to elites in the larger metropolitan centers, who rapidly moved to the suburbs after the 1880s. The development of an upper-class suburban neighborhood, away from the city center, was not a viable alternative for leaders in an extractive region because of the dispersed nature of the mining industry. Coal breakers and mining patch towns ringed the city; some were even located within Wilkes-Barre's boundaries. As a result, available land was limited. The descendants of the upper class had little choice but to maintain their residential integrity. Their living space did provide certain advantages. The residential district, which flanked the Susquehanna River, was the most attractive area in the city. The district continued to be the setting for social interaction among the members of the upper class. The Wyoming Valley Women's Club on North River Street, for example, provided quarters for luncheons, teas, and other social events among women in the upper class. Debutante balls, bridge parties, weekend dinner parties, and a variety of other functions occurred in the clubhouses and upper-class homes located in the residential district. In this sense, the district helped to reinforce the cohesiveness of the upper class.[7]

Figure 3. Kinship Ties among Select Families in Wilkes-Barre's Upper Class, 1920–1930

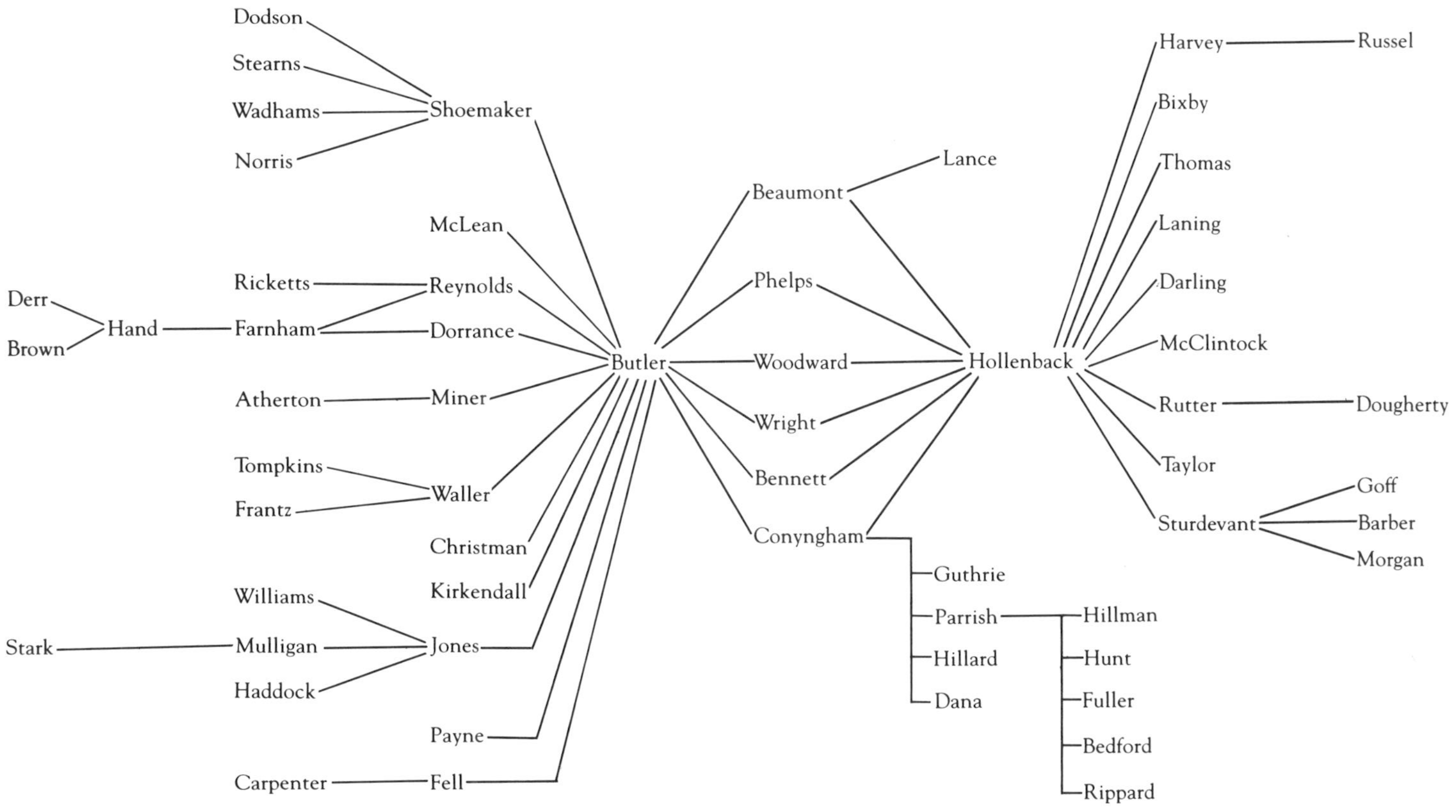

Table 4-3.   Social Characteristics of Wilkes-Barre's Upper Class, 1920–1930

Social Characteristics		%	N
Ethnicity	British	69	198
	Scotch-Irish	10	28
	Southern Irish	4	10
	German	15	43
	Other	2	8
		100%	287
Religion	Episcopalian	37	105
	Presbyterian	35	100
	Methodist	13	36
	Roman Catholic/Jewish	7	19
	Other	3	10
	Unknown	5	17
		100%	287
Education	Elementary	0.5	1
	High School	5.5	16
	Academy	18	52
	College	63	182
	Unknown	13	36
		100%	287
Occupation	Professional	46	132
	Coal mining	12	35
	Manufacturing	14	40
	Managerial	7	19
	Commerce	8	23
	Real estate/Insurance	6	17
	Finance	6	18
	Utility	0.7	2
	Contractor	0.3	1
		100%	287

Residence separated these men and their families from the rest of the community. The distinctive architectural design of the often lavish houses contrasted sharply with the small frame houses that accommodated the rest of Wilkes-Barre's population in the 1920s. These mansions were a physical link with the past, since they had housed the upper class, and often the same families, during the nineteenth century.

As Frederic Jaher pointed out in his study of the urban upper strata, residential proximity and retention of ancestral homes had become "class emblem[s]." Newcomers moved into the district to legitimize their status, while old-time residents preserved "the historical, genealogical and esthetic integrity of the neighborhood" through their mansions and historical associations, dating back to the nineteenth century. Like the Brahmins' Beacon Hill in Boston, this residential area had become an expression of Wilkes-Barre's upper class to those within the community.[8]

WILKES-BARRE'S UPPER CLASS AND THE INTRUSION OF THE LARGER SOCIETY

During the nineteenth century, the members of Wilkes-Barre's upper class had begun to develop ties with entrepreneurs in both New York City and Philadelphia. The demands for capital, the attempts by capitalists to exploit the coal reserves, and the emerging kinship ties between upper-class leaders and those in the metropolitan centers necessitated these ties. The railroads and the telegraph had made communications with New York City and Philadelphia possible as early as the 1850s.[9] Later, the telephone intensified these contacts. Upper-class leaders began to join social clubs and professional organizations in both cities as early as 1870. They also journeyed to New York for dinner engagements and business meetings on an irregular basis. At the same time, local entrepreneurs, such as Charles Parrish, served on the boards of metropolitan companies, including in Parrish's case the Central Railroad of New Jersey, the Pennsylvania Railroad, and the Lehigh Coal and Navigation Company of Philadelphia. Parrish also operated an office in New York City to maintain his business contacts and distribute his coal. Upper-class families even entertained prominent families and business allies from the metropolitan centers at parties, weddings, and other social events.[10]

These ties became more regular and increasingly overrode the relationships upper-class leaders had established with urban elite groups in the region. The corporation gradually forced members of Wilkes-Barre's upper class to look beyond the region and to realize that economic power ineluctably would gravitate toward these metropolitan centers, where the corporations were headquartered. At the same time, the rise of national trade and professional associations also helped to reorient urban leadership away from the community and the region and toward the larger society of the metropolitan center. At the top of the urban hierarchy and the most powerful group in the Wyoming Valley, the upper class developed the strongest ties with the leadership groups in New York City and Philadelphia.[11]

By the 1920s, Wilkes-Barre's upper class began to show the influences of these metropolitan centers. These influences became manifest in the social clubs, associational ties, and economic relationships of Wilkes-Barre's leaders. By the 1920s, the members of the upper class had established new clubs to accommodate the changing tastes of Wilkes-Barre's prominent families. These consisted of the Westmoreland Club, the Wyoming Valley Country Club, and the North Mountain Hunting and Fishing Club. The suburban clubs established by metropolitan upper classes and elites in New York and Philadelphia provided the model for the country club, which accommodated all the members of the upper class families and provided them with a location that was comfortably isolated from mining towns and their heterogeneous populations. Located outside the city, it was on the site of a country estate donated by one of the city's leading families for the recreational purposes of the upper class. The North Mountain

Club, also recreational in intent, limited its membership to males and only the most powerful among the community's upper class.[12]

Of the three, the Westmoreland Club, which grew out of the nineteenth-century Malt Club, was the most prestigious and the most cosmopolitan. Like its suburban counterpart and the Malt Club, the Westmoreland Club was modelled after a common metropolitan association, the men's luncheon club. The location of the club, on the edge of the upper-class residential quarters and adjoining the central business district, provided a convenient gathering place for the city's business and professional leaders. Admission to the club was based on the recommendation and a vote from the club's membership. Thus, membership was restricted to those in the upper class and business associates from other communities outside the Wyoming Valley. These included leaders from Hazleton and the surrounding anthracite communities at the southwestern end of Luzerne County and members of prominent families from communities in the Valley's hinterland to the north. Importantly, over one-half of the nonresident members were from New York City and Philadelphia. Members of what could be viewed as proper Philadelphia families such as the Coxes, who had made their fortunes in anthracite mining, belonged to the Westmoreland Club. These ties indicated a fairly close association between Wilkes-Barre's upper class and members of the upper class in Philadelphia.[13]

The upper class also participated in more than thirty prestigious clubs in New York City and Philadelphia. These included the full complement of suburban, athletic, political, men's luncheon, and Ivy League alumni clubs that encompassed all the social activities of the metropolitan leaders. The admission procedures of the Philadelphia clubs were the same as those for the Westmoreland Club, and the acceptance of a large number of Wilkes-Barre leaders suggested a growing association between the two leadership groups. In fact, 33 percent of the anthracite community leaders belonged to at least one of the metropolitan clubs in either New York City or Philadelphia, and often as many as eight separate associations. These men were found on the membership lists of such exclusive men's clubs as the Knickerbocker in New York and the Rittenhouse in Philadelphia. The Rittenhouse Club was the second most prestigious social organization among members of Philadelphia's upper class. The Knickerbocker Club in 1871 counted Morgans, Astors, and Rockefellers among its membership, which was obviously confined to men of wealth, power, and status. Other members of Wilkes-Barre's upper class belonged to the Union League Club in both cities and a variety of suburban and athletic clubs, including the New York Yacht Club and the exclusive Radnor Hunt Club in Philadelphia. These associations provided upper-class leaders with the opportunity to establish useful friendships through informal meetings with the top men in both New York and Philadelphia. The extensive intercity business relations that grew out of the nationalization of business demanded some basis for social interaction between leaders from the smaller cities and from the metropolitan centers, and the social club filled this need.[14]

Participation in fashionable metropolitan clubs was only one indication of the growing interaction among Wilkes-Barre, New York, and Philadelphia leaders. School was an important opportunity for sons of prominent Wilkes-Barre families to initiate this interaction with their counterparts from the two metropolitan centers. Exactly 16 percent of the Wilkes-Barre twentieth-century upper class attended one of the fashionable young men's prep schools supported by prominent families from New York and Philadelphia. Upper-class leaders matriculated at a variety of private boarding schools, such as Philips Andover, St. Paul's Episcopal, and Hotchkiss, which catered to the urban upper strata. The boarding school isolated the sons of urban leaders from the economic and ethnic diversity of the public schools and provided an atmosphere where lasting friendships could be established among future business leaders from a variety of communities.[15]

The graduates of these academies generally continued their education at Harvard, Yale, or Princeton. Among the city's male upper class, 28 percent of the members attended one of these Ivy League colleges, maintaining an upper-class tradition. These colleges continued to provide a socially exclusive environment, in general free of the class heterogeneity of the non–Ivy League institutions. On these campuses, future upper-class leaders were still able to socialize with young men of similar socioeconomic backgrounds. The sons of Philadelphia leaders began, for example, to drift away from the University of Pennsylvania and were most often attracted to Princeton, Harvard, and Yale after the 1880s. Prominent and wealthy families, such as the Vanderbilts and Morgans, sent their sons to these schools. The extent to which school ties persisted can be seen in the Ivy League alumni clubs in New York City and Philadelphia. In fact, members of the city's upper class established their own alumni clubs in the early 1880s. These clubs provided a haven for out-of-town guests and continued to be a part of the upper-class social season through their formal dances and frequent social gatherings. An additional 14 percent of the young men of the upper class attended one of the non–Ivy League schools, such as Amherst, which educated the members of leading families of the East Coast.[16]

An important function of extraregional associations was to separate the so-called Old Americans from the heterogeneous society that urban leaders encountered in their own communities, in other cities where they had business interests, and in the metropolitan centers to which they were drawn after the turn of the century. Around 1900, members of the upper class joined state and national organizations which seemed to serve this function on a broader scale. Members of the upper class affiliated with the Sons of the American Revolution, Daughters of the American Revolution, the Society of the Mayflower, the New England Society of Pennsylvania, and other similar groups. These organizations stressed genealogical and historical research and publications which concentrated on the historical roots of individual families. As would be expected, membership in these associations was reserved for men or women of colonial-stock lineage and reflected the desire of the upper class to preserve a quasi-ethnic character beyond the community.[17]

The growing social ties with leadership groups in New York City and Philadelphia reflected the integration of Wilkes-Barre's regional economy into the resource base of these metropolitan centers. Members of the metropolitan elites had been involved in the anthracite regions of eastern Pennsylvania since the mid-nineteenth century. In the Wyoming Valley, the upper class had managed to maintain considerable local control over the anthracite mining operations through the 1880s. After that decade, the anthracite railroad executives in New York and Philadelphia, through consolidation and mergers, gradually became the dominant force in the mining industry. In response to this intrusion, upper-class leaders began to transfer their investments to these and other corporations in New York and Philadelphia. In the process, they facilitated the upward movement in economic power from the region to the metropolitan center.[18]

By the 1920s, members of Wilkes-Barre's upper class had become major partners in these corporations. More than 33 percent of the leaders had established close economic ties with these corporations and their directors. For example, the president and four of the ten directors of the New York–controlled Lehigh Valley Railroad were local upper-class members. Coal company executives from the upper class dominated the Lehigh Valley Coal Corporation, a subsidiary of New York interests (House of Morgan). Similarly, the Lehigh and Wilkes-Barre Coal Company was run by a combination of leaders from Wilkes-Barre, New York, and Philadelphia. The makeup of these boards was typical of other companies, such as the Morris Run Coal Corporation of New York and Wilkes-Barre; the Coxe Brothers Coal Company of Philadelphia and Wilkes-Barre; the Lehigh Coal and Navigation Company of Philadelphia; and the Burns Brothers Retail Coal Corporation of New York City. These companies formed the backbone of the regional economy and constituted the basis of Wilkes-Barre's participation in the metropolitan-based economy. The associations of these companies, in part, facilitated the increasing social contact between Wilkes-Barre's upper class and the developing corporate world of New York and Philadelphia. More than 40 percent of those who belonged to exclusive clubs in these larger cities were also directors or officers in metropolitan-based corporations.[19]

Upper-class leaders also invested in coal and coal-related companies not directly controlled by members of the New York–Philadelphia leadership groups and served as directors or officers for mining companies in nearby Schuylkill and Northumberland counties, in West Virginia, and in the Far West. By the 1920s, members of upper-class families also became associated with the DuPont corporation, whose agents had consolidated control of explosive powder manufacturing. Wilkes-Barre leaders also invested in scores of corporations other than coal and coal-related companies. Members of the upper class held directorships and/or officers' posts in insurance, utility, railroad, and mass retailing corporations scattered over the country but concentrated primarily in the New York–Philadelphia area. These ranged from the Woolworth Chain Store Corporation to the Metropolitan Life Insurance Corporation, both located in New York City.

Members of the upper class also invested small to substantial sums of money in these types of corporations. Oil companies—Phillips Petroleum, Standard Oil of California, Humble Oil and Refining Company—steel corporations, and major manufacturing operations drew the attention and capital of investors in the upper class. These men also placed their money in municipal and state bonds, as well as in foreign countries. The amounts supplied to these operations varied from a few hundred dollars to more than $300,000. While still committed to the regional economy, entrepreneurs in the upper class did seek out profitable opportunities through the bond and stock markets as well as other means, no doubt pursued by other urban leaders throughout the Northeast.[20]

This increasing orientation beyond the community was also apparent in the number of professional associations that attracted members of the Wilkes-Barre upper class. The emergence of these national and state organizations occurred after the 1880s and coincided with the nationalization of American business. Such groups as the American Medical Association and the American Society for Civil Engineers successfully standardized training and codes for the members of their specialties, disseminated technical information, and often acted as effective lobbies in both the federal and state legislature. The American Society for Mining Engineers, for example, was vital to the interests of the upper class, since its members often worked to resolve technical problems that plagued the mining industry. All of these groups affected the professionals in the upper class, either through their licensure or professional-training powers. They compelled the lawyers, engineers, architects, and doctors to maintain ties with the extra-local organizations in order to keep up with the latest advances in their areas. At least 45 percent of the men in the Wilkes-Barre upper class belonged to professional associations beyond the community in the 1920s.[21]

National trade associations and other occupational groups also drew considerable participation from the members of the upper class. The growing importance of the federal government in the mining industry, the strength of the United Mine Workers Union, and the competition from other forms of energy compelled the coal company directors to join the Anthracite Operators Conference Committee and the American Mining Congress. The committee, for instance, defeated the miners' union in a bitter strike in 1925 and demonstrated the strength of organization. Similarly, bankers from the upper class affiliated with the American Bankers' Association and, on occasion, held national office. These associations ranged from the National Retailers Association to the Pennsylvania Manufacturers Association. These affiliations, found in more than 20 percent of the city's upper class, were typical of virtually every occupational and business pursuit among these men.[22]

THE WILKES-BARRE TWENTIETH-CENTURY ELITE

By the 1920s, Wilkes-Barre's leadership structure had also become far more complex than in the nineteenth century. The tremendous growth of Wilkes-Barre's economy in areas dependent upon coal, but outside the interests of the upper class, also created the basis for an urban elite. The members of this group were dependent on the continued economic success of the upper class for their own prosperity. Unlike their upper-class counterparts, these men had no contacts among the metropolitan leadership groups, nor did they participate in the major sectors of the regional economy, especially coal and coal-related industries. They did, however, perform critical functions in small business, local manufacturing, professional services, and a variety of other areas necessary to the urban and regional economies. Unlike the other communities in the Wyoming Valley, Wilkes-Barre's elite demonstrated a fairly even ethnic representation among its members (Table 4-4). The economic and locational advantages Wilkes-Barre offered by the 1920s drew equally from all ethnic groups who migrated to the region since the late nineteenth century. Before 1900, the city had well-developed Irish, German, and Welsh communities among its population. After the turn of the century, Wilkes-Barre's position as the regional center naturally attracted a sizable number of eastern and southern European immigrants, whose members had established substantial enclaves in Wilkes-Barre and began to penetrate the ranks of the emerging elite. Wilkes-Barre's newly developed elite did have a greater share—52 percent versus a low of 25 percent in Nanticoke and surrounding communities—of native-born leaders than elites in other communities of the Valley.[23]

Three of the five ethnic groups listed in Table 4-4 were predominantly Roman Catholic. As a result, leaders affiliated with the Catholic Church constituted the lion's share of the elite. Other members, associated with the Baptist, Congregational, Lutheran, and other non-upper-class denominations, formed the second largest category among the elite. So, too, were some leaders of Episcopal and Presbyterian persuasion numbered among the elite. They did not, however, participate in the upper-class churches because of the cultural and economic barriers erected by the upper-class leadership to lower socioeconomic groups. Elites who belonged to one of these denominations had established their own churches. Typically, they attended the Westminster Presbyterian and St. Clement's Episcopalian churches, located in south Wilkes-Barre, or the Grant Street Presbyterian Church, located on the Heights, where the members of the elite had been living since 1910.[24]

Church affiliation was as diverse as denominational ties among the elite. Irish Catholics patronized St. Mary's Irish Catholic Church, while their German counterparts affiliated with the St. Nicholas German Catholic Church, both located on the same street and separated by just one block. Leaders of Polish descent attended St. Mary's Polish Catholic Church on the Heights. Each group

Table 4-4. Social Characteristics of Wilkes-Barre's Twentieth-Century Elite,
Exclusive of the Upper Class, 1920–1930

Social Characteristics		%	N
Ethnicity	British*	26	35
	Southern Irish	23	31
	German	27	37
	Eastern and Southern European	15	20
	Welsh	9	13
		100%	136
Religion	Episcopalian/Presbyterian	20	28
	Other Protestant denominations[†]	28	38
	Roman Catholic[‡]	37	50
	Jewish	12	16
	Unknown	3	4
		100%	136
Education	None	4	5
	Elementary	16	22
	High School[§]	13	18
	Academy	10	13
	College	44	60
	Unknown	13	18
		100%	136
Occupation	Superintendent/Mine foreman	9	12
	Small business	21	29
	Local manufacturing	13	18
	Contract/Construction	7	9
	Professional	34	46
	Manager	4	5
	Insurance/Real estate	8	11
	Finance	4	6
		100%	136

* Includes Scotch-Irish, English, Scotch.

† Includes Baptists, Christians, Lutherans, Congregationalists, Methodists, and other
non-upper-class denominations.

‡ Includes Greek and Russian Orthodox.

§ Includes parochial high schools.

practiced its own brand of Catholicism. Each maintained its own schools and
parish organizations, which educated and socialized their sons and daughters.
Similar divisions existed among Jewish leaders. Those of German origin attended the B'nai B'rith Synagogue, founded by Jewish emigrés in the nineteenth
century. Blocked by culture and language, Jewish leaders from eastern Europe
established separate synagogues, where they and their families worshipped. Each
synagogue generally supported its own schools to maintain the traditions of the
homes of the worshippers. Each catered to a specific ethnic group. For example,
Hungarian and Lithuanian Jews had separate synagogues. Second- and third-

generation Jews, sons of eastern Europeans, worshipped at the Temple Israel, which offered a compromise between their Orthodox parents and Reformed brethren. Ties to the old country similarly divided leaders associated with the Lutheran Church. Those who were more assimilated, generally of the second and third generations, tended to worship at St. John's English Lutheran Church or St. Luke's Reformed Church, which conducted their services in English. In contrast, those who still favored services in German worshipped at the mother Lutheran Church, St. Paul's, or its daughter churches elsewhere in Wilkes-Barre.[25]

Like their colleagues in other communities in the region, the members of the Wilkes-Barre elite were well educated. Forty-four percent of the elite acquired college training or some form of post-secondary work (Table 4-4). The schools attended by the members of the elite consisted of parochial colleges, state universities, local business colleges, state normal schools, and university professional schools. Leaders who represented a cross section of the elite matriculated at the Wilkes-Barre Business School or the Wharton Business Extension School of the University of Pennsylvania. The skills acquired in these institutions were used by the members of the elite to establish successful small business operations ranging from clothing stores to electrical equipment dealerships, which were designed to meet the needs of local consumers. The popularity and the potential for success of the small business made it the second largest occupational category among the elite (Table 4-4). A high proportion of these leaders enrolled in professional schools to prepare for careers in law, medicine, dentistry, pharmacy, engineering, and architecture. These schools included the Medicio-chirurgical College in Philadelphia; Georgetown Law School in Washington, D.C.; the Jefferson Medical School in Philadelphia; the University of Pennsylvania Law School; and the Pennsylvania State University Engineering School, among others. In fact, professional occupations comprised the largest single category among the elite. These emerging professions provided numerous opportunities for the members of the elite and their sons, who often pursued similar careers.[26]

Members of the Wilkes-Barre elite also developed numerous associational ties. These ranged from affiliations with ethnic and social clubs to membership in the professional and extraregional organizations. As their upper-class counterparts had done, these leaders had established social institutions, such as the Fox Hill Country Club and the Irem Temple Country Club, each with its own ethnocultural membership. Partly as a response to their exclusion from upper-class clubs, Irish Catholic leaders formed the Fox Hill Country Club. This club drew the majority of its members from the Catholic and Jewish segments of the elite (Table 4-5), while the Irem Temple Club, which was Masonic, drew leaders from the British, Welsh, and German Protestant groups. Catholics, by papal order, could not become Masons after 1880 and, therefore, did not join the Irem Temple Club. These clubs integrated the two main ethnocultural groupings in the elite. Still, each subgroup supported its own organizations, which represented particular ethnic and religious heritages. Irish Catholics joined the An-

Table 4-5. Membership in the Irem Temple Country Club and the Fox Hill Country Club by Ethnocultural Group, Wilkes-Barre's Elite, 1920–1930

Ethnocultural Group	Fox Hill Country Club	Irem Temple Country Club
Irish Catholic	47%	0%
German Catholic	9	2
Eastern and Southern European	23	0
European Jewish	12	5
German Protestant	2	19
British Protestant	7	58
Welsh Protestant	0	16
	100%	100%
N = 88	(43)	(45)

cient Order of Hibernians, which had been a mainstay of the Irish community since the 1880s. Leaders from the Irish community also founded the Knights of Columbus, which by the 1920s drew leaders from all Catholic groups. Leaders of eastern and southern European descent participated in a number of ethnic associations, including the Tatra Club, the Polish Alliance, the Slavic Union, the American Sons of Italy, and the Greek Catholic Union.[27]

Members of the elite affiliated with Protestant denominations had established their own counterparts to the Catholic organizations. The Welsh, for example, participated in St. David's Society, founded in the late nineteenth century and by the 1920s the premier club in the Welsh community. Predominantly Protestant ethnic-group members also joined either the Patriotic Sons of America or the Junior Order of United American Mechanics, both of which were dominated by British elites. These two groups had a long history of anti-Catholicism, dating back to the mid-nineteenth century, when their national chapters were established. Representatives of the national organizations, in fact, lobbied heavily for the passage of the Johnson Immigration Act, the force of which was to restrict American immigration to nationals of Western European Protestant countries.[28]

Membership in professional and business organizations grew out of occupational and career pursuits, rather than ethnic or religious commonality. As a result, these ties cut across the cultural boundaries of the ethnic groups. Like their upper-class counterparts, the professionals in the elite belonged to the Luzerne County Medical and Bar Associations, among other organizations.[29] At the local level, members of the elite who were engaged in mercantile or other small business activity supported the Greater Wilkes-Barre Chamber of Commerce, the Rotary Club, and/or the Kiwanis Club, whose participants promoted the non-coal sectors of the regional economy. Members of the elite also joined a number of other business groups, such as the Wilkes-Barre Contractors' Association and the Wilkes-Barre Real Estate Association. These organizations often directly affected the business pursuits of the members of the elite, which compelled these men to join such associations. Without these ties, those in the elite would have had no way of influencing the fortunes of their particular businesses. Organization had become essential at all levels, whether in the communal or the national economy. For example, members of the Market Street Business Association, tied more by location than common occupational pursuits, pressured the city council for improved roads, police protection, and better sidewalks.

Both ethnic and occupational associations oriented the members of the elite toward the larger society. More than 70 percent of the 136 leaders in the elite had ties with a state or national organization. Poles and Slovaks belonged to the National Polish Alliance and the National Slovak Union, respectively. Small businessmen joined the Furniture Association of America, the National Electrical Association, and other similar groups. Similarly, local manufacturers joined the Pennsylvania Manufacturers' Association or specialty groups, such as the Lace Curtain Manufacturers' Association. These groups provided important information on market and technological conditions in a particular industry or business. Of necessity, they acted as lobbies for their various groups in both the state and national capitals. Through their conventions, these organizations facilitated the exchange of data on matters important to local merchants and dealers, whether the information had to do with wholesale prices or solvency of operations elsewhere in the state. These associational ties diverge sharply from those of the upper class, whose members were involved in vastly different kinds of business pursuits.[30]

Economic ties among the members of the elite also cut across these ethnic and cultural divisions. This was particularly true of the directors of banks which catered to small savers, the major incorporated operations among the elite. Representatives from all ethnocultural groups showed up on these financial boards. For example, among the directors and officers of the North End State Bank, three were British, three were Irish, two were German, two were Polish, and one was Welsh. Similarly, the directors of the Liberty State Bank and Trust Company were drawn from leaders who were Greek, Slovak, Polish, German, and Irish. Unlike the commercial banks that supported major economic activities, these institutions were primarily savings and loan associations or trust companies aimed at small savers, home buyers, and small businessmen. The boards were made up of such varied ethnic groups in order to attract a clientele from the ethnic enclaves that dotted the city. In contrast, the banks controlled by the upper class were linked to the large anthracite and coal-related corporations, the backbone of the regional economy. These banks were also tied to outside interests in New York City and Philadelphia.[31]

This contrast appears again in the associational and cultural ties of the bank directors in the two leadership groups. The ethnic differences between the two sets of directors typifies the contrast between the upper class and the elite as a whole. The majority of the families of directors in the upper class, 51 percent, were of colonial stock; in contrast, 69 percent of the families of directors in the

Table 4-6. Percentage of Leaders in Wilkes-Barre's Upper Class and Elite with Business, Ethnic, and Social Organizational Ties, 1920–1930

Organizational Ties	Upper Class	Elite
Upper-class social clubs	95%	0%
Director, national corporation	33	0
Director, anthracite coal-related corporation	34	0
New York City and/or Philadelphia social club	33	0
National and state business organizations	47	31
Local business and/or ethnic organizations	21*	86
Local and regional companies†	24‡	64
National ethnic organizations	0	40
Elite social clubs	11	65

*Those in the upper class belonged to the Sons of the American Revolution and other local groups which required colonial-stock lineage for entry. They also participated in the Chamber of Commerce and the Wilkes-Barre Real Estate Association.

†This category does not include banks or other financial institutions.

‡These operations generally consisted of utility and traction companies and manufacturing and milling companies founded in the nineteenth century by members of the upper class. These operations also included brokerage houses and investment companies aimed at national and East Coast markets.

elite came largely after 1880. Similarly, 83 percent of the board members in the upper class were British. In contrast, 74 percent of those in the elite belonged to ethnic groups other than British—19 percent, in fact, were from Eastern European families. The leaders in the upper class were also far more involved in activities centered in New York City and/or Philadelphia than were those in the elite (Table 4-6), who were more concerned with organizations tied to the local economy or the community. In fact, not a single member of the elite had economic or social ties with metropolitan leadership groups, whereas a significant proportion of the upper class were closely tied to the New York/Philadelphia leadership.[32]

LEADERSHIP GROUPS IN THE NORTHERN ANTHRACITE REGION OUTSIDE WILKES-BARRE

A dual structure of leadership similar to the one in Wilkes-Barre emerged in the other communities of the region. The remnants of the nineteenth-century elites still in the cities or towns constituted one group. The dispersal of the nineteenth-century leadership groups during the late 1800s created opportunities for members of immigrant groups, including those from southern and eastern Europe, to move into the vacuum left by the departing leaders of English descent and colonial-stock ancestry. The men moving into these positions represented a variety of ethnocultural groups, from Polish Catholics to Welsh Presbyterians, and constituted the new elites in the communities. These new elites mirrored the elite in Wilkes-Barre, while the descendants of the last century's leadership complemented the upper class.

The descendants who persisted in their cities and towns confronted the growing presence of corporate interests from metropolitan centers. At the same time, these men were still tied to Wilkes-Barre's upper-class leadership, whose continued prosperity insured their own fortunes. The regional networks that had been so disruptive to elites in the late nineteenth century were now vital in maintaining contact with the upper class and its economic and social institutions. In fact, improvements in transportation and communications facilitated these ties and brought members of both groups into far closer association.

No longer competitors with the upper class, the descendants of the nineteenth-century elites still shared the same social characteristics, cultural background, and kinship ties with members of Wilkes-Barre's upper class. These leaders were predominantly British, Episcopalian, or Presbyterian; they were as well educated as in the past tradition. They shared, therefore, the same cultural and socioeconomic backgrounds as their counterparts in Wilkes-Barre (Tables 4-7 and 4-8). The majority of these men had attended Wilkes-Barre academies and, for the most part, joined its upper-class churches. Over 50 percent of these men were related to prominent Wilkes-Barre families through blood or marriage. College educated, 29 percent of the descendants of the older elites in the other communities matriculated at Harvard, Yale, or Princeton (or other upper-class colleges) and were affiliated with the Ivy League Alumni clubs in Wilkes-Barre. The majority of the lawyers in these groups had trained under leading Wilkes-Barre attorneys, whose families had long been members of the city's upper class. Similarly, the doctors from these groups were usually affiliated with the Wilkes-Barre General Hospital, an institution founded and run by the upper class. More than 70 percent of these men belonged to either the Wyoming Historical and Geological Society, the Westmoreland Club, and/or the Wyoming Valley Country Club. The Historical Society identified these leaders with the founding of Wilkes-Barre and the settling of the Wyoming Valley during the late eighteenth century while the Westmoreland Club acknowledged the power and high social status of these men. These intense associations with the upper class had transformed these colonial-stock leaders into extensions of Wilkes-Barre's leadership. Their institutional identification, by and large, grew out of their ties with city leadership.[33]

The occupational and economic orientation of these men was also fixed on Wilkes-Barre. The largest single occupational category was the professional, made up of doctors and lawyers (Table 4-7). The men in this category had offices in and around Wilkes-Barre's central business district, a locational advantage, since they were near the region's primary political, legal, and philanthropic institutions. Among the lawyers, many were engaged in law partnerships with attorneys from the upper class or had full-time law practices in the city. Doctors

Table 4-7.   Birthplace, Lineage, and Proportion of Descendants of Nineteenth-Century Elites in Communities of the Wyoming Valley other than Wilkes-Barre, 1920–1930*

		%	N
Resident community in 1920s	Wyoming Valley	44	61
	Hinterland	30	42
	Outside region	22	31
	Foreign-born	4	5
		100%	139
Lineage	Colonial-stock	45	62
	Family pre-1880	33	46
	Family of leader post-1880	14	20
	Unknown	8	11
		100%	139
Proportion related to Wilkes-Barre's upper class	Proportion related to Wilkes-Barre's upper class through blood or marriage	52	72
	Proportion unrelated	48	67
		100%	139

*In the text, these elites are referred to either as older elites or as descendants of older elites. Technically, not all these men were descended from these elites. The greater portion, 37%, were. For the sake of description, all men who were leaders in these communities, who demonstrated characteristics shown in Tables 4-4 and 4-5, and who were tied to the upper class, are referred to as descendants of the nineteenth-century elites. Those not descended from nineteenth-century elite families within the Wyoming Valley came from elite families in the hinterland, managers from outside-based corporations, or were of unknown status. In some cases, the descendants of the nineteenth-century elites moved from their hometowns to communities in the Wyoming Valley other than Wilkes-Barre. For examples, see *Eastern Pennsylvanians* (Philadelphia: Eastern Pennsylvania Biographical Association, 1928), 99, 127; Oscar J. Harvey and Ernest G. Smith, *A History of Wilkes-Barre, Luzerne County, Pennsylvania*, 6 vols. (Wilkes-Barre: Rader Publishing House, 1909–1930), 5:204–5, 6:527–28; H. C. Hayden, Alfred Hand and John J. Jordan, *Genealogical and Family History of the Wyoming and Lackawanna Valleys*, 2 vols. (New York: Lewis Publishing Company, 1906), 1:566–67; *Wilkes-Barre Record*, 5 February 1925; and Estate Inventory, Register of Wills, Luzerne County Courthouse, Luzerne County, Wilkes-Barre, Pennsylvania, Estate number 164-1925.

and lawyers also belonged to the Luzerne County Medical and Bar associations, located in Wilkes-Barre. Similarly, architects, engineers, and other professionals often had their offices in Wilkes-Barre.[34]

As men of status and position, these individuals were involved in Wilkes-Barre's economic institutions. Forty-three percent were directors, officers, or partners in Wilkes-Barre companies, both large and small. They served on the boards of Wilkes-Barre utility, coal, and manufacturing companies, in addition to the major commercial banks. As participants in Wilkes-Barre's regionally oriented economy, over 40 percent belonged to the Greater Wilkes-Barre Cham-

Table 4-8. Social Characteristics of Descendants of Nineteenth-Century Elites in Communities of the Wyoming Valley other than Wilkes-Barre, 1920–1930

Social Characteristics		%	N
Ethnicity	British	77	108
	Scotch-Irish	4	6
	German	7	8
	Other*	12	17
		100%	139
Religion	Episcopalian	38	53
	Presbyterian	32	45
	Methodist	21	29
	Other	6	8
	Unknown	3	4
		100%	139
Education	Elementary	4	5
	High school	11	15
	Academy	31	44
	College	47	66
	Unknown	7	9
		100%	139
Occupation	Professional	29	40
	Coal mining	15	20
	Manufacturing	16	23
	Commerce	13	19
	Finance	10	14
	Managerial	5	7
	Real estate/Insurance	9	12
	Contractor	3	4
		100%	139

*Refers to Welsh and Irish.

ber of Commerce, the Wilkes-Barre Real Estate Board, and a variety of other business organizations in which members of the upper class participated.[35]

The break in the pattern of associational ties that occurred among the members of the upper class in Wilkes-Barre also transpired among these leaders. Significantly, these men affiliated with the same extralocal organizations as the Wilkes-Barre upper-class leaders. They or their wives joined the Sons of the American Revolution, the Daughters of the American Revolution, the Mayflower Society, and the New England Society of Pennsylvania. They participated in the same quasi-ethnic groups, and more than 10 percent were members of similar social clubs in New York and Philadelphia.

These men belonged to Ivy League Alumni, athletic, and social clubs patronized by members of the upper class and metropolitan leadership groups. They also sat on the boards of metropolitan-based corporations such as the National Publishing Corporation of New York City or Green, Ellis and Anderson of the New York Stock Exchange. Like their upper-class counterparts, these leaders also held board positions on companies outside the region and the metropolitan centers. Leaders from other communities served as directors on the Stonewall Iron Company of Alabama and the Springfield Coal Company of New Jersey. At the same time, they also placed their money in companies outside the region. Robert P. Brodhead invested his capital in midwestern, southern, and western railroads, as well as a utility company in Denver. He did, however, keep a substantial amount of money in his construction company, Brodhead and Garrett. Other leaders in this group invested their capital in municipal bonds (more than $300,000 in one case), oil companies, steel corporations, and a variety of other operations. Like their counterparts in Wilkes-Barre, these men were also associated with numerous professional and trade organizations on the national and state level.[36]

While these networks were still viable in the twentieth century, they had lost their critical economic functions of the nineteenth century. Issues of economic survival and development had been resolved by the 1880s, and after 1900, local economic and administrative control of the region had been tightly and irrevocably concentrated in Wilkes-Barre, which maintains its position as a regional center even into the 1980s. At the same time, the penetration of the region by the large-scale systems of New York and Philadelphia drew the focus of Wilkes-Barre's upper class away from the region and toward the metropolitan centers, where national economic power was becoming concentrated. Regional ties, in fact, became secondary to associations with elites in New York and Philadelphia. The crucial relationships in the twentieth century were no longer within the region but with leadership groups outside the Wyoming Valley and its hinterland to the north.

During the years when the old nineteenth-century leadership groups were breaking up, the new elites, whose members came from foreign-born groups, began to emerge; by the 1920s the new elites in these communities had become fairly heterogeneous (Table 4-9). These men shared neither lineage nor religious and socioeconomic backgrounds with the descendants of the older elites who persisted; they were equally dissimilar to the upper class in Wilkes-Barre. The new leaders from immigrant families had their own churches, economic activities, clubs, and associations.

These men were identified through their economic, political, and social standing within each community. The directors and officers of local savings and loan institutions, smaller commercial banks, construction companies, real estate firms, and insurance companies were included in these newly emerging elites. These institutions generally dealt with small savers, homeowners, and small-scale entrepreneurs from the newer ethnic groups and were outside the scope and interests of descendants of the older elites and their upper-class counterparts in Wilkes-Barre. The members of these elites also demonstrated social standing and political authority. As ethnic leaders, these men held public office in local and county government and were often local party figures. As prominent men within their communities and subcultures, they also headed local ethnic clubs, ran boards of trade, and were prominent in their churches. However, they lacked the powerful extraregional ties of the older leadership and had access to neither the corporations nor the large-scale agencies of national government.[37]

Almost all these men were engaged in activities that were both secondary to and dependent on mining and its related industries (Table 4-9). In nearby Plymouth, for example, all the leaders from first- or second-generation immigrant families were in contracting, small-scale manufacturing and mercantile operations, or services such as undertaking. Wilkes-Barre coal companies employed still other such men. In Nanticoke, Wilkes-Barre-owned and outside-owned anthracite corporations employed 20 percent of the largely Eastern European elite as superintendents, mining foremen, or fire bosses. None of these men participated in the major economic activities of the region or held power even remotely comparable to that of the descendants of the old elites despite the fact that they vastly outnumbered them. They were, moreover, rather isolated from the regional leadership in Wilkes-Barre, whose continued economic success insured the survival of these newer elite groups.[38]

The ethnic and religious content of these groups varied from community to community. In Nanticoke and the surrounding towns of Glen Lyon, Alden, and Wanamie, the majority of the urban elite were of Eastern European origin or descent; men of Welsh heritage were another important part of this group. These urban centers had grown exclusively on mining operations and largely after 1890, when the migration from Eastern Europe was rapidly increasing. The coal companies had, in fact, deliberately recruited workers from Slavic groups for new anthracite collieries because of their lower demands for wages. In contrast, leaders of British descent formed the largest component of Kingston's leadership. It had developed a strong commercial and small-scale manufacturing base after 1880 to support mining on the west side of the Wyoming Valley and to meet the demands of the growing regional population. These had attracted men with white-collar skills, most of them native-born. The majority of these elites had at least a high school education, and many had graduated from college (Table 4-8). This high level of education was reflected in the large proportion of leaders—25 percent to 33 percent—who were doctors, lawyers, engineers, or architects (Table 4-9).[39]

THE WILKES-BARRE ELITE, THE NEW ELITES IN THE COALFIELDS, AND THE INCIPIENT REGIONAL NETWORKS

The withering of the upper-class regional networks had created a vacuum that the new elites were starting to fill by the 1920s. In the years after 1920, the beginnings of the networks that tied together members of the new elites

Table 4-9. Social Characteristics of Urban Elites, Exclusive of Descendants of Nineteenth-Century Elites in Communities of the Wyoming Valley other than Wilkes-Barre, 1920–1930[*]

Social Characteristics		Pittston, Plains, and Wyoming	Nanticoke, Alden, Glen Lyon, and Wanamie	Plymouth and Larksville	Kingston, Forty-Fort, and Edwardsville
Ethnicity	British[†]	22%	19%	24%	48%
	Southern Irish	30	9	21	15
	German	6	13	12	12
	Eastern and Southern European	26	42	26	6
	Welsh	16	17	17	19
		100%	100%	100%	100%
Religion	Episcopalian/Presbyterian	16%	12%	9%	22%
	Other Protestant groups[‡]	8	12	16	7
	Methodist	12	11	11	26
	Roman Catholic[§]	56	46	45	22
	Jewish	2	8	13	3
	Unknown	6	11	6	20
		100%	100%	100%	100%
Education	None	2%	3%	4%	3%
	Elementary	22	32	16	11
	High School[‖]	21	22	41	23
	Academy	7	3	14	13
	College	42	38	22	38
	Unknown	6	2	3	12
		100%	100%	100%	100%

Table 4-9. *(Continued)*

Social Characteristics		Pittston, Plains, and Wyoming	Nanticoke, Alden, Glen Lyon, and Wanamie	Plymouth and Larksville	Kingston, Forty-Fort, and Edwardsville
Occupation	Superintendent/Mine foreman	14%	20%	15%	4%
	Small businessman	27	31	26	24
	Local manufacturer	14	8	9	6
	Contractor/Construction man	2	2	11	7
	Professional man	33	31	25	28[#]
	Manager	3	2	5	9
	Insurance/Realtor	2	0	5	11
	Financier	5	6	4	11
		100%	100%	100%	100%
		(86)	(106)	(76)	(95)

n = 363

[*]The term *descendants of nineteenth-century elites* refers to descendants of those nineteenth-century elites in Tables 4-3 and 4-4.

[†]Includes Scotch-Irish, English, and Scots.

[‡]Includes Christian, Lutheran, Congregational, and other Protestant denominations; excludes Methodists.

[§]Includes Greek and Russian Orthodox.

[‖]Includes those who attended parochial high school.

[#]Rounded up from 0.2736, so total equals 100%.

throughout the region were barely visible. The analysis of these networks is therefore not meant to be definitive or exhaustive but to underscore the continued importance of Wilkes-Barre as the center of regional society among the new leadership groups. The elite networks then developing around Wilkes-Barre's own elite lacked the cohesiveness of their upper-class counterparts in the nineteenth century. In fact, these new regional networks reflected the ethnic splits and business and occupational specialization found among Wilkes-Barre's elite. They also lacked a set of regionwide economic institutions, partly because of the small-scale business operations pursued by the members of the various elites. Blocked from participation in the regionally oriented anthracite, coal-related, transportation, and utility industries, the members of the elites had pursued service activities, which did not have strong extralocal orientations. Nonetheless, extralocal relationships in other areas remained an important aspect of Wilkes-Barre's newly emerging leadership.

The issue of regional hegemony, so important in the nineteenth century, had long been decided by the 1920s, and actually to the advantage of the Wilkes-Barre elite, which lacked the economic institutions comparable to those of the upper class of the last century. The economy of the Wyoming Valley revolved around Wilkes-Barre and tied virtually every elite in the region to the city, regardless of the business or occupational pursuits of its members. These ties facilitated the creation of a new set of extralocal relationships, centered on Wilkes-Barre, among the elites in the Valley. The city's position as the hub of the regional transit system and the primary point of contact with markets beyond the Valley offered attractions no other city could provide. Its comparatively diverse economy and its position as the regional center made it the natural focus of the new networks. Wilkes-Barre also acted as the headquarters of the major occupational, ethnic, business, and fraternal associations among the elites, a fact that added to the city's attractiveness.[40]

These elite associations drew their members from newer community elites throughout the Wyoming Valley. Members of these groups elsewhere in the region often conducted their business and professional activities in Wilkes-Barre because of the advantages it presented as the regional center and as the hub of the region's population (Table 4-10). The networks that arose from this type of interaction displayed some of the characteristics of the upper-class networks. Both oriented the newer elite groups in the Wyoming Valley toward Wilkes-Barre. Both penetrated the local society of the newer elite, and both tied the fortunes of those in these groups in the region to Wilkes-Barre and its continued economic success.

Wilkes-Barre's ethnic associations drew members from elites throughout the region. The Polish National Alliance, the American Sons of Italy, the Ancient Order of Hibernians, and the National Slovak Union, among others, operated chapters out of Wilkes-Barre. The regular meetings, in addition to activities on national holidays and religious occasions, created the basis for contact among the elites in the Wyoming Valley who also had chapters. The Knights of Colum-

Table 4-10. Proportion of Institutional, Economic, and Associational Ties between Wilkes-Barre and Its Elite and Other Elites in the Region, 1920–1930*

Institutional, Economic, and Associational Ties	Pittston, Plains,† and Wyoming	Nanticoke, Alden, Glen Lyon, and Wanamie	Plymouth and Larksville	Kingston, Forty-Fort, and Edwardsville
Ethnic club and fraternal lodge ties with Wilkes-Barre elite	37%	24%	32%	33%
Social club ties with Wilkes-Barre elite	23	25	11	16
Institutional ties with Wilkes-Barre elite	12	14	20	20
Business associational ties with Wilkes-Barre elite	9	10	15	11
Professional ties with Wilkes-Barre elite	11	8	10	9
Economic ties with Wilkes-Barre elite	8	19	12‡	11
Total	100%	100%	100%	100%
	(120)	(177)	(132)	(160)

n = 589

* Exclusive of descendants of nineteenth-century elites.

† Plains is actually a direct satellite of Wilkes-Barre.

‡ Rounded down from 12.8, so total equals 100 percent.

bus had an association in Wilkes-Barre which helped to maintain contact and coordinate activities among chapters scattered throughout the Wyoming Valley. Similarly, the Hibernians hosted St. Patrick's Day celebrations in Wilkes-Barre and drew members from all over the Valley. Other events, such as Easter Monday dances and balls, were equally popular throughout the region. Their Protestant counterparts belonged to the Patriotic Sons of America and/or the Junior Order of United American Mechanics, both with chapters in Wilkes-Barre. The St. David's Society, a Welsh counterpart to the Irish Catholic organizations, was headquartered in Wilkes-Barre and often held its meetings in the Hotel Sterling, near the center of the city. Members of newer elites in the Valley also participated in the fraternal lodges run by members of the Wilkes-Barre upper class and headquartered in the regional center. These lodges tended to recruit their members from the non-Catholic leaders in the region, though not exclusively. The Knights Templar and the Mystic Shrine, for example, appealed to the native-born Protestants, while the Cratfsmen's Club and the Elks Lodge drew from all ethnocultural groups.[41]

Wilkes-Barre offered businessmen and professionals numerous advantages. The presence of hospitals in the city drew doctors to Wilkes-Barre. Similarly, the community's position as the economic and professional hub of the region made it attractive both to lawyers and those engaged in politics. Attorneys conducted most of their formal business in the county courthouse, located in Wilkes-Barre. The courthouse contained land, criminal, title, and other records lawyers relied on to conduct much of their business; it was also a place where their clients often had to conclude their own affairs. The intense level of business activity in downtown Wilkes-Barre, where the coal companies, banks, and other financial institutions were often located, also created a demand for legal and other professional services. For attorneys involved in politics—and many still were—Wilkes-Barre's position as the political center for both the Republican and Democratic parties was especially attractive.[42]

These ties extended to a variety of other occupations. Among other elites located in Wilkes-Barre, merchants, real estate agents, and insurance agents, even building contractors, particularly those engaged throughout the region, had their offices in Wilkes-Barre. The city was especially appealing for national corporations with branches in the northern anthracite region. Central location in the transportation system, excellent communications, and diverse financial facilities drew these companies to the city. The managers employed by the corporations, whether they lived in Wilkes-Barre or elsewhere, had to work in the city. For instance, managers for companies such as the Remington Typewriter Corporation and the Mutual Life Insurance Company of New York City, who belonged to other elites, conducted their business in Wilkes-Barre. Leaders in other communities were often associated with Wilkes-Barre companies and banks. Members of the Kingston elite, for example, sat on the boards of the Wyoming Valley Building and Loan Association and the Wilkes-Barre Deposit and Savings Bank. Leaders from Plains and Ashley were directors for the Pennsylvania Bank and Trust Company, while those from Plymouth served on the Hanover Bank and Trust.[43]

Business associations in Wilkes-Barre also drew their members from elites over the Wyoming Valley. The Greater Wilkes-Barre Chamber of Commerce was the most prominent of these. Its membership included leaders from the city's upper class and its elite, as well as leaders from virtually every elite in the region. Leaders in communities other than Wilkes-Barre joined the Wilkes-Barre Underwriters Association, its real estate association, and a variety of other Wilkes-Barre-based groups. These groups provided regular channels of communication among leaders involved in similar kinds of business activity and helped to sustain contact among elites in the region.[44]

Members of newer elites participated in the institutions of Wilkes-Barre's elite. Catholics often joined St. Mary's Irish Catholic Church or the St. Nicholas German Catholic Church. Those who were Presbyterian affiliated with the Westminster Church or the Grant Street Church. Among those who were Jewish, most belonged to one of the synagogues in Wilkes-Barre. Members of newer elites often pursued their education in the regional center, where they encountered members of Wilkes-Barre's elite. These men attended the city's parochial high schools, the Wilkes-Barre Business College, or the Wharton Business School. Last, a large proportion of these elites belonged to the Irem Temple Country Club or the Fox Hill Country Club. Fox Hill drew its members from the Catholic and Jewish segment of these elites, while the Protestants joined the Irem Temple Country Club.[45]

The 1920s were probably the peak years of the northern anthracite region. The leadership groups flourished, the cities and towns grew, and the regional economy expanded. Subsequent decades would not be so kind. The Great Depression of the 1930s and competition from big oil would undercut the anthracite coal industry and, with it, the prosperity of all urban leadership groups in the region. The northern coalfields and the regional leadership would be among the early casualties of changing fuel sources and new patterns of industry.[46]

CHAPTER V

Pottsville's Entrepreneurial Elite in Prosperity and Depression

ILKES-BARRE'S UPPER CLASS provides one example of the evolution of urban leadership during the nineteenth century. To the south, in adjacent Schuylkill County, Pottsville's elite furnishes a second and contrasting case. Despite similarities in location, markets, and, above all, economic base, the two groups diverged sharply in their patterns of development. So, too, did the fate of their respective communities differ, in large measure, because of the varying entrepreneurial strategies pursued by each leadership group. Pottsville's elite never took on the characteristics of an upper class, nor did it transform the city into the regional center for the southern coalfields; it realized no potential for sustained population growth and economic development.

Until the 1870s, Pottsville leaders had sustained a thriving economic base, unrivalled in the region. Participation in this economic base also created the cohesiveness that maintained the elite. Primarily businessmen, this group had carved out a profitable niche in the mining industry; their entrepreneurial skills yielded substantial returns and gave the Pottsville leadership a measure of influence throughout the region. No other leadership group in the southern coalfields equalled the Pottsville elite in scale, capital, or productivity in the anthracite industry. At the same time, Pottsville leaders established a highly successful iron and steel industry, which depended on hard coal for its energy and which provided the city's elite with a continual source of profits and influence over other communities in the region.

These activities created a tremendous demand for money to sustain such diverse operations. In response, Pottsville leaders had built the largest financial institutions, in terms of money, and the greatest reserve of private capital in the southern coal region, one that rivalled the assets of Wilkes-Barre's upper class. By the early 1870s, Pottsville's leadership had fashioned an apparently stable, prosperous, and strong local economy with unlimited potential for expansion. In a very real sense, the entrepreneurial efforts of the elite tied them to the city and the region. Members of the elite owned profitable companies and banks, assets not easily abandoned, while the mutual involvement of the members of the city's leadership in similar activities had created the cohesiveness of the elite. The entrepreneurial efforts of the elite also made Pottsville into the largest community in the southern anthracite region and the hub of the coal trade. The elite's economic activities gave Pottsville the most diverse and prosperous economy, while the banks and capital originating through elite efforts transformed the city into the financial center of the region.

A series of economic reverses during the 1870s and 1880s undermined the prosperity and power of the Pottsville elite. Market pressures forced corporate leaders of the Philadelphia and Reading Railroad (PRRCO) to monopolize the anthracite industry in the southern region and force the coal entrepreneurs of Pottsville's elite, as well as all other leadership groups in the region, out of mining. Corporate leaders in Philadelphia also bought out almost all iron and steel operations in the region, thereby reducing further the independent economic activities of Pottsville's leadership. At the same time, the depression of the 1870s crippled the financial leaders in Pottsville's elite, who saw many of their banks go into receivership and then liquidate. Bankruptcies among individual entrepreneurs in the city's elite further exacerbated the deteriorating position of Pottsville's leadership.

Last, Pottsville's leaders faced a shift in the center of the mining industry from the southern rim, where their city was located, to the northern rim of the Schuylkill-Northumberland coalfields. This shift created new and rival leadership groups in the booming towns of this section, thus drawing capital and talent away from Pottsville's elite and contributing further to the erosion of its economic base. Pottsville leaders simultaneously saw their substantial capital holdings dwindle from the effects of the depression and their mining, iron and steel, and service operations fold under pressure from Philadelphia's corporate leaders. Independent action severely curtailed, Pottsville leaders now faced several decades of a stagnating economy and marginal population increases. These reverses had undermined the elite's main sources of entrepreneurial activity, power and wealth—its strongest attachments to the city. They also reduced Pottsville's position in the region, since the city was directly dependent on the array of activities its elite pursued. Pottsville could no longer be attractive to newcomers, who often moved to other communities in search of opportunities. So, too, would the sons of Pottsville's leaders depart, men who saw Pottsville's reduced economy and the declining fortunes of their fathers as a meager inheritance, one unlikely to promise a prosperous future. Philadelphia's leaders and the metropolitan center supplanted the Pottsville elite and its city as the focal point of the region.

EARLY HISTORY OF POTTSVILLE AND THE ANTHRACITE INDUSTRY

The anthracite coal boom of the 1820s sparked the rise of Pottsville and the development of the coal industry in the southern region. The city quickly

became the center of a brisk coal trade and the object of intense land speculation. Its leaders provided services to the growing number of coal operators, both
in Pottsville and the surrounding area. The future of these leaders and their
community was temporarily threatened when leaders in nearby Mount Carbon
opposed Pottsville's 1828 petition for incorporation by the Pennsylvania Legislature. As residents of the oldest community in Schuylkill County (founded in
1759), Mount Carbon's leaders carried some weight in the legislature. In its
position at the terminus of the Schuylkill Canal, Mount Carbon was also in a
position to compete effectively with Pottsville for supremacy in the newly developing region. With aid from political allies in the legislature, Pottsville leaders overcame this opposition and won full incorporation for their community in
1831. At the same time, they also used capital from business partners in Reading and also in Philadelphia to extend the Schuylkill Navigation Canal to
Pottsville, thereby overcoming Mount Carbon's locational advantage. By the
mid-thirties, Pottsville had emerged as the largest and most rapidly developing
community in the region. Its future, like that of the industry, seemed assured.[1]

Like the area, the mining industry experienced some growing pains during
the 1820s and 1830s. Anthracite operations consisted of small-scale collieries,
surface diggings, and land leasing to impecunious coal operators. This system
actually encouraged the rapid exploitation of available surface coal and, in 1825
to 1830, the first five years of intensive mining in the region, boosted production very greatly. The main elements of this decentralized system of mining were
low capital entry conditions, primitive technology, and rapid turnover, both of
operator and landowner. In the southern coal region, the decentralized system
made the coal industry vulnerable to penetration by outside investors and capitalists, as Pottsville's leaders did not hold sufficient economic power to resist
these outside entrepreneurs. Ultimately, the outsiders' presence would undercut
the efforts of Pottsville's elite to secure their position in the anthracite industries
and related activities. As a result, the city's leaders could not create a rapidly
expanding economy so necessary to their persistence.

The physical characteristics of the southern coalfields, where Pottsville's leaders operated, differed considerably from the densely settled and geographically
smaller northern coalfields. The Schuylkill-Northumberland fields consisted of
parallel hills, valleys, and mountains, each one succeeding the other. The
region was by far the larger of the two anthracite-producing fields. Totalling over
180 square miles, the southern rim stretched from Shenandoah in the north to
Schuylkill Haven in the south and from Tamaqua in the east to Shamokin in
the west. Although no major river cut through the two-county region, numerous
unnavigable streams broke up the rough terrain. With the assistance of a canal,
the headwaters of the Schuylkill River reached just below Pottsville and gave
the region its major source of transportation to the markets of Reading and
Philadelphia.

The combination of the river and the construction of the Schuylkill Navigation Canal in 1825 were the keys to economic growth in the region. Coal

operators capitalized on this water system to sell anthracite in Reading and Philadelphia, where consumers had begun to use coal as a home heating fuel. The canal and the river also made possible the marketing of large quantities of anthracite coal to the newly emerging iron and steel towns to the south. The low costs of shipping and the readily available markets boosted coal production tremendously from 1826 to 1830. During these five years, coal production soared 1,000 percent, while the average yearly coal shipment increased from 700 tons before 1826 to 45,311 tons after 1826.[2]

The railroad also contributed significantly to the rapid development of the coal industry. In response to the need for intraregional transportation, local entrepreneurs and outside capitalists built a series of short lateral rail lines. These lines connected mining sites with the canal and made possible the mining of new coal lands in the region. These laterals also provided transportation for every community in the region, from St. Clair and Tamaqua in the south and east to Shenandoah and Shamokin in the north and west.[3]

Railroad connections were also made with Danville, Pennsylvania; upstate New York, and the metropolitan centers. The first of these was completed in the 1830s on the strength of a $250,000 subsidy from the Stephen Girard estate in Philadelphia. The rail line connected the coal region with the rich agricultural and iron-producing area of Danville, along the Susquehanna. In less than ten years, the Philadelphia and Reading Railroad Company completed its own mainline to Pottsville. By the 1850s, the region had been joined with almost all the major markets. In that same decade, a series of additional spurs were built to the Shenandoah–Mahanoy City and the Shamokin–Mount Carmel sections, thereby completing the rail net.[4]

Pottsville was the chief beneficiary of these improvements in transportation. The community's pulling power as the center of the early coal trade drew thousands of rural and foreign-born migrants. The city grew overnight from a small, unpromising village into a thriving coal town and, potentially, the regional hub of the developing coalfields. Pottsville's growth outdistanced that of the rest of Schuylkill County and all other communities in the region until the 1860s. This pattern of boom-town growth was repeated in every other industrial community throughout the region during the nineteenth century. Communities such as Schuylkill Haven and Minersville sprang up in the early 1830s and grew with extraordinary speed. In the northern rim of the region, cities such as Mahanoy City and Shenandoah experienced similar rates of growth twenty years later, during the 1850s and 1860s.[5]

Pottsville's elite remained the most powerful and wealthiest leadership group in the southern coalfields. Its city, the largest and economically most diversified, reflected the power of Pottsville's elite. Pottsville's leaders benefitted from the city's position as the center of the anthracite industry, and their holdings scattered over the region. The strength of the city's elite in the anthracite industry was based on these leaders' successful participation in the small-scale mining system that typified the southern coal region. The coal industry was still in the midst of development during the 1830s and 1840s, a fact which contributed to its decentralized system. The primitive technology and easily accessible coal were probably the most important factors in shaping the early anthracite industry.

During the early mining of the southern coalfields, large amounts of anthracite, in the from of outcrop, were easy to dig. Mining this surface coal required little capital and technical knowledge, and early coal operators followed a very simple procedure to remove the coal. They usually dug holes into a surface vein, filled them with wet quicklime, and broke up the coal as the lime split the seam during the drying stage. The coal was then screened by hand, loaded into wooden carts, and hauled to a nearby rail line, after which it was taken to the canal and shipped to market. No costly pumps, machinery, or powder were needed in this process.[6]

When the surface coal had been exhausted, operators were forced to mine underground, frequently beneath the water level, in order to reach new veins. To mine underground, coal operators adopted the drift and slope technique. Drifts consisted of tunnels dug up and into a mountainside to an anthracite seam. The incline created by this technique drained the water, with no additional expense or labor required. The slope, on the other hand, ran downward toward the vein and demanded constant work to haul up the coal and pump out the water. Both techniques were fairly inexpensive; however, they were also inefficient and limited. Mining could often be done only to shallow depths.[7]

By using more sophisticated and productive methods, some experienced operators were able to avoid much of the waste. These operators were usually miners from England and Wales who were then living in Pottsville. The output of these men regularly accounted for at least 33 percent of the total production, although the miners made up less than 20 percent of all coal operators. But even these skilled and knowledgeable colliers were committed to small-scale, one- or two-man operations. Few of these men had sufficient long-term perspective or administrative experience to become involved in incorporated coal companies. The drift and slope methods quickly became the dominant mode of anthracite mining and remained so until the late nineteenth century.[8]

As a result, small-scale operators, landowners, and speculators were an important part of the anthracite industry in the southern coal regions. All three were primarily interested in immediate returns on their investments. Coal operators constantly shifted location when easily mined surface veins gave out. They seldom invested large amounts of capital to reach deep coal seams when surface veins elsewhere in the region promised sizable profits for small expenditures. The landholder, on the other hand, uninvolved in the actual mining, simply bought large tracts of coal lands and leased out parcels to as many operators as the tract would bear, in order to maximize his own profits. The land-holding speculator simply held onto the coal lands until the price rose sufficiently to make a substantial return by selling. This short-term investing attracted a large number of entrepreneurs into the industry. For example, by

1833, as many as fifty anthracite operators could be found mining in the Pottsville area alone. More than a thousand such entrepreneurs came and went during the years before the Philadelphia and Reading Railroad Company took control of the coal industry in the 1870s.[9]

The rising value of land prices during the early coal boom demonstrates the popularity of the short-term investment. In 1824, an average tract of coal land sold for $19,000. In five years, the price had jumped 110 percent, to $40,000, an enormous profit to those who had bought land in the early 1820s. This increase also reflected a tremendous rise in the price of coal and gave the operator a handsome return on a small investment. The large profits only reinforced the short-term view and encouraged the in-migration of more operators and land buyers.[10]

Small-scale mining and dispersed land ownership persisted through the 1850s, in spite of technological changes in the anthracite industry. After about 1850, sophisticated market demands and deeper coal seams required new and costly mining techniques and heavily capitalized coal companies. These coal companies consolidated control and better regulated production. In the southern region, incorporated companies began to appear after 1850, particularly in the developing mining districts of the Mahanoy coal basin and the Northumberland fields. Almost all, however, used outside financing, moderate capitalization, and slope and drift techniques. Most local coal operators in the southern region continued to operate one- or two-man-owned coal collieries, while landowners and speculators still exercised a powerful voice in the anthracite industry.[11]

POTTSVILLE'S ELITE AND THE MINING INDUSTRY

The entrepreneurial activities of the Pottsville elite were firmly rooted in this decentralized system of mining and the small rail companies associated with it. Pottsville's elite poured much of its time, effort, and capital into land speculation and leasing and one- or two-man-owned mining operations. Such men as Benjamin Haywood, Milton Boone, Burd Patterson, and George W. Snyder ran mining collieries throughout the region up through the 1870s. Of the 186 separate operations, 97 percent consisted of one- or two-man-controlled and land tracts/leasing operations (Table 5-1). Coal operators in the southern region seldom resorted to deep mine shafts, because of the expense and technical knowledge they required.[12]

Members of the elite used their capital to help finance the small lateral rail lines that provided intraregional transportation from the 1820s through the mid-1860s. Local figures such as John Shippen, Burd Patterson, and John M. Wetherill, with associates in Philadelphia and Reading, helped to finance, build, and maintain the first lateral rail line in the region—the Mine Hill and Schuylkill Haven Railroad Company. This pattern of cooperation between local leaders and capitalists from cities along the Schuylkill River was responsible for the

Table 5-1.   Types of Mining Activities Engaged in by Pottsville Leaders, 1820–1885

Type of Activity	N	%
One- or two-man-owned colliery	95	51
Land tracts/Leasing	86	46
Anthracite coal company	5	3
Total	186*	100

*The number of collieries and land tracts are rough estimates culled from biographies of coal operators and land speculators, state mining reports, newspapers, city directories, and private diaries and papers. In some cases, when the data only made reference to a leader as a landholder or coal operator, I have assumed that he owned at least one tract of land or one anthracite colliery.

Sources: See the appendix for a discussion of sources used to develop these data and those in subsequent tables. See also Edward J. Davies II, "The Urbanizing Region: Leadership and Urban Growth in the Anthracite Region, 1830–1885" (Ph.D. diss., University of Pittsburgh, 1977), Table VI–6, pp. 261–62.

construction of most of the lateral rails. For example, William Lawton of Pottsville relied partly on Philadelphia capital to build the Schuylkill Valley Railroad and the Tuscarora and Gold Run Tunnel and Railroad Company. Landowners and local coal operators strongly supported these lines, since they provided cheap transportation to main shipping points. In effect, the lateral rail lines reinforced the decentralized system of mining.[13]

In the short run, these entrepreneurial decisions seemed practical and rational. Capitalists in Philadelphia had provided and paid for the main canal and rail links with the urban markets to the southeast, thus relieving the coal operators of this responsibility. The small-scale and inexpensive mining operation presented the operator and the landowner with the quickest return on an investment. Not until the late 1850s and 1860s did Pottsville's leaders significantly increase the size of their coal operations or use their capital to incorporate coal companies.[14]

Pottsville leaders, in fact, invited outside penetration of the region through their joint participation in chartered companies with Philadelphia capitalists. Admittedly, these ventures never attracted the full resources of the elite, but they indicate a break with a long-standing policy within the ranks of local coal entrepreneurs. A majority of Pottsville's leaders had been longtime opponents of incorporation and outside-dominated companies and continued this opposition well into the 1850s. Yet, by the 1860s, members of the elite had become incorporators and/or directors on five chartered coal companies. The fate of these operations, however, suggests the increasing power of outside entrepreneurs, as well as the inability of Pottsville leaders to pursue this strategy successfully. Two of the companies were headquartered in Philadelphia, where metropolitan entrepreneurs exercised the dominant voice in company affairs. Two of the remaining three companies survived only a short period before collapsing under the market pressures and poor management. The last operation never ranked above the fiftieth percentile in coal production.[15]

Coal operators in the region were aware of the threat these corporations posed to their interests. Leading coal operators in the southern anthracite fields, such as Daniel Krebs, Lewis Audenreid, and Jacob Seitzinger, all of Pottsville, consistently opposed the intrusion of state-chartered companies during the early and mid-nineteenth century. These men and their allies in the Pennsylvania House and Senate attempted to block free participation in the industry by state-incorporated companies and coal-carrying railroads, whose resources and power overshadowed those of the local operators. The operators and their supporters were unable to maintain their unity through the 1850s. By that decade, excessive competition and the rising costs of mining deeper and more impure anthracite placed heavy demands on the capital of each local operator. As a result, major coal operators, such as John Wetherill and David Brown, had shifted their position and now favored incorporation. These men saw the state-chartered company as the only means of raising sufficient backing to remain effective in the mining industry. Opponents believed this strategy would reduce the profits they earned from speculation and one-man operations while also undermining their autonomy.[16]

The absence of major coal companies in Pottsville, combined with the constant migration of coal operators in search of new veins, meant the city never became sharply identified as an administrative hub of the anthracite industry as Wilkes-Barre had done. The city was home for the major coal entrepreneurs in the region and the area's coal exchanges; but, unlike Wilkes-Barre's upper class, its elite did not represent a concentration of power. The elite men of Pottsville generally reinvested their profits in Pottsville's economy and in developing new collieries. Enoch McGinnis is typical of coal entrepreneurs among Pottsville's elite. He repeatedly invested his money in exploring and opening up new coal veins. At the same time, he ran machine shops and sawmills in Pottsville, where he also joined in chartering two of the city's largest commercial banks.[17]

The constant movement of McGinnis and other coal entrepreneurs like him meant that resources were often wasted, while control of the land and the anthracite industry was never centralized. Coal mines were opened up, mined, and then abandoned. Often, this process was repeated several times in one area because of the discovery of new coal, each time requiring greater resources and effort. Without consolidation of their capital, members of the Pottsville elite were unable to compete effectively with outside-based entrepreneurs and their companies.

Not all coal operators pursued McGinnis's strategy. A second group of coal entrepreneurs eschewed his policy of reinvestment in Pottsville's local economy. This group successfully engaged in mining and coal-related operations, often on a fairly large scale. Once having achieved a substantial degree of success, they left the city and the region. Frequently, they had reinvested their profits in metropolitan-based activities as a prelude to their departure. This group of entrepreneurs shared an entirely different set of assumptions concerning the anthracite industry and Pottsville. They tended to see the city merely as a temporary place of residence, rather than as a family home whose fortunes were their own.[18]

George Potts typified this group of coal operators. Both in terms of wealth and scale of his activities, Potts was one of the top three or four operators in the region before the 1870s. By the 1850s, he operated at least eight different collieries and ranked among the top 5 percent of all producers in the coalfields. By that time, however, his interests had shifted to New York City, where he migrated in 1854. Potts continued to be a major force in the region, since he maintained and even expanded his operations in the coalfields. Shortly after his arrival, he joined the board of the National Park Bank of New York City, where he had invested much of his money. Potts remained active in the southern anthracite region through the early 1860s, when he served as an incorporator and director of the Wolf Creek Coal Company, one of the largest outside-controlled companies in the southern fields.[19]

The pattern of George Potts and similar coal operators persisted among Pottsville's leaders into the 1870s and 1880s. Often men of families who had been in the city for decades, such as Franklin P. Kaercher and George DeKeim, left Pottsville for more prosperous environments during these decades. DeKeim, in fact, had acted as agent for the PRRCO in purchasing coal lands and, subsequently, joined the corporation in Philadelphia. Throughout the mid- and late nineteenth century, entrepreneurs from among Pottsville's most powerful men participated in this migration to the metropolitan centers. At the end of the century, the booming coal towns of the northern rim in the Schuylkill-Northumberland coalfields also drew the attention of Pottsville's leaders, who saw these burgeoning communities as profitable urban centers where they could relocate their economic activities and/or reestablish new residences.[20] Pottsville's leaders, as these histories indicate, lacked a commonly shared perspective regarding the exploitation of hard coal and the advantages the elite and the city gained from this activity.

The pattern of out-migration continued into the 1870s, when coal operators, often newcomers in Pottsville, departed from the city, apparently under pressure from the PRRCO. The company's acquisition of coal lands and mining collieries undercut the resources of these operators, as well as their means of livelihood. This group of coal operators represented considerable skills, while their anthracite operations, regardless of size, enhanced the power of the city's leadership in the years before 1870. Often appearing only in the census and/or city directories, the coal operators had, most generally, moved to Pottsville because of the advantages it offered them and their industry. When the advantages began to disappear during the seventies so, too, did many of these operators and their families, probably in search of more promising communities. Typical was coal operator William Kendrick, who had arrived in Pottsville during the mid-sixties.

became involved in a lucrative partnership with James L. Dovey and John C. Northall. By the end of the decade, Kendrick, his relatives, and his partners had left the city. Similary, William and Michael Maize had engaged in mining operations at the same time as Kendrick and his colleagues. By 1865, the sixty-six-year-old father, Michael Maize, had left the city, though he returned by 1870. His son, William, continued his mining activities at New Philadelphia during the 1860s but had left Pottsville by 1870, when his father had returned. James Beatty, William Helfenstein, Francisco Socarraz, and William Wren also exemplify the coal operators who migrated from Pottsville during the 1870s. In fact, 62 percent of all those involved in anthracite producing, dealing, and shipping had left the city during the 1870s. Of the remaining 38 percent, all but one man had shifted into unrelated business activities. Theodore Garreston, a member of the elite, switched from coal mining to iron manufacturing and moved his operation from Pottsville to Lyons, Pennsylvania. His fellow member, Joshua Sigfried, had shifted from coal mining to insurance. Daniel Larer, a coal dealer, was selling wines and liquor by 1870. Baird Snyder joined these men in acquiring new occupations. A coal merchant in 1869 and 1870, he became a bookkeeper within the next ten years. Of the fifty-two men, fifty-one had abandoned the coal-mining industry and, often, the city itself.[21]

A third group of coal entrepreneurs, the landholders and speculators, pursued still another strategy in exploiting hard coal. These men made their money by leasing or selling coal lands. William Donaldson and John Wetherill were among the most affluent and prominent of this group. Donaldson came from Danville, in nearby Columbia County, where he had engaged in a profitable mercantile business along the Susquehanna River. Using money generated from this activity, he successfully pursued careers in land speculation and mining until the 1870s. Donaldson bought large tracts of land in the southwestern edge of the coalfields, after which he would lease them to numerous operators in the area, sell out to other speculators, or operate the tracts himself.[22]

John Wetherill came from a distinguished Philadelphia family and was a graduate of the University of Pennsylvania, although he resided in Pottsville, where he belonged to the city's elite. Wetherill used landholdings acquired by his father to earn sizable profits through leasing or selling small parcels to operators and speculators. In one year, Wetherill rented and sold ten separate tracts of coal lands to operators and other speculators. These tracts represented only a small part of his holdings, which stretched from New Philadelphia to Port Carbon. Neither Wetherill nor Donaldson reinvested a significant share of their capital in Pottsville's economy, but the range of their operations enhanced the influence of Pottsville's elite throughout the region.[23]

In contrast, Francis Hughes, neither the son of a prominent Philadelphia family nor even a native of the metropolitan center, used his skills as a laywer and Democratic party leader (he was state attorney general from 1853 to 1855 and state party chairman from 1862 to 1863) to acquire more than $250,000 in assets. Most of this sum was derived from his land speculation in the coalfields.

Originally from Montgomery County, Hughes owned large amounts of real estate and property in and around Pottsville and valuable tracts of coal land throughout the southern region. While Hughes did reinvest some of his profits in the regional economy, he also acquired a significant financial interest in real estate and economic activities in Philadelphia, Pottstown (also in southeastern Pennsylvania), and distant eastern Kentucky. Hughes, Charlemagne Tower, and other one-time Pottsville leaders relied heavily on land speculation to acquire their money and power.[24]

Coal companies owned by capitalists from Philadelphia, New England, and New York City frequently employed Pottsville coal entrepreneurs to direct mining collieries in the southern fields. The careers of several Pottsville leaders demonstrate this point. The first, David Brown, began his career in the 1840s, when he took control of his father's coal colliery. Within twenty years, he had abandoned his one-man operation to join the Philadelphia Coal Company as superintendent of its Packer collieries in the Mahanoy coal basins. Joshua Sigfried similarly gave up his coal-shipping agency to manage five collieries for the Wolf Creek Diamond Coal Company near St. Clair. Outside-owned companies, such as the Wolf Creek collieries, depended on the expertise and experience of men like Sigfried to run their mining operations in the southern anthracite region. The Mammoth Vein Consolidated Coal Company employed another prominent leader in Pottsville, William Sheafer, to oversee its eight collieries. Heber Thompson, a Yale-educated engineer, managed the entire Stephen Girard estates for several decades.[25]

The members of the Pottsville elite who worked for companies based outside the region supervised roughly fifty collieries during the years 1850 to 1870. The PRRCO adopted this practice after its takeover of the coal industry in the southern region. The company hired John Veith of Pottsville as mine inspector, and later superintendent, of its coal collieries. After a long period of service, men such as Veith frequently moved up in their companies to become officers or directors. George Keim, for example, eventually moved up from district supervisor of the Philadelphia and Reading Coal and Iron Company (PRC&ICO) to president and to head the PRRCO itself. These moves compelled Keim to take up permanent residence in Philadelphia. In losing these highly skilled coal operators, Pottsville also lost the talent and the potential profits that could have been earned from their operations. Members of Wilkes-Barre's upper class were the predominant investors, directors, or officers of incorporated companies. While intensely concerned with innovation and new technology, Wilkes-Barre investors seldom became directly involved in the day-to-day operations of either their own collieries or other companies.[26]

Pottsville's elite grew and prospered as long as the southern rim remained the center of the anthracite industry. The elite benefitted economically from the city's position as the main shipment point of the rim and the service center for a large number of communities in the area. Although rooted in the decentralized system of mining, the elite operated enough collieries and iron and steel foundries throughout the region to help sustain the city's rapid growth. The region was by far the greatest producer of anthracite, and Pottsville remained the largest coal town in eastern Pennsylvania until the 1860s. The shift in mining activity to the Mahanoy coal basin and the Northumberland fields in the 1850s triggered the explosive growth of Shenandoah, Mahanoy City, Shamokin, and Mount Carmel over the next three decades. The subsequent rise of the northern coal region in the mid-1850s significantly reduced Pottsville's rapid development and growth rate. The resulting urban populations in the northern rim accounted for over half the total population in the region by 1890.[27]

At the same time, investors and capitalists in Philadelphia, New York City, and New England began to organize coal companies that systematically took control of mining collieries and coal production in the northern rim. The members of the elite in Pottsville, locked into a system of small-scale mining, were unable to compete effectively with the better-organized coal companies owned by outside capitalists. Although the Pottsville operators were the largest local producers of coal, they never controlled more than 25 percent of the collieries or production in either the southern or northern rims. In fact, coal companies owned by outside interests and local coal operators in the Northumberland fields almost completely blocked the Pottsville coal entrepreneurs from penetrating the area. Moreover, elites in the newly developing Shenandoah, Mahanoy City, Shamokin, and Mount Carmel areas now performed the administrative, service, and transportation functions that the Pottsville leaders had provided for most of the coal towns in the southern rim.

These mining districts emerged in the north just as the near surface and shallow coal veins in the southern rim were rapidly being exhausted. The mining of deep coal seams required expensive machinery and sophisticated mining techniques. The sharp pitch of these underground veins also demanded extensive and costly tunnelling to reach the undulating seams. This tunnelling was usually beyond the technical knowledge or financial resources of most individual operators, but not the coal company. For example, the Pine Knot Coal Company, owned by Boston interests, invested considerable capital to mechanize and rehabilitate the West Pine Knot collieries. The owners introduced powerful steam engines and new techniques and greatly increased production. The Wolf Creek Diamond Coal Company followed a similar course in its dispersed coal collieries. Such increased costs forced many local coal operators out of business and hastened the penetration of coal companies such as the New York–controlled Wolf Creek Company. The extent of the costs can be seen in the amount of capital—$1 million—invested by the Philadelphia and Reading Coal and Iron Company, a subsidiary of the PRRCO, in its Pottsville operations.[28]

Outside-based entrepreneurs and their companies completely overshadowed Pottsville's elite in terms of coal produced and coal lands owned. In 1864, for example, the city's coal operators accounted for only 20 percent of the total production in the southern region, while operators from elsewhere in the region nearly equalled this output. Company executives with headquarters in New

England, New York City, and Philadelphia controlled 64 percent of the total anthracite production for that same year. The Mammoth Vein Consolidated Coal Company, for example, was the largest operation in the region. The company, which was owned by New York investors, ran seven coal collieries, which were spread throughout the entire region and produced 177,485 tons of coal. This tonnage accounted for 5 percent of the total production and represented the greatest single amount mined by any company or operator. Other investors and capitalists in New York City owned at least ten other companies. These New York companies constituted only a small fraction of the more than 150 companies active in the southern fields before the early 1870s. Outfits such as the Union Coal Company, the Delano Land Company, the Girard Mammoth Coal Company, and the Mahanoy Coal Company owned most of the coal lands, ran most of the anthracite collieries, and were controlled totally by outsiders. These large companies dominated coal production by the late 1860s. Even the Mountain Coal and Iron Company, which had been incorporated by members of the Pottsville elite, had headquarters in Philadelphia and was dominated by Philadelphia capitalists.[29]

Entrepreneurs from outside the region were also the most powerful landowners, according to the *Reports of the Inspectors of Coal Mines for 1870*. These outside entrepreneurs held 65 percent of all the coal lands in the southern anthracite region in 1870. More specifically, they controlled 58 percent of all coal lands in Pottsville, 72 percent in Mahanoy City, and 62 percent in Shamokin. In contrast, members of the Pottsville elite held only 21 percent of all coal lands in the region. Most of this land was concentrated in the Pottsville district, where the city's leaders held 34 percent of the land. They owned just 14 percent in the Mahanoy district and 17 percent in the Shamokin area. As these data show, the influence of Pottsville's leaders, compared to that of outside entrepreneurs, was weak in the newly developing mining districts. The prosperous and rapidly growing mining districts in the northern rim offered substantial profits and economic power that could have contributed to Pottsville's ascent in the urban hierarchy. Instead, these benefits were secured by outside-based land and coal companies and their owners, not the Pottsville elite.

Although they did not consistently do so, outside-controlled companies occasionally used their growing power to force Pottsville operators and landowners almost entirely out of the coal industry. Samuel Griscom, Alfred Lawton, and many others had to sell sizable holdings to firms such as the Boston-owned Delano Land Company. As the number of locally controlled companies dwindled, the Pottsville elite found it virtually impossible to compete successfully with capitalists from New England and the nearby multiregional centers.[30]

The shift of the coal-mining center from south to north in the 1850s and 1860s and the depression of 1857 were responsible for the drop in Pottsville's growth rate. Population growth per decade dropped from 75 percent in the 1840s to 25 percent in the 1850s, with only a marginal increase—31 percent—during the next decade. The elite had just enough influence in mining operations and other economic activities to prevent Pottsville from stagnating completely or losing population.

Despite the appearance of large outside-controlled companies, the decentralized system of mining persisted throughout the southern region. By 1870, more than 160 companies and operators in the southern region ran in excess of 200 collieries. In the north, roughly 25 coal companies operated 100 collieries and produced more anthracite coal. Almost all the mining collieries in the north used sophisticated techniques and considerable mechanization in mining and coal preparation. The southern-based operators almost always employed the more primitive drift and slope techniques. The difference in the scale of operations also was evident in the average number of men and the coal production per colliery. In the north, a mining operation employed a mean average of 311 men, while in the southern fields, the number was only 166. Similarly, an average colliery in the north produced 105,769 tons of coal, as compared to 41,197 tons in the southern fields. Clearly, the size and scale were considerably larger in the north than in the south.[31]

THE DECLINE OF POTTSVILLE'S ELITE

The two decades after 1870 saw the rapid eclipse of Pottsville's leadership as the most powerful elite in the southern region. By 1880, the city's elite had lost all of its influence in the mining industry as a result of the PRRCO's takeover of coal operations in the Schuylkill-Northumberland fields. The PRRCO or its subsidiary, the PRC&ICO, also took control of all local transportation and most of the coal-related industries, which had formed the backbone of the Pottsville elite's economy. The depression of the 1870s caused the failure of more than half the elite's major commercial banks and insurance companies, a severe loss, since their institutions had made the city the leading financial center of the region. These failures seriously eroded the elite's capital base, already sagging under the pressures of outside penetration of its primary industrial activities.

Adding to this erosion was the explosive development of the cities in the northern rim, which drained many of Pottsville's elite and substantial numbers of its middle sectors. In addition, some of the city's wealthiest men migrated to Philadelphia and further compounded the capital shortage of the late 1870s. The loss of this capital and talent and the withering of locally controlled industry and business fatally weakened Pottsville's elite and, therefore, the city's economy.

An analysis of the economic activities of the elite shows first the sources of the power and wealth of the group, as well as the seemingly insurmountable lead it had held over the other elites in the region in the early 1870s. Second, the analysis demonstrates the rapid and intense loss of this economic power in the two succeeding decades. The data in Table 5-2 demonstrate that the number

Table 5-2. Industries and Businesses in Communities of the Southern Coal Region, 1870–1875[*]

Location of Industries and Businesses	Collieries/ Land Tracts	Railroads	Coal-Related	Financial	Utilities Services	Traction	Insurance
				Industries and Businesses			
Pottsville	60%	73%	49%	33%	42%	43%	50%
Other communities in southern rim[†]	18	7	32	18	19	28.5	21
Communities in northern rim[‡]	22	20	19	49	39	28.5	29
Total	100% (150)	100% (15)	100% (65)	100% (49)	100% (48)	100% (7)	100% (14)
n = 348							

[*] These dates, besides their advantage in keeping the analysis manageable, moreover occur roughly before the city's economic structure begins to collapse. I wanted to give the reader a picture of Pottsville's economic strength before the disruption in the mid- and late 1870s.

[†] This category includes Pine Grove, Tamaqua, Schuylkill Haven, St. Clair, Minersville, Port Carbon, and Palo Alto.

[‡] This category includes Mahanoy City, Shenandoah, Mt. Carmel, Shamokin, Ashland, and Girardsville.

of solely elite-owned businesses and industries in Pottsville was almost equal to the combined total of all other businesses and industries in the region. The total capitalization for these institutions, moreover, exceeded the total capital for most financial operations of all other elites in the region. Pottsville's leaders remained the most powerful group among elites in the southern region as of the 1870s.

The dispersal of Pottsville's elite and its decline began with the forceful decision of the corporate leadership of the PRRCO to take complete control of all transportation, anthracite, and coal-related industries. The threat of competition from other major railroads and overproduction of the coal industry forced the company to move rapidly toward complete economic domination of the southern coal region. The PRRCO first consolidated ownership of all existing railroad companies in the region. These consisted of the Schuylkill Navigation Canal and the numerous lateral rail lines that primarily fed into it. The Schuylkill Navigation Company depended upon the strength of the coal trade to compete with the PRRCO in the 1840s and 1850s. In the early 1860s, the canal finally succumbed. Within ten years, the PRRCO had also absorbed all the lateral rail lines, such as the Mount Carbon Railroad, the Mill Creek Railroad, and the Little Schuylkill Navigation, Railroad and Coal Company. Most of these lines were partly owned by Pottsville's leaders, who suddenly found themselves pushed completely out of the local railroad business, a fate they had resisted over the preceding twenty years. By the early 1870s, the PRRCO had become the sole trafficker of coal, both within the region and that shipped to the urban markets, and had cut off Pottsville's leaders from important sources of revenue and influence throughout the region. Franklin B. Gowen, a former coal operator and lawyer in Pottsville, led the PRRCO's railroad executives, who now moved toward establishing their own hegemony over the anthracite industry.[32]

Prior to 1870, leaders in Pottsville and other communities feared large-scale companies, which had sufficient power to take control of the anthracite fields. Local leadership, in combination with other pressure groups, had successfully promoted legislation at the state level and prevented the main anthracite carriers from owning coal lands or coal companies. For more than thirty years, this measure effectively kept the PRRCO from becoming the dominant influence in the mining industry and helped secure the influence of Pottsville's leaders in the dispersed anthracite collieries.[33]

In 1870, Franklin Gowen engineered an amended law that finally allowed the rail corporations to participate directly in the industry by owning coal lands and companies. Within the space of five years, the PRRCO, through its holding company, the PRC&ICO, had taken control of 85 percent of all anthracite collieries in the Schuylkill-Northumberland coalfields. In order to achieve this control, the company spent $25 million to buy 100,000 acres of coal land; and the PRRCO finally achieved centralized control of the anthracite industry.[34]

In every county in the southern coalfields, the PRRCO, through the

PRC&ICO, owned over 70 percent of all the collieries and controlled the overwhelming share of coal production. The company's executives had taken complete control of the economic basis of every city, town, and industrial village in the region. With this power, Philadelphia interests, not the Pottsville elite, determined the future of the entire region.

The PRC&ICO agents also systematically recruited many of the leading coal operators in the region to supervise their massive holdings in the region. Pottsville coal entrepreneurs constituted an important part of this group. At least ten of the city's leading operators had joined the PRC&ICO, signifying the company's permanent controlling position within the anthracite industry. This hiring policy removed the last vestiges of Pottsville's direct economic influence in coal mining. These entrepreneurs, now superintendents and district managers for the PRC&ICO, only increased that company's ability to drain profits out of the region and away from Pottsville's elite.[35]

The PRRCO corporate leaders, through their subsidiary, the PRC&ICO, also took control of the region's coal-related industries, such as iron and steel, lumber, and explosives. Essential in coal production, these products—and the move to control them—seemed necessary to company leaders intent on preserving the overall stability of the industry. The operations, particularly iron and steel, comprised the second most important economic activity in the region, and one which the Pottsville elite clearly dominated. Until the mid-1870s, the city's leaders controlled 49 percent of these operations. Thirty-two were located in Pottsville, the majority of them iron and steel companies. Pottsville leaders also operated lumber, mining supply, and wholesale companies for their products, all of which formed a critical part of the city's economy. Leaders from Pottsville owned other iron and steel companies and four powder factories in neighboring towns and three more iron companies in the northern rim. Only Tamaqua's elite, with five iron and steel firms, even approached Pottsville's leadership in the number of companies or volume of output. In the communities of the northern rim, the Pottsville leaders controlled three out of the twelve coal-related companies, half of which were either small lumber mills or screen factories. The elite's unchallenged position of leadership in the coal-related industries generated considerable capital and profits, helped sustain the city's growth rate and economic development, and gave its elite an important measure of influence over many of the other communities in the region.[36]

The Pottsville elite had, in fact, pioneered the iron and steel industry in the region. City leaders were among the first to succeed in using anthracite as a fuel in the manufacture of iron and steel. This use of anthracite made Pottsville one of the leading iron centers in the northeast and also helped make American manufacturers competitive with their British counterparts. In the 1830s and 1840s, leaders such as Benjamin Haywood and George Snyder were among the first to establish mining machine and tool operations. Together, these two men built and operated five major manufacturing plants. By 1870, one of Haywood's companies employed 500 men, a substantial percentage of Pottsville's work force, and produced $1 million in mining equipment. Samuel Griscom, another local manufacturer, demonstrated the same type of aggressiveness that gave Pottsville its dominance of this industry. Griscom sought out the owners of the Pennsylvania Diamond Drill Company in Reading, which produced mining drills, and persuaded them to sell him the operation, after which he moved the company to Pottsville. With the financial support of other local leaders, Griscom enlarged the size of the company's plant and increased its production.[37] In the early 1870s, Pottsville's elite also controlled the majority of all coal-related companies in the southern rim and 27 percent in the northern rim.[38]

The influence of Pottsville's elite in coal-related industries ended abruptly in the late 1870s and early 1880s. During these years, corporate executives, through the PRC&ICO, conducted a systematic campaign to absorb most of the coal-related operations in the southern anthracite region. Gowen and the PRRCO board members directed these efforts primarily at the iron and steel industry. In short order, their agents bought out one company after another, including George Snyder's Colliery Iron Works and John Noble's Boiler Shops. By the mid-eighties, acting through PRC&ICO representatives, the PRRCO had taken over twenty-four of the forty-eight companies held by Pottsville's elite (Table 5-3). This takeover significantly reduced the influence of Pottsville's elite over a large number of communities in the region. This reduction was, of course, compounded by the depression of the late 1870s, which had forced the closing of four of the elite's companies.[39]

By 1890, Pottsville's leaders had lost control of all but 19 percent of the forty-eight companies they had controlled before 1870. The elite-controlled Pottsville Iron, Steel and Coal Company was one of the few coal-related companies to survive the PRC&ICO's takeover and the depression of the late 1870s. This firm was one of the few incorporated companies in the city; as such, it had access to sufficient resources to ward off outside control throughout the late eighties. The company's directors had absorbed the Pottsville Rolling Mill and Pioneer Furnace operations, also run by members of the city's elite. This merger brought added financial reserves, an enlarged market, and new facilities and enabled the company's stockholders and board members to retain control. In contrast, almost all of the city's iron and steel leaders held one- or two-man-owned operations, which were unable to resist the PRC&ICO. As a result, the majority of these small-scale companies failed or succumbed to outside investors during the depression. The Pottsville Steel, Iron and Coal Company fell prey to outside-based capitalists when, in the late 1880s, a Philadelphia syndicate bought the company. The local owners, financially crippled by the reverses of the last two decades, could not meet operating expenses and had no choice but to sell. Four additional companies had come under outside control in the late 1880s. The core of the elite's industrial power, which had at its peak included anthracite mining, local transportation, and coal-related industries, had almost entirely vanished within twenty years.

The pattern of involvement in the iron and steel industry of the Pottsville

Table 5-3. Pottsville-Controlled Enterprises, 1875, Absorbed by Outside Sources or Bankrupt by 1890

Sources of Control, 1880, 1890	Pottsville-Controlled Enterprises						
	Coal Enterprises	Coal-Related Enterprises	Railroad Companies	Banks	Service/ Utility	Traction	Insurance
% absorbed by PRRCO and PRC&ICO, 1880	100%	50%	100%	0%	0%	0%	0%
% Bankrupt: Depression, 1880	0	10	0	75	0	0	74
% absorbed by outside sources, 1890	0	21	0	0	0	100	13
% controlled by Pottsville elite, 1880–1890	0	19	0	25	100	0	13
	100%	100%	100%	100%	100%	100%	100%
	(90)	(48)	(11)	(16)	(23)	(3)	(8)

n = 202

leaders contrasted sharply with that of the Wilkes-Barre entrepreneurs. Members of the Pottsville elite seldom formed incorporated companies; instead, they relied on partnerships or their own individual resources to finance and run an iron and steel operation. This strategy, however, forced the entrepreneur to rely entirely on his own capital reserves, which might at most be pooled with those of a partner. Most of Pottsville's leaders who owned small-scale iron and steel companies were ill equipped to withstand pressure from the PRC&ICO. In the very years when the Wilkes-Barre upper class established control of the coal, iron, and steel industries, the Pottsville elite entirely lost its economic influence.

The depression of the 1870s accelerated the downward spiral of the elite's fortunes. It severely undermined the status of the elite as the leading financial group in the region. Until the late 1870s, Pottsville was the financial capital of the southern coal region. The elite-controlled banks performed essential functions, such as discounting, purchasing commercial paper, and transferring bills of exchange. Thirty-three percent of the forty-nine banks in the southern region were located in Pottsville. The money invested in Pottsville's banks by its elite constituted 54 percent of the total capital. Equally as important, the elite's commercial banks were the most powerful in the region. The amount of money the elite put into these institutions made up 52 percent of capital in commercial banks, as compared to the 36 percent in the cities of the northerm rim and 12 percent in the lower section. Clearly, the city's elite was the dominating force in the financial affairs of the region.

For example, the Miners' National and Government National banks, combined, capitalized at $1 million. This total accounted for almost as much investment capital as was held in all other commercial banks in the region. Members of the elite who were directors and officers of both institutions were among the wealthiest and most powerful in the region. The president of the Government National Bank, William Huntzinger, was a member of one of the richest families in Schuylkill County. His father, Jacob, was president of the Miners' Life Insurance Company and had total assets exceeding $1,000,000. All of the city's banks, whether commercial or savings, depended solely on local capital and remained entirely under the direction of Pottsville's elite.[40] Men from Pottsville's elite also helped to incorporate commercial banks in Ashland, Tamaqua, and Shamokin, where they also served as directors and shaped the policies of these institutions.[41]

The elite's banks provided financial services to many nearby towns and industrial villages. They drew investors, depositors, and savers from all over the county, but particularly from the southern rim. A natural result of this was that the city's direct influence, strongest in the southern rim, tapered off in the northern rim. In the north, leaders attempted to establish banks that would meet the needs of industrialists and savers in the area. These men formed a large number of banks in the early 1870s, most of which failed later in the decade. None of the elites in these communities were able to challenge Pottsville's position as the leading financial center in the Schuylkill-Northumberland coal-fields before the late 1870s.[42]

In the latter half of the 1870s, Pottsville's leaders suffered a series of financial reverses that weakened the city's position as the banking center of the southern coal region. Six of the city's largest commercial banks were forced to close or suspend operations because of loss of capital, poor investments, and withdrawals of money by other banks and local depositors. These failures resulted in the loss of $1,112,000, which constituted 59 percent of the capital invested in commercial banking in Pottsville. An additional $250,000 in investment capital was lost with the closing of three savings institutions. A number of stockholders and directors who lost considerable investment capital through these bank failures were members of Pottsville's elite. Thomas Wren, Henry C. Russel, Theodore Garreston, and Charles Dengler, for example, were financially crippled when the Mountain City Bank suspended operations and closed its doors in the mid-seventies. At least 46 percent of the city's leadership experienced some direct losses as a result of these failures.[43]

The failure of such banks as the Pottsville Bank, the Mountain City Bank, and the Mechanics Safe Deposit and Trust Bank not only hurt members of the elite but also small savers. These depositors and savers numbered in the thousands and represented all socioeconomic groups in the city and the region. Tailors, contractors, and printers, among a host of other savers from all occupations, saw years of savings vanish. Longtime residents such as merchant John Pollard and confectioner Charles Weber lost thousands of dollars as banks closed under pressure of major losses, massive withdrawals, and the recall of money deposited by companies and banks from outside the region. Sheriff Frank Warner alone lost more than $30,000 when the Government National Bank went bankrupt. Leading Pottsville families, including the Weissengers and Woltjens, and elite families from other places, such as the Basts in Schulykill Haven and the Christ family in Tamaqua, were among the legion of depositors and investors who lost their savings and business capital. The bank closings even crippled local lodges and societies. In Pottsville, the Mountain Lodge of the Knights of Pythias, the German Beneficial Society, and the GAR John Innes Post were deprived of their funds by these failures. Similarly, the Union Cemetery in Schuylkill Haven and the Beneficial Society of St. Clair also lost their operating capital when the Pottsville banks closed their doors.[44] The economic hard times of the seventies hit all levels of local society and seriously eroded Pottsville's capital base.

The leading family of Pottsville, the Huntzingers, had operated the Government National Bank and owned most of its stock. The closing of the bank and the collapse of the family meant a considerable loss of investment capital, both to the city and to the family. This, along with the failure of a family-controlled business and several other investments, brought the total financial losses of the Huntzingers to an amount in excess of $1 million. The family's ruin reverberated throughout the region. Its members owned hundreds of thousands of dollars in stocks and bonds of regionally based companies. These ranged from the Mammoth Vein Coal and Iron Company, the Ringgold Iron Company, and the Pottsville Water Company to the Philadelphia and Reading Coal and Iron Company and three powder mills in nearby Orwigsburg. By himself, head of the family Jacob Huntzinger controlled thousands of acres of valuable land throughout Schuylkill County and numerous mortgages in most of the communities of the region. He, like other members of the family, lost most of these investments by the early 1880s. The Huntzingers could not know that the Government National Bank would reopen by 1880; nor would such knowledge have helped. The bank's capitalization was reduced at the time of reopening from an 1876 figure of $500,000 to only $100,000 in 1880.[45]

By the 1880s, Pottsville's elite no longer held the dominant position in the financial affairs of the southern coal region. The decimation of the city's iron and steel industries, the takeover of mining and transportation by the PRRCO, and the loss of several of the major commercial banks reduced the elite's financial dealings to the savings market. The financial influence of the elite was thus restricted to an area bounded by St. Clair and Minersville in the east and west and Wadesville and Port Carbon in the north and south. The erosion of the elite's own economic base lessened the need for commercial banks and removed the possibility of their revival in the 1890s. The weakening of the economy of the business leaders and the failures in banking also seriously damaged the elite capital base. By the 1880s, the city's leadership saw its capital reserve almost completely exhausted.

Elite-controlled insurance companies also suffered from the strains of the depression. The city's elite had been the leader in the insurance business during the early 1870s, owning, in fact, most of the insurance companies that operated in the region. Headquartered in Pottsville, these companies represented 72 percent of all capital invested in insurance throughout the region. Outside Pottsville, the city's leaders also controlled the Schuylkill Haven Mutual Life and Health Insurance Company. They exercised some influence in Shamokin, where they constituted two of the five incorporators of the Shamokin Life Insurance Company, the largest operation in that section; but this dominance quickly vanished in the late 1870s.

Three major elite insurance companies failed early in the depression, resulting in the loss of $200,000 in investment capital to the members of the elite. Customers of the Miners' Life Insurance Company lost another $1 million in insurance policies. In the early 1880s, owners of a Philadelphia syndicate purchased control of the Pennsylvania Insurance Company and further reduced the influence of the city's leaders in the insurance business. By 1890, Pottsville's elite had lost more than half of its insurance companies, either through bankruptcy or takeover by outside capitalists.[46]

The failure of banks and insurance companies, the loss of industry, and the out-migration of wealth and talent crippled the capital base of the Pottsville elite, even though its members had been the top wealth holders among the elite

Table 5-4. Wealth Holdings of Members of Elites Who Held $30,000 or More in 1870

Location of Elites	Assessed Worth of Elites	Percentage of Total Assessed Regional Worth
Pottsville elite	$10,347,975	66%
Elites in other communities of southern rim*	2,490,300	16
Elites in communities of northern rim†	2,876,000	18
Total	$15,714,275	100%

* Includes Tamaqua, Schuylkill Haven, and Minersville.

† Includes Ashland, Mount Carmel, Trevorton, Shamokin, Mahanoy City, and Shenandoah.

Sources: *Manuscript Census Returns, Ninth Census of the United States, 1870, Schuylkill County, Pennsylvania,* M-593, Rolls 1447, 1448, 1449; *Manuscript Census Returns, Ninth Census of the United States, 1870, Northumberland County, Pennsylvania,* M-562, Roll 1384, M-563, Roll 1385.

the elite groups in the southern coal region (Table 5-4). This large capital base had supported a relatively diversified economic structure and sustained the city's high rate of growth. In 1870, for example, the Pottsville elite controlled more capital than any single competing group in the southern region and compared favorably with leadership groups in Wilkes-Barre, Scranton, Bethlehem, and other emerging regional centers.

Under the combined pressures of economic collapse and out-migration of wealth and talent, however, this substantial capital base withered rapidly. The takeover of the anthracite industry by the PRRCO cost Pottsville leaders $200,000 in small-scale mining collieries. In addition, Pottsville landholders and speculators had no choice but to sell their holdings and primary source of revenue to PRC&ICO agents. Leaders such as John Wetherill, Jeremiah Seitzinger, and Frank Carter, who had owned considerable coal lands in the anthracite region, saw the core of their economic activity vanish within one year. Major coal operators such as Charles Atkins and Theodore Garreston also lost substantial investments.[47]

Through bankruptcy or purchase by PRC&ICO agents, the Pottsville elite lost an additional $420,000 in iron and steel companies. The corporate executives simply had the plants dismantled, thus removing a major source of employment and wages in Pottsville. These losses crippled the economic base of the elite and eroded the wealth holdings of most of its leaders. The new outside owners drained almost 100 percent of the profits from the major industries that had formerly constituted Pottsville's main revenue.

Added to these major setbacks were even greater capital losses in banking and insurance. Bank and insurance failures experienced by Pottsville leaders accounted for over $1,362,000, or 34 percent, of all capital lost between 1875 and 1885 and seriously damaged the economic position of many of Pottsville's leaders who specialized in these businesses. John Ryon, who had already lost his coal lands and anthracite collieries to outside interests, also lost his investments in the Pottsville Bank and the Pottsville Title Insurance Company when those concerns went bankrupt. The failure of these two investments obviously, but nonetheless significantly, reduced his financial holdings. Francis Alstatt suffered similar reverses. Three of the companies and banks on which he held director- ships failed during the last half of the 1870s, and Alstatt suffered substantial capital losses in these two economic activities.[48]

At the same time, Pottsville's elite lost considerable capital or access to it through out-migration of leaders and their families. (Men such as Jacob Hunt- zinger and Edward Patterson, for example, left the city during the seventies and eighties.) The economic reverses of these decades also forced new entrepreneur- ial strategies on the members of the elite. Clifford Pomeroy, who inherited Benjamin Pomeroy's iron works, was left without a viable company. Crippled by the depression and the policies of the PRRCO, Pomeroy's son switched into a flour and feed operation, where he hoped to regain the prosperity his family had enjoyed in an earlier period. By 1890, however, he had left the city. Similarly, John T. Noble, who had run a profitable boiler works into the 1870s, had by 1880 moved into a new career as a manufacturer of boots and shoes. Highly successful real estate speculator and coal entrepreneur John M. Wetherill saw his participation in the industry shrink as a result of the PRRCO's policies. His son, John Price Wetherill, became a mining engineer for the PRRCO, an occupational pursuit that reflected the changing economic environment of Pottsville's elite. By the 1890s, the family had left the city entirely. Besides the Wetherills, such families as the Donaldsons and the Shippens, whose members had been entrepreneurs in the city for decades, had left Pottsville by the 1890s. The shrinking of Pottsville's entrepreneurial ranks occurred at all levels, not just in the elite. Non-elite merchants, manufacturers, and prosperous skilled artisans with assets between $10,000 and $30,000 joined the flow of talent out of Pottsville during these decades. Though the figures are necessarily rough, it is safe to say that these substantial assets, combined with the capital lost through the elite and coal operators described earlier, exceeded a total loss of $2 million.[49]

In addition to this money, Pottsville also lost a large number of capable young men with little or no assets—but with great potential earnings—from its middle income sector to newly developing cities in the north. These men soon joined the leadership ranks in the major cities in the northern rim, as shown in Table 5-5. For example, migrants from the Pottsville area constituted 47 percent of the leaders in Shenandoah and 59 percent of the leaders in Mahanoy City. Without a regional contact network, the Pottsville elite was unable to control the outward flow of capital and talent. Pottsville's leadership was never in a position to drain critical resources from the other communities, as Wilkes-Barre's upper class had done so successfully in the northern region. The resulting loss of capital and talent and the economic disasters in industry and business under- mined the stability and cohesiveness of Pottsville's elite. Its members found

Table 5-5. Proportion of Elites in Shenandoah, Mahanoy City, Shamokin, and Ashland Formed by Migrants from Pottsville and Nearby Communities, 1875–1885

	Communities			
Origins of Leaders	Shenandoah	Mahanoy	Shamokin	Ashland
Pottsville area	47%	59%	21%	43%
Communities outside Pottsville area	53	41	79	57
	100%	100%	100%	100%
N = 195	(44)	(37)	(84)	(30)

themselves reduced to a subordinate status in the region, as Philadelphia corporate leaders took over control of their economic activities.

The Pottsville elite also experienced a similar fate in the traction and utility industries. Elite-controlled traction and utility companies provided service to the city itself or to nearby communities. The People's Railway Company, incorporated by the city's leaders in 1865, was the first and only traction company formed prior to 1880. This company served Pottsville and nearby towns, including Palo Alto, Port Carbon, and Patterson. In the early 1880s, several of Pottsville's leaders joined with entrepreneurs in Tamaqua and Ashland to build transit lines between the three communities, but the elite never established a traction net that encompassed the cities of the northern rim, such as Shenandoah and Shamokin. In these northern communities, local elites built and maintained their own trolley lines.[50]

The nearest attempt at a comprehensive system occurred in the late 1880s, when Pottsville's leaders chartered the Schuylkill Electric Company. The owners of this firm constructed a series of electrified traction lines that connected all the cities, towns, and villages of the southern tier and extended to Shenandoah and Mahanoy City in the north. Weakened by the economic collapse of the 1870s, however, the Pottsville elite was unable to provide much of the needed capital and had to rely on investors from New York City and Philadelphia. The largest stockholder in the company was the PRRCO, which owned 50 percent of the shares. Despite vigorous opposition from Pottsville leaders, a traction syndicate backed by Philadelphia financiers eventually bought out the Schuylkill Electric Company and consolidated control of all traction companies in the region. Pottsville's elite had neither the money nor economic power to block the takeover.[51]

The elite-owned utility companies served the needs of the city and adjacent communities. Pottsville leaders incorporated and maintained their own utility companies and only infrequently became involved in establishing similar operations in other communities. Some Pottsville leaders helped charter gas and water companies in nearby towns, such as Schuylkill Haven and Minersville, and subsequently served as directors or officers on these firms. These, however, were the exception. Pottsville's own utility companies provided services to the small industrial villages of Llewellyn, Patterson, and Wadesville, as well as the nearby town of Port Carbon; but they did not extend beyond this close range.

CHAPTER VI

A Social Analysis of Pottsville's Late Nineteenth-Century Elite

HE SOCIAL PROFILE of the Pottsville elite contrasts sharply with that of the colonial-stock, kinship-oriented upper class of Wilkes-Barre. The cultural commonality among the members of the upper class in Wilkes-Barre sustained institutions and family ties into the twentieth century. These were critical in the persistence of the upper class and its economic success in the region. In Pottsville, leaders shared little by way of class origins, lineage, or ethnocultural traits. As a result, the community could not depend to any significant degree on these sources of cohesiveness.

Boom-town growth had produced an extremely heterogeneous elite, whose members shared only entrepreneurial and occupational experiences. These, rather than social institutions and kinship, formed the cornerstone of the elite. These associations generated a sense of identity with the city and the group. Involvement in similar types of entrepreneurial ventures and financial institutions created and maintained a sense of familiarity among the members of the elite. Their persistence in Pottsville depended on their rising fortunes, a product of these activities. Loyalties established through entrepreneurial cooperation, economic investments, and participation in the anthracite industry collapsed under the severe economic pressures of the 1870s and 1880s.

By the 1870s and 1880s, the elite in Pottsville was beginning to create somewhat permanent bases for its social, economic, and political institutions, a process which, if completed, could have insured the city's continued growth and dominant position, at least in the southern rim of the Schuylkill-Northumberland coalfields. However, these were neither all-inclusive nor sufficiently mature to survive the reverses of the late nineteenth century. Economic pressures eroded the sense of attachment among Pottsville's leaders and their families and contributed to the departure of many. As a result, Pottsville experienced instability and high turnover in its leadership ranks.

SOCIAL ANALYSIS OF POTTSVILLE'S ELITE

The members of Pottsville's elite were generally longtime residents of the city, with the majority having been in the community since the 1840s and some in residence since the 1830s. Within thirty or forty years, by the 1860s and 1870s, the members of the elite were beginning to organize a number of clubs and formal social groups confined largely to the leadership. These ranged from lodges and athletic clubs to annual parties and clubs whose purpose was to underscore the prominence of these men and to provide an exclusive environment for their recreation. High social status was beginning to take on an air of importance in defining the membership of the elite; however, not all the community's leaders joined such organizations, and status had not become the critical attribute in penetrating the ranks of a largely economic group.

Status, economic power, and political authority were starting to take on an overlapping character by the late nineteenth century. Pottsville leaders who held both economic power and high social status constituted 22 percent of the 216 leaders represented in Table 6-1. Each of these men belonged to one of the leading clubs and owned local business and industrial concerns or served on their boards. Many of these leaders were also ranked among the top wealth holders, according to the 1870 manuscript census or the R. G. Dun and Company Credit Records. A slightly larger proportion—29 percent—held economic and political power. Still, only a small percentage demonstrated all three attributes, and 39 percent possessed only economic power.

An examination of the social characteristics of these leaders shows an elite of diverse social, economic, and cultural origins. Pottsville leaders frequently came from non-elite or foreign-born families. They also came from a broad variety of cultural groups, which ranged from German Lutheran and German Reformed to Irish Catholic and Scotch-Irish Presbyterian. Religious and ethnic barriers impeded intermarriage among the families in the elite and divided them into separate institutions, each reflecting a particular heritage. Educational achievement varied as much as cultural origins. Substantial numbers of leaders were found at all levels of achievement, from common schools to colleges. A sizable proportion of the elite never went beyond the secondary level and had attended public, rather than private, schools. As a result, many of the city's leaders opted for apprenticeships in the trades, such as tinsmithing, blacksmithing, and leather making, rather than furthering their formal education.

Ties among these diverse ethnic and religious groups emerged slowly and were still in the formative stages during the seventies and early eighties. By this time, no clearly defined residential district had yet appeared, although many of the city's elite were beginning to move to Mahantongo Street, which was slowly developing into an exclusive reserve. In 1880, those in the city's elite lived on seventeen different streets, located throughout the entire city. The basis of the elite tended to be common occupational experiences in similar economic activities, such as mining, iron making, and banking. This emphasis on career

Table 6-1. Overlapping Dimensions of Power: Economic Power, Political
Authority, and High Social Status among Members of Pottsville's Elite, 1870–1885

Dimensions of Power	%	N
Economic power, political authority, and high social status	10	21
Economic power and high social status	22	48
Economic power and political authority	29	63
Economic power	39	84
Total	100%	216*

*In 6% of these cases, political power was used in lieu of economic power as an indicator.

Sources: See the appendix for a discussion of the sources used to develop these data and those in Table 6-2. For workers' challenges to the power of leadership groups in the region, see Harold Aurand, *From the Molly Maguires to the United Mine Workers: The Social Ecology of an Industrial Union, 1869–1897* (Philadelphia: Temple University Press, 1971). During the Molly Maguire years of the seventies, these challenges were particularly violent.

patterns and entrepreneurial achievement appeared in the nineteenth-century histories of Pottsville and the biographies of the city's prominent men. These locally sponsored city, county, and family narratives stressed the self-made character of the leaders and their economic or political accomplishments. They meticulously traced their frequent occupational and geographic moves and the successes that resulted from them. Information gathered from the R. G. Dun and Company records for Schuylkill County confirms these histories, showing the elite to be an extremely mobile group. In fact, moving was likely the most commonly shared experience among the members of the elite. The histories published before 1900 only infrequently emphasize colonial lineage, institutional affiliations, or blood and marriage ties. These factors were relatively unimportant in Pottsville's nineteenth-century leadership.

The men in the elite came from a variety of geographic locations (Table 6-2). Those born in Pottsville or other communities in Schuylkill County made up the second largest proportion of the elite. More than half of these leaders were natives of Pottsville, though a sizable number came from rural villages scattered throughout the county. Another group originated in the nearby counties of Berks, Dauphin, Montgomery, and Northampton. Many of the migrants from southeastern Pennsylvania were descendants of the early Pennsylvania German settlers who pioneered the farm belt and established the market towns of this area. The Germans also constituted the majority of the foreign-born leaders. They alone comprised 11 percent of the entire elite, ranking third, behind newcomers from the southeastern counties and those native to Schuylkill County. The majority of the Germans had been born in the provinces of Hanover, Wurtemburg, Hesse, and Rhenish Palatinate and were frequently Catholic or Lutheran, the dominant religions of their native states. The remaining immigrants were from southern and northern Ireland, Scotland, Wales, and England.[1]

No single ethnic group dominated the composition of the Pottsville elite as

Table 6-2. Social Characteristics of Members of Pottsville's Elite by
Birthplace, 1870–1885

Social Characteristics		Schuylkill County	Areas outside Region	Foreign-Born	Total
Ethnicity	English	36%	66%	22%	48%
	German	45	21	50	34
	Scotch-Irish/Irish	14	3	15	9
	Scottish	1	3	4	3
	Welsh	4	7	9	6
		100%	100%	100%	100%
Religion	Presbyterian	27%	22%	21%	24%
	Episcopalian	13	18	2	13
	Methodist	9	7	7	7
	Evangelical	8	0	0	2
	Lutheran	23	12	26	18
	German Reformed	2	1	7	3
	Catholic	8	1	13	6
	Society of Friends (Quakers)	0	5	0	2
	Unknown	10	34	24	25
		100%	100%	100%	100%
Education	No formal education	0%	4%	4%	3%
	Common school	25	26	39	28
	Public high school	28	14	13	18
	Academy	13	11	2	10
	College	24	16	5	16
	Unknown	10	29	37	25
		100%	100%	100%	100%
		(66)	(104)	(46)	(216)
Birthplace N = 216		30%*	48%	22%	100%

*18% in Pottsville and 12% in Schuylkill County.

did the colonial stock in Wilkes-Barre. As Table 6-2 shows, the majority of the men from Schuylkill County were English and German; however, 18 percent were Scotch-Irish, Irish, or Welsh. The same pattern was typical of leaders from the other geographic sections represented in the table. This cultural diversity resulted from the fluid nature of Pottsville's early society and the undeveloped character of its elite structure, which enabled successful entrepreneurs, regardless of origin, to achieve economic power and communitywide influence.

The religious affiliations of the Pottsville elite were as diverse as their ethnic backgrounds. Eight different denominations and sects were represented among the city's leaders. Members of the elite who were of English ethnicity tended to be Presbyterian, Episcopalian, and Methodist. The leaders of German ethnicity usually belonged to the Lutheran or German Reformed denominations, although a small portion were Evangelical Protestants. Leaders of German nationality were also found among Roman Catholic, Presbyterian, and Episcopalian congregations. Like the English, the majority of Scots and Scotch-Irish were either Presbyterian, Episcopalian, or Methodist. Some of the Scottish and Irish leaders were Catholic or Quaker. The large number of disparate religious faiths underscores the lack of cultural commonality among the members of the elite. Church membership naturally reflected the diversity of religious preferences among these men. The Pottsville leaders attended eleven separate churches, which represented various denominations, such as the First and Second Presbyterian churches or the German Lutheran and St. Matthew's Lutheran churches. The religious institutions were among the earliest to be found in Pottsville; yet none of them were originally intended as elite-oriented churches. Exclusively elite churches did not appear in Pottsville for another seventy years. The Trinity Episcopal Church, which eventually became elite dominated, was not even founded until the late 1830s and had difficulty sustaining its membership. The problem of maintaining a viable congregation plagued all of Pottsville's early churches and demonstrated the unstable nature of these early institutions and the lack of cohesiveness among the city's prominent men. Of all the religious institutions, only the First Presbyterian, German Lutheran, and Trinity Episcopal developed predominantly elite congregations.[2]

Analysis of educational experience among the Pottsville elite shows a wide range of achievement, reflected in Table 6-2. Only a small proportion of all the men in the elite had no education. Most had a few years of elementary schooling, and some attended public high schools. The foreign-born among the elite were the least educated. The majority finished only a few years of common school and then entered the work force. Within this economic context, many immigrants found such pursuits feasible and reasonable.

Benjamin Haywood provides one example. He left school at the age of twelve to join his father's hardware-manufacturing business. This experience taught him valuable skills in iron making and business, which he later parlayed into a small fortune in Pottsville. David Brown also had only a few years of common school before he began working as a screen boy in his father's colliery. For thirteen years, he moved from job to job until he had mastered all the skills needed to run a mining operation. Adolf Schalck pursued a somewhat different course. Although he left school at an early age, he decided not to learn his father's trade of gunsmithing; instead, the young Schalck went to work as a clerk in a wholesale house in Philadelphia. After a short period, he moved back to Pottsville and worked for a German weekly newspaper. At seventeen, he became a clerk for Franklin Gowen, one of the city's best lawyers and later president of the PRRCO. This preparation with Gowen enabled Schalck to pass his bar examinations in 1866, only four years after; and he then began a successful career in law.[3]

Although educational achievement still varied widely, levels of schooling were generally higher among the native-born in the elite. Among these leaders, the majority completed common school or attended public high school. A substantial proportion of them were even able to attend private academies, colleges, business and law schools. The experiences of leaders native to Schuylk- ill County demonstrated a high level of achievement: 13 percent and 24 percent, respectively, had academy or collegiate training. Among this group were sons of Pottsville's first generation of leaders, young men who were able to take advan- tage of their fathers' success, wealth, and position in the community to acquire the best education available.[4]

No family tradition of attending certain colleges developed among the mem- bers of the Pottsville elite, nor had these men successfully established and maintained their own local academies. The city had two private schools, the Pottsville Academy, founded in 1832, and the Pottsville Seminary, created in 1834. Neither attracted an exclusively elite following, and neither survived past the early 1870s. The boys' academy, unable to compete effectively with the developing public school system, closed in 1862, while the girls' seminary lasted only nine years longer before declining enrollments forced its demise. The members of the elite did not uniformly support the schools, nor did they develop a practice of consistently enrolling their children in them.[5]

The members of the elite did not gravitate toward any particular set of private schools outside the community as Wilkes-Barre's upper class had done; there was nothing comparable to the Ivy League to entice this group. Men in the elite graduated from twenty-one different private schools, including the Foley Semi- nary in New York and St. Mary's Private Catholic School in Baltimore, Mary- land. Moreover, no more than two leaders attended the same school. The Pottsville leaders who went beyond high school matriculated at twenty separate colleges and business and law schools; and no more than three leaders attended the same school. These colleges and other schools also ranged in location from Connecticut to Maryland and varied greatly in quality, from Yale College in Connecticut to Hahnemann College in Philadelphia. Clearly, the educational experiences of the Pottsville leaders differed both in levels of achievement and types of schools from those of Wilkes-Barre's upper class.[6]

Members of Pottsville's elite often came from modest circumstances (Table 6-3). Their fathers pursued a number of occupations; they ranged from skilled workers and coal operators to peasant farmers and coal miners. This pattern contrasts sharply with that of Wilkes-Barre's upper-class leaders, whose fathers were lawyers, wealthy coal operators, or highly successful merchants. None of the fathers whose sons were in the Wilkes-Barre upper class were peasants, laborers, or skilled craftsmen; 18 percent of the fathers of those in the Pottsville elite pursued these occupations. The few Pottsville leaders from powerful fami- lies, such as the Pattersons, the Shippens, and the Wetherills, usually came from the Philadelphia leadership, whose members had considerable investments in the coal region.[7]

The occupational pursuits of these fathers tell us much about the class origins of the Pottsville elite. For example, the father of Levi Laubenstein, a Pottsville leader, owned a farm in Berks County, where the family had settled in the pre-

Table 6-3.   Occupations of Fathers of Members of the Pottsville Elite, 1870–1885

Occupation	%	N
Merchant	15%	32
Skilled work/Artisanal	12	27
Coal operator	8	18
Lawyer/Politician	11	24
Manufacturer	7	14
Laborer/Peasant	5	10
Farmer	5	11
Professional	2	4
Banker/Real estate	3	6
Contractor	2	4
Unknown	30	66
Total	100%	216

Revolutionary period. James Moreton, father of Pottsville leader Daniel Moreton, was a native of Staffordshire, England, and a skilled canal-lock builder,
who practiced his trade in Lowell, Massachusetts. The younger Moreton began
his career as an apprentice in the tin trade and eventually opened up his own
shop when he moved to Pottsville. He later shifted into plumbing and gas-
fitting supplies. James Reilly's father was an unskilled laborer from southern
Ireland; his first job in America was as a railroad laborer in Schuylkill County.
Later, he became a railroad contractor.[8]

Members of the elite also originated in artisan families. The Kaerchers, whose
members achieved considerable prominence in Pottsville and Philadelphia, began in modest circumstances. Franklin B. Kaercher was the first family member
to acquire economic power and prominence in Pottsville. His father had been a
cabinetmaker who learned his trade in Hamburg, Berks County, and subsequently worked in communities scattered over the southern coalfields and, finally, in Philadelphia.[9]

A small proportion of Pottsville leaders were born into families of status and
power from outside Philadelphia's leadership. The fathers of these men were
successful coal entrepreneurs, bankers, lawyers, and politicians. John Ryon, Sr.,
for example, served as a state representative from Luzerne County, as superintendent of state canals, and as a judge in Tioga County. Peter Sheafer's father,
in contrast, was a skilled coal entrepreneur, the first to introduce anthracite coal
into the lower Susquehanna Valley markets. He served as superintendent of the
Lykens Valley Coal Mines and president of the Lykens Valley Railroad, both
located in Dauphin County.[10]

The non-elite origins of a large proportion of Pottsville's prominent men was
reflected in their lineage (Table 6-4). The majority of these men came from
non-colonial-stock families, many of whom had been in America only one
generation before their sons achieved economic success. This pattern was consistent throughout the elite, regardless of birthplace. It meant that upper-class

Table 6-4.   Lineage and Kinship of Members of Pottsville's Elite
by Birthplace, 1870–1885

Lineage, Kinship		Schuylkill County	Areas outside Region	Foreign-Born	Total
Lineage:	First Family[*]	6%	2%	2%[†]	3%
	Colonial stock	23	18	4[‡]	17
	Non–colonial stock	58	48	89	60
	Unknown	13	32	5	20
		100%	100%	100%	100%
Kinship:	Related to another member of Pottsville elite through blood or marriage[§]	55%[#]	32%	35%	40%
	Unrelated to other members of Pottsville elite	45	68	65	60
		100%	100%	100%	100%
		(66)	(104)	(46)	(216)

[*] Includes percentage of leaders from both colonial and non-colonial-stock families.

[†] Includes percentage of foreign-born leaders who married women descended from one of Pottsville's First Families.

[‡] Includes percentage of foreign-born leaders who married women descended from colonial-stock families.

[§] Indicates only that a member of the elite was related to another family in the elite, not that an individual was part of a kinship group.

[#] The high proportion of leaders related in the category reflects the presence, in many cases, of sons rather than intermarriage.

family traditions comparable to those in Wilkes-Barre played no role in the formation of Pottsville's elite and its development in the nineteenth century. First Families in Pottsville did not embody the same historic importance as their counterparts did in Wilkes-Barre; nor did they leave an enduring legacy for their successors. As a result, the city's founding and historical evolution played a minor part in the symbolism of the elite, most of whom stressed their lower socioeconomic origins, their Horatio Alger–like struggles against adversity, and their eventual success. Unlike Wilkes-Barre's upper class, the members of the city's elite did not rely on an historical society as a sign of status from the 1850s through the early 1880s. The absence of such an institution demonstrated the recent origins of the elite, and the fact that Pottsville's prominent families had only dim ties, if any, with the community's early beginnings. The elite, therefore, had little to build on, except the recent, and substantial, achievements of its members; and these decreased rapidly after the reverses of the seventies and eighties, when their fortunes went into marked decline.[11]

The lack of a separate and clearly defined residential district reflected the young age of the elite and the absence of upper-class traditions. The city's leaders built their homes mainly on five streets: Mahantongo, Center, Market (East and West), Norwegian (East and West) and Second; however, their residences were found on twelve other streets and lanes in the city. The members of the elite lived as close as possible to the center of Pottsville, yet leaders were found throughout the center of the city. Members of the Boone, Reilly, and Ryon families lived on four separate streets, from North Second and West Market Street to Schuylkill Avenue and North George Street. George Snyder's family house was built on Mauch Chunk Street; John Roseberry lived on Hardware Avenue; and George Mortimer had his home at 644 North Second Street.[12]

The members of the elite did not exclusively dominate these five streets. Center Street, for example, was the core of the city's rapidly emerging central business district and, as such, contained business establishments, mercantile stores, banks, merchants' homes, and boardinghouses. Moreover, side streets and alleyways, which housed members of working and middle-income groups, cut through these five main streets. A large proportion of the elite—20 percent—continued to work out of their places of residence, while another 20 percent lived adjacent to their business. Only Mahantongo Street would, by the twentieth century, develop into an exclusively elite district.

Pottsville leaders had begun to move to Mahantongo Street in the 1860s. In 1867, Burd Patterson was one of the first to build a mansion on the avenue. Other members of the elite, such as Heber and Lewis Thompson and Bernard Reilly, also left their Market Street homes to join the slow migration to Mahantongo Street, where each established a family mansion. The elite also began to set up churches and social organizations—for example, the Trinity Episcopal Church and the First Presbyterian Church—on Mahantongo Street, although many other institutions, such as the First Reformed Church, the German Lutheran Church, and the Pulaski Lodge, were located elsewhere in the city. As late as the seventies and eighties, Pottsville's leaders were scattered throughout the city, from the northern to southern edges of the community.[13]

ENTREPRENEURIAL AND OCCUPATIONAL BASIS OF POTTSVILLE'S ELITE

Although a generally diverse group, Pottsville's elite showed considerable commonality in their occupations and career patterns (Table 6-5). Slightly over 50 percent of all leaders were involved in mining, law, or manufacturing as their main occupation. Only among the foreign-born did members of the elite engage in other choices, such as meat packing or publishing.

These men also shared similar patterns of occupational change and career experiences. Unlike the Wilkes-Barre upper class, to whom advantages such as wealth and family influence were common, only a small minority of the future

Table 6-5.   Occupations of Members of Pottsville's Elite, 1870–1885

Occupation	Schuylkill County	Areas outside Region	Foreign-Born	Pottsville Elite, Combined Total
Coal entrepreneur	24%	25%	22%	24%
Lawyer	21	21	7	18
Manufacturer	9	11	24	13
Merchant	11	11	17	12
Services	8	11	22	13
Politician	3	4	0	2
Banker	9	8	0	7
Professional	6	4	4	5
Real estate/Insurance agent	6	0	0	2
Contractor	3	5	4	4
	100%	100%	100%	100%
	(66)	(104)	(46)	(216)

Pottsville elite were advantaged at birth. As a result, the rising young entrepreneurs were forced to make several occupational and geographic changes as they attempted to reach the next economic plateau in the course of upward mobility. This pattern occurred even among members of the elite who had academy training, as well as among those who only had a few years of common schooling. In some cases, even the careers of those Pottsville leaders who finished college followed an almost identical course of frequent job and locational movement as they tried to establish themselves in the social structure.

The most active of the groups were the foreign-born, who moved into new occupations a mean average of 2.7 times during the course of their careers. Leaders in the other two groups were somewhat less active. Those born in Schuylkill County averaged 2.56 changes, while their counterparts from Pennsylvania and neighboring states switched jobs with a slightly lesser frequency, at 2.46.

The men in the elite changed jobs with greater frequency than did the members of Wilkes-Barre's upper class. The Pottsville leaders had a mean average of 2.57 occupational changes during their careers, while the men in Wilkes-Barre's upper class averaged only 1.2 moves. The Pottsville elite also showed a far greater number of moves despite its considerably smaller number of leaders. The substance of careers also differed between the two leadership groups. In Wilkes-Barre, those in the upper class pursued a course of academy training, followed by college and entry into law or a locally owned company. Their early careers drew them into the city's tightly knit leadership group and created a series of powerful contacts critical for later economic ventures. For the rising talent in Wilkes-Barre, occupational mobility was rigidly structured. The following examples contrast the career experiences of the Pottsville elite and the Wilkes-Barre upper class.

Like the many Pottsville leaders who began their careers with only a common school education, Franklin B. Kaercher, a native of Friedensburg in Schuylkill County, left school at age twelve and began to work as a boatman on the Schuylkill Navigation Canal from Pottsville to Philadelphia. The limited opportunities of this job compelled him to shift into the printing business as an apprentice to Benjamin Bannon, publisher and editor of a Pottsville newspaper. After mastering this trade, Kaercher moved to Philadelphia, where he briefly worked for the *Daily Sun*. Returning to Pottsville, Kaercher established the *Anthracite Gazette*, which survived only a few years. After holding public office during the late 1850s, he eventually opened up the Exchange Hotel of Pottsville, which provided a sound financial base from which to invest in other local businesses and industrial ventures. In all, he had held six jobs and moved three times.[14]

Solomon Foster had only a few years of common school before he apprenticed as a shoemaker in Newburg, Massachusetts, near his home in Ipswich. After several years, he opened his own business in Newburg; but he soon migrated to Reading, Pennsylvania (1818), where he reopened his shoe shop. He moved to Philadelphia in 1836 and manufactured whips for eight years. In 1840, he acquired coal lands in Schuylkill County and used his profits to open a boot and shoe store in Pottsville. By 1870, the money earned from these activities ranked Foster among the city's top wealth holders.[15]

Edward Davis was educated beyond the secondary level; yet he followed mobility patterns comparable to those of Parker and Foster in frequent job and residential change. Davis, a native of Chestertown, Maryland, attended Washington College in Lexington, Virginia, where he learned mechanical engineering. Then, in 1866, he joined the merchant marines for three years. In 1869, he moved to Philadelphia to apprentice in Brinton and Henderson's machinery foundry. Two years later, Davis took a job as draftsman for Hay, Kennedy and Company in New Castle, Delaware, where he remained until 1873. In that year, he joined the office of George Snyder's iron and steel company in Pottsville. During the next eight years, Davis's career included positions as assistant superintendent of the Pottsville Iron, Steel and Coal Company, draftsman for the PRC&ICO and superintendent of the PRC&ICO's mechanical engineering departments in the region, a post of considerable power. From 1866 until 1880, Davis had moved five times and changed jobs six times before establishing himself as a member of the Pottsville elite. During this time, he also married the daughter of a prominent local leader, herself a relative of the city's founding Pott family.[16]

These patterns of career movement and locational change almost never occurred among the members of Wilkes-Barre's upper class. The difference in the substances of their careers can be seen in a brief examination of Stanley Woodward's early years. Woodward was born into Wilkes-Barre's upper class. His father came to Wilkes-Barre from Pike County in northeastern Pennsylvania to attend the city's academy and returned after finishing college to study law under Judge Garrick Mallery. The younger Woodward went to the Wyoming Seminary, the Episcopal High School in Alexandria, Virginia, and Yale University. Upon completion of his studies, Woodward came back to Wilkes-Barre, where his father was then a noted judge, to train under lawyer Martin Hoyt, a future Pennsylvania governor. After passing his bar exams, Woodward successfully engaged in politics as a state senator, county judge, and city council member. He also became director of several local banks and traction companies. In addition to these activities, Woodward headed a law firm and acted as legal counsel for the Delaware, Lackawanna and Western Railroad and the Delaware and Hudson Canal Company. His social and kinship ties cemented his position in the city's upper class. As a member of St. Stephen's Episcopal Church, the Masonic Lodge 61, the Wyoming Historical and Geological Society, and the Cheese and Crackers Club, he was in daily contact with a large proportion of the city's elite. Woodward also married into the prestigious Butler family.[17]

Woodward clearly depended on birth rather than frequent occupational and locational changes to move into the upper class, a pattern that was typical of most members of Wilkes-Barre's upper class. No real mobility actually occurred for these men, since each pursued a prescribed course—the best educational training, valuable experience, and the establishment of useful social, familial, and economic contacts—all of which prepared the young leader to enter Wilkes-Barre's upper class.

The process of skill acquisition and career development common to all members of the Pottsville elite tended to delay age of marriage among the community's leaders. The majority married between the ages of twenty-five and twenty-nine. This similarity in the life-cycle pattern can be seen in the careers of several Pottsville leaders. O. P. Bechtel delayed marriage until he had acquired academy training, taught school in Mahanoy City, worked as a bookkeeper for a coal company in Girardville, and started his law practice. Heber Thompson and William Sheafer both finished their educations, gained practical experience in their professions, and had opened their own offices before each married and began a family. In almost all cases, education, skill acquisition, apprenticeships, and the establishment of a career preceded marriage.[18]

Even those men who had almost no schooling and had married in their early twenties had acquired necessary career skills before settling down. Leonard Weissenger was married at age twenty-one, yet he had gained skills and experience in his occupation by that time. Weissenger had worked as a helper in several butchers' shops and meat markets for over five years and was operating his own business before his marriage.[19]

In addition to occupational choices and career patterns, the members of the Pottsville elite also engaged in similar types of entrepreneurial activities (Table 6-6). Participation in mining, politics, manufacturing, and banking gave rise to a common set of experiences that provided the basis for interaction among these men. These overlapping economic and political ties cut across cultural boundaries that divided the elite and were far more pervasive and stronger than kinship or institutional ties. Men of the elite almost always engaged in a number of

Table 6-6. Proportion of Entrepreneurial Activities Engaged in by Members of Pottsville's Elite by Birthplace, 1870–1885

Entrepreneurial Activity	Schuylkill County	Areas outside Region	Foreign-Born
Mining	24%	22%	16%
Manufacturing	9	14	19
Politics	21	21	21
Banking	14	16	8
Services	9	9	13
Utilities	9	4	8
Insurance	7	4	7
Commerce	7	10	8
	100%	100%	100%
N = 472	(155)	(210)	(107)

entrepreneurial activities that encompassed the primary sectors of the local and regional economies. The mean number of these activities among the leaders from Schuylkill County was 2.35, while for those in the other two categories, the averages were 2.01 and 2.32, respectively, and overall, 2.19.

The careers of David Greene and Francis W. Hughes, who combined economic and political activities, demonstrate these shared entrepreneurial efforts. David Greene, a native of Reading, pursued a successful career as a lawyer and prominent Republican politician and served as director of the Safe Deposit Bank and the Pennsylvania Life Insurance Company. His colleague, Francis Hughes of Montgomery County, was also an attorney, a Democratic political leader, and a director of the Safe Deposit Bank. In addition, he was an incorporator of the Pennsylvania Mutual and Joint Stock Association and the Pottsville Gas Company.[20]

Other leaders specialized in mining and coal-related industries. Benjamin Haywood, a native of England, and Charles Atkins, George W. Snyder, and Benjamin Pomeroy, all from southeastern Pennsylvania, were well known and successful coal entrepreneurs, and operated extremely profitable iron and steel companies. Iron manufacturer John Roseberry, who also speculated in coal lands, held directorships on the Miners' National Bank and the Pennsylvania National Bank. Merchant Jacob Ulmer, a native of Germany, owned two meat-packing houses and directed the Miners' National Bank and the Schuylkill Electric Railway. As Ulmer's case suggests, leaders from various ethnic groups frequently were directors of the same companies and banks. Jesse Drumheller and George Rosengarten, who were Germans, served with Heber Thompson, a Scotch-Irish Presbyterian, and John Shippen, a colonial-stock Episcopalian, as directors on the Miners' National Bank.[21]

In addition to these shared activities in the regional and local companies, members of Pottsville's elite also established close ties through apprenticeships, legal training, and business and law partnerships, common to most. Involvement in incorporated companies and banks formed the largest proportion—34 percent—of these activities, but not the majority. Business and law partnerships almost equalled this percentage, and when added to other economic associations, such as mining superintendency, actually equalled the percentage. This total does not even include independent operations, which constituted 18 percent of all entrepreneurial efforts. These joint ventures formed the basis of the elite and facilitated close and frequent contact among its members. For example, 173 partnerships engaged in by community leaders involved over half of the elite. Through these ties, a young man was exposed to a large portion of the city's leadership. These contacts were often not sustained, since they usually lasted only a few years; but they were sufficient to separate the elite from the rest of the population and to generate interaction among Pottsville's emerging leadership. Charles Baber and L. F. Whitney, for instance, used their combined resources to speculate in the prosperous coal and land markets, which returned large profits to both parties. Similarly, Samuel Griscom and George DeKeim joined their resources to capitalize on the thriving speculative markets in anthracite and landholdings.[22]

As coal entrepreneurs, Pottsville's leaders often established business partnerships to acquire mining collieries throughout the region. George Potts and Joshua Sigfried engaged in joint mining operations in and around Pottsville during the 1850s. Collieries such as those at Mt. Laffee, near Pottsville, returned large profits and sustained their ventures for several years. This pattern continued through the 1870s, despite the reverses of those years. In the early part of the decade, John Phillips and William Sheafer combined their resources to lease the profitable Kolima Colliery, near Shenandoah City in the northern rim of the coalfields. They mined the colliery until the latter part of the decade, when financial pressures and the PRRCO forced them out of business.[23]

Occupationally mobile, Pottsville leaders frequently worked for one another as they moved up the social and economic ladders. In 1833, Thomas Wren, then barely ten years old, began apprenticeship in the Benjamin Haywood and George W. Snyder machine shop. By 1845, Wren had sufficiently mastered the business to open up the Eagle Foundry with his brothers. Riollary F. Lee also acquired training under Haywood and Snyder. Lee was a clerk for merchant James B. Beatty of Pottsville. He then assumed a similar position in Harrisburg and finally returned to Pottsville where he became chief clerk in the Haywood and Snyder operation. Similarly, Leonard W. Weissenger, who pursued a career in packing, worked in the Seltzer and Stoeffregen families' meat markets during the 1850s before opening up his own stockyard.[24] Partnerships and occupational ties provided Pottsville leaders with associations that bound them together.

The frequency of such partnerships can be seen in the career of George Bright. From 1852 through 1872, he engaged in five separate partnerships, which ranged from commerce to real estate. First, he operated a hardware store with George Potts. Then, in 1855, he joined his brother-in-law in a second mercantile venture. Two years later, he shifted his capital into the mining company of Haywood, Lee & Co. By 1860, he and Charles Lawton had acquired mining collieries near St. Clair. Shortly, he moved out on his own until 1866, when he and Peter Buck opened up mining operations in the southern rim. By 1872, he had a new partner, William Marr. During these years, Bright also invested in real estate in the Ashland and St. Clair area of Schuylkill County and in communities located in nearby Columbia County.[25]

These business ventures occasionally drew Pottsville leaders out of the city and even the region. Often, these ventures involved moving to other communities within the region. More frequently, Pottsville entrepreneurs had to leave the region to pursue seemingly profitable ventures elsewhere. L. P. Brooke provides a case in point. He arrived in Pottsville from southeastern Pennsylvania during the 1830s. In 1844, he returned to Philadelphia for two years and then came back to Pottsville. Once in the region, he engaged in mining operations, along with George Potts. Together, they ran several collieries and provided necessary commercial services to their work force. In 1864, Brooke journeyed to Lynchburg, Virginia, where he directed a union rolling mill and remained there until 1869, when he retired to Pottsville.[26] All told, members of the elite left the city a total of 127 times for periods of a few months to several years.

Members of the Sheafer, Haeseler, Shumway, and Wren families, to cite a few, left the city for a number of years to engage in entrepreneurial and professional activities in other communities. Even Benjamin Haywood, one of the leading entrepreneurs in the community, abandoned his operations and Pottsville to pursue ventures out of the region. In 1850, he sold his iron foundries and machine shops and migrated to San Francisco in order to capitalize on the gold rush. Not until 1856, after he had lost all his money, did he return to the southern coalfields. Haywood also invested his capital outside the southern anthracite region. He owned machine shops in Danville, Pennsylvania, and an iron mill and railroad in Allentown, also in the Keystone State. Ultimately, Haywood established his own independent operations in and around Pottsville. Members of the Pottsville elite often pursued this strategy. They conducted at least 120 separate activities, financed and directed by the leaders themselves. These filled the complement of operations, from mercantile and manufacturing to mining and coal-related.[27]

White-collar occupations also generated a large number of these associations. L. C. Thompson and Charles Dengler jointly owned a banking and exchange house that served many of the region's entrepreneurs and acted as an important link with Philadelphia and New York money markets. David B. Greene, lawyer, entrepreneur, and political leader, encountered fellow leader O. P. Bechtel in a hard-fought contest for county judge.[28]

The professions served as an arena where Pottsville leaders initiated business, occupational, and political ties. O. P. Bechtel acquired his legal training under Judge Francis Hughes, a prominent entrepreneur and Democratic party leader. Bechtel used this contact to break into the inner circle of county Democratic leadership and later establish his own reputation within the party. James B.

Reilly also studied under Hughes, whose patronage no doubt helped Reilly's political career. He later went on to hold several public offices and pursue several judicial posts. Even doctors in the Pottsville elite acquired a portion of their training under colleagues who were also members of the city's leadership. Francis Boyer served under C. H. Haeseler. Both had been associated with the Hahnemann College of Philadelphia, Haeseler as chair of pathology and practical medicine and Boyer as a student, although at different times. The presence and widespread character of these ties indicated a slow but steadily developing set of associations among these men, which formed the basis for the elite.[29]

SOCIAL INSTITUTIONS OF POTTSVILLE'S ELITE

The interaction generated through these economic and political ties did give rise to a number of social and benevolent organizations. Despite their prominence, none of these included most of the city's leaders and, occasionally, such organizations drew members from outside the elite. The oldest of the social organizations was the Pulaski Masonic Lodge. The membership tended to be economic and political leaders, but this was not an exclusive situation. Established in 1831, the lodge, named after the great Polish hero, was originally intended for all local residents who possessed certain ethnic and religious qualifications. For over twenty years, the lodge floundered, apparently because its members were unwilling to support it or participate in its activities. Faced with a chronic shortage of funds, the lodge was on the brink of dissolving in 1853, when members of Pottsville's emerging elite decided to join the organization and save it from extinction. The leaders developed a more selective membership, stiffened the admission policies, and pumped needed money into the lodge's treasury. By the 1870s, the lodge had recovered and had developed into one of the more popular associations among the elite.[30]

The Pottsville Fishing Party was the most prominent and exclusive group among the community's leadership. The party was not an ongoing concern with regular meetings and a clubhouse. Instead, it was an annual party, whose purpose was to underscore the high socioeconomic position of those invited. Its members included such prominent local figures as Judge William Donaldson, iron manufacturer Charles Atkins, State Attorney General Francis Hughes and Franklin P. Kaercher, later a PRRCO executive. The party did not become part of the social calendar of the emerging elite until the late 1850s and did not survive the economic decline of the seventies and eighties. The Pottsville Athletic Association (1878) was a relatively young organization and one not exclusively dominated by members of the elite.[31]

The members of the elite also established benevolent associations, intended to deal with the social problems that accompanied industrialization. Some of these organizations, such as the Female Bible Society, were religious, their purpose being to aid the destitute and indoctrinate them with Christianity. The Pottsville Benevolent Association also directed its efforts toward the less well-off in the community. Both groups were composed of the leaders (or their wives and daughters) who had the capital and the time to engage in such activities. These and other similar organizations, such as the Miners' Hospital, reflected the patronizing attitude of the members of the elite toward their fellow citizens at the bottom of the social structure. As instruments of charity, they never dealt effectively with the widespread poverty and the social problems of high seasonal unemployment, both chronic to mining-based regions. These organizations did, however, demonstrate the high social and economic position of their members and were a mark of community leadership.[32]

In contrast to these charitable and self-help associations, members of the elite established a branch of the National Guard to protect the propertied elements in the community. It was a reaction to the violence of the great Railroad Strike of 1877, in which destruction of property was commonplace. In Pottsville, Civil War Major Joshua Sigfried headed the guard. He was a member of one of the leading families in the city and had earned a reputation as a successful coal entrepreneur. The guard, despite its original intentions, evolved into a ceremonial organization, rather than an association designed to combat the laboring elements in the region.[33]

Pottsville leaders and their families also engaged in a number of literary and scientific organizations. By their very nature, these were confined to a select number of citizens who were almost always members of the elite. Several of these groups, such as the Pottsville Athenaeum, were not founded until the late 1860s, while others, including the Pottsville Literary Society and the Pottsville Scientific Association, had been in existence since the late 1850s. These drew their membership from the leading families, among whom were the Gowens, the Wetherills, and the Sheafers, whose members were longtime members of the elite and leading entrepreneurs. These groups provided an exclusive environment for socializing and entertaining among those in the leadership. Few would continue to draw their membership predominantly from the elite into the twentieth century.[34]

Funerals provide the last example of social interaction among the members of Pottsville's elite. On most such occasions, pallbearers were immediate business associates or members of the deceased's ethnic group. The five pallbearers at Benjamin Haywood's funeral were all iron manufacturers who had been in the business with him for more than twenty years. Those who acted in this capacity at the funeral of German brewer David Yuengling were Germans, Lutherans, and fellow church members. The rest of the funeral processions of these men often included members of non-elite groups, for example, clerks or neighbors of the deceased. The community's leaders were buried in a number of different cemeteries, the choice usually a reflection of their ethnocultural origins, although the Charles Baber Cemetery would become an increasingly common burial site for these men and their families.[35]

KINSHIP AND POTTSVILLE'S ELITE

The social and entrepreneurial associations formed the basis for increasing inter-marriage among the community's leading families after 1860 (Table 6-7). Until that decade, only fourteen of Pottsville's families whose members were in the elite were related through marriage. The presence of so many diverse cultural groups and the migration and mobility patterns of the elite had retarded the rate of intermarriage among the community's leaders. A large portion of the men of the elite were migrants who often had married before they arrived in Pottsville. Many had also married while they were moving from one socioeconomic plateau to another and, as a result, their wives frequently came from non-elite families. Kinship had, similarly, played a minor role in attracting these men to Pottsville; so few had familial ties to community leaders upon migrating to the city. Charles Atkins, John Roseberry, and David Greene, for example, had come to Pottsville already married. Other leaders, such as John Ryon, once in the city, married women from the communities where they had themselves last resided. Until the 1860s, most of these men selected wives on the basis of ethnocultural com-monality, women whom the men most often encountered in social situations and who demonstrated perceptions and values most appealing to Pottsville's leaders.[36]

Consequently, most of the marriage ties that existed in these years were between members of similar cultural groups and connected only two or three families. While this was less true of the post-1860 decades, ethnicity and reli-gion still tended to be important characteristics of kinship among the elite. The ties between the Yuenglings and Luthers and those among the Kaerchers, Na-gles, and Huntzingers, all of whom were German and most of whom were Lutheran, demonstrate this point. The Callens and Reillys were both Irish, Catholic, and of foreign-born parents. The kinship ties, however, often followed long periods of association in the same industry and frequent interaction in political affairs, occasionally in the same business. For example, Charles Atkins and Riollary F. Lee had been engaged in mining and coal land speculation for two decades before their offspring married in the late 1870s. The Parkers and the Sparkses had been engaged in the Schuylkill County Machine Depot oper-ation for some time before the two families were joined through the marriages of Mary Sparks, and later her sister, Julia Sparks, to Hiram Parker, Jr.[37]

By the seventies and eighties, three distinct kinship groups had emerged among the Pottsville elite. These groups centered around the Atkins, Nagle, and Mortimer families. The Mortimers, for instance, were related directly by blood and/or marriage to the Seltzer and Muir families and, distantly, to the Bertram family. Similarly, members of the Atkins clan were kinsmen of the Henning, Baber, Greene, Lee, Sheafer, and Roseberry families, who contributed many of Pottsville's most visible and powerful men. This same pattern of ties appeared among the relatives of the Nagle family. The Kaerchers, Rosengartens, Bowens, and Huntzingers, whose members ranked among the elite's most prom-

Table 6-7. Number, Proportion, and Cumulative Percentage of 158 Elite Families in Pottsville Related by Marriage, 1830–1890*

Decade	Number of Families Interrelated	Percentage by Decade	Cumulative Percentage
1830–1839	3	2%	2%
1840–1849	3	2	4
1850–1859	8	5	9
1860–1869	12	8	17.8
1870–1879	12	8	26
1880–1889	11	7	33
N = 158			

*Rates cover the years of intermarriage and differ from the dates (1870–1885) used in the majority of tables.

inent and wealthy, belonged to the Nagle kinship group.[38] These familial ties occurred most often in the second generation of leaders and frequently overcame the sharp ethnic and religious differences among families in the elite (these data appear in the "Kinship" section of Table 6-4). For instance, Franklin P. Kaercher, son of a prominent Pottsville clan, married Helen R. Reilly, also a member of a local elite family. He was German Lutheran and affiliated with the Trinity Lutheran Church. She was Irish Catholic and a member of St. Patrick's Irish Catholic Church. A similar cultural mix occurred in the marriage of F. P. Mortimer, English and Presbyterian, to Clara Seltzer, who was German and Lutheran.

Despite the growing frequency of these marriages, only 31 percent of the families in Pottsville's elite were related through marriage by the 1880s. Moreover, none of the three kinship groups overlapped. Nor did these familial ties reflect an emerging entrepreneurial network sustained through family. The familial and economic ties did at times overlap but involved only two or three families. The stagnation and economic decline of the city and the southern rim, in general, after 1870, in many cases, removed the industries to which these families had committed their resources and on which their business relationships were based. As important, these familial ties followed, rather than preceded, the joint economic ventures. They also occurred after Pottsville had reached its peak of power, rather than before. After the 1880s, the elite experienced considerable instability and out-migration, which undermined the basis of these embryonic kinship groups.[39]

CHAPTER VII

Pottsville's Elite and Regional Society

OTTSVILLE'S ELITE complemented its entrepreneurial activities, which sustained the local economy, with a network of regional ties. Members of Pottsville's leadership had begun constructing this network in the decades before 1870, the beginning of the city's decline. Not mature by that date, this series of extralocal ties was strongest among the elites and communities in the southern rim, where Pottsville's leaders had the majority of their investments and entrepreneurial activities. These men also had a far longer time to establish these ties, since the leadership groups and cities and towns in the southern rim were the oldest in the region. In the northern rim, these ties were far weaker. The urban elites and their communities had only begun to emerge in the 1860s. In addition, the presence of powerful outside interests also blunted the efforts of Pottsville's leadership to build a set of extralocal associations comparable to those in the southern rim.

The elite network, consisting mainly of economic and entrepreneurial ties, reflected the character of Pottsville's leadership; and the similarities of background and common experiences in the regional economy shared by elites throughout the southern coalfields facilitated the spread of this network. Rapid growth and instant cities had produced heterogeneous leadership groups over the entire region. Linked only by their common entrepreneurial ambitions and participation in the anthracite and coal-related industries, these elites differed little from Pottsville's leadership in either makeup or aspirations. By the 1860s, these elites, primarily those in the southern rim, had begun to depend on Pottsville's elite for credit, marketing ties, and other functions, while their communities relied on Pottsville-controlled enterprises for employment and income.

The emergence of a competing network fashioned by metropolitan-based entrepreneurs, corporate leaders, and their companies seriously challenged the persistence of Pottsville's network of regional ties. This network challenged

Pottsville's elite for influence throughout the region. The men who had begun to build this network of extraregional ties drained resources and capital needed for diversification and growth within the region. The consolidation of these ties by corporate leaders in Philadelphia during the 1870s and 1880s undermined the network of Pottsville's elite. Cut off from their sources of power and stressed by a weakened local economy, these men or their sons began to leave the city and the coalfields in large numbers after those decades. Similarly, members of other elites also joined this out-migration. Reduced to complete dependency by Philadelphia interests and, often without their own resources, these men sought opportunity outside the region.

The following chapter consists of four sections. The first will consider the social and entrepreneurial characteristics of elites throughout the region. The second section deals with the network of extralocal ties Pottsville's leaders fashioned with these men and their communities. The next section focuses on the network of extraregional ties and the metropolitan leaders who established these associations. The last section includes an analysis of the dispersal of urban elites in the region through 1930.

SOCIAL ANALYSIS OF URBAN ELITES IN COMMUNITIES OUTSIDE POTTSVILLE

Leadership groups in communities outside Pottsville developed under much the same conditions as Pottsville's elite and, therefore, depended on entrepreneurial and other economic ties for their cohesiveness. Virtually all the communities in the region were true boomtowns, with no past and futures tied to rapid economic growth. Like Pottsville, these cities and towns had fluid social structures and, therefore, heterogeneous elites. Mobility, rather than birth, was the main route to prominence and power in urban centers such as Mahanoy City and Shenandoah. As a result, these elites demonstrated the same cultural diversity as the Pottsville leadership group and, like that elite, drew a large share of their members from non–leadership groups. The powerful men in the communities of the Schuylkill-Northumberland coalfields also shared similar occupational and geographic mobility patterns as the leaders in Pottsville and, generally, adopted the same entrepreneurial strategies. Because of this diversity, cultural and social ties played a small role in the formation of these elites and in sustaining the extralocal relationships with Pottsville and its leadership.

For purposes of analysis, I have divided the communities in the region outside Pottsville into three categories, based on location. These formed the economic heart of the region before the 1870s. They had been founded at roughly the same time, or within a decade of Pottsville's incorporation. Among these communities, Tamaqua (elite under 1 percent of population in 1870), St. Clair, and Minersville were the largest, although all were considerably smaller than Pottsville and remained so through the 1920s. Schuylkill Haven, Port Carbon, Palo

Alto, and Tremont all ranged between 1,700 and 3,000, while urban villages such as Middleport and New Philadelphia were under 600 population in 1870.

Mahanoy City (elite under 1 percent of population in 1870) and Shenandoah (elite 1 percent of population in 1870) were the largest urban centers in the northern rim. Both eventually rivalled Pottsville in size, economic power, and political influence. Under 6,000 in 1870, the two communities surpassed 15,000 by 1920, while Shenandoah would reach 21,000 within a decade. Ashland (elite under 1 percent of population), Girardville, and Frackville constituted the second tier of communities in the northern rim, all less than a few thousand residents in 1870. Their growth occurred in spurts over the next fifty years, with Frackville becoming the largest, at roughly 8,000 by 1930.

The cities and towns in Northumberland County, at the northwestern edge of the region, comprised the third category. Shamokin (elite 3 percent of population in 1870) and Mt. Carmel ranked as the two largest communities in this area. Both, however, were still under 2,300 in 1870. By the 1920s, both had surpassed 17,000, while Shamokin, roughly at 20,000, had become the third largest city in the entire region, behind Pottsville and Shenandoah. Trevorton and Kulpmont were the other two important mining towns in the county during the late nineteenth century. In the shadow of Shamokin and Mt. Carmel, these two towns acted only as small service centers for the local mining populations and depended on the larger communities for a host of economic activities, from banking to utilities. Neither grew very rapidly after the 1890s, and both were still relatively small in the 1920s. Comparatively young in the late nineteenth century, the communities in the northern rim and Northumberland County were just in the first stages of urban growth and not fully integrated into the regional network by that decade. On the periphery before 1870, these sections became the core of the southern coalfields during the subsequent years, as population and industry shifted away from Pottsville and the southern rim. By the 1920s, the majority of the urban population in the southern coalfields resided in the communities of the northern rim and Northumberland County.[1]

As true boomtowns, these communities lacked indigenous elites before industrialization. As a result, the majority of their leaders were usually natives of other localities (Table 7-1). This was particularly true of elites in the northern rim and Northumberland County, whose cities and towns were only a few years old by the 1870s. The foreign-born also comprised a significant share of the elites in all three locations. The fluid social structures contributed greatly to the presence of so many foreign-born leaders, who confronted none of the social barriers present in communities with a developed upper class.[2]

The career of Charles Kaier of Mahanoy City was representative of those of many immigrant leaders in the region. A native of Baden, Germany, Kaier had accompanied his family to America in 1839. They landed in Philadelphia, where the family temporarily settled. Attracted inland, the Kaiers then moved to Norristown, northwest of Philadelphia and, finally, took roots in St. Clair, where Kaier's father engaged in a blacksmith business. As the son of an artisan,

Table 7-1.   Birthplace and Social Characteristics of Leaders in Communities of
the Southern Anthracite Region, 1870–1885

Birthplace and Social Characteristics		Communities in Southern Rim	Communities in Northern Rim	Communities in Northumberland County
Birthplace:	Community of residence	15%	2%	4%
	Schuylkill County	24	31	40
	Areas outside region	37	32	35
	Foreign-born	24	35	21
		100%	100%	100%
Ethnicity:	English	28	34	39
	German	48	36	43
	Scotch-Irish/Irish	10	19	8
	Welsh	13	8	3
	Scottish	1	3	7
		100%	100%	100%
Religion:	Presbyterian	8	9	12
	Episcopalian	4	6	6
	Methodist	20	6	18
	Evangelical*	10	7	5
	Lutheran	7	14	16
	German Reformed	11	3	8
	Catholic	13	24	12
	Unknown	27	31	23
		100%	100%	100%
Education:	No education	11	5	17
	Common school	30	33	52
	Public high school	16	12	9
	Private academy	13	3	4
	College	15	15	13
	Unknown	15	32	5
		100%	100%	100%
Occupation:	Merchant	27	38	39
	Coal operator	23	21	31
	Professional	17	13	10
	Manufacturer	15	9	10
	Contractor	6	2	3
	Hotel owner†	3	1	3
	Politician	3	4	0
	Banker	3	6	2
	Insurance/Real estate agent	3	6	2
		100%	100%	100%
		(71)	(101)	(94)

N = 266

* Includes Baptist, Congregationalist, Independent Church of God, and other German sects.

† Includes all service occupations.

Sources: See discussion of sources in Appendix.

Kaier's position in St. Clair offered him little opportunity for economic power. The community's small size and narrow range of industry further impeded his efforts to achieve wealth. In contrast, Mahanoy City's explosive growth during the 1860s seemed to promise abundant opportunities for a better future. In 1862, Kaier left St. Clair for the northern rim.[3]

The circumstances that enabled Kaier to achieve his economic success also produced elites with varied ethnocultural backgrounds. No single ethnic group dominated the leadership groups in any of the sections, as Table 7-1 shows. Leaders of English and German ancestry were the largest contingents in each of the three areas; however, the Irish and Scotch-Irish also formed a sizable proportion—19 percent—among elites in the northern rim. These leadership groups also fragmented along religious lines. Their members participated in over ten denominations and sects, from Presbyterian and Episcopalian to German Lutheran and German Evangelical. In the northern rim, the Roman Catholic Church drew the largest proportion of leaders—24 percent—of any religious denomination. The presence of a large number of Irish Catholic leaders in the communities of this section accounts for the strength of the Catholic Church among the elites, also shown in Table 7-1.[4]

Without common religious affiliation, the members of these leadership groups never developed upper-class churches, which could have served as important institutions in binding these elites together. The leaders in the communities of the northern rim and Northumberland County belonged to a number of churches that, in general, reflected their ethnic and religious heritages. For example, leaders in Tamaqua belonged to the Trinity Reformed Church, the Evangelical Church of Tamaqua, the Primitive Methodist Church, the St. Jerome's Roman Catholic Church, and the Episcopal Church of Tamaqua. Members of the elite in Ashland participated in at least eight separate churches, including Presbyterian, German Lutheran, Baptist, and Irish Catholic.[5]

Education played a minor role in the makeup of these elites. A large portion of these leaders had only a few years of common school before they joined the work force (see Table 7-1). Born into families without educational backgrounds to speak of, urban leaders saw job experience as more valuable than formal schooling in their quest for wealth and economic power. Apprenticeships in the trades, clerking in general stores, or even unskilled positions in industry seemed to hold more promise than education. Only a small number of these men attended college, and even a smaller proportion went to private secondary schools. As community leaders, these men continued to show little interest in education and made no efforts to establish private academies within the region. Conspicuous by their absence, educational institutions were simply not important in the formation of these elites or their survival into the twentieth century.[6]

Robert Aucker's educational experience was typical of that of leaders in the region. Aucker completed just three years of common school in his native Snyder County, Pennsylvania, before joining the work force. After years of hard work and some good luck, Aucker had acquired wealth and economic power in

Shamokin, where he served as director of several local companies. Aucker depended exclusively on job experience, rather than education, for his success.[7]

The absence of an educational tradition among leaders in the southern anthracite region is even apparent among the men who enrolled in private academies. No two attended the same school. They matriculated at private schools scattered over five states, rather than concentrating in one city or county. For example, John Kistler of Shenandoah graduated from the Union Seminary in New Berlin, Ohio, while his colleague, J. K. Haas of Shamokin, enrolled at Freeburg Academy in Snyder County and, later, Allentown Seminary in Lehigh County, Pennsylvania. Colleges and post-secondary schools were as varied as the academies. They ranged from state-supported schools, such as Pennsylvania State College, to prestigious Ivy League colleges.[8]

The traditions of an upper class were decidedly absent in the families of these leaders. The majority of them had been in America only a generation before the sons achieved economic success (Table 7-2). Most were also situated in non–leadership groups, unable to contribute to their sons' quest for power and wealth. Inheritance, customs, and emotional ties to the family name played a small part in the maturing of urban leaders in the southern coalfields. Pride in family, if it existed at all, took on a different meaning than in the upper class, where family was all-important. This was apparent in the local histories, which stress the lowly origins of the community's prominent men and their struggles to overcome the disadvantages of birth. The rhetoric downplayed even the most powerful of community symbols, the First Families. Mobility and achievement, not lineage and tradition, were the hallmarks of these elites.[9]

The largest single group among these leaders were born into families in which the fathers were artisans or skilled workers, often coal miners. Among the members of urban elites in the three sections, no less than 26 percent of these men and as high as 34 percent fell into this category. A substantial proportion of leaders from communities outside Pottsville had also grown up in agricultural families and depended on fathers who engaged in farming as their primary means of support. A. A. Heim's family background demonstrates a common pattern among the urban leaders in the region. His father was a silk weaver who migrated from his native Alsace-Lorraine to Wurtemberg, Germany, in search of work. From there, he emigrated to America, landing in Philadelphia in 1826. Compelled by economic necessity, the elder Heim moved to Lycoming County, in central Pennsylvania, then to Montour and Columbia counties, and eventually to Sullivan County, where he settled in the small town of Dushore. Having none of the advantages of birth, the son began his career as a day laborer before apprenticing in the carpenter's trade.[10]

Kinship played a minor role in sustaining these elites. The cultural pluralism and diverse economic backgrounds of these men slowed intermarriage among the leading families. No more than 15 percent of the prominent families in any community were joined through marriage or blood. At the same time, these characteristics reduced the importance of marriage ties with Pottsville elite

Table 7-2.   Lineage, Occupation of Father, and Kinship of Leaders in Communities of the Southern Anthracite Region, 1870–1885

		Communities in Southern Rim	Communities in Northern Rim	Communities in Northumberland County
Lineage:	First Family	1%	1%	1%
	Colonial stock	12	5	4
	Non–colonial stock	65	71	64
	Unknown	22	23	31
		100%	100%	100%
Occupation of Father:	Artisan/Skilled worker*	28	34	26
	Farmer	17	9	19
	Merchant	13	10	5
	Coal operator	12	3	6
	Professional	1	2	6
	Laborer/Peasant	3	4	7
	Lawyer	1	2	1
	Manufacturer	3	1	1
	Contractor	1	0	2
	Unknown	21	35	27
		100%	100%	100%
Kinship:	Related to Pottsville elite	25	9	7
	Unrelated to Pottsville elite	75	91	93
		100%	100%	100%
		(71)	(101)	(94)
N = 266				

* Includes coal miners.

families. Only in the southern rim had a significant proportion of the urban leaders established familial ties with the city's elites. Still, just 25 percent of the leaders in this section were related to leading Pottsville families, as Table 7-2 shows.

Most frequently, these men chose wives from non-elite families that were similar to their own economic origins. Often, they married before permanently settling down in the region. Conrad Graeber of Shamokin had married twice before arriving in Northumberland County. Neither of his wives came from families with power or status. Having once established themselves, leaders continued to choose wives from non-elite backgrounds. William McCarthy was typical. He married into the Sullivan family of St. Clair and went on to achieve financial, economic, and political power. His in-laws, unaffected, remained obscure and powerless.[11]

Despite the overwhelming importance of economic ties in sustaining these elites, urban leaders did participate in a number of social organizations. Few, however, were clearly confined to the upper strata. Their members often came from non-elite groups and carried no visible influence in the community. Even the local histories seldom mention these associations, other than merely to list their names; the individual biographical sketches stressed economic success almost to the exclusion of social ties. This was particularly true among the elites still in the early stages of development in the northern rim. On occasion, fraternal lodges drew disproportionate numbers of leaders for their membership, as in the case of Masonic Lodge No. 38 F&AM of Tamaqua.[12]

ENTREPRENEURIAL BASIS OF ELITES IN COMMUNITIES OUTSIDE POTTSVILLE

As economic elites, these groups depended upon ties generated through entrepreneurial activities. Urban leaders jointly exercised power over the community, its population, and industry through involvement in similar economic and financial activities. This interaction generated common economic interests among these men, which were not shared with other groups in the community. As successful entrepreneurs, the leaders in urban centers such as Mount Carmel and Shamokin had engaged in the arduous climb up the social ladder and, as a result, were firmly committed to Horatio Alger–like notions of hard work, thrift, and achievement. For all leaders, the continued growth of the region was essential, since they had capitalized on the burgeoning population and thriving industry to build their fortunes.

Commercial pursuits, which depended exclusively on this growth, were the most prevalent occupations among these men (see Table 7-1). The backbone of the urban elites, merchants also served as full-scale entrepreneurs, using their time and money to finance banking, utility, service, and transit companies which were central to the independent economic activities in the cities and towns of the region. Coal entrepreneurs comprised the second largest occupational category. During the early years of settlement, the explosive nature of the anthracite industry promised huge profits and a secure future. Coal operators responded to these opportunities in large numbers and, by the 1860s, had become an important component of local leadership. While a force in the industry, these men experienced intense pressure from Pottsville coal operators and outside-based capitalists, both of whom saw the rich coal deposits as vital sources of wealth and power. Many of these locally based operators lost control of their landholdings and mining collieries during this decade. In spite of this pressure, leaders often remained in the industry, either by leasing coal mines or joining the managerial staffs of outside-controlled companies.[13]

A significant proportion of these coal entrepreneurs acted as superintendents or general managers for coal companies based in New York or Philadelphia. As supervisors for these large operations, urban leaders exercised enormous power over the local work force and regulated a significant proportion of total family income in the community. The intrusion of the PRRCO simply changed employers; it did not displace these men. The PRRCO, like its predecessors, relied on the skills of local coal operators to insure the continuous flow of anthracite coal to the markets. By the end of the nineteenth century, former coal entrepreneurs throughout the region had become superintendents, district managers, or mine inspectors for the Philadelphia corporation.[14]

Lewis Riley of Ashland was perhaps a typical example of urban leaders who represented outside interests before the late 1870s. At one point, Riley had owned and operated the Logan Colliery near Centralia, just south of Ashland. Later, he abandoned what had become a marginal operation and assumed the managerial duties for the Locust Mountain Coal and Iron Company. By the early 1870s, he had taken over direction of the Lehigh Valley Coal Company's interest from Delano in Schuylkill County to Trevorton in Northumberland County. Riley was able to parlay these positions into an important source of capital. By the seventies, he had become director of the Citizens National Bank of Ashland and an entrenched member of the community's elite.[15]

As indicated in Table 7-1, the boom in the anthracite industry also stimulated a rise in coal-related manufacturing that attracted a sizable number of entrepreneurs. These men established lumber mills, machine shops, iron-making operations, and explosive and specialty machine tool plants. Their products in turn sustained mining collieries and fed into non-coal sectors, such as housing and construction. By 1870, entrepreneurs throughout the region had expanded beyond the regional markets and were beginning to export their goods to urban centers as far away as Wilmington, Delaware. But the depression of the seventies and the intrusion of the PRRCO were as crippling in these industries as they had been in anthracite mining. Faced with financial ruin and the loss of their main source of income, manufacturers switched into new entrepreneurial ventures by the 1890s. Many had completely left the region by that decade.[16]

job changes among these urban leaders, producing high mobility among them. The most volatile elites were those of the coal-producing communities of Northumberland County. Urban leaders in this section moved into new occupations 2.72 times during their careers and changed places of residence 3.4 times before settling more or less permanent places of residence. This geographic mobility was greater than among the leaders in the northern and southern rims, who migrated 2.65 and 2.84 times, respectively. Overall, the mean number of job changes for these leaders was 2.68 (N = 641), while the mean number of geographic moves for the entire group was 2.99 (N = 713).[17]

The career of William Grant demonstrates this rapid geographic and occupational mobility. As a young man in Scotland, Grant started work as a laborer in a local textile factory. In 1836, he left this job to pursue a career in coal mining and six years later migrated to Nova Scotia, leaving for Pottsville in 1843, after only one year. In Pennsylvania, he used past experience to become inside foreman for local operator George Potts. In 1854, Grant assumed the duties of

Table 7-3. Entrepreneurial Relationships among the Leaders in the
Southern Anthracite Region, 1850–1885

Entrepreneurial Relationships and Operations	Southern Rim	Northern Rim	Northumberland County
Other economic associations	6%	14%	11%
Apprenticeships and clerkships	9	6	12
Independent operations	23	15	16
Business and law partnerships	29	26	24
Ties with incorporated companies	33	39	37
Total	100%	100%	100%
n = 871	(245)	(275)	(351)

mine superintendent for hard-coal operations in Dauphin and Susquehanna counties, but he returned to his old position early in 1855. In the same year, he became inside boss in George W. Snyder's Pine Forest Colliery. At the end of 1855, Grant moved to New Hope, Pennsylvania, and in 1863 arrived in Shenandoah. For several years, he directed successful coal collieries for Pottsville leaders such as R. F. Lee. Grant switched into iron manufacturing during the 1860s and, in 1870, into banking.[18] Similar patterns occurred in the careers of most urban leaders from this region.[19]

Given their frequent mobility, urban leaders seldom established permanent bonds with future colleagues, a common event among members of upper-class leadership groups. As successful entrepreneurs, however, these men engaged in a number of common economic activities which sustained contact among the members of the elite (Table 7-3). These entrepreneurial ties overrode the cultural and ethnic barriers that divided elites throughout the region and provided cohesiveness for these groups. Board members of the Tamaqua Manufacturing Company provide a case in point. Emmanuel J. Fry and Henry Weldy, both prominent men in Tamaqua, were directors in the company. Fry was English, Episcopalian, and of recent lineage, while Weldy was French, Huguenot, and of colonial stock. Similarly, the men who ran the First National Bank of Minersville were drawn from cultural groups as disparate as Welsh Baptist and Irish Catholic. Longtime director Jacob Lawrence was native-born, of English descent, and a man of little formal education. His colleague, William Kear, was Methodist, foreign-born, and academy trained. A similar pattern was apparent among the directors and officers of the Shenandoah First National Bank, where board member John Kistler was native-born and German Evangelical; and his fellow director, Patrick Ferguson, was Irish, foreign-born and Roman Catholic. Without exception, cultural pluralism typified every financial, utility, service, and manufacturing company in the region. Participation in these enterprises constituted between 33 percent and 38 percent of all entrepreneurial activities among the urban leaders in the three sections of the region (see Table 7-3).[20]

As the table also shows, entrepreneurs oftentimes formed associations through

Table 7-4. Mean and Total Numbers of Occupational Changes and Geographic Moves among Leaders in the Southern Anthracite Region, 1850–1885*

Occupational Changes and Geographic Moves	Southern Rim	Northern Rim	Northumberland County	Overall
Mean number of occupational changes	2.78	2.59	2.72	2.69
Total number of occupational changes	175	213	253	641
Mean number of geographic moves	2.84	2.65	3.4	2.99
Total number of geographic moves	179	218	316	713
N = 871				

*In 10 percent of the cases (eight men in the southern rim, nineteen in the northern rim, and one in Northumberland County), information was insufficient for inclusion in the table.

partnerships. The frequency and duration of these varied enormously. Members of the Carter, Allen, and Shoener families in Tamaqua operated an iron foundry and machine shop for years. Family members also served on the board of the First National Bank of Tamaqua, which provided short-term capital for family entrepreneurial activities. From 1871 through 1878, Peter Buck and Edward Heaton, both of Ashland, were involved in a number of joint ventures, from banking and commerce to real estate. Buck also engaged in partnerships of much shorter duration with entrepreneurs from Pottsville and Shamokin.[21]

Leaders also pursued their own independent operations. These formed between 15 percent and 23 percent of economic activities listed in Table 7-3. For instance, Marmaduke Fowler of Shenandoah built up a $100,000 fortune through his commercial coal mining and flour and grain activities. Fowler then used profits from these operations to acquire real estate, other properties, and stocks, thus solidifying his financial position.[22]

While Fowler made his fortune in Shenandoah, leaders throughout the region often left their communities to pursue entrepreneurial activities in other cities and towns. Opportunities in other mining centers drew these men away for periods as long as five years. More often, they left the region entirely, either for Pennsylvania cities outside the coalfields or communities in surrounding states (Table 7-4). Alexander Fulton of Shamokin abandoned his investments and a promising career as a coal operator to exploit the coal boom in the northern anthracite region. After stops in the Lackawanna Valley, Nova Scotia, and Schuylkill County, he returned to Shamokin in 1867 to build a successful career in banking and utilities.[23]

Occupational and geographic mobility complemented such entrepreneurial strategies. Mobility provided aspiring young men exposure to urban economies, familiarized them with the resources of the southern coalfields, and helped them acquire skills in a number of economic activities. In a region with few institutions distributing this information, mobility was a virtual necessity for the rise of an entrepreneur. Urban leaders from all three sections spent much of their early careers travelling in search of opportunities. For leaders in the southern rim, these journeys often took them through as many as five communities, where they stayed for periods of six months to five years. Prominent men in the northern rim had also used this way of building successful careers. But unlike their counterparts to the south, the northern leaders had travelled through the cities and towns of both sections as economic booms or opportunities shifted from one community to another. Similar patterns existed among the urban leaders in Northumberland County. Many of these men had begun their careers in small rural villages or commercial centers of Northumberland or surrounding communities. In order to achieve economic success, leaders of Shamokin or Mount Carmel had to migrate from their native communities to mining patch towns—essentially industrial villages—to larger coal towns and, finally, to the major cities in the county. During these migrations, urban leaders mastered the art of locating natural resources, assessing their potential for exploitation, and evaluating the costs of these undertakings, all critical skills for entrepreneurial success. They also became familiar with investment opportunities and saw first-hand failing or prospering enterprises that later served as guides in their own careers.

Occupational mobility was also vital for the entrepreneurial leaders in the Schuylkill-Northumberland coalfields. It gave them a working knowledge of a number of economic ventures, from iron manufacturing to coal mining. It also helped them understand market fluctuations in a wide variety of industries and the demands for setting up new operations, whether in commerce or land speculation. Both forms of mobility were indispensable for creating partnerships or securing needed capital to finance new business operations. Because of their experiences as mobile young men, urban leaders were better able in maturity to evaluate potential associates, capital sources, the feasibility of new ventures, and the best locations for these activities.

POTTSVILLE ELITE'S REGIONAL NETWORK

Proximity brought elites from throughout the region into contact with Pottsville's leadership. Similar economic base, competition for scarce resources, and common markets contributed to this interaction. Above all, the decision of Pottsville's leaders to exploit the region's rich coal deposits and to build industry tied to anthracite made this contact inevitable. In the process of acquiring resources and pioneering new entrepreneurial activities, Pottsville's leaders penetrated the economies of other cities and towns in the region and began to fashion a series of economic ties that formed the basis for their regional network (Table 7-5). Leaders throughout the region eventually came to depend on Pottsville for capital, credit, and commercial goods while their communities relied on Pottsville-owned or subsidized industry for employment, income and prosperity. The city further provided marketing ties, a service that sustained this industry and made its expansion throughout the nineteenth century possible.

Pottsville's leaders actively exploited their own geographic and occupational

Table 7-5. Entrepreneurial Relationships among Pottsville's Elite and Other
Leaders in the Southern Anthracite Region, 1850–1885

Economic, Social, and Familial Ties		Southern Rim	Northern Rim	Northumberland County
Economic ties	Financial	12%	14%	9%
	Entrepreneurial	13	12	30
	Subordinate*	40	31	38
	Investments†	16	27	4
	Reciprocal/Trade	1	1	0
	Subtotal	82	85	81
Social and familial ties		18	15	19
Total		100%	100%	100%
		(256)	(97)	(47)
n = 400				

*Includes mercantile operations such as clothing stores, general stores, and hardware stores;
service operations such as hotels; and commercial operations tied directly to the coal industry.
Also included are coal-related, mining, and manufacturing operations.

†Refers primarily to investments in land, mineral rights, coal lands, real estate, and such
property as buildings and factories.

Sources: See Appendix, Note on Table Sources.

mobility to further the elite's position in the region. As young men, they, too,
had journeyed from community to community in order to make their way up
the economic ladder. In the process, they acquired the same knowledge of the
region's natural resources as their competitors elsewhere in the coalfields. They
also established an array of contacts with business interests in the cities and
towns of the region. These ties were later useful in acquiring coal lands, building
coal collieries, setting up coal-related industries, and opening mercantile outlets. These ties gave Pottsville's leaders an intimate knowledge of the region's
entrepreneurs and the feasibility of new industry. With access to the financial
and economic affairs of urban leaders in the region, Pottsville's leaders were
better able to appraise entrepreneurs who solicited money or proposed joint
ventures. Members of the city's elite were in a position to judge the capital needs
for new industry, their potential returns, and the conditions of the market, all
of which were crucial in lending money or collaborating in entrepreneurial
ventures with other businessmen.

Despite appearances, this network lacked the cohesiveness and resiliency of
its counterpart in the Wyoming Valley. The Pottsville elite had not yet solidified
the city's position as the regional center by the 1870s, and it weakened dramatically in the northern rim and Northumberland County. Ties with communities
in these sections were still few in number and not sufficiently strong to bring
these cities and towns under the control of Pottsville's elite. Pottsville's elite
also lacked the social, familial, and informal ties to cement this emerging regional network. Since institutions that would generate these ties were not central to the Pottsville elite, its members were forced to rely on economic and

entrepreneurial relationships, created mainly by the individual leader to maintain this network. The continued economic success of these men was crucial for the survival of the regional network. Yet the reverses of the seventies and eighties hit this group hardest and fractured the regional network. Last, Pottsville's leaders had to compete directly with extraregional agencies also attempting to exploit the natural resources of the region; these were threatening before the 1870s and ruinous after that decade.

The strength of these extralocal ties varied by industry. In anthracite, the city's leaders had clearly established themselves as the dominant group of regional coal operators (see Table 7-5, under "Subordinate"). Yet, their economic ties via the industry were not comparable to those generated by Wilkes-Barre's coal companies in the Wyoming Valley. In Pottsville, entrepreneurs, rather than companies, established the majority of locally controlled mining operations in the region. The amount of money invested in these collieries and their life expectancy depended on the entrepreneur's willingness to commit his resources on a long-term basis. Often, the thinning out of a coal vein was sufficient to discourage further exploration, and the colliery would be shut down. At other times, the Pottsville entrepreneurs switched their capital to other, seemingly more profitable enterprises. Financial reverses often forced the city's coal operators to withdraw their investments. Therefore, ties generated through the anthracite industry often persisted for only short periods, while their location and density constantly shifted from community to community.[24]

Obviously, these investments varied dramatically in size, value, and productivity. William Donaldson probably had the most extensive coal operations in the region. His mining operations in the Tremont district, at the southwestern edge of the coalfields, were valued at $450,000 and employed hundreds of men and boys. In contrast, his counterparts, Benjamin Mines and Benjamin Haywood, ran an anthracite mine in Blythe Township estimated only at $80,000 in 1870. It produced less and employed significantly fewer workers than Donaldson's operation. Yet this colliery was still large when compared to Haywood's Newcastle mine, valued at only $10,000. Nor were the Miles and Haywood operations exceptional. Pottsville leaders such as George Pomeroy and Edward Patterson frequently engaged in such small-scale operations. Still, no other elite could compete with Pottsville's leadership in the amount of capital, size of investment, or number of collieries, particularly in the southern rim (see Table 7-5, under "Subordinate"). In the other two sections, Pottsville's leaders encountered still more opposition from outside-based coal companies. They were never able to establish a firm hold in either the northern rim or Northumberland County.[25]

Coal-related operations were far stronger sources of economic power. Iron manufacturing, lumber mills, and machine shops required considerable capital, equipment, and real estate, a fact that necessitated long-term investments (see Table 7-5, under "Subordinate"). These created permanent lines of communication and thus gave the city's elite access to urban economies throughout the coalfields. The majority of the activities were located in the southern rim, where many dated back to the 1840s. In towns such as Palo Alto, Port Carbon, and Tremont, factories and mills controlled by members of Pottsville's elite provided work for a large share of the local work force and were essential in generating income for laboring families in the community. Pottsville's leaders owned or subsidized mine-related operations in Pinegrove, Schuylkill Haven, and Miners-ville, reinforcing the city's grip on the southern rim and holding the regional network together. Pottsville's leaders controlled iron and lumber companies in Mahanoy City, Shenandoah, Shamokin, and Ashland; obviously, this extended the city's influence into the newly developing sections of the region.[26]

Pottsville leaders complemented these entrepreneurial efforts with a series of commercial outlets scattered over the coalfields (see Table 7-5, under "Subordinate"). These ranged from general stores to more specialized outlets, such as warehouses and furniture stores. Solomon Hoover owned tin stove outlets throughout the southern rim and in Ashland; the products were built in Pottsville. Similarly, the Huntzinger family ran dry goods and grocery stores in a number of the smaller communities surrounding Pottsville.[27]

The participation of Pottsville's leaders in land speculation also spread their influence throughout the region (see Table 7-5, under "Investments"). Benjamin Haywood, William Donaldson, and Jacob Huntzinger relied on vast landhold-ings to sustain their fortunes. Donaldson owned and actively mined 15,000 acres in the Tremont district while Haywood controlled land tracts in and around Palo Alto, where he also had a major manufacturing operation. Hunt-zinger may well have been the largest investor of the Pottsville elite. He owned tracts in Barry, Rattling, Hegan, Foster, and Blythe townships, to cite a few examples. He also owned real estate in Ashland, Schuylkill Haven, Tremont, and Orwigsburg. In addition, Huntzinger controlled considerable property in ten different communities and ran powder mills in Orwigsburg. Although smaller in his scale of operations, George Bright was also an active investor. He held title to $20,000 worth of real estate in Ashland and operated hardware stores in St. Clair, Ashland, and Pottsville, where he was headquartered.[28]

This large capital base enabled Pottsville entrepreneurs to become the major creditors in the region (see Table 7-5, under "Finance"). They directly subsidized numerous economic activities in all sections of the southern coalfields, and their loans often saved other urban leaders from bankruptcy. For example, Jacob Huntzinger's advance of $55,000 enabled iron manufacturer Z. P. Boyer to maintain his business in Schuylkill Haven. Hard hit by the depression of the seventies, Boyer lacked sufficient capital reserves to cope with a sharp drop in the market. Only Huntzinger's loan kept him afloat. Huntzinger also lent money to coal operators, iron companies, merchants, and even cities and towns in need of short-term capital. Such practice was common among members of Pottsville's elite, including the Moorheads, the Fochts, the Atkinses, and the Wrens, whose capital supported entrepreneurial endeavors in Ashland, Mahanoy City, Shen-andoah, New Philadelphia, and Mt. Laffee. Urban leaders such as John Wadlinger of Minersville, William Grant of Shenandoah, and George Wren of Mahanoy City depended heavily on credit from members of Pottsville's financial community to maintain their operations.[29]

Pottsville leaders used the city's banks to extend its influence in the financial affairs of the region. The Miners' Trust Company was typical. It supplied money for a wide range of enterprises, from the Schuylkill and Ringgold Iron Companies in the southern rim to the First National Bank of Mahanoy City and the Northumberland Bank of Shamokin to the north. Similarly, the Mountain City Bank lent capital to the First National Bank of Minersville, the Miners Trust of Shamokin, and the First National Bank of Tremont. The amount of these investments varied from a few hundred dollars for short-term expenses to thousands of dollars for company securities and heavy capital improvements.[30]

Pottsville's leaders engaged in numerous entrepreneurial activities with members of elites throughout the coalfields (see Table 7-5, under "Entrepreneurial"). These ranged from large, heavily capitalized companies to smaller-scale business partnerships of shorter duration. As financial sources for many regional ventures, Pottsville's leading men also served as directors and/or officers in companies and banks located in other communities. Members of the city's elite held board positions in the Shamokin Banking Company, the Anthracite Bank of Tamaqua, and the Orwigsburg Shoe Manufacturing Company, among others. The success of Pottsville's elite attracted entrepreneurial leaders, who saw in the city's economic ventures steady profits, access to a large capital reserve, and well-developed ties with outside markets. Occasionally, entrepreneurs relocated their operations to Pottsville. For instance, Henry Saylor, whose family exercised considerable power in Schuylkill Haven, moved his insurance company to the city, and rechartered it as the Pottsville Bank. He was able to secure strong local backing to help revive his flagging company. More frequently, leaders from Minersville, Tamaqua, Port Carbon, and Schuylkill Haven—all in the southern rim—acted as directors of Pottsville-controlled companies. These were generally in finance, utilities, and services, rather than in coal and coal-related industries, wherein Pottsville leaders usually pursued independent operations or business partnerships as their primary entrepreneurial strategies.[31]

Business partnerships between Pottsville's leaders and those elsewhere in the region depended on common economic interests, similar entrepreneurial objectives, and some means of establishing contact. These ventures also covered the full range of economic activity, from coal mining to commercial operations. Mining operator J. J. Connor of Pottsville frequently entered into joint business ventures with entrepreneurs from communities scattered over the region. For example, he and Jacob Rhoads of Tamaqua (and later Shenandoah) held mining collieries and commercial outlets in the New Philadelphia area during the 1850s. He also operated collieries in the Ashland area. Andrew Robertson of Pottsville, Henry Guiterman of Port Carbon, and Robert Allison of Schuylkill Haven all held coal properties in Schuylkill County. They all marketed their coal through agencies in Pottsville, and all invested in the city. The three combined their skills and capital to open up anthracite-mining operations in Northumberland County, where Robertson owned considerable coal lands. Unlike Robertson and his partners, George Bright of Pottsville and Peter Buck of Ashland (later Mahanoy City) specialized in mercantile operations and real estate. Both ran hardware stores in their communities and both owned considerable land and property. Together, they established major hardware outlets in Pottsville and Ashland. Charles Kear of Minersville relied on his son-in-law, Charles Barker of Pottsville, to conduct his brokerage business in that city. As a member of the Pottsville elite, Barker had useful contacts with the city's leading entrepreneurs; Kear was able to exploit these connections. Despite the frequency of such entrepreneurial associations, they still accounted for only 13 percent of the economic ties in the southern rim and 13 percent in the northern rim (see Table 7-5, under "Entrepreneurial").[32]

Kinship and social ties were not central in Pottsville's network of extralocal ties (see Table 7-5, under "Social and Familial Ties"). Combined, these accounted for only 18 percent of all contacts beyond the community. Pottsville's own social institutions were just beginning to mature in the seventies and had not been an important part of the elite's efforts to build a regional network. Leaders from other communities rarely participated in Pottsville's elite clubs and lodges; but on occasion, members of leading families—for example, the Heebners in Port Carbon or the Pattersons in Ashland—joined the city's elite-sponsored annual Fishing Party. Others belonged to the newly formed Athletic Club or the older Pottsville Literary Society. Still, these outsiders comprised only a small portion of the membership in these organizations.[33]

Familial ties contributed little to Pottsville's economic power. Its leaders usually married into families with little power or wealth. Such marriages, in fact, outnumbered those with elite families by five to one. Similarly, most of the city's leaders came from non-elite families, whose kinship ties proved of little use to Pottsville in its quest for urban power. These patterns of kinship ties become apparent in a study of several Pottsville leaders and their families. Typical was the case of Levi Laubenstein. Born in Berks County, he moved in 1822 to Schuylkill County with his family; at the time, he was still quite young. Laubenstein's father was a moderately successful farmer and part-time merchant who achieved a comfortable living; but he never acquired economic ranking, appeared on the boards of Schuylkill Haven companies and banks, or held notable wealth. The younger Laubenstein migrated to Pottsville at age eighteen. Other than the relationship with his family, he did not maintain visible social, cultural, or economic ties with Schuylkill Haven. Like so many of his peers, he had kinship ties of insufficient closeness or power to use in any attempts to channel wealth and talent into Pottsville or exert influence over the economy in Schuylkill Haven.[34]

Familial ties with members of other cities and towns often were the product of out-migration among the sons of leading families, who no longer saw Pottsville as a viable community for entrepreneurial endeavors. During the seventies and eighties, many of these young men abandoned the city and its stagnating economy for the seemingly more vital cities of the northern rim and Northumberland County.

The career of Millard Nagle illustrates the point. Nagle, son of Daniel and nephew of James Nagle, both prominent Pottsville leaders, married Jeanne Meck of Schuylkill Haven. Her father was a fairly wealthy merchant who also had a thriving lumber business. The potential in this attachment, however, dissolved when Nagle migrated first to Schuylkill Haven and then to Shamokin, where he established a seemingly profitable mercantile operation. Later, he was joined by his younger brother, who worked in the business. But neither son moved into Shamokin's elite ranks, acquired any form of economic power, nor kept up any ties with Pottsville.[35]

Most ties among elite families in the region, although not great in number, were concentrated in the southern rim. Often, the families were located in the smaller and economically weaker towns and villages, such as Orwigsburg, that provided few advantages to Pottsville. At the same time, Pottsville's leaders had developed few ties with powerful families in larger and rapidly growing cities in the northern rim and Northumberland County, whose economies had much greater potential for exploitation. Some members of Pottsville's elite were related to leading families in these sections, including the Kistlers of Mahanoy City and the Pattersons of Ashland, both in the northern rim, and the Llewellyns of Shamokin. These associations, however, seldom overlapped with entrepreneurial ties; nor did they promote economic cooperation with urban elites in the area.[36]

OUTSIDE-CONTROLLED COMPANIES AND COMPETING REGIONAL NETWORKS

Outside agencies presented a major threat to the regional network of Pottsville's elite. Representatives of metropolitan-based coal companies, banks, brokerage houses, and railroads were fashioning their own ties with entrepreneurs and communities in the region (Table 7-6). These extraregional ties rivalled Pottsville's own network. Still, they were not concentrated in one community but scattered among several metropolitan centers and even larger cities close to the region. Leaders from Philadelphia and New York City dominated these extraregional associations, though entrepreneurs and companies from Boston, Harrisburg, and Wilmington, Delaware, were also active in the southern coalfields. As a result, outside companies and their agents were not able to develop a concerted effort to undermine Pottsville's own economic power or its regional network. Nor did evidence exist to suggest these companies even raised this option as a possibility.

The ties made by metropolitan leaders and their companies differed little from those in Pottsville's network.[37] Entrepreneurs within the region frequently

Table 7-6.   Proportion of Economic, Social, and Familial Ties between Elites and Communities in the Southern Anthracite Region and Entrepreneurs outside the Region, 1850–1875

Economic, Social, and Familial Ties*		%	N
Economic ties	Financial	17	48
	Entrepreneurial	6	18
	Subordinate	44	123
	Investments	25	70
	Reciprocal/Trade	6	16
	Subtotal	98	275
Social and familial ties		2	5
Total		100%	280†

* The greater part of the data was taken from sources after the mid-1850s.

† These totals do not include the acquisitions by the PRRCO during the 1870s nor those by other Philadelphia companies that moved into traction, utilities, and other areas in the years following 1880.

Sources: See Appendix.

sought loans and other credit from outside-based financial institutions. Charles Kopitzsch of Pottsville helped maintain his soap-manufacturing operations with loans secured from the Guarantee Trust Company of Philadelphia. Similarly, David Clearly, who operated dry-goods stores in Mahanoy City, relied on loans from Wood, Brown and Company of Philadelphia to sustain his business. Nearby, Shenandoah's Valley Bank invested its capital in the Union Banking Company of Philadelphia. At the same time, it borrowed money from New York City banks and other Philadelphia financial institutions. Bankers in the coalfields also depended on metropolitan brokers to sell their stocks and bonds in order to raise cash for entrepreneurial activities in the region. This net of financial ties joined the southern anthracite region with the broader world of eastern banking establishments.[38]

Urban leaders in the region frequently acted as agents for companies and investment houses in Boston, Philadelphia, and New York City. In this capacity, they helped direct local investments, handled administrative duties, and facilitated the transfer of capital in and out of the region. These men came from all leadership groups in the region. Charles Baber, for example, a longtime community leader, was one of the wealthiest men in Pottsville. In addition to his investments, he worked as an agent for the Lombard Investment Company of Boston, passing this position on to his son William in the late eighties. Baber's colleague, Heber S. Thompson, served as an agent for the Girard Estate of Philadelphia, which owned large tracts of coal lands in the region and leased numerous collieries to local operators. In the northern rim, Patrick J. Ferguson, director and officer in several Shenandoah companies and banks, worked for the Lehigh Valley Railroad, headquartered in Philadelphia. In neighboring Ashland, William H. Bright, in addition to his entrepreneurial activities, acted as agent for the Towanda Erie Company of New York. This phenomenon was common throughout the region and enabled outside interests to penetrate every facet of the regional economy.[39]

The economic ties created by outside-controlled anthracite companies competed directly with the elite's own network of entrepreneurial associations. The Hickory Coal Company, the New Boston Coal Company, the Philadelphia Coal Company, and the Bear Ridge Coal Company owned collieries in the northern rim. The first two were controlled by capitalists in New York City, while the last two were headquartered in Philadelphia. New York City interests owned the New Philadelphia Mining Company, which operated just east of Pottsville in the southern rim. Philadelphia capitalists controlled the Greenwood Coal Company, which owned mining collieries in and around Tamaqua. Investors from Philadelphia also established companies in the Northumberland County section. The Green Ridge Improvement Company and the Coal Run Improvement Company, among others, built and operated numerous mining collieries and purchased valuable tracts of coal lands. These companies gave the southern coalfields a strong extraregional orientation and, in the cities of Northumberland County, almost displaced Pottsville's entrepreneurs.[40]

While this series of ties competed with those established by the Pottsville elite, it neither preempted them nor removed the city's leaders from the broad range of entrepreneurial operations. Pottsville continued to grow, its economy expanded, its leaders continued to exploit the resources of the region, and they still carried on the full complement of economic activities. They also retained their hold on coal-related industries and still constituted the wealthiest group in the region. They were able to maintain the series of extralocal ties which had made Pottsville the hub of an emerging regional network and the largest and most powerful community in the southern coalfields. Outside agencies made no active attempt, whether in mining or coal-related industries, to undermine Pottsville's extralocal ties. Nor did companies and entrepreneurs seek to buy out Pottsville's landholdings or commercial operations. Only with the intrusion of the PRRCO would these strategies embody a consistent corporate strategy pursued by railroad owners.

THE COLLAPSE OF THE REGIONAL NETWORK OF THE POTTSVILLE ELITE

These ties sustained Pottsville's elite in the region, while its future growth depended on the extension of the ties into the northern rim and Northumberland County. Elite-controlled industry, commerce, and landholdings were concentrated in the southern rim, although elite members were active elsewhere in the region. The continued prosperity of the communities where Pottsville had major investments was vital to the city's own economic interests. Its future was linked to this emerging network as much as to its own economy. The reverses of the seventies and eighties severed these ties and crippled the economies of the cities and towns in the region. In the southern rim, they stripped the more rapidly growing communities of their potential for diversified growth and severely weakened the economic base of their elites. The Pottsville elite suffered a dual loss: its own economy was undermined, and its regional network had collapsed.

The PRRCO undermined the elite's network of economic ties. The PRRCO simply eliminated the partnerships, the independent operations, and the few Pottsville-controlled companies in the anthracite industry. The PRRCO also systematically bought out the majority of the Pottsville-owned or subsidized iron-manufacturing and machine shops, which in many communities were the major sources of employment and the primary means to dominate their economies. Coal-related operations in Palo Alto and Port Carbon, for example, were permanently shut down. At the same time, the depression forced the closing of Pottsville-owned iron companies in Pinegrove, Mahanoy City, Tremont, and a number of other cities and towns, with resultant loss of capital and influence over the economic activities of these communities. The collapse of the Schuylkill Iron Company, for instance, cost Jacob Huntzinger alone $55,000. Similarly, executives and agents of the Philadelphia corporation bought out all the valuable coal lands owned by the Pottsville elite. Lewis Thompson, one of the major landowners among the city's leaders, sold all of his holdings to the PRRCO. The collapse of Pottsville's banks was a final disaster, as it removed the city's credit ties and significantly reduced its influence in the financial and economic affairs of the region.[41]

Bankruptcies or the near-collapse of individual entrepreneurs among Pottsville's elite accompanied these reverses. Almost half of the city's elite experienced financial difficulties. Members of the Sheafer, Baber, Huntzinger, Haeseler, Woltjen, Ulmer, and Seltzer families either verged on declarations of bankruptcy or actually filed for liquidation in the county court. Through their economic activities, these men were often the origin of a large number of extralocal ties with elites and communities throughout the region; with their collapse, these ties vanished. Many of the city's entrepreneurs, in an effort to stem the tide of failures, began to shift their capital out of the region to what appeared to be safer investments in other communities.[42]

As with Pottsville, the reverses of these decades severely damaged the economies of these communities in the southern rim and, therefore, the fortunes of their elites. Never a major factor in the anthracite industry, the leaders of these communities were completely unable to cope with the intrusion of the PRRCO or the northward shift in mining operations. At the same time, locally controlled coal-related industries collapsed. For example, the Palo Alto Rolling Mills created jobs for 500 men and a monthly payroll of $20,000. In the late 1870s, the PRC&ICO purchased the company from its Pottsville owners and tore down the plant. Already slowed to a −9 percent population growth, the city lost an additional 10 percent during the 1880s as a result of this loss (Table

7-7). Port Carbon experienced a similar fate. The Port Carbon Iron Works, which produced mining machinery and T-rails, constituted one of the main industries of both the elite and the town. After its takeover by the PRC&ICO in the early 1880s, the company eventually closed the plant down. This shutdown put 135 men out of work and removed a critical source of profits for Port Carbon's leaders. The same pattern occurred in Minersville, Mount Carbon, Schuylkill Haven, and every other community in the southern rim.[43]

As in Pottsville, banks and entrepreneurs in the communities of the southern rim failed in large numbers. Financial institutions in Minersville, Tamaqua, and Tremont closed their doors during the depression. The economic distress of these years created enormous financial difficulties for the powerful families in the communities outside Pottsville. William Kear of Minersville, whose family had been the wealthiest and most powerful in his community, declared bankruptcy. Henry Heil of Tremont came near bankruptcy in the early seventies and almost lost his major investment in a locally controlled iron company. Eventually, the strains of the depression overwhelmed Heil and, in 1874, the county sheriff sold his property and real estate.[44]

The impact of outside economic control, coupled with the depression of the 1870s, can be seen in Table 7-7. The population growth rate of all communities in the southern rim declined sharply between 1870 and 1890. With the exception of New Philadelphia and Middleport, none of the communities grew more than 8 percent per decade through 1890. Many towns and villages actually lost population. Other than Pottsville, only Tamaqua exceeded 12,000 in population by the 1920s. Most of the communities reached only a 2,000 to 7,000 population range by this decade.

All the cities, towns, and villages of the southern rim were now tied irrevocably to Philadelphia, whose corporations and entrepreneurs controlled the regional economies and the main industries. The PRRCO and its representatives were primarily interested in profit, not the diversified growth of the community or the region. It closed most of the coal-related operations in the section and consolidated them into central points to avoid competition and needless duplication, an economic necessity for corporate leaders whose own resources were dangerously thin by the late 1870s. Corporate leaders shut down unprofitable mining collieries and shifted the capital north to the newly discovered coal deposits in the northern rim and Northumberland County. Members of these elites were never able to make up their capital losses nor restore the local companies. Philadelphia entrepreneurs and companies significantly reduced the economic basis of elites in these cities and towns and made them dependent on Philadelphia corporate leaders. The once-prosperous and growing southern rim and its elites now faced decades of stagnation. Broken up internally and cut off from the Pottsville elite, the leadership groups in the communities of this section looked beyond the southern anthracite fields for regional unity and their economic fate.[45]

The cities in the northern rim continued to develop at a brisk pace from 1870

Table 7-7. Growth Rates of Communities in the Southern Anthracite Region, 1870–1930

Southern Rim	Population (1870)	Growth Rate by Decade						Population (1930)
		1880	1890	1900	1910	1920	1930	
Pottsville	12,384	7%	6%	11%	29%	8%	11%	24,300
Tamaqua	5,960	-4	6	17	3	31	5	12,363
St. Clair	5,726	-28	-11	21	39	1	12	7,296
Minersville	3,690	-12	8	37	50	8	19	9,392
Schuylkill Haven	2,946	4	1	18	30	15	19	6,514
Port Carbon	2,251	4	-18	10	23	8	12	3,225
Palo Alto	1,740	-9	-10	2	10	-11	14	1,908
New Philadelphia	558	-35	56	135	89	1	1	2,557
Middleport	377	-39	6	42	104	-11	24	1,225
Mount Carbon	364	-10	1	-24	32	-1	-6	311
Northern Rim								
Ashland	5,714	6%	21%	-12%	7%	-2%	8%	7,164
Mahanoy City	5,533	30	57	20	18	-2	-5	14,784
Shenandoah	2,951	244	57	55	4	-21	7	21,782
Shamokin	2,282	258	76	26	7	8	-4	20,274
Mt. Carmel	1,289	84	248	60	33	-1	3	17,962
Frackville	1,707*	—	48	3	20	79	44	8,037
Girardville	2,730†	—	31	2	20	2	9	4,891

*Figure indicates population in 1880, when Frackville was incorporated as a borough.
†Figure indicates population in 1880, when Girardville was incorporated as a borough.

through 1900, but corporate leaders from Philadelphia controlled the economic destinies of elites in this section. They too became solely dependent on the exploitation of coal for survival. None of the elites in these communities had sufficient resources to sustain independent growth through diversification. These leaders actually faced the same long-term problems as those in the southern rim, despite the appearance of rapid industrial and population growth. The elites in the developing cities of Mahanoy City, Shenandoah, and Shamokin had not established economic activities of sufficient productivity to generate large amounts of capital. Moreover, the depression of the 1870s caused the failure of major commercial banks in Shenandoah, Shamokin, and Mahanoy City. These bankruptcies resulted in the loss of almost $1,000,000 in investment capital to the leadership groups in this section.[46]

The depression also crippled entrepreneurs in the northern rim and Northumberland County. Leaders in Shamokin, Shenandoah, Mahanoy City, and Ashland lost hundreds of thousands of dollars through bankruptcies. Admittedly, capital and talent did flow northward from the cities and towns in the southern rim; but they were not sufficient to reverse the economic trends in the northern rim nor in Northumberland County. The elites in these emerging communities had neither the resources nor the internal cohesiveness to cope with the PRRCO and the marketing pressures which forced it to take control of the anthracite industry. Later, as other Philadelphia entrepreneurs and their companies absorbed service and utility operations, these leadership groups no longer had the capacity to resist. Growth would come within the parameters of the anthracite industry, as it had in the past; but entrepreneurs and corporate leaders outside the region would make key decisions. Moreover, these men retained a narrow range of investment and transferred all other profits to economic activities and communities beyond the coalfields.[47]

This penetration of the local economies by Philadelphia entrepreneurs and company executives destroyed any basis for sustained growth in the northern rim and Northumberland County. The rapid population growth during the years between 1870 and 1890 resembled the explosive development of the southern rim from 1826 through the early 1850s. Like these communities, those to the north did not have the economic base necessary to maintain this fast rate of development. By the early twentieth century, the growth rates in almost every city and town had begun to decline. Shenandoah dropped from 55 percent in the 1890s to 4 percent during the next ten years and actually lost 21 percent of its population in the following decade. With the exception of Frackville, every community in Table 7-7 reflected the downward trend. None of these cities exceeded 21,000 by 1920, nor would any surpass 25,000 by the end of the decade. Therefore, the potential for full-scale economic development and regional hegemony comparable to that sustained by Wilkes-Barre's upper class was limited for the communities of the northern rim after 1870, as it was for Pottsville's leadership and the elites in the communities in the southern rim.[48]

Philadelphia's corporate leaders, entrepreneurs, and their companies now provided the cohesion for the entire region. Pottsville's elite, whose members had created an integrated urban order for the southern rim, now found itself in one of several medium-sized cities. Its economic strength in Northumberland County, comparatively weak before the 1870s, was now nonexistent. The uniform penetration of the regional economy by Philadelphia's interests severely limited the autonomy of the coalfields (Table 7-8). Through its takeover of the main economic activities, Philadelphia's corporate leaders in the PRRCO and other companies had significantly weakened the economic power of Pottsville's elite, the only leadership group capable of dominating even a portion of the southern coalfields. Pottsville, Shenandoah, Shamokin, and Mahanoy City emerged as the largest cities by the late 1890s, yet none of their elites could dominate the region. Instead, PRRCO executives and other Philadelphia capitalists integrated the communities of the southern coalfields through consolidation of all main industries, the traction companies, and, eventually, the public utilities. In an effort to stabilize the anthracite industry, the PRRCO corporate leaders reduced the autonomy of urban leaders in the region.

These changes disrupted elites throughout the region. Weakened by the depression and undercut by the PRRCO, these men saw opportunities shrink dramatically by the turn of the century. As a result, leaders and their families were often unable to maintain their positions in local society. By 1930, only 36 percent of the prominent nineteenth-century families in the southern rim had male members in positions of power. The proportional difference was even greater in the northern section, where 70 percent of the nineteenth-century leaders and their families did not perpetuate their status into the twentieth century. Philadelphia corporate leaders now controlled the main economic activities which ultimately sustained even urban leaders in the regional communities.[49]

Pottsville's elite, the most powerful before 1870, experienced the same consequences as the other elites. It lost over 10 percent of its members even before the end of the 1880s, with many children of the families who remained joining the exodus during the 1890s. Information on 192 offspring of the nineteenth-century Pottsville elite demonstrates that only 33 percent of these children remained in the community by 1900. The majority—51 percent—migrated out of the coalfields entirely, while a smaller proportion—16 percent—moved to other communities in the region. This persistence rate was even lower for nineteenth-century elite families. Only 30 percent remained by the 1920s and still held economic power. Their institutions also did not last into the twentieth century. The churches remained; but the clubs, lodges, economic institutions, and political institutions had long since vanished or had been displaced by newer organizations, which drew leading members of the community. Of these groups, the Pottsville Club and the Schuylkill Country Club were the most popular. Yet, 20 percent to 25 percent of the members and officers in the years after their founding were descended from the nineteenth-century elite families as late as the 1930s.[50]

Table 7-8. Elite Enterprises in the Southern Anthracite Region in 1870, Absorbed by Outside Sources or Bankrupt before 1890*

				Economic Activity			
Sources of Control in 1890(%)	Coal Enterprises	Coal-Related Enterprises	Railroads	Banks	Service/Utility Companies	Traction Companies	Insurance Companies
Absorbed by PRRCO and PRC&ICO	100%	35%	100%	0%	0%	0%	0%
Absorbed by other outside sources	0	12	0	0	0	100	0
Bankrupted by depression	0	6	0	39	0	0	14
Controlled by elites in region	0	47	0	61	100	0	86
Total	100%	100%	100%	100%	100%	100%	100%
n = 149	(60)	(17)	(4)	(33)	(25)	(4)	(6)

*The enterprises represented in this table are not among those controlled by the Pottsville elite.

By 1930, such prominent families as the Shippens, Donaldsons, Wetherills, Haywoods, Babers, and Derrs no longer had members among the elite ranks of Pottsville. Some nineteenth-century families weathered the hard times of the seventies and eighties and survived the fluctuating regional economy into the twentieth century but lost all visible power. The Drumhellers provide a case in point. Members of this family had been community leaders since the 1850s; they were among the wealthiest residents during the 1870s. By the 1930s, the one surviving member, David Drumheller, was a salesman for the Pottsville Supply Company. In contrast, members of the Atkinses, Kaerchers, Mortimers, Ulmers, Yuenglings, and Luthers had maintained their positions as economic leaders in the city. These men ran their own manufacturing enterprises or sat on the local bank boards, institutions that still generated considerable power within the city. Still, such men were few in number and no longer the dominant group in the city.[51]

Pottsville leaders also reallocated their capital to accommodate the economic realities of the post-1885 years. Reduced to a subordinate position and ruled largely through the PRRCO, community leaders had few choices available to them. In the early eighties, local journalists who recognized that Pottsville would never become a major industrial center urged its economic leaders to concentrate their efforts on transforming the community into a commercial center. In fact, this was one of the very few options open to the elite. By the late eighties, Pottsville's leaders had shifted their remaining capital into textile plants, boot and shoe factories, small electric companies, publishing operations, and hat and cap companies. These became the heart of Pottsville's rebuilt economy. Few, however, lasted into the 1920s. By that decade, hosiery and knitting mills, broom works, a box-producing plant, a candy-manufacturing company, and a new utility company had replaced the older operations. Textiles were still present, but these were now owned by outside concerns. The financial institutions had also undergone a transformation. Most had closed, and those that survived fed into a much smaller local economy, with few ties to other parts of the region. Small savings and loan associations, which handled the banking needs of the largely blue-collar and white-collar clerical population, now dominated the financial landscape.[52]

The populations of Pottsville and several other communities in the southern rim did experience a growth period in the early part of the twentieth century, but this expansion in the southern rim resulted from increased coal production financed by the PRRCO and merely reflected the area's dependence. Pottsville, once the only city in the region with a population larger than 10,000, was now just one of five such communities. Moreover, it constituted only 21 percent of the urban population in mining communities with populations greater than 10,000. Its two closest rivals, Shenandoah and Shamokin, combined, made up 37 percent of this population, considerably more than Pottsville's proportion. After 1930, Pottsville and the entire region faced five decades of uninterrupted decline and economic deterioration. Long before leadership groups in Wilkes-

Barre and the Wyoming Valley had become tied to outside agencies, the elites in the cities and towns in the southern region had become subordinate to corporate leaders and their companies in the metropolitan centers. The metropolitan elite disrupted the elites in the southern anthracite region, unlike Wilkes-Barre's upper class, which co-opted its competition. Yet the results were similar. The gradual dissolution of elites in the northern coal region resembled the breakup of leadership groups in the Schuylkill-Northumberland coalfields, while cities in the Wyoming Valley—Pittston, Kingston, and Plymouth—approximated the population sizes of comparable communities in the southern coalfields.

CHAPTER VIII

Urban Leadership in the Industrializing Region, 1800–1930

UNDAMENTAL DIFFERENCES in the formation and evolution of the urban leadership groups account for the persistence of Wilkes-Barre's upper class and the dispersal of Pottsville's elite. In Wilkes-Barre, an incipient upper class, whose roots stretched back to the eighteenth century, was fairly well developed as the city began to industrialize. Its members had already created a strong set of familial, cultural, and social institutions by 1850; and these proved remarkably durable in sustaining the cohesiveness of the upper class throughout the remainder of the nineteenth century. Sharing similar social traits and ancestral backgrounds, the upper-class leaders also developed common economic objectives and institutions, a process that was reinforced by widespread cooperation among these men in their entrepreneurial activities. Participation in banks, coal companies, land ventures, and coal-related activities brought together men who engaged in an intense and close social interaction and whose families were joined through blood and marriage. As a result, the members of the upper class remained committed to the city and the region.

In Pottsville, on the other hand, the elite developed as the city industrialized, largely on the efforts of its leaders. These men were usually new to the city and the region and, therefore, rather unfamiliar with their colleagues in the exercise of economic power. Drawn from families of diverse social, ethnic, and economic backgrounds, these men also shared little by the way of cultural heritage, rearing patterns, or institutional participation. They relied primarily on their similar occupational experiences and shared entrepreneurial activities to sustain the cohesiveness of the elite. Without a long-term identification with the city, Pottsville's leaders often pursued varied and conflicting entrepreneurial strategies. These men engaged in small-scale operations and one- or two-man entrepreneurial activities. Frequently, they worked for outside-based companies and occasionally left the city for a period of months or years to pursue economic activities elsewhere. When active and powerful within the city, members of the elite also engaged in numerous operations outside. They joined in building and/ or directing a system of short lateral railroads within the region. The members of the elite opened up new coal veins in the region and set up coal-related industries in numerous communities throughout the coalfields. Whether in the community or the region, these activities brought the men of the Pottsville elite together in business and social interaction.

Activities beyond the community were important in the rising or falling fortunes of these two leadership groups. In Wilkes-Barre, such operations facilitated a sustained expansion of the economic power of the upper class. In regional expansion as well as within their city, the Wilkes-Barre upper class relied on a combination of social, familial, and cultural ties, on the one hand, and economic on the other, to maintain the growing power of their group. Wilkes-Barre's upper class had built a series of familial, social, cultural, and economic institutions that drew from community elites all over the region. This participation was crucial in making Wilkes-Barre the hub of regional society in the northern anthracite fields. It oriented the leadership groups in the Wyoming Valley and hinterland toward Wilkes-Barre. It was also instrumental in transferring capital, talent, and power to Wilkes-Barre's upper class, all of which added to the prosperity of its members and secured their commitment to the city.

The upper-class leaders in Wilkes-Barre also relied heavily on the city's economic institutions, particularly the coal companies, to extend its power throughout the region. Through these institutions, Wilkes-Barre's upper-class members were able to gain at least partial and, frequently, total control of mining operations in the region. This consolidation of power extended into other regionwide activities, such as traction, utilities, and communications. Those in the upper class also established the most powerful banking houses in the northern coalfields, a feat that made the city the financial capital of the region. In addition, members of the upper class built up the largest coal-related companies in the Valley. These provided additional sources of profit and labor and thus promoted the upper class's economic power. Men in the upper class also used their institutions to acquire control over the region's critical resources of land and coal, assets vital in securing the upper class's power in the anthracite industry and real estate markets. Together, the social and economic power of the upper class made it the most powerful leadership group in the region and its city the focus of economic and entrepreneurial activity among the urban upper strata throughout the northern coalfields.

Through this power, Wilkes-Barre's upper class also co-opted urban elites throughout the region and drew their members into the social and economic world of the city's leadership. The ties fashioned by Wilkes-Barre's leaders sustained their interaction with outsiders. The regional orientation of the upper-class institutions eroded the integrity of the clubs, churches, lodges, and economic institutions that formed the basis of regional elites. Through migration, this process moved considerable economic power into Wilkes-Barre. The leaders who moved to Wilkes-Barre from Plymouth, Kingston, or Pittston continued to exploit the resources and economic opportunities of their native communities; but they did this as Wilkes-Barreans, and as members of its upper class. They also maintained series of familial, economic, and informal ties with those leaders who remained in their original homes. Such ties strengthened the lines of communication between the expanding upper class of Wilkes-Barre and the elites in the Valley and the hinterland. They also facilitated penetration of the local economies in the coalfields by other members of the upper class, thereby augmenting its power.

The upper class used these relationships to strengthen and augment its fortunes at the expense of other leadership groups in the region. An understanding of the extralocal ties with the members of these elites and their communities is central to understanding the growing power of the upper class and its persistence. The economic influence and prosperity derived from these ties only further anchored the members of the upper class to Wilkes-Barre. At the same time, the movement of resources from other leadership groups into Wilkes-Barre's upper class only further eroded the autonomy of entrepreneurs in these elites. These men saw Wilkes-Barre's upper class as the only viable alternative to leaving the region. As potential members of the upper class, members of these elites would have access to financial and economic opportunities and capital not present in their cities and towns; this access would enable them to maintain their own power. The upper class, then, consolidated the power of various leadership groups throughout the region.

Members of the upper class were able to use this consolidated power to maintain an important measure of local control into the twentieth century, when leaders from metropolitan-based corporations began to exert significant influence over the northern coalfields. Confronted by these corporate leaders from New York City and Philadelphia, members of the Wilkes-Barre upper class found themselves in a position similar to that of urban elites in the Wyoming Valley and hinterland during the nineteenth century, when members of those groups had been forced to cope with Wilkes-Barre's upper class. The center of power was beginning to shift out of the region and into the metropolitan centers by the 1920s. In response, those in the upper class began to transfer their investments to corporations in New York and Philadelphia, where they served on the boards of major coal companies, anthracite railroads, and service and utility corporations. Yet the power base of the upper class still remained in anthracite coal and the Wyoming Valley. In addition to these economic ties, members of the Wilkes-Barre upper class developed a series of familial and social ties with leaders in these major cities in much the same fashion as leaders in the smaller communities of the Wyoming Valley had with Wilkes-Barre's upper class in the last century. These associations oriented the city's upper class away from the region and toward the metropolitan centers. The upper class maintained its cosmopolitan perspective, but in the twentieth century it focused on power centers outside the Wyoming Valley. This shift is reflective of general changes that occurred throughout the nonmetropolitan leadership groups in the northeast and elsewhere in the country. From Wheeling, West Virginia, to Youngstown, Ohio, urban leaders were increasingly drawn into a larger network of economic and cultural associations, the consequences of which have only been suggested to this point. Still, these changes underscore the importance of understanding the character of extralocal ties, whether within the region or with agencies outside it.

This shift toward the outside and the increasing specialization in economic activities beyond the region had an important impact on the leadership structure in the Valley. The changes created the need for a new group of leaders, both in Wilkes-Barre and throughout the region, who could meet the needs of growing ethnic populations. These new elites, including the one in Wilkes-Barre, drew their members from immigrant groups very different in character from the twentieth-century upper class of Wilkes-Barre. These men were often Catholic, Jewish, Baptist, or Methodist. They came from Irish, German, Polish, Russian, and other ethnic groups whose members had little in common with those in the upper class. The elite members filled in at the secondary and tertiary levels of the regional economy, where profits were marginal, business small-scale, and power was much diminished. These leaders had none of the power of their upper-class colleagues; nor did they have such an array of contacts with large-scale systems. The elite in Wilkes-Barre capitalized on the locational advantages inherent in the city by the 1920s, and this elite became central in an emerging network of extralocal ties among the new elites in the Valley. This extralocal dimension remained a critical feature of leadership, despite the massive changes of the twentieth century, and the network demonstrates the continuing importance of associations beyond the community, regardless of the type of leadership or the time period. The technological innovations of the post-1920 period serve to accentuate their importance.

The development of elites in the southern coalfields contrasts sharply with the evolution of leadership groups in the northern anthracite region. Its leaders capitalized on the economic boom that followed to secure locational advantage by extending the canal to Pottsville and, by the 1850s, making that city the county seat, despite opposition from elites in the older communities such as Mount Carbon and Orwigsburg. The growth and prosperity of Pottsville's elite derived from the network of economic and entrepreneurial ties with urban elites and their communities throughout the southern coalfields.

By the 1870s, Pottsville's elite was the best-organized leadership group in the region. Its members had created strong financial institutions that made the city the banking hub of the developing region. These men had also become the major coal operators and iron and steel producers within the coalfields, with assets unmatched by other leadership groups in the region. Although an economic elite, the city's leaders had begun to establish exclusive clubs and lodges and even started to produce a second generation of leaders. The Pottsville leaders used their economic power, augmented by the largest capital base in the region, to build a series of entrepreneurial, financial, and economic ties that spanned the region. Pottsville relied more on these ties than on social or familial ones, a reflection of the nature of its elite.

Neither the city's elite nor the region was fully matured by the late nineteenth century. The elite was just beginning to stabilize, and its social and cultural institutions were still in the process of development by the seventies. The members of the elite were still divided along ethnic and religious lines and participated in the institutions of their cultural groups, even tending to choose their wives on the basis of their ethnocultural orientation. The evolution of Pottsville's leadership was in sharp contrast to that of Wilkes-Barre's upper class, whose members shared a common background and who had developed a strong set of social, cultural, familial, and economic institutions before industrialization.

The region, even as late as the 1870s, was still in the process of development. Its core was located in the southern rim of the coalfields. The communities in the other two sections—the northern rim and Northumberland County—were only in the first stages of growth by that decade; therefore, their resources were not fully exploited, and their potential was untapped. As a result, Pottsville's network of economic, entrepreneurial, and financial ties were still concentrated in the southern rim. Its leaders were just beginning to move into the other two sections by the seventies. However, they encountered stiff competition from outside sources, who kept the presence of Pottsville's elite to a minimum, particularly in Northumberland County, where Philadelphia, Reading, and other southeastern Pennsylvania–based companies had moved in rapidly to capitalize on the rich anthracite reserves.

Neither the economic base of Pottsville's elite nor its network of extralocal ties survived the strains of the depression of the seventies or the intrusion of the Philadelphia and Reading Railroad Corporation (PRRCO) intact. Together, these economic reverses disrupted the city's network and led to the dispersal of its elites. The depression undermined the elite's financial position in the region, while the PRRCO took control of its coal and coal-related operations throughout the city and the region. The few coal-related activities of the elite that survived as independent activities in Pottsville folded within fifteen years because of business losses and poor management. These reverses also crippled many of Pottsville's entrepreneurs. The activities of these men formed the basis of the city's economy and its network of extralocal ties. Bankruptcies, business failures, and capital losses undermined the elite and severely curtailed its power throughout the region. Combined, these losses cut the city's elite off from its mining collieries, lumber operations, iron-producing plants, other coal-related activities, and mercantile outlets, which had been the sources of Pottsville's economic power in the region, critical to its continued rapid growth. By 1890, the elite had become a satellite of Philadelphia, whose corporate leadership had taken over virtually all of the elite's main economic activities and significantly reduced the autonomy of Pottsville's leadership.

These reverses also crippled elites in other communities in the southern rim where the Pottsville elite had the majority of its investments. These investments had sustained growth in smaller cities and towns, as they had also helped sustain the prosperity of their leadership groups. The severing of these ties therefore undercut the growth of these communities and the prosperity of their leaders, who were tied to Pottsville's elite and had a considerable stake in its survival. Pottsville's elite had begun to build a network of extralocal ties, but it cracked under these strains; and the leadership groups and their cities and towns in this section now came under the complete control of members of Philadelphia's corporate leadership.

The diverse entrepreneurial strategies of the Pottsville elite made the city leadership vulnerable to the power of Philadelphia's corporations and the depression of the seventies. Members of the Pottsville elite did not opt for the strategy of the incorporated coal and coal-related companies, as had Wilkes-Barre's upper class, nor for the large-scale manufacturing companies, as had Scranton's elite. Built on successful iron and steel operations of the Scranton family and its relatives, Scranton became the largest city in northeastern Pennsylvania. The members of its elite, like Pottsville's leadership, came from diverse ethnocultural and socioeconomic backgrounds. Their entrepreneurial strategy, however, yielded greater results and sustained the city's growth during the 1900s and into the twentieth century. The elite fared less well. It lacked the strong social and familial institutions and the dedication to sustaining its power that Wilkes-Barre's upper class had. As a result, most of its prominent families were gone by the 1920s or no longer major economic leaders. Pottsville's elite, with neither the enduring social and kinship basis of the upper class nor the large-scale strategy of Scranton's elite, did not persist; nor did it build a flourishing urban economy that would survive the demise of Pottsville's leadership group. Committed to small-scale operations run independently or through partnerships, Pottsville's elite never effectively capitalized on its resources nor maintained its power.

The decision of the PRRCO and Philadelphia company executives to take control of mining, commercial, manufacturing, and service companies removed local control over industry and shifted power to the metropolitan leadership in Philadelphia. This decision also reduced the scope of entrepreneurial activities for urban leaders throughout the region and undermined the autonomy these men experienced before the 1870s. Pottsville's elite and leadership groups in neighboring cities and towns of the southern rim faced the decline of their numbers and the erosion of their economic power. Indeed, decisions made by corporate leaders in Philadelphia now set the parameters for all elites in the Schuylkill-Northumberland coalfields. By the end of the nineteenth century, the region had become a colony of Philadelphia's corporate leadership, the autonomy of its urban elites severely limited.

The persistence of urban leadership derived in part from its economic strategies. It also depended on the durability of its economic and social, familial and cultural institutions, and their strength beyond the community. In both regions, this combination of internal cohesiveness and economic and social influence throughout the region determined, in large measure, the evolution of urban leadership. The change in the basis of leadership in the smaller communities of the Wyoming Valley was intimately tied to the participation of their elites in the regional networks centered in Wilkes-Barre. The long-term stability of these elites was clearly disrupted as a result of the intrusion of the upper class into the social and familial world of leaders in other communities of the Valley. To a great extent, the institutions and kinship system of the upper class shaped a myriad of decisions concerning marriages, investments, church affiliations, club memberships, and business partnerships. These irrevocably tied the elites to Wilkes-Barre's upper class and ultimately undermined the institutions and cohesiveness of the leadership groups outside Wilkes-Barre. The locally oriented institutions of the elites in the smaller communities collapsed under pressure from the regional institutions and kinship system of Wilkes-Barre's upper class. Only at this point were men from other social and economic backgrounds able to assume leadership status within these communities. Their power, however, was clearly inferior to that of their predecessors; and they were subordinate to the upper class.

Similarly, the continuity of Wilkes-Barre's upper class was also a product of participation in regional networks. On first sight, Wilkes-Barre's nineteenth-century upper class appears to resemble the traditional leadership that scholars have argued preserved the sense of community and stability in a rapidly changing economic world. New England in origin, Episcopal or Presbyterian in religious affiliation, and bound by the ties of family, Wilkes-Barre's leadership certainly suggests stereotypical images of the proper upper class. Yet the images are deceiving. The upper class was at the center of a series of dynamic social, familial, and economic networks that triggered and sustained economic growth, long-term social change, and an integrated urban system. Participation in these networks encouraged migration to Wilkes-Barre and facilitated assimilation into the upper class, at the same time preserving the leaders' ethnic and cultural character. Newcomers from communities in the region or even from outside failed to compete as power groups or to disrupt the equilibrium because of Wilkes-Barre's control of the broader regional networks and ability to recruit selectively. Wilkes-Barre's upper class grew at the expense of these other leadership groups.

In the twentieth century, Wilkes-Barre's upper class began to interact with corporate leadership in the metropolitan centers of New York City and Philadelphia. The process whereby elites in the Wyoming Valley and its hinterland linked into Wilkes-Barre during the nineteenth century was now being duplicated on a higher level, as power moved to the metropolitan centers. The city's upper-class leaders increasingly tied their fortunes to corporations and other investments in New York City and Philadelphia and, as a result, began to develop social, institutional, and even familial ties with leadership groups in these metropolitan centers. Members of the upper class still relied on the anthracite industry for their power, however, and remained in the Valley into the 1930s.

In the southern anthracite region, the dispersal of urban elites also occurred during the late nineteenth century and into the twentieth century, as it had in the leadership groups outside Wilkes-Barre in the north. The basis of the elites in Schuylkill and Northumberland counties was economic, and the reversals of the seventies and eighties unhinged the loyalty of their members and precipitated a steady out-migration or downward mobility of these men and their families that continued into the twentieth century. Bankruptcy, business failures, and loss of control over key industries undermined the power of leaders from Pottsville, Tamaqua, and Schuylkill Haven and compelled many of these men and/or their male heirs to leave the region between 1880 and 1930. In the communities of the northern rim and Northumberland County, growth continued through 1900, but the range of entrepreneurial activity narrowed as Philadelphia corporations colonized these areas. After 1900, growth slowed and out-migration increased as economic decisions made in Philadelphia adversely affected the local economies of Shenandoah, Mahanoy City, and other communities in these sections. Loyalty based on prosperity and rapid growth severely weakened during the late nineteenth and early twentieth centuries. As a result, the integrity of nineteenth-century elites was eroded throughout the region, and none of these groups persisted intact through the 1920s. In both the northern and southern coalfields, the regional network was the key to understanding the process of social change.

Description of Sources

LOCAL HISTORIES AND BIBLIOGRAPHIC COLLECTIONS

City and County Histories

Over the last decade and a half, city and county histories have taken on new importance in historical research as valuable sources for scholars studying the relationship between process and structure. For the most part, however, these local histories have been secondary to manuscript censuses, tax records, and other sources covering all residents in a community. City and county histories, on the other hand, are biased toward the more stable elements in the community and toward the upper levels of society. As a result, they have only limited usefulness in the study of the community. Yet this limitation offers considerable potential for the study of leadership and its social and economic basis.

City and county histories and their extensive biographical addenda are actually histories of urban leadership. They were usually written by or compiled from local leaders who had an intimate knowledge of their families, their colleagues, and their community. These men also had a stake in advertising the achievements and social characteristics of their fellow leaders to demonstrate their preeminence in the community. Consequently, the local histories contain an inordinate amount of data on the individual and the family, often extending back three or more generations. Despite their breadth of information, rarely have these sources been exploited in the study of local elites.

In the early stages of my research, I noted that the city and the county histories differ significantly, with the latter containing a short description of every community in the county, regardless of size; rural communities and their leaders, generally grouped by township, are included; and these brief descriptions cover the major institutions and a few of the more prominent men in the community. The authors of these volumes give greater attention to community fathers, to men who run the city's institutions and local organizations such as clubs and lodges. The authors list all the economic activities of any importance, the directors and officers of local companies, and private clubs and associations. While the city histories contain more information, they are available for only a limited number of cities. The county histories were vital in collecting data on leadership whose communities left no comparable records. All of these data are critical for the analysis of leadership, since members of leadership groups tend to dominate these economic and social institutions and organizations.

In addition to the information in the texts, both the city and county histories have biographical addenda. These generally number between one and four volumes, each 400 to 600 pages. The number and length depend on the size and importance of the community or county. The biographies contain very detailed information on the life history of the individual and his family, including spouse, brothers, sisters, and children. Often, these sketches extend back two or more generations. The data touch on all the processes such as migration, geographic mobility, and the formation of family networks as these affect the individual.

The city and county histories are vital in analyzing three dimensions of urban leadership. First, the main text and the biographical sketches of the individual and the family record all the person's economic, social, political, and familial associations and provide the basis for a systematic description of internal class structure. Second, the histories in the addenda have considerable information on the broader social, economic, and kinship networks in which leaders operated, both in and beyond the community. These extracommunity ties usually provided the basis for the urban system and for the interaction among urban elites that gave the system its cohesiveness. The data show that urban leaders were deeply involved in these networks, and the nature of that interaction often shaped the patterns of urban growth and dominance-subordination in an urban system. Last, the publication of these sources, from the late nineteenth century through the 1920s, when many industrial communities had matured, enables the historian to examine long-term social change in the nature of leadership. These three facets of leadership were the core of the research on leadership and regional urban growth.

In researching this topic, I found the need for information on class structure. The city and county history provide invaluable data on family, migration, the social characteristics of the leaders, and their institutional and economic affiliations. The information in the biographical volumes is particularly useful for the study of family ties. The brief histories list the marriages of all the leaders and members of their families, as well as similar information on the spouses' families. In my own study, the genealogical data on marriages in the previous generations were also critical in connecting the prominent families in the city in the late nineteenth century. These descriptions noted the marriages of all the children, making it possible to see whether the offspring also continued to marry within the group or at least to marry into families of comparable status elsewhere.

The city and county histories were also useful in analyzing the migration and occupational patterns among urban leaders. The biographical sketches in the addenda contain the birthplace of the leaders and every change of residence throughout their lives. The sketches include the date of each move and the birthdate of each leader, making it possible to gauge the timing of this migration. Along with the record of each move, the sketches also detail occupational change, if any occurred. In combination, these data make it possible to study migration and occupational mobility.

The social and institutional basis of leadership constitutes an important element to the understanding of urban elites. The local histories and their biographical addenda probably have the most information on these characteristics of urban leaders. The biographical sketches include the national origin, religious and church affiliation, and educational background of almost all community leaders. The biographies, in addition, list the club and lodge memberships and associations with philanthropic groups, such as the YMCA. This information enables the historian to detail the ethnocultural characteristics of urban leadership and systematically compare the social basis of urban elites. The evidence of institutional ties demonstrates the extent to which members of a leadership group participated in a common set of institutions and indicates the degree of cohesiveness among a community's leaders.

The economic and political data in the city and county histories are as valuable in outlining the dimensions of the local power structure as the social and institutional information. The main texts of the local histories inevitably list all the directors and officers in local companies at the time of publication, while the biographical sketches record similar positions of economic power held by the individual leaders. This information is repeated for public and party officeholders. Both types of data have proven effective in establishing a positional definition of leadership, particularly when wealth figures are not available. These data can be combined with the information on family ties to learn whether kinship played a major role in economic development and power.

The city and county histories probably are among the best sources to contain complete data on the broader social, familial, and economic networks that extended beyond the community, the least explored of all dimensions of urban leadership. Piecing together these networks requires combining various types of information on migration, family, economic activities, and marriage. In communities where migrants constitute a majority of the leaders, the city and/or county history generally has information on ties with the native cities or towns. Those who migrated from within the urban system tended to maintain some social and most economic ties with their native communities, as opposed to the migrants from outside the region, who apparently kept few active associations with their last places of residence. The migrants from urban centers in the region also had kinship ties extending beyond their immediate families which served as the basis for interaction with colleagues in their new cities and those in their native towns. An investigation of marriage selection by leaders provides another means to trace extralocal ties. Leaders who married outside the community but within the region often selected mates from families of comparable status in neighboring cities and towns. These ties frequently served as the basis for economic cooperations between husbands and fathers-in-law. Leaders also maintained social and economic associations with elites in other communities. These ranged from club and church memberships to directorships in major companies and mercantile activities, and the sketches in the biographical addenda always list these associations. Moreover, since these sources extend back for at least two generations, it is possible to investigate the strength and persistence of extralocal ties.

While these local histories are useful tools for analysis of urban leadership in the nineteenth century, local histories also exist for the twentieth century. Publication of the local histories first occurred between 1875 and roughly 1900; a second group appeared between 1915 and 1929. The availability of these sources for two different time periods enables the historian to examine the long-term impact of mobility, assimilation, and communication on urban leadership. The local histories of the twentieth century contain the same type of information on a far greater scale, since the numbers of leaders had increased considerably by the 1920s, along with the size of most communities. Therefore, it is possible to reconstruct the basis of leadership with the same thoroughness and accuracy as for the nineteenth century, as well as to make systematic comparisons of leadership at two widely separated points in time.

In summary, the city and county histories provide the historian with considerable data for the analysis of the social composition and long-term social change in urban leadership. With these sources, the historian can study several different types of leadership, make systematic comparisons, and learn which types of leadership are associated with different economic bases and patterns of economic development. Leadership clearly varied from community to community and from region to region. The data in these local histories also make it possible to define an urban system and to pinpoint the variety of social, economic, and institutional ties that give the system its cohesiveness. The nature of interaction among urban elites may vary widely from region to region, particularly since regional economic development and urban leadership demonstrate such vastly different patterns. The interaction among urban elites in these networks is a critical determinant of urban growth and hegemony. Last, the city and county histories give insight into the nature of long-term social and organizational change in urban leadership. To a significant extent, the information in the city and county history can increase our understanding of the relationship between structure and process.

Other Local Histories and Biographical Collections

Entrepreneurs, particularly in the southern anthracite region, published articles on methods of coal mining and descriptions of the early stages of the coal industry and its development into the late nineteenth century. These appeared in the journals of the local historical societies. In the same journals, members of leadership groups also wrote descriptions of local institutions, such as the churches, academies, and clubs. These were useful in reconstructing the patterns of social interaction among urban leaders and in dating the emergence of leadership groups.

On occasion, biographical collections of legislative districts and of northeastern or eastern Pennsylvania were also available. These ranged between 400 and 800 pages in length and contained biographical data comparable to the city and county histories. They were generally published later in the nineteenth century or in the 1920s, and they updated earlier works. In the twentieth century, they also supplemented city and county histories. These histories provided data on occupational changes and geographic moves, as well as familial ties.

Family histories were rarer but quite useful in linking prominent men in a community. They also extend back to the eighteenth century or earlier. Of that material, I generally relied only on the data closest to the year 1790.

CONTEMPORARY PUBLICATIONS

These sources generally concentrated on economic data. Material focusing on the mining industry gave solid descriptions of coal-mining techniques, the evolution of the industry, the influence of companies outside the region, and the development of anthracite-related industries. They contained the amount of coal production by region, the destination of the anthracite once it left the coalfields, and occasionally the coal mined by operators and companies in the regions. Equally important, these sources included detailed descriptions of the physical environment in each region and pictures of the communities, the coal mines, the rivers and streams, and the business districts of the larger cities in each region.

The data on finance, utilities, and transit were also fairly detailed. The descriptions of the financial institutions included short histories of the banks, banking houses, savings and loan associations, and mortgage companies. These accounts contained discussions of the financial status of these institutions, their founders, and current directors and officers. In my study, these data were essential to the reconstruction of the financial community, its leaders, and ties to other industries. The accounts of the utility and transit industries contained similar kinds of information, as well as descriptions of their operations and the physical extent of their activities.

The Moody and Poor reports covered a variety of industries, from utilities and anthracite to railroads and manufacturing. All but one of these reports were published after 1900. They contained data on the major companies in each region, including financial histories, analyses of the firms' current market conditions, lists of their officers and directors and their residences, and, last, their area of operations.

Last, company and bank histories were particularly useful in gathering data on the economic base of the region and biographical information on the industrial leaders. These accounts covered the complete history of the institution, from its creation to the date of publication. These sources included biographies of most incorporators, directors, and officers active in the institution's development. As important, the histories noted company or bank expansions, financial changes, and absorption of competing enterprises.

GOVERNMENT PUBLICATIONS

These sources contained economic and population data. The federal census report listed populations of the communities and the counties studied, from the mid-nineteenth century through 1940. For this study, these records were essential in tracing shifts in population within a region.

State reports were similarly invaluable in studying the economic evolution of the coal regions. The *Digest of Corporations, 1700–1866* noted all companies and banks incorporated under state law in the nineteenth century up to 1866, a fact that greatly facilitated use of the state laws of Pennsylvania. The volumes listing the state laws contained the acts of incorporation for companies, banks, and communities in the state. Up to 1875, the acts specified the incorporators, the amount of capitalization, the area of operation, and the year of incorporation. After that date, the laws simply stated the year of incorporation, the amount of capitalization, and the name of the company. The laws also noted changes in the company subsequent to 1875.

The annual reports of the secretary of internal affairs, the Bureau of Mines, and the State Banking Commission covered all types of economic activity in the regions. The number and types of mines, companies, and banks, as well as financial institutions, were included. The reports specified the area of operation, the amount of production, the number of men employed, and the current capitalization. The banking reports listed the officers of the bank, its financial picture, and its location. The last source of importance to me was the industrial directory of Pennsylvania, which was published from 1914 through the 1920s. It contained the lists of every economic operation by county, number employed, the headquarters of the company and its area of operation, the amount of productivity, and a brief history of the county.

CITY DIRECTORIES

Directories were available for the larger communities. They occasionally included lists of residents in nearby communities and business directories of most of the cities and towns in the region. The directories were vital in locating the residences of the members of the leadership groups, the location of their institutions, and their occupations. The business directories and yellow pages enabled me to check the distribution of economic activities, the directors and officers, the amount of capitalization, the products, and the potential markets (with the exception of the distribution of economic activities, these were listed only in the yellow pages). The directories also contained lists of all the clubs, lodges, banks, companies, churches, and other organizations in the community. Officers, ministers, and occasionally directors of companies and banks were included in these lists. The city directories facilitated my examination of persistence, geographic and occupational mobility among urban leaders, and the extent to which kin resided with their families. Last, the directories were the primary source used to reconstruct the neighborhoods of the urban leaders.

NEWSPAPERS AND ALMANACS

These proved to be rich sources of economic and social data. Their continuous run for most of the period under consideration made it possible to gather similar kinds of data for several decades. The newspapers listed the names of directors, officers, owners of local enterprises, and the law and business partners active in the community or region. The papers also contained the election of new company or bank officers and directors, changes in business partnerships, or the closing of independent operations. The editors faithfully recorded the bankruptcies of most enterprises in the region, descriptions of their ventures, the reasons for failure, and occasionally their stockholders, creditors, and depositors. In addition, the stories included the residences of the depositors, stockholders, and creditors, as well as the types and locations of the banks' investments. In the case of the Huntzinger family in the southern coal region, the Pottsville papers carried verbatim reports of the trial of the family heads for embezzlement of hundreds of thousands of dollars of bank funds. The trial records contained detailed accounts of the Huntzingers, their bank's financial dealings, and their ties throughout the region and beyond the coalfields. These included real estate holdings, property owned, coal lands purchased, and range of investments and creditors.

The papers were indispensable sources of social data. They listed the meetings of local societies, lodges, and clubs, as well as many of those members in attendance, and the business conducted at the meeting. Officers of these organizations were also named in these accounts. The papers, particularly after 1870, contained notices of balls, informal gatherings, parties of local notables, dinner dances, anniversary celebrations, and the participants in such events and their residences. In addition, editors recorded marriages, biographies of the partners, notes on their families, and names and residences of individuals invited to the marriage. In the later nineteenth century, the papers reported funerals of local leaders in the region, their biographies, the pallbearers, and the names of the persons who eulogized the deceased. On occasion, the editors noted local leaders who went on trips to Europe and printed their accounts of the journeys. These kinds of data were invaluable in piecing together the social and economic lives of urban leadership and the regional networks.

Almanacs listed sundry information, such as the names of local officials, major events in the communities, and a regional calendar. The almanacs also noted populations of the communities in the region.

MANUSCRIPTS: PUBLIC AND PRIVATE

Private

These sources ranged from personal correspondence to club records. The club material contained membership lists, invitation notices to local notables (as well as those from outside the community or region), names of persons who attended, and their residences. Personal correspondence was particularly useful in tracing economic ties among prominent men in the community, between communities in the region, and with entrepreneurs outside the region. The letters also made it possible to specify the nature of these relationships, the range of the person's investments, and his creditors and debtors. Diaries, on the other hand, were more useful in collecting social data. The notations in the diary generally contained dinner invitations, parties attended and the names of persons encountered at them, and attitudes toward colleagues. The diaries also recorded trips outside the region, as well as economic and social contacts throughout the region and beyond.

Scattered records uncovered in local historical societies contained descriptions of local industry, from mining to coal-related. These accounts also included names of the prominent men in each industry, descriptions of their operations and discussions of the evolution of technology in each industry. Coal company records occasionally included names of the directors, all the stockholders, and the number of shares owned. The private collection of transit company records in the Wyoming Valley contained minutes of almost all the companies in operation from the 1850s through the 1920s, outlines of their tracks and stations, lists of stockholders, and decisions on allocation of available resources. Wills proved an invaluable source on kinship ties. They often listed, besides the names of those persons who would receive money, the names of relatives and the nature of their ties. Occasionally, the wills listed the range of investments by the deceased.

The R. G. Dun and Company records were one of the most useful sources I explored. They were indispensable in tracing extralocal and extraregional ties, the location of a leader's investments, his net worth, his business partners, his credit ties, his debtors, his financial backers, and his business ability. The records also covered the histories of most local companies and banks, evaluations of their financial conditions, areas of their investments, and similar kinds of data. The records enabled me to determine who controlled many of the local enterprises, the extent of landholdings and real estate ventures carried on by local entrepreneurs, and the financial status of hundreds of urban leaders in the regions. The records were also useful in examining migrations, occupational changes, and the range and location of economic activities conducted both by the individual leader and his leadership group. The records also noted the activities of outside-controlled companies, the residences of their directors, and the area of their operations.

Public

The manuscript censuses of population and manufacturing were important sources. They listed the wealth of each person in the community, individuals residing in each household, and their birthplaces. Boarders were included in these descriptions. The manufacturing censuses indicated the size of an economic operation, its owners, the number employed, its worth, and the nature of the product. I used both sources to reconstruct the economic and family basis of leadership groups.

PERSONAL INTERVIEWS

I had the good fortune to conduct interviews with the curators of the historical societies in Schuylkill and Luzerne counties. The late Ralph Hazeltine of Luzerne County was an important source of data who became a good personal friend. As curator, he knew the records of many of the leaders of the Wyoming Valley. As an amateur historian, he knew the history of the Valley and Wilkes-Barre's hinterland extremely well. He was also an employee of the Conyngham family for more than twenty years and, at various times, was tax assessor for the county, the Republican party leader, and Republican county political leader. As a lifelong resident and active participant in the regional economy from 1918 to 1970, he was an indispensable source of personal information on many of the leaders in the twentieth century.

Reginald Rix of Schuylkill was also cooperative. He had spent most of his adult life in the county and was quite knowledgeable on its history in the twentieth century. He shared with me many of his experiences and his understanding of the southern region's decline.

DEATH REGISTERS AND ESTATE INVENTORIES

Both sources were useful in tracing leadership in the twentieth century. By reviewing the death registers, whether in cemetery, church, or county archives, I was able to pinpoint the death date of a given leader and then search the newspapers for his or her obituary. At the same time, I was also able to locate the leader's estate inventory in the county records. These gave me a good idea of the investment and wealth of the particular person.

A NOTE ON TABLE SOURCES

Local histories, legislation, financial reports, private papers, city directories, and manuscript census records were, as throughout this study, of great assistance in preparing the tabular matter for this book. In most of the tables, I have listed the sources where the table occurs. Some, however, require lists of such length that a separate listing appeared desirable. They are as follows.

Table 3-1
J. H. Battle, ed., *History of Columbia and Montour Counties, Pennsylvania* (Chicago: Brown, Runk and Company, 1887); H. C. Bradsby, ed., *History of Bradford County, Pennsylvania with Biographical Selections* (Chicago: S. B. Nelson and Company, Publishers, 1891); Bradsby, ed., *History of Luzerne County, Pennsylvania with Biographical Selections* (Chicago: S. B. Nelson and Company, 1893); *Commemorative Biographical Record of Northeastern Pennsylvania* (Chicago: J. H. Beers Co., 1900); *Eastern Pennsylvanians* (Philadelphia: Eastern Pennsylvania Biographical Association, 1928); Samuel L. French, *Reminiscences of Plymouth, Luzerne County, Pennsylvania* (Plymouth: n.p., 1915); Oscar J. Harvey, *A History of Lodge 61* (Wilkes-Barre: Yardley, 1897); Harvey, *A History of the Miners National Bank of Wilkes-Barre, Pennsylvania* (Wilkes-Barre: Board of Directors of the Bank, 1918); Harvey and Ernest G. Smith, *A History of Wilkes-Barre, Luzerne County, Pennsylvania*, 6 vols. (Wilkes-Barre: Rader Publishing House, 1909–1930); Harvey, *The Harvey Book* (Wilkes-Barre: E. B. Yordy and Company, Printer); Horace C. Hayden, Alfred Hand and J. W. Jordan, *Genealogical and Family History of the Wyoming and Lackawanna Valleys*, 2 vols. (New York: Lewis Publishing Company, 1906); *Historical and Biographical Annals of Columbia and Montour Counties, Pennsylvania*, 2 vols. (Chicago: J. H. Beers, 1915); *History of Bradford County, Pennsylvania* (Philadelphia: L. H. Everts and Company, 1878); Frederick C. Johnson, comp., *The Historical Record of Wilkes-Barre*, 16 vols. (Wilkes-Barre: The Wilkes-Barre Record, 1909); George B. Kulp, *Families of the Wyoming Valley*, 3 vols. (Wilkes-Barre: Wyoming Historical and Geological Society, 1885); Charles Miner, *History of Wyoming in a Series of Letters to His Son, John Miner* (Philadelphia: J. Crissy, 1845); W. W. Munsell and Company, *A History of Luzerne, Lackawanna and Wyoming Counties, with Illustrations and Biographical Sketches of Some of Their Prominent Men and Pioneers* (New York: W. W. Munsell and Company, 1880); Stewart Pearce, *Annals of Luzerne County*, 2d ed. (Philadelphia: J. B. Lippincott and Company, 1866); *Principal Cities and Towns on the Bloomsburg Division of the Delaware, Lackawanna and Western Railroad* (Wilkes-Barre: J. S. Miller and Company, 1889); George Raddin, *The Wilderness and the City: The Story of a Parish* (Wilkes-Barre: St. Stephen's Episcopal Church, 1968); Charles Robeson, *The Manufactories and Manufacturers of Pennsylvania of the Nineteenth Century* (Philadelphia: Galaxy Publishing Company, 1875); S. R. Smith, *The Wyoming Valley in 1892* (Wilkes-Barre: Wilkes-Barre Leader, Printer, 1894); Dwight J. Stoddard, *Prominent Men in Scranton*

and the Vicinity and Wilkes-Barre and the Vicinity (Scranton: Press of the Tribune Publishing Company, 1906); Rhamanthus M. Stocker, *Centennial History of Susquehanna County, Pennsylvania* (Philadelphia: R. J. Peck and Company, 1887); J. H. Sutherland, *The City of Wilkes-Barre and Vicinity and Their Resources* (Wilkes-Barre: Wilkes-Barre Leader Publishing House, 1897); *The Biographical Encyclopedia of Pennsylvania in the Nineteenth Century* (Philadephia: Galaxy Publishing Company, 1874); *Wilkes-Barre, The Diamond City, Its History, Its Industries, 1769–1906* (Wilkes-Barre: Rader Publishing House, 1906); *Wilkes-Barre: The Progressive City, 1889* (Wilkes-Barre: Enterprise Review, 1890); Blair T. Williams, *The Michael Shoemaker Book* (Scranton: International Textbook Press, 1924); Hendrick B. Wright, *Historical Sketches of Plymouth, Luzerne County, Pennsylvania* (Philadelphia: T. B. Paterson and Brothers, 1873); *Laws of the General Assembly of the State of Pennsylvania, 1838–1890* (Harrisburg: Publisher varies, 1838–1890); *Luzerne Union* (Wilkes-Barre, Pennsylvania); *Republican Farmer and Democratic Journal* (Wilkes-Barre, Pennsylvania); George R. Wright diaries, 1874–1930, Wyoming Historical and Geological Society, Wilkes-Barre, Pennsylvania; R. G. Dun and Company Collection, Harvard University, Baker Library, Manuscript Division, All Counties Volume, Luzerne County, vols. 91–100; *Will Books A–Z*, Luzerne County Courthouse, Wilkes-Barre, Pennsylvania. Unless others are cited, these serve as the main sources for subsequent tables and charts in Chapters 3 and 4. Additional sources follow: *Wilkes-Barre Record Almanac, 1913*, Wilkes-Barre: Wilkes-Barre Record, 1914; *Wilkes-Barre Record Almanac, 1918*, Wilkes-Barre: Wilkes-Barre Record, 1919; *Wilkes-Barre Record Almanac, 1919*, Wilkes-Barre: Wilkes-Barre Record, 1920; *Wilkes-Barre Record Almanac, 1921*, Wilkes-Barre: Wilkes-Barre Record, 1922; *Wilkes-Barre Record Alamanc, 1922*, Wilkes-Barre: Wilkes-Barre Record, 1923; *Wilkes-Barre Record Almanac, 1923*, Wilkes-Barre: Wilkes-Barre Record, 1924; *Wilkes-Barre Record Almanac, 1924*, Wilkes-Barre: Wilkes-Barre Record, 1925; *Wilkes-Barre Record Almanac, 1926*, Wilkes-Barre: Wilkes-Barre Record, 1927; *Wilkes-Barre Record Almanac, 1927*, Wilkes-Barre: Wilkes-Barre Record, 1928; *Wilkes-Barre Record Almanac, 1929*, Wilkes-Barre: Wilkes-Barre Record, 1930; *Wilkes-Barre Record Almanac, 1930*, Wilkes-Barre: Wilkes-Barre Record, 1931; *Wilkes-Barre Record Almanac, 1931*, Wilkes-Barre: Wilkes-Barre Record, 1932; *Wilkes-Barre Record Almanac, 1932*, Wilkes-Barre: Wilkes-Barre Record, 1933; Death Register, First Presbyterian Church, Wilkes-Barre, Pennsylvania; Death Register, Hollenback Cemetery, Wilkes-Barre, Pennsylvania; Death Register, Forty-Fort Cemetery, Forty-Fort, Pennsylvania; Death Register, Register of Wills Office, Luzerne County Courthouse, Wilkes-Barre, Pennsylvania; Death Register, St. Stephen's Episcopal Church, Wilkes-Barre, Pennsylvania; Estate Inventories, 1919–1967, Luzerne County Courthouse, Luzerne County, Wilkes-Barre, Pennsylvania.

Table 3-9

In addition to the sources noted in Table 3-1, I consulted the following: Henry Poor, *Poor's Manual of Railroads of the United States, 1872–1873* (New York:

H. V. and H. W. Poor, 1873); *Laws of the General Assembly of the State of Pennsylvania, 1860–1873* (Harrisburg: Publisher varies, 1860–1873). These laws contained descriptions of areas of operations engaged in by local companies and the men involved: the city and business directories runs for the Wyoming Valley and Wilkes-Barre during the nineteenth century cited throughout the text and in the bibliography; George Hollenback papers, Wyoming Historical and Geological Society, Wilkes-Barre, Pennsylvania (hereafter WHGS); Lehigh and Wilkes-Barre Coal Company Papers, WHGS; Wilkes-Barre Street Railway Collection, Wilkes College Library, Wilkes-Barre, Pennsylvania; *Will Books A–K, 1790–1885*, Luzerne County Courthouse, Wilkes-Barre, Pennsylvania; *Pennsylvania Census Records, 1850, 1860, 1870, 1880, Luzerne County, Manufacturing*, Bell and Howell, MicroPhoto Division, Worcester, Ohio; *Annual Report of the Secretary of Internal Affairs of the Commonwealth of Pennsylvania, Part III, Industrial Statistics, 1872–1891* (Harrisburg: Publisher varies, 1872–1891). See also Bibliography and the remainder of this appendix.

Table 6-2

J. H. Beers, *Schuylkill County, Pennsylvania*, 2 vols. (Chicago: J. H. Beers and Company, 1916); Herbert Bell, ed., *History of Northumberland County* (Chicago: Brown, Runk and Company, 1891); *Book of Biographies: Biographical Sketches of Leading Citizens of the Seventeenth Congressional District, Pennsylvania* (Chicago: Biographical Publications Comp., 1899); *Centennial Anniversary, Orwigsburg, Pennsylvania, 1813–1913* (Pottsville: Seiders Printers, 1914); Centennial Committee, *Mahanoy City, Schuylkill County, Pennsylvania, 1863–1963: A History* (Mahanoy City: Centennial Committee, 1963); George Chambers, *Historical Sketch of Pottsville, Schuylkill County, Pa.* (Pottsville: Standard Publishing Company Printer, 1876); *Genealogical and Biographical Annals of Northumberland County, Pennsylvania* (Chicago: J. L. Floyd & Co., 1911); John S. Bird, "Early Shamokin," *Northumberland County Historical Society* 16 (1934): 145–69; Mrs. Ella Zerbey Elliot, *Blue Book of Schuylkill County* (Pottsville: Joseph A. Zerbey, Proprietor Publishers, 1916); *History Compiled for the First Methodist Church, Pottsville, Pennsylvania, on the Occasion of Its Centennial Anniversary by Pottsville Evening Republican and Pottsville Morning Paper* (Pottsville: Zerbey Newspapers, 1932); the Rev. Jonathan W. Miller, *History of Frackville, Schuylkill County, Pennsylvania* (Frackville: Miners Journal, 1904); W. W. Munsell and Company, ed., *History of Schuylkill County, Pennsylvania* (New York: W. W. Munsell and Company, 1881); Harry Rockman, *The Path of Progress: Shenandoah, Pennsylvania, Centennial, 1866–1966* (Reading: Reading Eagle Press, 1967); Daniel Rupp, *History of Northampton, Lehigh, Monroe and Schuylkill Counties* (Harrisburg: Hill, Lancaster, Hickock and Contini, 1845); Adolph W. Schalck and the Honorable D. C. Henning, eds., *History of Schuylkill County, Pennsylvania*, 2 vols. (Harrisburg: State Historical Association, 1907); *The Biographical Encyclopedia of Pennsylvania of the Nineteenth Century* (Philadelphia: Galaxy Publishing Company, 1874); *The 175th Anniversary, Schuylkill Haven* (Schuylkill Haven: Civic Clerk of Schuylkill Haven, 1925); Samuel Wiley and Henry Ruoff, *Biographical and Portrait Cyclopedia of Schuylkill County, Pennsylvania* (Philadelphia: Rush, West and Company, 1893); Joseph H. Zerbey, *History of Pottsville and Schuylkill County, Pennsylvania* (Pottsville: J. H. Zerbey Newspapers, 1934–1935); *The Reading Railroad* (Philadelphia: Burk & McFetridge Printers, 1898); *Pottsville* (Pennsylvania) *Daily Republican; Pottsville* (Pennsylvania) *Weekly Miners Journal; Miners Journal* (Pottsville, Pennsylvania); "People of Importance," Historical Society of Schuylkill County, Pottsville, Pennsylvania; R. G. Dun and Company Collection, Harvard University, Baker Library, Manuscript Division, All Counties Volumes, Northumberland County (vols. 124–25) and Schuylkill County (vols. 172–75); untitled papers on the iron and steel industry, Historical Society of Schuylkill County, Pottsville, Pennsylvania; Supplement to the Pottsville *Weekly Miners Journal,* January–April 1875; *Miners Journal,* Pottsville, Schuylkill County, Pennsylvania, Marriages, Deaths, Burials, Obituaries, 1829– *Minutes of the Sessions of the Presbyterian Church,* First Presbyterian Church of Pottsville, 1834–1927, 2 vols. (Philadelphia: Presbyterian Book of Publications); *Minutes of the Sessions of the Presbyterian Church,* First Presbyterian Church of Port Carbon, 1834–1927, 2 vols. (Philadelphia: Presbyterian Book of Publications); *Will Books,* 1886–1913, 12 vols., Register and Recorder, Northumberland County Courthouse, Sunbury. The preceding five citations, from the two miners' journals, the Presbyterian minutes, and the *Will Books,* are located in the Microfilm Archives of the Church of Jesus Christ of Latter-Day Saints, American Section, Salt Lake City, Utah. These citations also serve as sources for subsequent tables unless otherwise noted.

Table 7-5
In addition to sources cited in Table 6-2, see also Samuel Daddow and Benjamin Bannon, *Coal, Iron and Oil or the Practical American Miner* (Philadelphia: J. B. Lippincott and Company, 1866); *The Reading Railroad* (Philadelphia: Burk & McFetridge, Printers, 1898); *Annual Reports of the Secretary of Internal Affairs of the Commonwealth of Pennsylvania, Part III, Industrial Statistics, 1872–1891* (Harrisburg: Publisher varies, 1872–1891); city and business directory runs for Schuylkill and Northumberland counties and Pottsville (see Bibliography and rest of appendix); Anniversary Dinner Invitation of the Pottsville Fishing Club, 1883 and 1885, Historical Society of Schuylkill County, Pottsville, Pennsylvania (hereafter HSSCO); untitled papers on the anthracite industry, HSSCO; untitled papers on the iron and steel industry, HSSCO; untitled papers on the Philadelphia and Reading Railroad Company, HSSCO; untitled papers on the railroads in Schuylkill County, HSSCO; *Pennsylvania Census Records, 1850, 1860, 1870, 1880, Northumberland and Schuylkill Counties, Manufacturing,* Bell and Howell, MicroPhoto Division, Worcester, Ohio.

Notes

NOTES TO CHAPTER 1

1. For a work on the Lackawanna Valley, a center of anthracite production and iron manufacturing, see Burton W. Folsom, Jr., *Urban Capitalists: Entrepreneurs and City Growth in Pennsylvania's Lackawanna and Lehigh Regions, 1800–1920* (Baltimore: Johns Hopkins University Press, 1981).

2. Julius Rubin, *Canal or Railroad? Imitation in Response to the Erie Canal in Philadelphia, Baltimore and Boston* (Philadelphia: American Philosophical Society, 1961); Blake McKelvey, *Rochester, The Flower City: 1854–1890* (Cambridge, Mass.: Harvard University Press, 1949); Blake McKelvey, "The Emergence of Industrial Cities," in *American Urban History: An Interpretive Reader with Commentaries*, ed. Alexander B. Callow, Jr. (New York: Oxford University Press, 1973), pp. 160–71; Bayrd Still, "Patterns of Mid-Nineteenth-Century Urbanization in the Middle West," in *American Urban History*, pp. 122–35; Daniel S. Boorstein, "The Businessman as City Booster," in *American Urban History*, pp. 146–53; Arthur C. Cole, *Business Enterprise in Its Social Setting* (Cambridge: Harvard University Press, 1959); Joseph A. Schumpter, "The Creative Response in Economic History," *Journal of Economic History* 7 (1959): 149–59; Folsom, *Urban Capitalists*.

3. John N. Ingham, *The Iron Barons: A Social Analysis of an American Urban Elite, 1874–1965* (Westport, Conn.: Greenwood Press, 1978); Frederic Cople Jaher, *The Urban Establishment: The Upper Strata in Boston, New York, Charleston, Chicago and Los Angeles* (Chicago: University of Illinois Press, 1982); E. Digby Baltzell, *Philadelphia Gentlemen: The Making of a National Upper Class* (Philadelphia: University of Pennsylvania Press, 1979); Edward Pessen, "The Egalitarian Myth and American Social Reality: Wealth, Mobility and Equality in the 'Era of the Common Man,'" *American Historical Review* 76 (1971): 989–1034. For examples of other studies, see Peter Decker, *Fortunes and Failures: White Collar Mobility in Nineteenth-Century San Francisco* (Cambridge, Mass.: Harvard University Press, 1976); Richard Jensen, "Quantitative Collective Biography: An Application to Metropolitan Elites," in *Quantification in American History: Theory and Research*, ed. Robert P. Swierenga (New

York: Atheneum, 1970); Whitman Ridgeway, *Community Leadership in Maryland, 1790–1840* (Chapel Hill, N.C.: University of North Carolina Press, 1979).

4. Diane Lindstrom, *Economic Development in the Philadelphia Region, 1810–1850* (New York: Columbia University Press, 1978); Roberta B. Miller, *City and Hinterland: A Case Study of Urban Growth and Regional Development* (Westport, Conn.: Greenwood Press, 1979); James Lemon, *The Best Poor Man's Country* (New York: W. W. Norton & Company, 1976); Allan Pred, *Urban Growth and the Circulation of Information: The United States System of Cities, 1790–1840* (Cambridge, Mass.: Harvard University Press, 1973); Robert Doherty, *Society and Power: Five New England Towns, 1800–1860* (Amherst, Mass.: University of Massachusetts Press, 1977); Michael P. Conzen, "The Maturing Urban System in the United States, 1840–1910," *Annals, Association of American Geographers* 67 (1977): 88–108; Edward K. Muller, "Selective Urban Growth in the Middle Ohio Valley, 1800–1860," *Geographical Review* 66 (1976): 178–99; Muller, "Regional Urbanization and Selective Growth of Towns in North American Regions," *Journal of Historical Geography* 3 (1977): 22–39; F. A. Dahms, "The Evolution of Settlement Systems: A Canadian Example, 1851–1970," *Journal of Urban History* 7 (1981): 169–204; G. William Skinner, "Marketing and Social Structure in Rural China, Part I," *Journal of Asian Studies* 24 (1969): 3–43; Skinner, "Cities and the Hierarchy of Local Systems," in *The City in Late Imperial China*, ed. G. William Skinner (Stanford, Calif.: Stanford University Press, 1976), pp. 275–315; Stuart Blumin, *The Urban Threshold: Growth and Change in a Nineteenth-Century American Community* (Chicago: University of Chicago Press, 1976); Francis Blouin, *The Boston Region, 1810–1850: A Study in Urbanization* (Ann Arbor, Mich.: UMI Research, 1980); William Silag, "City, Town and Countryside: Northwest Iowa and the Ecology of Urbanization, 1854–1900" (Ph.D. diss., University of Iowa, 1979).

5. Baltzell, *Philadelphia Gentlemen*; Jaher, "Nineteenth-Century Elites in Boston and New York," *Journal of Social History* 6 (1972): 30–72; Jaher, "Businessman and Gentleman: Nathan and Thomas Gold Appleton—An Exploration in Intergenerational History," *Explorations in Entrepreneurial History* 4 (1966): 17–38.

6. Folsom, *Urban Capitalists*; Spyridon G. Patten, "Some Impacts of the Reading Railroad on the Industrialization of Reading, Pa.; 1838–1910" (Ph.D. diss., University of Pittsburgh, 1979); James Soltow, "The Small City Industrialist, 1900–1950: A Case Study of Norristown, Pennsylvania," *Business History Review* 32 (1958): 102–15; Carol E. Hoffecker, *Wilmington, Delaware: Portrait of an Industrial City* (Charlottesville, Va.: University of Virginia Press, 1974).

7. Ingham, *Iron Barons*, pp. 10–11; Baltzell, *Philadelphia Gentlemen*, pp. 6, 7–12; C. Wright Mills, *The Power Elite* (New York: Oxford University Press, 1956), 30–46, 48–68, 271–78; W. Lloyd Warner and Paul S. Lunt, *The Social Life of the Modern Community* (New Haven, Conn.: Yale University Press, 1941); Bernard Barber, *Social Stratification: A Comparative Analysis of Structure and Process* (New York: Oxford University Press, 1968).

8. For ways of defining the term *elite*, see Richard S. Alcorn, "Leadership and Stability in Mid-Nineteenth-Century America: A Case Study of an Illinois Town," *Journal of American History* 61 (1974): 685–702; Robert V. Schulze, "The Bifurcation of Power in a City," in *Community Political Systems*, ed. Morris Janowitz (Glencoe, Ill.: Free Press, 1961), 19–80; Jensen, "Quantitative Collective Biography," pp. 390–92; Clyde Griffen and Sally Griffen, *Natives and Newcomers: The Ordering of Oppor-*

tunity in Mid-Nineteenth-Century Poughkeepsie (Cambridge, Mass.: Harvard University Press, 1978), 85–86; Pessen, "The Egalitarian Myth," pp. 993–95. For a discussion of sources used to identify leaders, see Appendix: Description of Sources.

9. Jaher, *The Urban Establishment,* pp. 317–98.

10. Ibid., pp. 173–249.

11. For other important works which stress the values of urban networks and the external relationships of the community, see Van Beck Hall, *Politics without Parties: Massachusetts, 1780–1790* (Pittsburgh: University of Pittsburgh Press, 1972); Van Beck Hall, "A Fond Farewell to Henry Adams: Ideas Relating Political History to Social Change during the Early National Period," in *The Human Dimensions of Nation Making,* ed. James Kirby Martin (Madison, Wis.: University of Wisconsin Press, 1976), 323–61; John Walton, "The Vertical Axis of Community Organization and the Structure of Power," in *The Search for Community Power,* ed. Willis D. Hawley and Frederick M. Wirt (Englewood Cliffs, N.J.: Prentice Hall, 1968), 353–69; Arthur J. Vidich and Joseph Bensman, *Small Town in Mass Society: Class, Power and Religion,* rev. ed. (Princeton, N.J.: Princeton University Press, 1968), 79–101, 155–67, 186–95, and 198–222.

12. Baltzell, *Philadelphia Gentlemen,* pp. 6, 7–12, 158–72, 335–63; Ingham, *Iron Barons,* pp. 11, 85–102, 117–36.

13. Horace C. Hayden, Alfred Hand, and John W. Jordan, *Genealogical and Family History of the Wyoming and Lackawanna Valleys, Pennsylvania,* 2 vols. (New York: Lewis Publishing Company, 1906), 1:435, Oscar J. Harvey and Ernest G. Smith, *A History of Wilkes-Barre, Luzerne County, Pennsylvania,* 6 vols. (Wilkes-Barre, Pa.: Rader Publishing House, 1909–1930), 5:250–51; W. W. Munsell and Company, *History of Luzerne, Lackawanna and Wyoming Counties, Pennsylvania, with Illustrations and Biographical Sketches of Some of Their Prominent Men and Pioneers* (New York: W. W. Munsell and Company, 1880), 226, 228, 230, 232, 235, 315–16; Baltzell, *Philadelphia Gentlemen,* pp. 335–63; Ingham, *Iron Barons,* pp. 96–98; Jaher, *The Urban Establishment,* pp. 9–10, 73–74; coal-mining superintendents and supervisory officials of the Pennsylvania and Reading Railroad Company and the Philadelphia and Reading Coal & Iron Company are included.

14. Floyd Hunter, *Community Power Structure: A Study in Decision-Makers* (New York: Anchor Books, 1961).

15. Ridgeway, *Community Leadership,* esp. Appendix I, "Methodological Procedures," pp. 195–209.

NOTES TO CHAPTER 2

1. S. F. Smith, *The Wyoming Valley in the Nineteenth Century* (Wilkes-Barre: Wilkes-Barre Leader, 1894), 142; W. W. Munsell and Company, *History of Luzerne, Lackawanna and Wyoming Counties, Pennsylvania, with Illustrations and Biographical Sketches of Some of Their Prominent Men and Pioneers* (New York: W. W. Munsell and Company, 1880), 236R–236S; Stewart Pearce, *Annals of Luzerne County,* 2d ed. (Philadelphia: J. B. Lippincott and Company, 1866), 370–74; H. B. Plumb, *History of Hanover Township, Including Nanticoke, Ashley and Sugar Notch and also a History of Wyoming Valley* (Wilkes-Barre: R. Baller, 1885), 329–30; Hendrick B. Wright, *Historical Sketches of Plymouth, Luzerne County, Pennsylvania* (Philadelphia: T. B. Patterson and

Brothers, 1873), 313–15; H. C. Bradsby, ed., *History of Luzerne County, Pennsylvania, with Biographical Selections* (Chicago: S. B. Nelson and Company, 1893), 277–80; H. Benjamin Powell, *Philadelphia's First Fuel Crisis* (University Park, Pa: Pennsylvania State University Press, 1978); Edward Phillips, "History of the Wyoming Valley," unpublished manuscript (Wilkes-Barre, Pennsylvania, Wyoming Historical and Geological Society, hereafter, WHGS).

2. Wright, *Historical Sketches*, pp. 317–18; *Wilkes-Barre: The Diamond City: Its History, Its Resources, Its Industries, 1769–1906* (Wilkes-Barre: Rader Publishing House, 1906), 110–11.

3. Bradsby, *History of Luzerne County*, pp. 258–60; Oscar J. Harvey and Ernest G. Smith, *A History of Wilkes-Barre, Luzerne County, Pennsylvania*, 6 vols. (Wilkes-Barre: Rader Publishing House, 1909–1930), 5:252; Oscar J. Harvey, *The Harvey Book* (Wilkes-Barre: E. B. Yordy and Company, Printer, 1899), 737–78; Horace E. Hayden, Alfred Hand, and John W. Jordan, *Genealogical and Family History of the Wyoming and Lackawanna Valleys*, 2 vols. (New York: Lewis Publishing Company, 1906), 1:81–82, 357–58; Munsell, *A History of Luzerne, Lackawanna and Wyoming Counties*, pp. 236J–236K, 236A, 236M–236N, 516B; George B. Kulp, *Families of the Wyoming Valley*, 3 vols. (Wilkes-Barre: Wyoming Historical and Geological Society, 1885), 2:551–53; Pearce, *Annals*, pp. 374–81.

4. Alfred D. Chandler, Jr., "Anthracite Coal and the Beginnings of the Industrial Revolution in the United States," *Business History Review* 46 (1972): 141–81; Samuel Daddow and Benjamin Bannan, *Coal, Iron and Oil, or the Practical American Miner* (Philadelphia: J. B. Lippincott and Company, 1866), 705–10; Eliot Jones, *The Anthracite Coal Combinations in the United States with Some Accounts of the Early Development of the Anthracite Industry* (Cambridge, Mass.: Harvard University Press, 1914), 81–85; Plumb, *History of Hanover Township*, pp. 286–89; Ralph Trego, *A Geography of Pennsylvania* (Philadelphia: Edward G. Biddle, 1843), 121. For accounts of continued local support of the canal system and the North Branch Canal, in particular, see *Republican Farmer and Democratic Journal* (Wilkes-Barre, Pennsylvania), 31 May 1853; *Luzerne Union* (Wilkes-Barre, Pennsylvania), 7 February 1855, 11 May 1855, and 16 February 1859. Merchants relied on the North Branch Canal to reach Philadelphia through the 1850s; see William H. Shank, P.E., *The Amazing Pennsylvania Canals* (York, Penn.: American Canal and Transportation Center, 1973), 39–41.

5. Hayden, Hand, and Jordan, *Genealogical and Family History*, 1:36, 81–82, and 357–58; Harvey and Smith, *A History of Wilkes-Barre*, 4:1985; *Republican Farmer and Democratic Journal*, 8 May 1850, 17 May 1850, and 16 June 1852; *Luzerne Union*, 28 November 1855, 15 May 1857, 16 February 1859, and 23 January 1861; Wright, *Historical Sketches*, pp. 365–67; Bradsby, *History of Luzerne County*, pp. 260–61, 263, 280, 282–83, 1280; *Laws of the General Assembly of the State of Pennsylvania, 1852*, C. 391, p. 669; *Laws, 1853*, C. 131, p. 179. The Pennsylvania Assembly used various publishers; facts of publication for all cited *Laws* may be found in the Bibliography.

6. Jules I. Bogen, *The Anthracite Railroads: A Study in American Enterprise* (New York: Ronald Press, 1927), 109, 113, 115, 123–27; Bradsby, *History of Luzerne County*, pp. 260–61, 263, 280, 290; *Boyd's City Directory for Wilkes-Barre, Hazleton, Scranton and Surrounding Communities, 1873* (Wilkes-Barre: William H. Boyd, 1873); Harvey and Smith, *A History of Wilkes-Barre*, 5:62–66.

7. See H. Benjamin Powell, "Pioneering the Anthracite Industry: The Case of the Smith Coal Company" (unpublished ms., written for the Department of History,

Bloomsburg State College, 1975). See also citations in note 8 below.

8. Bradsby, *History of Luzerne County*, pp. 1364, 1367; Harvey, *Harvey Book*, pp. 735, 782, 815–19, 841–43, 873–79; Harvey and Smith, *A History of Wilkes-Barre*, 4:2090–91, and 5:162, 293; Hayden, Hand, and Jordan, *Genealogical and Family History*, 7:163–64, 2:371–73, 509–10; Frederick C. Johnson, comp., *The Historical Record of Wilkes-Barre* (Wilkes-Barre: *Wilkes-Barre Record*, 1906), 3:13–15, 4:39, 4:162, and 13:123–25; Munsell, *A History of Luzerne, Lackawanna and Wyoming Counties*, pp. 236E, 236L, 329; Smith, *The Wyoming Valley*, pp. 33, 64, 93; Wright, *Historical Sketches*, p. 315.

9. For a complete list of coal companies, see Edward J. Davies II, "The Urbanizing Region: Leadership and Urban Growth in the Anthracite Regions, 1830–1885" (Ph.D. diss., University of Pittsburgh, 1977), p. 94 (Table II-3); Smith, *History of Wilkes-Barre*, 5:205; Munsell, *A History of Luzerne, Lackawanna and Wyoming Counties*, pp. 304–5; Phillips, "History of the Wyoming Valley," 7:196–98, 7:202–3, and 7:207; Smith, *The Wyoming Valley*, p. 49; *Laws of the General Assembly of the State of Pennsylvania*, 1849, C. 129, p. 149; *Laws*, 1850, C. 336, pp. 531–32; *Laws*, 1853, C. 335, pp. 567–69; *Laws*, 1856, C. 277, pp. 253–55, and C. 753, pp. 765–66; *Laws*, 1838, C. 406, p. 422; *Laws*, 1864, C. 832, p. 940, and C. 345, pp. 412–13; *Laws*, 1869, C. 1279, p. 1312. The 1838 company was the one exception.

10. The figure $17 million was gathered from incorporated capital. Often, this was not fully paid up and would be paid only slowly over the years of the company's existence. For example, see R. G. Dun and Company Collection, All-Counties Volumes, Harvard University, Baker Library, Manuscript Division. (The Dun Collection is divided by county. All-Counties volumes accompany each county and contain names of the evaluators, almost all of them lawyers, for each county.) Luzerne County is in vols. 91–100; see 100:106 (Hanover Coal Company). Frequently, the capital was paid in full, but the property and real estate inflated beyond the initial investment. See R. G. Dun and Company Collection, 95:424 (Ellenwood Coal Company), 228 (Warrior Run Coal Company); 96:65 (Riverside Coal Company); 97:181 (Riverside Coal Company) 60 (Forty-Fort Coal Company). The Ellenwood Company capitalized at $100,000, yet the value of the company totalled $500,000.

11. Harvey and Smith, *History of Wilkes-Barre*, 4:2090-91, and 5:255; Phillips, "History of the Wyoming Valley," 7:196, 7:198, and 7:205–7; Munsell, *A History of Luzerne, Lackawanna and Wyoming Counties*, pp. 305, 236D, 236S–T; *Laws of the General Assembly of the State of Pennsylvania*, 1867, C. 867, p. 922; *Luzerne Union*, 18 July 1855; *Annual Report of the Secretary of Internal Affairs of the Commonwealth of Pennsylvania, Part III: Industrial Statistics, 1872–1873* (Harrisburg: Benjamin Singerly, 1874), 278–79, 294, 305; *Annual Report of the Secretary of Internal Affairs of the Commonwealth of Pennsylvania, Part III: Industrial Statistics, 1875–1876* (Harrisburg: Benjamin Singerly, 1877), 411–24, 428–31, 433, 452, 455; *Annual Report of the Secretary of Internal Affairs of the Commonwealth of Pennsylvania, Part III: Industrial Statistics, 1878–1879* (Harrisburg: Lane S. Hart, State Printer, 1880), 19–22; *Reports of the Inspectors of Coal Mines of the Anthracite Regions of Pennsylvania for the Year 1870*, vol. 1 (Harrisburg: B. Singerly, State Printer, 1870), 232–33; Bradsby, *History of Luzerne County*, pp. 316–19. For some examples of ownership of coal lands, see R. G. Dun and Company Collection, 91:138, 149 (William P. Miner); 92:37 (E. C. Wadhams); 93:546 (Washington Lee, Jr.), 892 (Harvey Brothers), 861 (Charles Parrish); 94:118 (Franklin J. Leavenworth), 1184–85 (Charles Parrish); 95:59 (J. H.

Swoyer), 219 (Charles A. Miner), 228 (Warrior Run Coal Company), 262 (William Stoddard), 261 (Joseph Brown & Alexander Gray); 96:19 (T. S. & W. S. Hillard), 65 (Riverside Coal Company); 97:A (W. W. Loomis), 62 (Arnold Bertels), 64, 67, 478 (B. G. Carpenter & Co.), 86 (J. R. Coollaugh), 194 (C. A. Miner and J. W. Thomas), 233 (Kirkendall & Whiteman), 455 (R. Scott & Co.); 98:317 (Lewis Landmesser); 99:126 (Bennett Hardware Co., Red Ash Coal Company); 100:15, 209 (Charles P. Hunt & Bro.); *Will Books A–Z*, Luzerne County Courthouse, Wilkes-Barre, Pennsylvania. See in particular *Will Book A*, pp. 13, 47–48; *Will Book B*, pp. 79–80, 153–54, 210, 266, 532, 544, 550; *Will Book C*, pp. 39, 166, 409; *Will Book D*, pp. 276, 355–57, 436–40; *Will Book E*, pp. 266, 308; *Will Book G*, pp. 1, 93, 415; *Will Book H*, p. 445; *Will Book K*, pp. 120–21, 172–79; *Will Book L*, p. 32; and the *Wilkes-Barre Record*, 30 July 1883. Leaders from other communities also owned coal lands. For example, see R. G. Dun and Company Collection, 91:276 (John B. Smith/Plymouth & Kingston); 92:62 (John B. and L. M. Smith/Plymouth & Kingston); 92:22 (Joel Bowlkley and Benjamin Beyea/Pittston); 95:128 (Benjamin and Edward Bowlkley/Pittston); 98:302 (Daniel Edwards/Plymouth & Kingston); 92:8 and 92:9 (Turner Brothers/Plymouth Township).

12. Hayden, Hand, and Jordan, *Genealogical and Family History*, 7:81–82; *Laws of the General Assembly of the State of Pennsylvania*, 1849, C. 129, p. 149; Munsell, *A History of Luzerne, Lackawanna and Wyoming Counties*, pp. 236A, 236M–36N; Phillips, "A History of the Wyoming Valley," 1:207.

13. *The Biographical Encyclopedia of Pennsylvania of the Nineteenth Century* (Philadelphia: Galaxy Publishing Company, 1874), 532–33; Hayden, Hand, and Jordan, *Genealogical and Family History*, 1:78, 84–85, and 117–19; *Laws of the General Assembly of the State of Pennsylvania*, 1864, C. 526, p. 629; Munsell, *A History of Luzerne, Lackawanna and Wyoming Counties*, p. 236F; Johnson, *Historical Record*, 2:166 and 7:74–77; *Annual Report of the Secretary of Internal Affairs of the Commonwealth of Pennsylvania*, 1875–1876, pp. 411–24, 428–31, 433, 438, 452, 455; and 1878–1879, pp. 19–22.

14. *Laws of the General Assembly of the State of Pennsylvania*, 1864, C. 832, p. 940; *Annual Report of the Secretary of Internal Affairs of the Commonwealth of Pennsylvania*, 1872–1873, pp. 278–89, 294, 305; 1876–1877, pp. 411–24, 428–31, 433, 438, 452, 455; *Annual Report of the Secretary of Internal Affairs of the Commonwealth*, 1878–1879, pp. 19–22; Bradsby, *History of Luzerne County*, pp. 1232–33; Hayden, Hand, and Jordan, *Genealogical and Family History*, 1:81–82, 111–13, and 117–19; *Biographical Encyclopedia*, pp. 532–33; Kulp, *Families of the Wyoming Valley*, 1:88–89, 95, and 2:455–56; Munsell, *History of Luzerne, Lackawanna and Wyoming Counties*, pp. 236A–N; Smith, *The Wyoming Valley*, p. 99; *Luzerne Union*, 27 September 1871; R. G. Dun and Company Collection, 93:860 (Wilkes-Barre Coal & Iron Co.); *Will Book G*, p. 410. The Lehigh Coal and Navigation Company at one point owned the majority of the stock in the Wilkes-Barre Coal and Iron Company.

15. R. G. Dun and Company Collection, 93:860 (Wilkes-Barre Coal and Iron Co.); 94:1096 (Charles Parrish); 95:3 (Hazard Manufacturing Company); 96:115 (Lehigh and Wilkes-Barre Coal Company), 299 (Charles Parrish & Co.); 100:15, 209 (Charles Parrish Hunt & Bro.), 316 (Charles Parrish & Co.); *Biographical Encyclopedia*, pp. 532–33; Hayden, Hand, and Jordan, *Genealogical and Family History*, 1:117–19; Munsell, *A History of Luzerne, Lackawanna and Wyoming Counties*, pp. 278–79, 326–27, 356; Johnson, *Historical Record*, 7:474–77; *Laws of the General Assembly of*

the State of Pennsylvania, 1864, C. 489, pp. 554–55; Annual Report of the Secretary of Internal Affairs of the Commonwealth of Pennsylvania, 1872–1873, pp. 278–89, 294, 305; 1875–1876, pp. 411–24, 428–31, 433, 438, 455, and 1878–1879, pp. 19–22. Hazleton and the mining communities surrounding it in the southern part of Luzerne County were not completely integrated into Wilkes-Barre's region until the early 1900s. Because members of the upper class did take control of many of the mining operations in this area, and Hazleton was politically and administratively tied to Wilkes-Barre (the county seat), it is included in this analysis but nowhere else.

16. Biographical Encyclopedia, pp. 532–33; Hayden, Hand, and Jordan, Genealogical and Family History, 1:117–19; Johnson, Historical Record, 7:74–77; R. G. Dun and Company Collection, 95:3 (Hazard Wire Rope Company).

17. In addition to citations in note 19 below, see R. G. Dun and Company Collection, 95:A, F, G (H. H. Ashley & Co.), 262 (Conyngham & Paine); 97:174, 253, 239 (Conyngham & Co.); and 100:303 (Conyngham, Schrage & Co.).

18. Hayden, Hand, and Jordan, Genealogical and Family History, 1:10–14, 117–19, 542–44; Harvey and Smith, A History of the Wyoming Valley, 5:188, and 6:321–22, 485–86; Kulp, Families of the Wyoming Valley, 1:206–7, and 2:593–95; Johnson, Historical Record, 3:181–84.

19. Hayden, Hand, and Jordan, Genealogical and Family History, 1:12–14; Harvey and Smith, A History of Wilkes-Barre, 5:321–22, and 6:484–85; Johnson, Historical Record, 3:181–84; Kulp, Families of the Wyoming Valley, 1:118–19, 206–7, 542–44, and 2:593–95; Munsell, A History of Luzerne, Lackawanna and Wyoming Counties, p. 236L.

20. For examples of Wilkes-Barre's penetration into the hinterland, see Hayden, Hand, and Jordan, Genealogical and Family History, 1:196–203, 2:816–17, and 3:1087–90; Munsell, A History of Luzerne, Lackawanna and Wyoming Counties, p. 217; Will Book C, pp. 39, 166; Will Book E, p. 10; Sterling to Hollenback (hereafter referred to as GMH), 23 April to 15 June 1860, 13 February to 21 December 1861, Meshoppen, Wyoming County; Overfield to GMH, 22 April to 10 June 1854 and 20 November 1860, Braintrim, Wyoming County; Loomis to GMH, 15 October to 4 December 1861, Meshoppen; Welles to GHM, 4 June 1861, Meshoppen; Osterhout to GMH, 22 April to 10 June 1854, Tunkhannock, Wyoming County; Shipman and C. L. Welles to GMH, 21 December 1853 to 25 July 1854, Athens, Bradford County; George Hollenback Collection, Wyoming Historical and Geological Society, Wilkes-Barre, Pennsylvania.

21. Bradsby, History of Luzerne County, pp. 607, 614–15; Bogen, The Anthracite Railroads, pp. 96–98, 161–70, 187–89; Jones, The Anthracite Coal Combinations in the United States, pp. 23–28; Munsell, A History of Luzerne, Lackawanna and Wyoming Counties, pp. 273, 342, 346; Phillips, "History of Wyoming Valley," 1:203, 206; W. F. Roberts, The Everhart Coal Company (Boston: J. E. Farwell Company, 1864), 85–87; Laws of the General Assembly of the State of Pennsylvania, 1864, C. 525, pp. 627–28.

22. Luzerne Union, 7 January 1855.

23. Kulp, Families of the Wyoming Valley, 2:799; Will Book B, p. 210; Munsell, A History of Luzerne, Lackawanna and Wyoming Counties, p. 236D; Luzerne Union, 18 September 1872; R. G. Dun and Company Collection, 93:892 (H. H. & William J. Harvey); Wilkes-Barre Record, 13 July 1883.

24. R. G. Dun and Company Collection, 95:262 (William and Charles Conyngham), 379 (H. H. Ashley), 3 (Hazard Wire Rope); 96:299 (Charles Parrish & Co.),

115 (Lehigh and Wilkes-Barre Coal Company); 97:20 (Charles P. Hunt), 47 (Hazard Wire Rope Co.), and 102 (L. C. & J. C. Paine). See John A. James, *Money and Capital Markets in Postbellum America* (Princeton: Princeton University Press, 1978), 28–39, 32–36.

25. R. G. Dun and Company Collection, 95:59 (John Swoyer), 261 (Bennett, Phelps & Co.); 96:65 (Riverside Coal Co.); 97:60 (Forty-Fort Coal Co.); *Wilkes-Barre Record*, 12 December 1885; Johnson, *Historical Record*, 2:166.

26. R. G. Dun and Company Collection, 93:861 (Charles Parrish); 94:1184–85 (Charles Parrish); 95:228 (Warrior Run Coal Company), 59 (John H. Swoyer); 96:65 (Riverside Coal Company); 97:60 (Forty-Fort Coal Company); 99:391 (Red Ash Coal Company); 98:284, 404 (Wyoming Valley Coal Company); 100:51 (Leavenworth & Co.), 146 (Hanover Coal Company), 316 (Parrish & Co.). From the Dundee Coal Company Papers Collection of the Wyoming Historical and Geological Society in Wilkes-Barre, the following are of note: *Journal*, p. 1; and Minutes of the Meeting in Wilkes-Barre, 22 February 1856. See also Phillips, "History of Wilkes-Barre," 1:207; *Laws of the General Assembly of the State of Pennsylvania, 1869*, C. 1279, p. 1312, Hillside Coal & Iron Company.

27. Francis Walker and Charles W. Seaton, Supts., *Report of the Mining Industries of the United States* (Washington, D.C.: Government Printing Office, 1886), 625–26; Munsell, *A History of Luzerne, Lackawanna and Wyoming Counties*, p. 195.

28. For some examples of these mining operations, see R. G. Dun and Company Collection, 92:114 (Eno & Fuller), 175 (Thomas Broderick & Co.); 93:728 (Broderick & Conyngham & Co.), 860 (Wilkes-Barre Coal and Iron Co.); 94:977 (Mineral Spring Coal Co.); 95:59 (J. H. Swoyer), 228 (Warrior Run Coal Co.), 424 (Ellenwood Coal Co.); 96:65 (Riverside Coal Co.), 115 (Lehigh and Wilkes-Barre Coal Co.), 304 (W. G. Payne & Co.); 97:30 (Riverside Coal Co.), 60 (Forty-Fort Coal Co.), 182 (Plymouth Coal Company), 253 (Conyngham & Co.), 258 (Dickson & Sturdevant); 98:284, 409 (Wyoming Valley Coal Co.); 99:391 (Red Ash Coal Co.); 100:51 (Leavenworth & Co.), 146 (Hanover Coal Co.), and 316 (Parrish Coal Co.).

29. Bradsby, *A History of Luzerne County*, pp. 608, 614; Harvey and Smith, *A History of Wilkes-Barre*, 5:128–29, 164–65, 194, 223–24, 245–46, 330–31; Hayden, Hand, and Jordan, *Genealogical and Family History*, 1:109, 157, 235, 386–88, 566, and 2:54–57; Johnson, *Historical Record*, 3:56 57, 9:123 27; Kulp, *Families of the Wyoming Valley*, 1:128–29, 2:541–51, and 3:1388–89; Munsell, *A History of Luzerne, Lackawanna and Wyoming Counties*, pp. 236A, 236Q–36R, 256, 278–79, 326–27; Smith, *The Wyoming Valley*, pp. 50, 69, 93, 98; Wright, *Historical Sketches*, pp. 367–71. See also the city and business directories, WHGS.

30. Bradsby, *History of Luzerne County*, pp. 623–25, 634–35; Munsell, *A History of Luzerne, Lackawanna and Wyoming Counties*, pp. 252–53, 306–9, 329–31, 355–60; Phillips, "History of Wyoming Valley," 3:625, 628, 652, 654, 656–57.

31. Bradsby, *History of Luzerne County*, pp. 634–35; Harvey and Smith, *History of Wilkes-Barre*, 5:358; *Laws of the General Assembly of the State of Pennsylvania, 1883*, C. 100, p. 298; R. G. Dun and Company Collection, 97:278 (Harvey Brothers & Co).

32. J. H. Battle, ed., *History of Columbia and Montour Counties, Pennsylvania* (Chicago: Brown, Runk and Company, 1887), 250–52; Harvey, *A History of the Miners' National Bank of Wilkes-Barre, Pennsylvania* (Wilkes-Barre: Miners' National Bank,

1918), 18–20; Harvey, *Harvey Book*, pp. 782, 790, 807, 810, 815–19; *Historical and Biographical Annals of Columbia and Montour Counties, Pennsylvania* (Chicago: J. H. Beers, 1915), 1:256–59; Hayden, Hand, and Jordan, *Genealogical and Family History*, 1:163–64, 357–58, 475–76, 535–36; Johnson, *Historical Record*, 7:251–52; Pearce, *Annals*, pp. 354–62; Bradsby, *History of Luzerne County*, p. 513; *Wilkes-Barre: The Diamond City*, pp. 113–15; Munsell, *A History of Luzerne, Lackawanna and Wyoming Counties*, p. 316; R. G. Dun and Company Collection, 91:267 (J. Sturdevant); 92:150 (Sturdevant and Goff); 94:957 (J. E. Patterson & Co.); 97:62 (Arnold Bertels), 86 (J. R. Coollaugh & Co.), 112 (Sturdevant and Goff), 232 (A. Ryman's Sons), and 278 (Harvey Brothers & Co.); *Will Book C*, pp. 39, 166; *Will Book E*, pp. 266, 308.

33. Pearce, *Annals*, pp. 507–8; R. G. Dun and Company Collection, 93:860 (Vulcan Iron Works), 892 (Harvey Brothers); 94:1140 (Wyoming Valley Manufacturing Company), 1096 (Charles Parrish); 95:264 (Wyoming Valley Ice Company), 3 (Hazard Manufacturing Company); 98:389, 415 (Sheldon Axle Company); 100:31 (Wilkes-Barre Paper Company).

34. *Wilkes-Barre: The Diamond City*, p. 115; R. G. Dun and Company Collection, 98:218 (Hazard Manufacturing Company).

35. Munsell, *A History of Luzerne, Lackawanna and Wyoming Counties*, pp. 217–18; *Wilkes-Barre: The Diamond City*, p. 115; R. G. Dun and Company Collection, 98:389, 415 (Sheldon Axle Company).

36. Harvey and Smith, *A History of Wilkes-Barre*, 4:2151; *Wilkes-Barre: The Diamond City*, pp. 117–18; R. G. Dun and Company Collection, 94:1140 (Wyoming Valley Manufacturing Company); 100:A, 160 (Wilkes-Barre Lace Manufacturing Company).

37. *Wilkes-Barre: The Diamond City*, p. 124; R. G. Dun and Company Collection, 92:150 (Baer & Stegmaier), 153 (George Reichard); 96:163 (Charles Stegmaier), 422 (John Reichard & H. Stauff); 97:371 (John Reichard and Son); 99:197 (Charles Stegmaier & Son); Kulp, *Families of the Wyoming Valley*, 3:1299–1300; Hayden, Hand, and Jordan, *Genealogical and Family History*, 1:281–82; *Wilkes-Barre Record*, 28 August and 22 September 1881; *Luzerne Union*, 12 August 1868, 18 September 1872.

38. R. G. Dun and Company Collection, 95:261 (Charles Morgan), 3 (Hazard Manufacturing Company), 264 (Wyoming Valley Ice); 97:184 (Wilkes-Barre Publishing Company), 254 (J. & W. P. Morgan Bros.), 31 (Charles and Jesse Morgan); 98:218 (Hazard Manufacturing Company), 389, 415 (Sheldon Axle Company); 100:A, 160 (Wilkes-Barre Lace Manufacturing Company), 251 (Pennsylvania Oil Company Limited), 31 (Wilkes-Barre Paper Company).

39. *Laws of the General Assembly of the State of Pennsylvania, 1851*, C. 55, p. 71; *Laws, 1852*, C. 391, p. 669; *Laws, 1853*, C. 160, p. 179; *Laws, 1859*, C. 691, p. 857; *Laws, 1860*, appendix 1859, p. 886; *Laws, 1874*, C. 270, p. 336; *Laws, 1871*, C. 1327, p. 1444, C. 1247, p. 1343; Munsell, *A History of Luzerne, Lackawanna and Wyoming Counties*, pp. 236C–36D; Smith, *The Wyoming Valley*, p. 46; *City Directory for Wilkes-Barre, 1873*; Wilkes-Barre Street Railway Collection, Wilkes College Library, Wilkes-Barre, Pennsylvania; *Wilkes-Barre, The Progressive City* (Wilkes-Barre: Enterprise Review, 1890), pp. 42–46.

40. Bradsby, *History of Luzerne County*, pp. 634, 658–59, 1280–81; Harvey, *History of the Miners' National Bank*, pp. 65–69, 92–94; Harvey and Smith, *A History of Wilkes-Barre*, 4:2008, and 5:158–59, 245–46, 250–51, 260–61; Hayden, Hand, and

Jordan, *Genealogical and Family History,* 1:43–46, 115, 157, 235, 556; Munsell, *A History of Luzerne, Lackawanna and Wyoming Counties,* pp. 213, 236D, 236Q–36R, 358; Wright, *Historical Sketches,* pp. 367–71; *Laws of the General Assembly of the State of Pennsylvania, 1851,* C. 480, p. 762; *Laws, 1871,* C. 1324, pp. 1439–1442.

41. For a description of the functions of banks, see George D. Green, *Finance and Economic Development in the Old South: Louisiana Banking, 1804–1861* (Stanford, Calif.: Stanford University Press, 1972), esp. chap. 1, "Banking and the Allocation of Credit," and 2, "Finance and Economic Development"; Richard H. Timerlake, Jr., *Money, Banking and Central Banking* (New York: Harper & Row, 1965); James, *Money and Capital Markets;* Richard Sylla, "Federal Policy, Banking Market Structure and Capital Mobilization in the United States, 1863–1913," *Journal of Economic History* 29 (1969): 657–86.

42. James, *Money and Capital Markets,* pp. 28–39, 226; R. G. Dun and Company Collection, 93:546 (Washington Lee), 570 (Lawrence Myers), 892 (Harvey Brothers); 94:897 (Bennet & Phelps), 977 (Wilkes-Barre Deposit Bank, J. P. Williamson & Co.), 978 (F. V. Rockefellow & Co.); 95:22 (Wilkes-Barre Savings Bank), 86 (People's Bank), 95 (E. P. Darling), 216 (Miners' Savings Bank), 230 (Wood, Flannigan & Co.), 245 (Anthracite Savings Bank), 261 (Brown & Gray; Bennett, Phelps & Co). For examples of investments in real estate, see R. G. Dun and Company Collection, 91:138, 149 (William P. Miner); 95:F, A (H. H. Ashley & Co.), 59 (J. H. Swoyer); 97:30 (Riverside Coal Company), 64, 67, (B. G. Carpenter & Co.), 233 (J. W. Patten & Co.); Richard Sylla, "Forgotten Men of Money: Private Bankers in Early U.S. History," *Journal of Economic History* 36 (1976): 173–88.

43. On private banking houses, see R. G. Dun and Company Collection, 93:546 (Washington Lee), 570 (Lawrence Myers Stock and Exchange Brokers); 94:897 (Bennett & Phelps Co.), 977 (J. P. Williamson & Co.), 978 (F. V. Rockefellow & Company); 95:261 (Lawrence Myers Stock and Exchange Brokers), 261 (Brown & Gray), and 228, 230 (Wood, Flannigan & Co.). On national banks, see the Dun Collection, 91:144 (Wyoming National Bank); 93:730 (First National Bank); 94:1147 (First National Bank), 1096 (Second National Bank); and on state banks, the Dun Collection, 95:22 (Wilkes-Barre Savings Bank); 86 (People's Bank), 216 (Miners' Savings Bank); Davies, "Urbanizing Region," p. 123 (Table III-13).

44. Bradsby, *History of Luzerne County,* p. 624; Harvey, *History of the Miners' National Bank,* pp. 18, 29–30, 51–52; Harvey and Smith, *A History of Wilkes-Barre,* 5:214–15; 6:561, 649; Hayden, Hand, and Jordan, *Genealogical and Family History,* 1:81–82, 88, 103–4, 489; Johnson, *Historical Record,* 2:64–66, and 6:75; Munsell, *A History of Luzerne, Lackawanna and Wyoming Counties,* pp. 306E, 306O, 336A, 336M–36N, 332; Burton W. Folsom II, "Urban Networks: The Economic and Social Order of the Lackawanna and Lehigh Valleys during Early Industrialization, 1850–1880" (Ph.D. diss., University of Pittsburgh, 1976), pp. 114–17; *Laws of the General Assembly of the State of Pennsylvania, 1871,* C. 390, pp. 424–25.

45. Harvey, *Harvey Book,* pp. 782, 807, 810, 815–19; Harvey and Smith, *A History of Wilkes-Barre,* 5:49, 330–31; Johnson, *Historical Record,* 3:13–15, and 13:56–57; Hayden, Hand, and Jordan, *Genealogical and Family History,* 1:163–64, 476, 566; Kulp, *Families of the Wyoming Valley,* 2:541–51, and 3:1388–89; Munsell, *A History of Luzerne, Lackawanna and Wyoming Counties,* pp. 236F, 236L, 335–56; *Laws of the General Assembly of the State of Pennsylvania, 1871,* C. 392, p. 428, C. 2294, p. 1384.

46. James, *Money and Capital Markets,* pp. 27–29, 48–52, 54–55, 59–63, 90–91,

93–103, 105, 120; R. G. Dun and Company Collection, 92:150 (A. Ryman); 93:730 (First National Bank), 861 (Charles Parrish); 94:917 (John Laning), 1096 (Second National Bank), 1147 (First National Bank), 1184–85 (Charles Parrish); 95:59 (J. H. Swoyer), 86 (People's Bank), 261 (Bennett, Phelps & Co.), 262 (Conyngham & Payne [These entrepreneurs were part of the private market for commercial paper. They owned $80,000 in paper from the Lehigh and Wilkes-Barre Coal Company.]), 379 (H. H. Ashley); 96:20 (McNeish & Williamson), 65 (Riverside Coal Company), 60 (Forty-Fort Coal Company), 127 (A. Ryman & Sons); 97:20 (Charles P. Hunt), 47 (Hazard Manufacturing Company), 194 (C. A. & J. W. Thomas), 232 (A. Ryman & Son).

47. For examples of ties between Wilkes-Barre banks and leaders elsewhere in the region, see R. G. Dun and Company Collection, 95:119 (Joseph P. Schooley); 96:20 (McNeish & Williamson), 176 (Sharpe, Weiss & Co.); 97:127, 232 (A. Ryman & Son); 100:268 (Ashley, McClarney & Co.).

NOTES TO CHAPTER 3

1. For a study that connects class and social ties with economic endeavor, see Frederic Cople Jaher, *The Urban Establishment: The Upper Strata in Boston, New York, Charleston, Chicago and Los Angeles* (Chicago: University of Illinois Press, 1982).

2. For a general discussion of large-scale systems and the organizational changes they precipitated in American society after the end of the nineteenth century, see Jerry Israel, ed., *Building the Organizational Society* (New York: Free Press, 1972), particularly Samuel P. Hays's introduction (pp. 1–17); W. Lloyd Warner, ed., *The Emergent American Society* (New Haven: Yale University Press, 1967), particularly the introduction and chaps. 2, 4, 12, and 14.

3. Burton W. Folsom, Jr., *Urban Capitalists: Entrepreneurs and City Growth in Pennsylvania's Lackawanna and Lehigh Regions, 1800–1920* (Baltimore: Johns Hopkins University Press, 1981); Clyde Griffen and Sally Griffen, *Natives and Newcomers: The Ordering of Opportunity in Mid-Nineteenth-Century Poughkeepsie* (Cambridge, Mass.: Harvard University Press, 1978), 84–102; Michael B. Katz, *The People of Hamilton, Canada West: Family and Class in a Mid-Nineteenth-Century City* (Cambridge, Mass.: Harvard University Press, 1975), 176–208.

4. Edward M. Cook, Jr., *Fathers of the Towns: Leadership and Community in Eighteenth-Century New England* (Baltimore: Johns Hopkins University Press, 1976), 97–104, 114–16, 129–41.

5. The best history of Wilkes-Barre before 1850 is Charles Miner's *History of Wyoming in a Series of Letters to His Son, John Miner* (Philadelphia: J. Crisay, 1845). See also *Republican Farmer and Democratic Journal* (Wilkes-Barre, Pennsylvania), 18 May 1850 and 17 April 1850; *Luzerne Union* (Wilkes-Barre, Pennsylvania), 30 May 1855; Stewart Pearce, *Annals of Luzerne County,* 2d ed. (Philadelphia: J. B. Lippincott and Company, 1866), 424, 426, 430–32; George P. Kulp, *Families of the Wyoming Valley* (Wilkes-Barre: Wyoming Historical and Geological Society, 1885), 1:2–13; 3:1079–80, and 3:1225–26; Horace C. Hayden, Alfred Hand, and John W. Jordan, *Genealogical and Family History of the Wyoming and Lackawanna Valleys, Pennsylvania* (New York: Lewis Publishing Company, 1906), 1:10 and 1:48–54.

6. Hayden, Hand, and Jordan, *Genealogical and Family History,* 1:146–47; Kulp, *Families of the Wyoming Valley,* 3:1274–75; Bradsby, ed., *History of Luzerne County,*

Pennsylvania, with Biographical Selections, pp. 700–701; Raddin, *The Wilderness and the City: The Story of a Parish,* pp. 489, 491.

7. For the Hollenbacks, see Hayden, Hand, and Jordan, *Genealogical and Family History,* 1:10–11, 1:81–82, 1:96–97, 1:102, 1:119–20, 1:355–358. For other examples, see Kulp, *Families of the Wyoming Valley,* 1:206–7, 3:1083–85, 3:1126–27, 3:1218–19; W. W. Munsell and Company, *History of Luzerne, Lackawanna and Wyoming Counties, Pennsylvania, with Illustrations and Biographical Sketches of Some of Their Prominent Men and Pioneers* (New York: W. W. Munsell and Company, 1880), pp. 236A, 236I–J, 236F, 236O, 236Q–R; Oscar J. Harvey and Ernest G. Smith, *A History of Wilkes-Barre, Pennsylvania* (Wilkes-Barre: Rader Publishing House, 1909–1930), 5:190–91, 138, 188, 231–33; Raddin, *The Wilderness and the City,* pp. 497–501, 518; Frederick C. Johnson, comp., *The Historical Record of Wilkes-Barre* (Wilkes-Barre Record, 1909), 12:112; *Luzerne Union,* 27 September 1871, 14 August 1868.

8. For the importance of these overlapping dimensions of power, see Walter S. Glazer, "Participation and Power: Voluntary Associations and Functional Organizations of Cincinnati in 1840," *Historical Methods Newsletter* 4 (1972): 150–68.

9. For an analysis of sponsored and contested mobility, see Ralph H. Turner, "Sponsored and Contested Mobility and the School System," *American Sociological Review* 25 (1960): 350–62; see also John N. Ingham, *The Iron Barons: A Social Analysis of an American Urban Elite, 1874–1965* (Westport, Conn.: Greenwood Press, 1978), 84–85. For discussions of elite continuity, see Richard S. Alcorn, "Leadership and Stability in Mid-Nineteenth-Century America: A Case Study of an Illinois Town," *Journal of American History* 61 (1974): 685–702; and Edward Pessen, "The Egalitarian Myth and the American Social Reality: Wealth, Mobility and Equality in the 'Era of the Common Man,' " *American Historical Review* 76 (1971): 989–1034. For discussions of elite discontinuity, see Herbert Gutman, "The Reality of the Rags to Riches 'Myth': The Case of Paterson, New Jersey, Locomotive, Iron and Machinery Manufacturers, 1830–1880," in *Nineteenth Century Cities,* ed. Stephen Thernstrom and Richard Sennett (New Haven: Yale University Press, 1969), pp. 98–124; Peter Decker, *Fortunes and Failures: White Collar Mobility in Nineteenth-Century San Francisco* (Cambridge, Mass.: Harvard University Press, 1978), particularly chaps. 4 and 9; Griffen and Griffen, *Natives and Newcomers,* chap. 4; and Robert Dahl, *Who Governs? Democracy in an American City* (New Haven: Yale University Press, 1961), especially chaps. 2 through 4. These positions reflect the two major interpretations of late nineteenth-century American society, social disorder, and social continuity. For the main statements on these interpretations, see Roland Berthoff on disorder: *An Unsettled People: Social Order and Disorder in American History* (New York: Harper and Row, 1971); and, on continuity, Robert H. Wiebe, *The Search for Order, 1877–1920* (New York: Hill and Wang, 1967).

10. Oscar J. Harvey, *History of the Miners' National Bank of Wilkes-Barre, Pennsylvania* (Wilkes-Barre: Board of Directors of the Miners' National Bank, 1918), 18–19; Harvey and Smith, *History of Wilkes-Barre,* 6:606; *Luzerne Union,* 20 December 1854.

11. Hayden, Hand, and Jordan, *Genealogical and Family History,* 3:213–15; Harvey and Smith, *A History of Wilkes-Barre,* 5:370–71, and 6:602–4, 606–7; Munsell, *History of Luzerne, Lackawanna and Wyoming Counties,* pp. 236E, 236O, 236P, 236S; Bradsby, *History of Luzerne,* p. 1086; Kulp, *Families of the Wyoming Valley,* 1:798–99, 63–64, and 2:816–17; Raddin, *The Wilderness and the City,* pp. 470, 475, 496; J. H. Battle, ed., *History of Columbia and Montour Counties, Pennsylvania* (Chicago: Brown, Runk

and Company, 1887), 252–53; R. G. Dun and Company Collection, 94:917 (John Laning), Harvard University, Baker Library, Manuscript Division. For other examples, see Hayden, Hand, and Jordan, *Genealogical and Family History,* 1:36, 40–42, 45, 82–83, 94, 119–21, 321–22; Harvey and Smith, *A History of Wilkes-Barre,* 5:313, 321–22, 370–71, 138, and 6:604; Bradsby, *History of Luzerne County,* pp. 1127–28, 1280; Kulp, *Families of the Wyoming Valley,* 3:1257–59; Munsell, *A History of Luzerne, Lackawanna and Wyoming Counties,* pp. 236D, 236F, 236M, 236S; Johnson, *Historical Record,* 4:133–42, 146, 109–13, 9:76–80, and 13:139–42; R. G. Dun and Company Collection, 95:429 (Ziba Bennett), 261 (Bennett, Phelps & Co.), All Counties Volume: 259 (Asa R. Brundage); 94:977 (J. P. Williamson & Co.); 96:20 (McNeish and Williamson); *Wilkes-Barre Record,* 12 September 1883.

12. Bradsby, *History of Luzerne County,* pp. 1280–81; Harvey, *History of the Miners' National Bank,* pp. 65–69; Harvey and Smith, *A History of Wilkes-Barre,* 6:604; Hayden, Hand, and Jordan, *Genealogical and Family History,* 1:36, 43–46; Kulp, *Families of the Wyoming Valley,* 3:1083; Hendrick B. Wright, *Historical Sketches of Plymouth, Luzerne County, Pennsylvania* (Philadelphia: T. B. Paterson and Brothers, 1873), 365–67, 376; Ingham, *Iron Barons,* pp. 93–96; E. Digby Baltzell, *Philadelphia Gentlemen: The Making of a National Upper Class* (Philadelphia: University of Pennsylvania Press, 1979), 293–94, 319–33.

13. N. J. Demerath, "Religion and Social Class in America," in *Sociology of Religion,* ed. Roland Robertson (Baltimore: Penguin Books, 1969), 333–51; Baltzell, *Philadelphia Gentlemen,* pp. 173–261, 335–63; Ingham, *Iron Barons,* pp. 88–92; Robert Presthus, *Men at the Top: A Study in Community Power* (New York: Oxford University Press, 1964), 76–78, 186–203; Johnson, *Historical Record,* 9:81–83.

14. Harvey and Smith, *History of Wilkes-Barre,* 5:250–51; Hayden, Hand, and Jordan, *Genealogical and Family History,* 2:435; Munsell, *A History of Luzerne, Lackawanna and Wyoming Counties,* pp. 226, 228, 230, 232, 235, 315–16. For a description of the role of religion in class, see Cook, *Fathers of the Towns,* pp. 119–24, 126–28, 131–36. This source is particularly useful as a source of background information on the Connecticut towns where many of Wilkes-Barre's prominent families originated. Most of the settlers in Wilkes-Barre and the Wyoming Valley belonged to dissenting sects in Connecticut; see Decker, *Fortunes and Failures,* pp. 112–14, 235–41; Ingham, *Iron Barons,* pp. 87–92; and Liston Pope, "Religion and Class Structure," *Annals of the American Academy of Political and Social Science* 265 (1949): 75–90. The quotation is from Ingham.

15. For a description of Wilkes-Barre's academies, see Bradsby, *History of Luzerne County,* 1:346–48; Johnson, *Historical Record,* 10:165–266; Baltzell, *Philadelphia Gentlemen,* pp. 311–15; and Ingham, *Iron Barons,* pp. 117–27, 162–67.

16. Complete-membership lists are available only for the Wyoming Historical and Geological Society, the Triton Fire House Company, and the Wyoming Athenaeum; see Stanley Woodward correspondence, 1856–1862, Triton Fire House Company, *Ledger,* 1849–1851; Wyoming Historical and Geological Society, Wilkes-Barre, Pennsylvania (hereafter cited as WHGS); WHGS, Wyoming Athenaeum Records, 2 vols., WHGS, membership lists of the WHGS; Oscar J. Harvey, *A History of Lodge 61 F&AM* (Wilkes-Barre: Yordy, 1897); *Proceedings and Collections of the Wyoming Historical and Geological Society* (Wilkes-Barre: Wilkes-Barre Record, 1886–1938). These volumes contain membership lists, obituaries of members of prominent families, and marriage and death notices. They also contain numerous articles written by members of the upper class, describing local institutions, New England ancestors, and local

events. Members also discussed science and technological matters related to coal mining. I ascertained memberships in the other organizations through newspaper notices of meetings and through the biographies in the local histories and the partial membership lists in these works. City directories were also of help. The other clubs and organizations consisted of the Cheese and Crackers Club, the Daughters of the American Revolution, the Wilkes-Barre Law and Library Association, and the Wilkes-Barre Light Dragons. Conversations with the late Ralph Hazeltine proved enormously useful. While I have cited several formal interviews, Mr. Hazeltine and I talked frequently about Wilkes-Barre's upper class, including its social clubs. Much of my information on the Malt Club and the Cheese and Crackers Club derived from these talks. Mr. Hazeltine also showed me newspaper clippings on the Malt Club and the Cheese and Crackers Club. For a description of the social life of an urban elite, see Edward Pessen, "The Lifestyle of the Antebellum Urban Elite," *Mid-America* 55 (1973): 163–80; Baltzell, *Philadelphia Gentlemen*, pp. 334–38; Ingham, *Iron Barons*, pp. 162–67, 117–27. For a history of the Malt Club and its successor, the Westmoreland Club, see *Westmoreland Club*, a recently printed pamphlet (Wilkes-Barre: Westmoreland Club, 59 South Franklin Street, 1984), 9–15.

17. For biographical examples of Wilkes-Barre leaders who began their careers as lawyers—and the role of the apprenticeship in such cases—see Edward J. Davies, "The Urbanizing Region: Leadership and Urban Growth in the Anthracite Coal Regions, 1830–1885" (Ph.D. diss., University of Pittsburgh, 1977), pp. 166–68. On the importance of the legal apprenticeship as a means of preserving power and transferring status, see Gary B. Nash, "The Philadelphia Bench and Bar, 1800–1861," *Comparative Studies in Society and History* 7 (1965): 203–20.

18. Morton J. Horowitz, *The Transformation of American Law, 1780–1860* (Cambridge, Mass.: Harvard University Press, 1977), chaps. 2, 4, and 7; James W. Hurst, "The Release of Energy," in *New Perspectives on American History*, ed. Stanley N. Katz and Stanley I. Kutler, 1st ed. (Boston: Little, Brown and Company, 1968): 354–88; Jonathan Lurie, "Lawyers, Judges and Legal Change, 1852–1916: New York as a Case Study," *Working Papers from the Regional Economic History Research Center* 3 (1980): 31–57; James W. Hurst, *Law and the Social Order in the United States* (Ithaca, N.Y.: Cornell University Press, 1977).

19. Davies, "Urbanizing Region," pp. 48–51, 54–55, 62–63.

20. These figures were drawn from the city directories, 1871–1885, located at the WHGS. For examples, see *Boyd's City Directory of Wilkes-Barre, Hazleton, Scranton and Surrounding Communities, 1871–72* (Wilkes-Barre: Andrew Boyd and W. Harry Boyd, 1871); *Wilkes-Barre, Pittston Directory for 1879–80 Containing the Names of the Inhabitants of Wilkes-Barre, Pittston, West Pittston and a Business Directory of Ashley, Kingston, Nanticoke, Parsons, Plains, Plymouth and Wyoming, 1879* (Wilkes-Barre: Lant & Company, 1879); *Boyd's Wilkes-Barre City Directory 1880–1882 Containing the Names of the Citizens Together with a Business Directory of Ashley, Carbondale, Hazleton, Kingston, Pittston, Plymouth, Scranton and White Haven* (Wilkes-Barre: Boyd's Cousins, 1880).

21. *Boyd's Wilkes-Barre City Directory 1880–1882*; Bradsby, *History of Luzerne County*, p. 511; Harvey and Smith, *History of Wilkes-Barre*, 5:211; Munsell, *A History of Luzerne, Lackawanna and Wyoming Counties*, pp. 205–10, 226–32.

22. WHGS, George R. Wright diaries of the 1870s and 1880s. See Pessen, "Lifestyle of the Antebellum Urban Elite," for similar activities among other elites.

23. This description of McClintock's funeral differs in no significant way from those

of the funerals of Samuel G. Turner, Lewis G. Paine, Elisha Harvey, and Calvin Parsons, among others. For examples, see *Luzerne Union*, 19 February 1873; *Wilkes-Barre Record*, 13 July 1883; Johnson, *Historical Record*, 3:181–84; and Hayden, Hand, and Jordan, *Genealogical and Family History*, 1:119–20, 163, 386–88, 542–44. For similar phenomena among other urban leadership groups, see Edward Pessen, "Philip Hone Set: The Social World of the New York City Elite in the 'Age of Egalitarianism,' " *New York Historical Society Quarterly* 56 (1972): 285–308, and, by the same writer, "The Lifestyle of the Antebellum Urban Elite," ibid., pp. 163–83.

24. Bradsby, *History of Luzerne County*, pp. 511, 1128; *City Directory for Wilkes-Barre, 1873*, p. 86; Harvey, *History of the Miners' National Bank*, pp. 31–33, 86, 92–94; Harvey and Smith, *History of Wilkes-Barre*, 5:2–11, 184, 321–23; Hayden, Hand, and Jordan, *Genealogical and Family History*, 1:40–42, 82–83, 111–12, 119–20, 143–46, 206–7, 235, 245–47, 542–44, 549; Munsell, *A History of Luzerne, Lackawanna and Wyoming Counties*, pp. 208–10, 236D, 236F, 236H–36I, 236Q–36R.

25. For an excellent example of the role of kinship in economic activities, see Bernard Farber, *Guardians of Virtue: Salem Families in 1800* (New York: Basic Books, 1972), 25–28, 70–75, 83–85, 117–24, 120–27; Bernard Farber, *Kinship and Class: A Midwestern City* (New York: Basic Books, 1971), 31–33, 42–45; Peter D. Hall, "Marital Selection and Business in Massachusetts Merchant Families," in *The American Family in Social Historical Perspective*, ed. Michael Gordon (New York: St. Martin's Press, 1978), 101–14; Ingham, *Iron Barons*, pp. 98–99; Cook, *Fathers of the Towns*, pp. 115–17.

26. Harvey and Smith, *A History of Wilkes-Barre*, 5:138, 173, 178–79, 188, 190–91, 310; Hayden, Hand, and Jordan, *Genealogical and Family History*, 1:10–14, 17–18, 111–13, 119–21, 235, 320–21, 357–58; Kulp, *Families of the Wyoming Valley*, 1:88–95, 109–14, 128–29, 288–90, 455–56; Raddin, *The Wilderness and the City*, p. 492; *Wilkes-Barre Record*, 21 February 1885, 24 February 1885; Munsell, *A History of Luzerne, Lackawanna and Wyoming Counties*, pp. 236Q–36R; see also Kulp, *Families of the Wyoming Valley*, 2:551–53, 586–93, 593–603, 1131, and 3:1240–42, 1299–1300; Munsell, *A History of Luzerne, Lackawanna and Wyoming Counties*, pp. 236J–K, 516B; Harvey and Smith, *A History of Wilkes-Barre*, 5:242, 326, 321–22; Hayden, Hand, and Jordan, *Genealogical and Family History*, 1:117–19, 281–82, 544, 521–23; Bradsby, *History of Luzerne County*, pp. 1232–33; Johnson, *Historical Record*, 7:74–77.

27. Bradsby, *History of Luzerne County*, pp. 1143–44; Harvey and Smith, *History of Wilkes-Barre*, 6:538; Hayden, Hand, and Jordan, *Genealogical and Family History*, 1:178–82; Munsell, *A History of Luzerne, Lackawanna and Wyoming Counties*, p. 236F; *Manuscript Census Returns, Eighth Census of the United States, 1860, Luzerne County, Pennsylvania*, National Archives Microfilm Series M-650, Rolls 1132, 1133; *Manuscript Census Returns, Ninth Census of the United States, 1870, Luzerne County, Pennsylvania*, M-593, Rolls 1365, 1366, 1367; R. G. Dun and Company Collection, 91:160 (Alexander McLean).

28. R. G. Dun and Company Collection, 91:160 (Alexander McLean).

29. Harvey, *History of the Miners' National Bank*, pp. 92–94; Harvey and Smith, *History of Wilkes-Barre*, 5:111–13, 138, 197–98, 313, 231–33, and 6:606–7; Hayden, Hand, and Jordan, *Genealogical and Family History*, 1:94, 111–12, 119–20, 215, 320–21, 475–76, and 2:213–15; Kulp, *Families of the Wyoming Valley*, 1:88–89, 95, and 3:1225–26; Munsell, *A History of Luzerne, Lackawanna and Wyoming Counties*, pp. 236D–F, 236O, 236P, 236S–T; Bradsby, *History of Luzerne County*, p. 1097; Johnson,

Historical Record, 9:76–80, and 12:109–13; R. G. Dun and Company Collection, 91:144 (Wyoming National Bank).

30. R. G. Dun and Company Collection, 95: A, F, B, 3, 379 (H. H. Ashley & Co.), 261, 263, 429 (Bennett, Phelps & Co.); 96:115, 299 (Lehigh & Wilkes-Barre Coal Company); 97:659, 60, 181 (J. H. Swoyer), 20, 248 (Charles Parrish Hunt), 234, 390 (Charles M. Conyngham); 100:316 (Parrish Coal Company). For a description of the importance of family in business, see Clyde Griffen and Sally Griffen, "Family and Business in a Small City, Poughkeepsie, New York, 1850–1880," *Journal of Urban History* 1 (1975): 316–38; and Farber, *Guardians of Virtue,* pp. 75–80, 120–27.

31. R. G. Dun and Company Collection, 92:153 (George Reichard); 95:59 (J. H. Swoyer), 261 (Bennett, Phelps & Co.); 96:65 (Riverside Coal Co.), 422 (John Reichard and H. Stauff); 97:30, 181 (Riverside Coal Company), 60 (Forty-Fort Coal Company), 371 (John Reichard & Son); and 98:284, 409 (Wyoming Valley Coal Company).

32. For the importance of extralocal ties, see G. William Skinner, "Marketing and Social Structure in Rural China, Part I," *Journal of Asian Studies* 24 (1964): 3–43. For an elaboration of these ideas, see G. William Skinner, "Cities and the Hierarchy of Local Systems," in *The City in Late Imperial China,* ed. G. William Skinner (Stanford, Calif.: Stanford University Press, 1976): 275–315, and G. William Skinner, "Mobility Strategies in Late Imperial China: A Regional Systems Analysis," in *Regional Analysis,* ed. Carol Smith, 2 vols. (New York: Academic Press, 1976), 1:327–61; Roland Warren, *The Community in America,* 3d. ed. (Chicago: Rand, McNally, 1978), chaps. 6 and 8. For the vertical dimension of the American community, see also John Walton, "The Vertical Axis of Community Organizations and the Structure of Power," in *The Search for Community Power,* ed. Willis D. Hawley and Frederick M. Wirt (Englewood Cliffs, N.J.: Prentice Hall, 1968), 353–69; and Arthur Vidich and Joseph Bensman, *Small Town in Mass Society: Class, Power and Region in a Rural Community* (Chicago: University of Chicago Press, 1976). For a bibliographic review, see John B. Sharpless and Sam B. Warner, Jr., "Urban History," *American Behavioral Scientist* 21 (1977): 227–32. For innovative studies of leadership types by community rank position in the eighteenth century, see Cook, *Fathers of the Towns;* Burton W. Folsom, "A Regional Analysis of Urban History: City Building in the Lackawanna Valley during Early Industrialization," *Working Papers from the Regional Economic History Research Center* 2 (1979): 71–100; and Diane Lindstrom, *Economic Development in the Philadelphia Region, 1810–1850* (New York: Columbia University Press, 1976). The idea of region is well developed in the literature of economics and geography. For some examples, see Michael P. Conzen, "The Maturing Urban System in the United States, 1840–1910," *Annals, Association of American Geographers* 67 (1977): 88–106; Michael P. Conzen, "A Transport Interpretation of the Growth of Urban Regions: An American Example," *Journal of Historical Geography* 1 (1975): 361–82; Edward K. Muller, "Selective Urban Growth in the Middle Ohio Valley, 1800–1860," *Geographical Review* 66 (1976): 178–99; Edward K. Muller, "Regional Urbanization and the Selective Growth of Towns in North American Regions," *Journal of Historical Geography* 3 (1977): 22–39. For an analysis of social and kinship networks, see Darrett B. Rutman, "Community Study," *Historical Methods* 13 (1980): 29–41, as a work of important heuristic value for historians. See also J. A. Barnes, "Networks and Political Process," in *Social Networks and Urban Situations: Analysis of Personal Relationships*

in *Central African Towns*, ed. J. Clyde Mitchell (Manchester, England: Manchester University Press, 1971), 50–70; Elizabeth Bott, *Family and Social Network* (New York: Free Press, 1971); J. A. Barnes, "Class and Committees in a Norwegian Parish," *Human Relations: Studies toward the Integration of the Social Sciences* 7 (1954): 39–58; Lawrence Rosen and Robert Hall, "Mate Selection in the Upper Class," *Sociological Quarterly* 7 (1966): 157–96; Farber, *Guardians of Virtue*, pp. 25–28, 70–75, 83–85; and Ingham, *Iron Barons*, particularly chap. 4, on the Pittsburgh elite.

33. For examples of the activities of these entrepreneurs during the 1840s and after, see R. G. Dun and Company Collection, 91:100; Pittston is recorded in 92:14 (Ralph Lacoe), 22 (Bowlkley & Beya), 14, 15 (Abraham Price & Co.), 16 (J. R. Schooley), 38 (Alva Tompkins); 95:128, 130 (William and J. J. Bryden); 96:307 (Michael Mangan). For Kingston, see 91:176 (Ziba A. Hoyt), 276 (Philip & Abram Goodwin), 95:51 (R. R. Phelps), 95:235 and 96:49 (Charles Hutchinson); 98:302 (Daniel Edwards & Co.). For Plymouth, see 91:104 (Smith, Blair & Davenport), 237, 246 (Peter Shupp), 294 (Abram H. Reynolds), 276 and 92:62 (J. R. & L. M. Smith), 92:8, 9 (Turner Brothers). For Wyoming, see 91:213 (Payne Pettebone), 273 (J. C. Shoemaker & Son), 277 (William Swetland); 97:329 (Pringle & Laycock).

34. Harvey and Smith, *A History of Wilkes-Barre*, 6:561; Hayden, Hand, and Jordan, *Genealogical and Family History*, 2:489; Kulp, *Families of the Wyoming Valley*, 2:724–25.

35. The manuscript census was used to locate boarders; see *Manuscript Census Returns, Seventh Census of the United States, 1850, Luzerne County, Pennsylvania*; *Manuscript Census Returns, Eighth Census of the United States, 1860, Luzerne County*; *Manuscript Census Returns, Ninth Census of the United States, 1870, Luzerne County*; Hayden, Hand, and Jordan, *Genealogical and Family History*, 1:162–65, 233–34, 535–37; Harvey and Smith, *A History of Wilkes-Barre*, 5:358, 6:669; Kulp, *Families of the Wyoming Valley*, 2:551–53; Johnson, *Historical Record*, 8:251–53.

36. Hayden, Hand, and Jordan, *Genealogical and Family History*, 1:519–60, and 2:389; Harvey and Smith, *A History of Wilkes-Barre*, 6:584–85; Munsell, *A History of Luzerne, Lackawanna and Wyoming Counties*, pp. 236E, 330B; Raddin, *The Wilderness and the City*, pp. 346–47; Bradsby, *History of Luzerne County*, 2:1909–91; *Will Book D*, Luzerne County Courthouse, Wilkes-Barre, Pennsylvania, pp. 355–57.

37. Hayden, Hand, and Jordan, *Genealogical and Family History*, 1:61–63; Harvey and Smith, *A History of Wilkes-Barre*, 5:274; Johnson, *Historical Record*, 4:145–47; Bradsby, *History of Luzerne County*, 2:850–51.

38. Bradsby, *History of Luzerne County*, 2:824–25.

39. For a contrasting view of region, see Muller, "Selective Urban Growth," pp. 178–99. Muller relies more on transportation routes and geography in his analysis and neglects export because of the economic mix in the Ohio Valley. The extractive base of the Wyoming Valley and the long-established trading relationships with communities north along the Susquehanna River obviate the problem of defining a region.

40. For an analysis of political networks beyond the community, see Whitman Ridgway, *Community Leadership in Maryland, 1790–1849* (Chapel Hill: University of North Carolina Press, 1979); Kathleen Smith Kutlowski, "The Janus Face of New York's Local Parties: Genesee County, 1821–1827," *New York History* 59 (1978): 145–72; Van Beck Hall, "A Fond Farewell to Henry Adams: Ideas on Relating Political History to Social Change during the Early National Period," in *The Human Dimensions of Nation Making*, ed. James Kirby Martin (Madison: University of Wisconsin Press, 1976): 323–61. The essay is a work of tremendous heuristic value.

41. Samuel L. French, *Reminiscences of Plymouth, Luzerne County, Penna.* (Plymouth: n.p., 1915), 43–47; Kulp, *Families of the Wyoming Valley*, pp. 756–59. For example, members of the Shonk, Turner, Rickard, Reynolds, Wadhams, Lee, and French families sent their sons to Wilkes-Barre academies.

42. Raddin, in *The Wilderness and the City*, lists the incorporators, along with biographical information on them and their children (pp. 687–89). For similar information on the incorporators of the St. James Episcopal Church in Pittston, see Raddin, pp. 679–86. For an example of Plymouth leaders' denominational changes, see the Harvey family, in Hayden, Hand, and Jordan, *Genealogical and Family History*, 1:163–64; Harvey and Smith, *A History of Wilkes-Barre*, 6:669; and in *Will Book J*, p. 220. For Patten and Turner, see *Luzerne Union*, 19 February 1873; Bradsby, *History of Luzerne County*, pp. 1234–36; and the R. G. Dun and Company Collection, 97:233, and 100:238, 293 (J. W. Patten & Co.).

43. French, *Reminiscences*, pp. 74–75; George R. Wright diaries (entries of 4 and 11 May 1874; 11, 20, and 25 December 1874; 2 and 6 February 1875; 3 March 1876), WHGS, Wilkes-Barre, Pennsylvania. The data on the twentieth-century leadership were gathered from biographical information on eighty-two men identified as leaders through indicators used for nineteenth-century leadership.

44. Hayden, Hand and Jordan, *Genealogical and Family History*, 1:162–64; Harvey and Smith, *A History of Wilkes-Barre*, 6:669; Munsell, *A History of Luzerne, Lackawanna and Wyoming Counties*, p. 236D; *Luzerne Union*, 19 February 1873; *Will Book J*, p. 220.

45. H. Benjamin Powell, "Pioneering the Anthracite Industry: The Case of the Smith Coal Company"; Munsell, *A History of Luzerne, Lackawanna and Wyoming Counties*, pp. 356–57; Kulp, *Families of the Wyoming Valley*, 2:759–62; Hayden, Hand, and Jordan, *Genealogical and Family History*, 1:163–64, 475–76; *Will Book A*, pp. 13, 47–48; *Will Book B*, pp. 266, 532; *Will Book D*, pp. 355–57; *Will Book E*, p. 308; *Will Book G*, pp. 1, 415; *Will Book H*, p. 455; *Will Book I*, pp. 19, 495; and *Will Book J*, p. 220.

46. Munsell, *A History of Luzerne, Lackawanna and Wyoming Counties*, pp. 306C, 313–14; Hayden, Hand, and Jordan, *Genealogical and Family History*, 1:176; Johnson, *Historical Record*, 6:198–200; Kulp, *Families of the Wyoming Valley*, 2:226–32.

47. For a brief description of Pittston's elite, see Folsom, *Urban Capitalists*, pp. 92–95; *Laws of the General Assembly of the State of Pennsylvania, 1853*, C. 335, pp. 567–69.

48. Harvey and Smith, *A History of Wilkes-Barre*, 5:131; Munsell, *A History of Luzerne, Lackawanna and Wyoming Counties*, pp. 329–32; Bradsby, *History of Luzerne County*, pp. 619–23; Kulp, *Families of the Wyoming Valley*, 3:1083–85, 1126–27, 1218–19; Hayden, Hand, and Jordan, *Genealogical and Family History*, 1:51–54.

49. Munsell, *A History of Luzerne, Lackawanna and Wyoming Counties*, pp. 329–32; Harvey and Smith, *A History of Wilkes-Barre*, 5:162; Folsom, *Urban Capitalists*, pp. 92–95.

50. Folsom, *Urban Capitalists*, pp. 92–95.

51. Hayden, Hand, and Jordan, *Genealogical and Family History*, 1:109, 132–33; Bradsby, *History of Luzerne County*, p. 1382; Raddin, *The Wilderness and the City*, pp. 346–47.

52. Kulp, *Families of the Wyoming Valley*, 1:114–20.

53. Hayden, Hand, and Jordan, *Genealogical and Family History*, 1:436–37, 489, and 2:464–65; R. G. Dun and Company Collection, 92:14 (Ralph Lacoe), and 93:926

(Ralph Lacoe). For other examples, see Bradsby, *History of Luzerne County*, pp. 897, 937; and Kulp, *Families of the Wyoming Valley*, 2:724–25, and 3:1306–7; Munsell, *A History of Luzerne, Lackawanna and Wyoming Counties*, pp. 330A–B; and Harvey and Smith, *A History of Wilkes-Barre*, 6:561.

54. Folsom, *Urban Capitalists*, pp. 92–94. For examples of leaders of Welsh descent, see Bradsby, *History of Luzerne County*, pp. 886, 1000–1001; Kulp, *Families of the Wyoming Valley*, 2:569–70; R. G. Dun and Company Collection, 92:14, 15 (Abraham Price & Co.), 95:100–101 (John Howell), and 95:128 (Benjamin & Edward Bowlkley). For leaders of Scottish ancestry, see Bradsby, *History of Luzerne County*, pp. 752–53, 1090–91; Hayden, Hand, and Jordan, *Genealogical and Family History*, 2:111–12, 381–82; R. G. Dun and Company Collection, 95:131 (Andrew Bryden); and Munsell, *A History of Luzerne, Lackawanna and Wyoming Counties*, pp. 330B, 330E.

55. *Laws of the General Assembly of the State of Pennsylvania, 1883*, p. 286; Bradsby, *History of Luzerne County*, pp. 621, 625, 1243; *Will Book H*, p. 445; R. G. Dun and Company Collection, 91:10 (Miners' Savings Bank of Pittston), 213 (Payne Pettebone), 277 (William Swetland), 273 (J. Shoemaker & Son); 93:546 (Washington Lee, Jr.), 905 (Pittston Stove Company), 95:59 (John H. Swoyer), 68 (Hillside Coal Company), 128, 130 (J. J. & William Bryden), 121 (Pittston Water Co.), 131 (Pittston Gas & Light Co.), 130 (Charles Pugh); 96:6 (Riverside Coal Company), 307 (W. G. Payne), 304 (William G. Payne & Co.), 376 (George M. Stock), 458 (Payne & Perrin); 97:30 (Riverside Coal Company), 158 (Pittston Arms Company), 331 (Lee Arms Company); 98:235 (Pittston Manufacturing Company), 261 (Lee Arms Company); Bradsby, *History of Luzerne County*, pp. 621, 1243; Munsell, *A History of Luzerne, Lackawanna and Wyoming Counties*, p. 331; Hayden, Hand, and Jordan, *Genealogical and Family History*, 2:447–48.

56. Persistence was determined by identifying leaders in these communities during the 1920s and comparing them with the nineteenth-century group. I also checked the city directories for the 1920s to locate specific families. Additionally, I consulted the following sources for biographical information pertaining to the 1920s: *Eastern Pennsylvanians* (Philadelphia: Eastern Pennsylvania Biographical Association, 1928); John Jordan, ed., *Encyclopedia of Pennsylvania: Biography* (New York: Lewis Historical Publishing Company, 1918); Dwight Stoddard, *Prominent Men in Scranton and the Vicinity and Wilkes-Barre and the Vicinity* (Scranton: Tribune Publishing Company, 1929); and *Wilkes-Barre Times Leader*.

57. For works on disorder and order associated with industrialization, see Berthoff, *An Unsettled People*; Gutman, "The Reality of Rags to Riches 'Myth'," pp. 98–124, and Stephen Thernstrom and Peter R. Knights, "Men in Motion: Some Data and Speculation about Urban Population Mobility in Nineteenth-Century America," *Journal of Interdisciplinary History* 1 (1970): 9–32. For other examples of the disruptive impact of economic growth on leadership, see Decker, *Fortunes and Failures*, particularly chaps. 4 and 9; Griffen and Griffen, *Natives and Newcomers*, chap. 4; and Dahl, *Who Governs?*, especially chaps. 2 through 4. For a summary of the order, or "island community," thesis and elite continuity, see Wiebe, *The Search for Order, 1877–1920*; Alcorn, "Leadership and Stability in Mid-Nineteenth-Century America," pp. 685–702; and Pessen, "The Egalitarian Myth and the American Social Reality," pp. 989–1034. Pessen, in "The Social Configuration of the Antebellum City: An Historical and Theoretical Inquiry" (*Journal of Urban History* 2 [1976]: 267–306), reviews much of this literature.

NOTES TO CHAPTER 4

1. The studies of twentieth-century leadership and power by social scientists are legion. For some examples, see Peter H. Rossi, "Power and Community Structure," in *Political Sociology*, ed. Lewis A. Coser (New York: Harper Torch, 1967): 132–45; Floyd Hunter, *Community Power Structure: A Study of Decision Makers* (Chapel Hill, N.C.: University of North Carolina Press, 1953); and Robert Presthus, *Men at the Top: A Study in Community Power* (New York: Oxford University Press, 1964). The primary historical studies of the twentieth-century leadership include E. Digby Baltzell, *Philadelphia Gentlemen: The Making of a National Upper Class* (Philadelphia: University of Pennsylvania Press, 1979); John N. Ingham, *The Iron Barons: A Social Analysis of an American Urban Elite, 1874–1965* (Westport, Conn.: Greenwood Press, 1978); and Frederic Cople Jaher, *The Urban Establishment: The Upper Strata in Boston, New York, Charleston, Chicago and Los Angeles* (Chicago: University of Illinois Press, 1982). For a description of Wilkes-Barre and the region, see U.S., Bureau of the Census, *Fourteenth Census of the United States, Population* (Washington, D.C.: Government Printing Office, 1920), 2:955; U.S., Census Bureau, *Financial Statistics of Cities Having a Population over 30,000* (Washington, D.C.: U.S. Government Printing Office, 1919), 110–11, 347–49; Peter Roberts, *Anthracite Coal Communities* (New York: Macmillan Company, 1904), 25–36, 209; *McGraw Electric Railway Manual, 1912* (New York: McGraw Publishing Company, 1913), 353; *Poor's Manual or Register of Directors and Corporation Securities* (New York: Poor's Publishing Company, 1922), 38, 503–4, 518, 686, 691, 696, 744, 749, 1029, 1639; Oscar J. Harvey and Ernest G. Smith, *A History of Wilkes-Barre, Luzerne County, Pennsylvania*, 6 vols. (Wilkes-Barre: Rader Publishing House, 1909–1930), 4:2149–52, 2167–69, 5:44–54, and 6:614, 616, 618, 623, 630, 633. For a list of all economic activity in Wilkes-Barre and the Wyoming Valley that also provides the number of employees, location of plant, headquarters, and product, see Pennsylvania Department of Internal Affairs, *Fourth Industrial Directory of the Commonwealth of Pennsylvania* (Harrisburg: J. L. Kuhn, Printers, 1923), 339–55; H. T. Adolph, *Industrial Survey of the Wyoming Valley, 1930* (Wilkes-Barre. Lockwood Greene Engineers, 1930); "Stock Ledger of the Wilkes-Barre Railway Corporation, 1912–1922," Wilkes-Barre Street Railroad Collection, Wilkes College Library, Wilkes-Barre, Pennsylvania; *Twenty-Fourth Annual Report of the Commission of Banking* (Harrisburg: J. L. Kuhn, Printer to the Commonwealth, 1918); and *Financing an Empire: History of Banking in Pennsylvania*, 4 vols., (Philadelphia: S. J. Clarke Publishing Company, 1928), 3:118–19, 295–96, 363, 375–77, 4:337–38. For examples of persistence among families in the upper class, see Harvey and Smith, *A History of Wilkes-Barre*, 5:174, 177–79, 180, 194–96, 190–91, 200, 202–3, 216, 219–20, 224–25, 257, 239–40, 260–61, 269, 313, 321–23, 352, and 6:441–42, 443, 461–62, 484–85, 539–40, 562–63, 574, 608, 689–90, 696; *Eastern Pennsylvanians* (Philadelphia: Eastern Pennsylvania Biographical Association, 1928), pp. 100, 101, 108, 124, 135, 150, 154, 126, 217, 231, 233, 235–36; Oscar J. Harvey, *History of the Miners' National Bank of Wilkes-Barre, Pennsylvania* (Wilkes-Barre: Miners' National Bank 1918), pp. 31–33, 92–94; *Wilkes-Barre Record*, 3 February 1924, 3 May 1944; *Wilkes-Barre Times-Leader*, 3 February 1934 (Hillard), 8 May 1925 (Sturdevant), 7 September 1925 (Woodward), 31 March 1930, 24 February 1932 (Goff), 25 June 1935, 5 June 1932, and 21 August 1959 (Bixby), 30 October 1932 (Wright), 12 December 1932 (Hunt), 29 January 1931 (Parrish), 23 November 1931 (Carpenter), 10 November 1928 (Morgan), 30 November 1930 (Harvey), 22 May 1931, 16 Feb-

ruary 1956 (Hand), 21 October 1933 (McLean), 7 June 1944 (Brown), 24 November 1944 (Beaumont), 10 November 1959 (Haddock). The name of the *Wilkes-Barre Times-Leader* varies. After February 1944 it became the *Wilkes-Barre Times Leader Evening News* and in May 1978 reverted to the *Wilkes-Barre Times Leader.* I am grateful to Carol Leavesly, librarian for the *Wilkes-Barre Times Leader,* for this information.

2. For examples, see H. C. Bradsby, ed., *History of Luzerne, Lackawanna and Wyoming Counties, Pennsylvania, with Biographical Selections* (Chicago: S. B. Nelson and Company, 1893), 769; *Eastern Pennsylvanians,* pp. 103–4, 106, 114–15, 124, 127, 156, 233, 252, 236; Harvey and Smith, A *History of Wilkes-Barre,* 5:219–20, 257, 260–61, 352; H. C. Hayden, Alfred Hand, and John W. Jordan, *Genealogical and Family History of the Wyoming and Lackawanna Valleys,* 2 vols. (New York: Lewis Publishing Company, 1906), 1:63–64, 81–83, 346; Harvey, *History of the Miners' National Bank of Wilkes-Barre, Pennsylvania,* p. 18; Oscar J. Harvey, *The Harvey Book* (Wilkes-Barre: E. B. Yordy and Company, Printer, 1899), 782, 790, 810, 807; George B. Kulp, *Families of the Wyoming Valley,* 3 vols. (Wilkes-Barre: Wyoming Historical and Geological Society, 1885), 1:224–26; W. W. Munsell and Company, A *History of Luzerne, Lackawanna and Wyoming Counties, with Illustrations and Biographical Sketches of Some of Their Prominent Men and Pioneers* (New York: W. W. Munsell and Company, 1880), 236A–N; *Proceedings and Collections of the Wyoming Historical and Geological Society,* s.v. "Necrology" in vols. 9 and 20; George Raddin, *The Wilderness and the City: The Story of a Parish* (Wilkes-Barre: St. Stephen's Episcopal Church, 1968), 408; S. R. Smith, *The Wyoming Valley in the Nineteenth Century* (Wilkes-Barre: Wilkes-Barre Leader, Printer, 1894), 45, 51, 90, 92; Smith, *The Wyoming Valley in 1892* (Wilkes-Barre: Scranton Republican, 1892), 54–55, 58–59; *Will Book G,* p. 410, and *Will Book J,* p. 22, Luzerne County Courthouse, Wilkes-Barre, Pennsylvania.

3. For accounts of some of these organizations, see Munsell, *History of Luzerne, Lackawanna and Wyoming Counties,* pp. 208–9; Harvey and Smith, *History of Wilkes-Barre,* 4:2168–69; Bradsby, *History of Luzerne County,* pp. 454, 512; *Wilkes-Barre Record,* 13 June 1884.

4. For examples of kinship among families in the upper class, see Bradsby, *History of Luzerne County,* pp. 703–4, 1127–28; Harvey and Smith, A *History of Wilkes-Barre,* 5:179–80, 187, 202, 209, 219, 220, 224–25, 313, 321–22, 326, 345, and 6:439–40, 461–67, 497, 540–41, 602–4, 655; Harvey, *History of the Miners' National Bank,* pp. 92–94, 107–8; *Eastern Pennsylvanians,* pp. 101, 103, 106, 126–27, 135, 233, 236, 154, 329; Hayden, Hand, and Jordan, *Genealogical and Family History,* 1:104–5; 120–21, 312–13, 317–18; 351–52; Kulp, *Families of the Wyoming Valley,* 2:800–801, 816–17, 593–603, and 3:1174–77, 1131; Smith, *The Wyoming Valley,* pp. 64, 66–67, 99; Raddin, *The Wilderness and the City,* pp. 408, 468, 473, 475, 503; Munsell, *History of Luzerne, Lackawanna and Wyoming Counties,* p. 236F; *Proceedings and Collections of the Wyoming Historical and Geological Society,* s.v. "Necrology," 19 (1926): li–liii; *Wilkes-Barre Record,* 6 May 1884; Darret B. Rutman, "Community Study," *Historical Methods* 13 (1980): 29–41. For examples of biographical data on women in the upper class, see *Wilkes-Barre Record,* 7 September 1922 (Mrs. Jennie DeWitte Harvey), 25 August 1925 (Miss Elizabeth Loveland), 21 May 1926 (Mrs. Harold Mercer Shoemaker), 26 September 1927 (Mrs. George Shoemaker), 27 November 1928 (Mrs. Ellen Woodward Bennett), 28 June 1930 (Mrs. J. Eva Loomis), 11 November 1930 (Mrs. Charles D. Foster), 1 November 1931 (Mrs. Esther Wadhams Shoemaker Norris), 2 April 1932 (Mrs. Mary Butler Ayres), 3 February 1934 (Amy Sturdevant Barber), 17 Feb-

ruary 1934 (Mrs. Esther Fuller Hillard), 28 March 1936 (Mrs. Charles Parrish Hunt), 2 January 1937 (Mrs. Helen M. Reynolds Miller), 7 August 1937 (Mrs. Elizabeth Woodward Scott), 28 July 1938 (Miss Ella Bowman), 13 October 1943 (Mary E. Hillard), 21 December 1964 (Miss Anna Chadhoon Lewis), 24 November 1967 (Mrs. Elizabeth Ayres Tompkins), 3 July 1969 (Mrs. Dorothy D. Darte). The obituaries vary from a paragraph to several columns.

5. Ingham, *Iron Barons*, pp. 87–92; Baltzell, *Philadelphia Gentlemen*, pp. 292–334.

6. Ingham, *Iron Barons*, pp. 87–92; N. J. Demerath, "Religion and Social Class in America," in *Sociology of Religion*, ed. Roland Robertson (Baltimore: Penguin Books, 1969), 333–51; Presthus, *Men at the Top*, pp. 76–78, 186–203.

7. Ingham, *Iron Barons*, pp. 85–87, 106–17; Baltzell, *Philadelphia Gentlemen*, pp. 173–322; *Wilkes-Barre Record*, 24 December 1928, 22 October 1929, 29 November 1929, 26 July 1932, 3 January 1935, 6 December 1937. The social section of the paper noted in considerable detail the interaction among the members of the upper class. Guest lists for parties, luncheons, teas, and other such events were included in each description of the social activities of the upper class. Today, the residential district is occupied largely by Wilkes College, which began to take over the district in the 1940s and 1950s. During the 1960s, when I attended the school, it attracted a large portion of its student body from working-class families in the Wyoming Valley. As a student of that school, I sat in these mansions, taking classes there, and of course unaware that the people who had lived in my classrooms were those I would study in later years.

8. *Wilkes-Barre City Tax Records, 1910–1950*, Wilkes-Barre, Pennsylvania, Ward 7, 1920–1940, located in Wilkes College, Wilkes College Special Collections.

9. For a summary of the impact of the corporation and organizational change in the twentieth century, see Jerry Israel, ed., *Building the Organizational Society: Essays on Associational Activities in Modern America* (New York: Free Press, 1972), especially Samuel P. Hays's introduction, "The New Organizational Society" (pp. 1–16); Maurice R. Stein, *The Eclipse of Community: An Interpretation of American Studies* (New York: Harper & Row Publishers, 1960), 70–116 and Part 3; Louis Galambos, "The Emerging Organizational Synthesis in American History," and Alfred D. Chandler, Jr., and Louis Galambos, "The Development of Large-Scale Economic Organizations in Modern America," both in *Men and Organizations*, ed. Edwin J. Perkins (New York: G. P. Putnam's Sons, 1977), 3–15 and 188–201, respectively; W. Lloyd Warner, *Yankee City*, abridged ed. (New Haven: Yale University Press, 1963), 301–56; Roland L. Warren, *The Community in America* (Chicago: Rand McNally College Publishing Company, 1978), chaps. 3, 4, 9, and especially 8, "The Community's Vertical Pattern: Ties to the Larger Society"; Richard Jensen, "Quantitative Collective Biography: An Application to Metropolitan Elites," in *Quantification in American History: Theory and Research*, ed. Robert P. Swierenga (New York: Atheneum, 1970), 386–405; John Walton, "The Vertical Axis of Community Organizations and the Structure of Power," in *The Search For Community Power*, ed. Willis D. Hawley and Frederick M. Wirt (Englewood Cliffs, N.J.: Prentice-Hall, 1968), 353–66. For a discussion of these ties among metropolitan elites, see Edward Pessen, "The Lifestyle of the Antebellum Urban Elite," *Mid-America* 55 (1973): 163–80, and, by the same author, "The Egalitarian Myth and the American Social Reality: Wealth, Mobility, and Equality in the 'Era of the Common Man,' " *American Historical Review* 76 (1971): 999–1000.

10. These were drawn from the local newspapers; R. G. Dun and Company Collec-

218 : notes to pages 80 to 83

tion, All Counties Volume, Luzerne County, vols. 91–100, Baker Library, Manuscript Division, Harvard University; biographies in local histories; genealogies, and the George R. Wright Diaries, 1874–1930, Wyoming Historical and Geological Society, Wilkes-Barre, Pennsylvania.

11. For a general discussion of professional and trade associations, see W. Lloyd Warner, ed., *Emergent American Society* (New Haven: Yale University Press, 1967).

12. Ingham, *Iron Barons*, pp. 96–98, 117–27; Baltzell, *Philadelphia Gentlemen*, pp. 335–63.

13. Baltzell, *Philadelphia Gentlemen*, pp. 72, 119–20, 336–43, 375; Westmoreland Club Papers, 1896–1927, WHGS; Ralph Hazeltine, interview with author, 20 and 21 March 1972, Wilkes-Barre, Pennsylvania. Mr. Hazeltine, the retired director of the Wyoming Valley Historical and Geological Society, and his father were tied to the Eastern Pennsylvania Supply Company and the Conyngham family, its owners for much of the twentieth century and one of the most powerful old-line families in the Valley. Ralph Hazeltine was also county tax assessor, county Republican committeeman and party leader for more than thirty years. Membership in the Westmoreland Club was largely drawn from the biographical sketches.

14. Baltzell, *Philadelphia Gentlemen*, pp. 342–43; Jaher, *The Urban Establishment*, pp. 103–4, 277–78.

15. Ingham, *Iron Barons*, pp. 96–98; Baltzell, *Philadelphia Gentlemen*, pp. 296–99, 301–13; James McLachan, *American Boarding Schools: A Historical Study* (New York: Charles Scribner's Sons, 1970); Jaher, *The Urban Establishment*, pp. 102–3.

16. Baltzell, *Philadelphia Gentlemen*, pp. 326–34; Ingham, *Iron Barons*, pp. 94–95; Jaher, *The Urban Establishment*, pp. 103–4, 266–67, 277–78.

17. These societies also worried about the deleterious effects of southern and eastern Europeans and conducted campaigns aimed at making them good citizens. See John Higham, *Strangers in the Land: Patterns of American Nativism, 1860–1925* (New York: Atheneum, 1967), pp. 326–63. The local branches of these organizations often cooperated in a variety of local events. These were generally noted in the reports of each volume of the *Proceedings* published by the WHGS. The branches also hosted statewide conventions and frequently reported on national meetings through the various *Proceedings*. For an example, see "Reports," *Proceedings and Collections of the Wyoming Historical and Geological Society* 22 (1938): xii–xv; Jaher, *The Urban Establishment*, p. 276.

18. For a general description of the intrusion of New York City corporations, see Jules I. Bogen, *The Anthracite Railroads: A Study in American Enterprise* (New York: Ronald Press, 1927); see also Eliot Jones, *The Anthracite Coal Corporations in the United States with Some Account of the Early Development of the Anthracite Industry* (Cambridge, Mass.: Harvard University Press, 1914); G. O. Virtue, "The Anthracite Combination," *Quarterly Journal of Economics* 19 (1896): 296–323. On the issue of absentee ownership, see R. J. Pellegrin and C. H. Coates, "Absentee-Owned Corporations and Community Power Structure," *American Journal of Sociology* 61 (1956): 413–19.

19. For railroads and coal companies, see *Poor's Manual or Register of Directors and Corporation Securities*, pp. 38, 504, 518–19, 686, 749, 1503, 1629, 1639. For leaders who served as directors of these companies, see Harvey and Smith, *A History of Wilkes-Barre*, 5:118–19, 158, 179–80, 193, 224, 329, 6:484–85, 539–40; and *Eastern*

Pennsylvanians, pp. 100–101, 105, 115, 126–27, 159. For listings of number of employees, locations of plants, headquarters and products, see Pennsylvania Department of Internal Affairs, *Fourth Industrial Directory of the Commonwealth of Pennsylvania*, pp. 339–55; Burton W. Folsom, Jr., *Urban Capitalists: Entrepreneurs and City Growth in Pennsylvania's Lackawanna and Lehigh Regions, 1800–1920* (Baltimore: Johns Hopkins University Press, 1981), 137–38.

20. A large portion of these leaders served in the four main commercial banks (i.e., the Wyoming National Bank, the First National Bank, the Second National Bank, and the Miners' National Bank). See Harvey and Smith, *A History of Wilkes-Barre*, 5:381–83. Estate Inventories, Register of Wills, Luzerne County Courthouse, Luzerne County, Wilkes-Barre, Pennsylvania. The inventory numbers, followed by the years of filing, are 1166 in 1920; 61, 187, 816, and 833 in 1924; 254 in 1925 (Cabinet #2, first can in second row); 22 in 1928; 982 in 1930; 1054 and 1420 in 1931; 1293 in 1932; 378 in 1933; 215 and 805 in 1934; 233 in 1937; 1262 in 1940 (File Cabinet #2, can on bottom row, second from right to left); 473 (Cabinet #5, can #29) and 1661 in 1943; 511 in 1944; 326 in 1950; 240 in 1956; 1143 in 1959; and 1243 in 1967. The coal company stocks generally had no value by the 1950s; see Estate Inventory #1143, from 1959.

21. Monte Calvert, *The Mechanical Engineer in America, 1830–1910: Professional Cultures in Conflict* (Baltimore: Johns Hopkins University Press, 1967); Daniel H. Calhoun, *The American Civil Engineer: Origins and Conflict* (Cambridge, Mass.: M.I.T. Press, 1960); Robert Reid, "The Professionalization of Public School Teachers: The Chicago Experience" (Ph.D. diss., Northwestern University, 1968); Warner, *Emergent American Society*, pp. 276–346; Hays, "The New Organizational Society," pp. 5–11.

22. Baltzell, *Philadelphia Gentlemen*, p. 375.

23. Bureau of the Census, *Fourteenth Census*, 2:955; Bureau of the Census, *Financial Statistics of Cities*, pp. 110–11, 347–49.

Although they did not meet the criteria for economic or political power, I have included doctors from the ethnic groups as members of the elite in the Wyoming Valley. There are several reasons to do so. First, the occupation carried considerable prestige within the ethnic subcultures. Second, it required a college and postgraduate education, both comparatively rare among the immigrant groups during this decade. The education imparted professional skills of enormous value, also rare among the immigrant subcultures. Third, while the income of a doctor varied, it was probably several times greater than the income for coal mining or other occupations generally found among these groups. These men also participated in the elite social, ethnic, and fraternal clubs patronized by those who held economic and/or political power. Moreover, their biographies also appeared with the men of visible substance. For examples, see Harvey and Smith, *A History of Wilkes-Barre*, 5:219, 320, 360–63, and 6:400, 422–23, 430–31, 444, 453, 458, 514–16, 534–35, 616–17, 641, 655–56, 726–27, 731, 734–35, 739–40. These men comprised 7 percent of the 499 leaders. For a discussion of ethnic leadership, see Ewa Morowska, "The Internal Status Hierarchy in the East European Communities in Johnstown, Pa., 1890–1930's," *Journal of Social History* 16 (1982): 75–108; and Barrington Moore, "Historical Notes on the Doctors' Work Ethic," *Journal of Social History* 17 (1984): 547–72, especially p. 559 (salaries).

24. Harvey and Smith, *A History of Wilkes-Barre*, vol. 4. For an excellent account

of these churches and the Wyoming Valley in general, see Edward F. Hanlon, *The Wyoming Valley, An American Portrait* (Woodland, Calif.: Windsor Publications, 1983).

25. Harvey and Smith, *A History of Wilkes-Barre.* Vols. 5 and 6 index each church and give histories of each institution. The biographies of the members of the elite also list their church affiliation. For the founding of several of these churches, see Munsell, *History of Luzerne, Lackawanna and Wyoming Counties,* pp. 232–36; and Hanlon, *The Wyoming Valley, An American Portrait.*

26. For some examples, see Harvey and Smith, *A History of Wilkes-Barre,* 6:476, 650, 759; and *Eastern Pennsylvanians,* pp. 180, 238, 345.

27. The clubs and several of the ethnic organizations were discussed in Harvey and Smith, *A History of Wilkes-Barre,* vol. 6. See also the *Wilkes-Barre Record* and the *Wilkes-Barre Times Leader,* particularly the holiday issues and those which occurred around religious celebrations, such as Easter and St. Patrick's Day. The *Wilkes-Barre Record* occasionally ran short biographies of prominent men in the Valley. These contained useful information on the members of Wilkes-Barre's and other urban elites in the Valley. For example, see *Wilkes-Barre Record,* January through April, 1932. Generally, the biographies appeared in the second section, the second or later pages. A picture of the leader accompanied the biography. The biographies in the local histories also listed club and ethnic associations of members of the elite. My thanks to E. G. Hartmann, Professor Emeritus, Suffolk University, Boston, for information on the restriction against Catholics joining Masonic organizations.

28. For a general history of these groups, see Higham, *Strangers in the Land.*

29. The *Wilkes-Barre Record* contained information on these groups, while the biographies list membership in each.

30. For a discussion of associational ties, see Israel, *Building the Organizational Society;* Warner, ed., *Emergent American Society.*

31. Harvey and Smith, *A History of Wilkes-Barre,* 4:2149–52, 2167–69, 5:44–54, and 6:614, 616, 618, 623, 630, 633. For biographies of bank directors, including those in the North End State Bank and the Liberty State Bank and Trust Company, see *Eastern Pennsylvanians,* pp. 122, 211, 233, 257; and Harvey and Smith, *A History of Wilkes-Barre,* 5:222, 278, 328, 333–35, 337, 339, 360, and 6:432, 508, 525, 535, 558, 592, 616, 623, 634, 640, 659, 662, 739, 743.

32. Bernard Barber, "Family Status, Local Community Status and Social Stratification: Three Types of Social Ranking," *Pacific Sociological Review* 4 (1961): 463–69; H. Goldhammer and E. Shils, "Types of Power and Status," *American Journal of Sociology* 45 (1939): 171–82. The bank directors in the upper class were drawn from the boards of the Miners' National Bank, the First National Bank, the Second National Bank, and the Wyoming National Bank. The bank directors in the elite were drawn from the boards of the Wilkes-Barre Deposit and Savings Bank, the Wyoming Valley Trust Company of Wilkes-Barre, the South Side Bank and Trust Company, the North End State Bank, the Heights Deposit Bank, the Liberty State Bank and Trust Company, the Pennsylvania Bank and Trust Company, the Dime Bank Title and Trust Company, the Wyoming Valley Building and Loan Association, the Wilkes-Barre Union Savings Bank and Trust Company, the Hanover Bank and Trust Company, the Lincoln Bank and Trust Company, and the Susquehanna Savings and Loan Association. Members of the upper class and the elite on occasion did serve on the same bank boards. The Wilkes-Barre Deposit and Savings Bank and the Union Bank and

Trust Company were prominent examples. See Harvey and Smith, *A History of Wilkes-Barre*, 5:177–78, 351–52, and 6:608–9; *Eastern Pennsylvanians*, 106, 127; and *Wilkes-Barre Record*, 7 September 1925.

33. For examples, see Harvey and Smith, *A History of Wilkes-Barre*, 5:246, and 6:547–48, 570, 614, 663–64. For examples of these families, see Harvey and Smith, *A History of Wilkes-Barre*, 5:233 (French), 246 (Nesbitt), 390 (Reynolds), 243 (Schooley), 312–13 (Morris), and 6:386–87 (Lees), 375 (McMillan), 414 (Howell), 527–28 (Richard), 594–95 (Stark), 615 (Blackman); and *Eastern Pennsylvanians*, pp. 312 (Spry), and 359, 365 (Foster).

34. For examples, see Harvey and Smith, *A History of Wilkes-Barre*, 5:180, 246, 312–13, 343, and 6:394, 414; and *Eastern Pennsylvanians*, p. 219; *Wilkes-Barre Record Almanac, 1922* (Wilkes-Barre: Wilkes-Barre Record, 1922), "Deaths."

35. Harvey and Smith, *A History of Wilkes-Barre*, 5:187, 247, 200, 264, and 6:543, 594–95; *Eastern Pennsylvanians*, pp. 157, 213, 278.

36. Harvey and Smith, *A History of Wilkes-Barre*, 5:204–7, 246, 255–56, 259–60, 297–98, 318, 338, 346–47, 358, and 6:375, 378, 413–14, 478–80, 543, 570, 586, 588, 697, 760; *Eastern Pennsylvanians*, pp. 99, 127, 151, 236, 294, 308, 312; *Wilkes-Barre Record*, 9 February 1925 (Harry Ash), 14 April 1926 (William G. Payne), 31 August 1923 (George Wall), 24 February 1936 (William T. Payne); Estate Inventory number 580 in 1922; 1089 in 1920 (Special Box, top row against west wall, Abram Nesbitt), 583 in 1926 (Special Box, top row against west wall, Abram Nesbitt, Jr.), 164 in 1925.

37. Harvey and Smith, *A History of Wilkes-Barre*, 5:286, 290, and 6:443–44, 504–5, 522–23, 556–57, 554–55, 614, 638, 660, 662, 690–91, 701, 752; *Eastern Pennsylvanians*, pp. 94, 330.

38. Harvey and Smith, *A History of Wilkes-Barre*, 5:300, and 6:412–13, 524, 528, 654, 703, 731–32; *Eastern Pennsylvanians*, p. 267. I use comparatively instead of completely isolated, as I had done in an earlier publication, for a number of reasons. At that time, I had not done a club analysis of the urban elites nor a study of their ties with Wilkes-Barre and its elite. I also had not examined Kingston's elite, nor the Wilkes-Barre elite. The members of the urban elites in the Wyoming Valley had developed several types of ties with the upper class, as had the leaders in Wilkes-Barre's 1920 elite. The Wilkes-Barre Chamber of Commerce, other professional associations, and the elite country clubs were the main points of contact. These ties were far more intense among Kingston's elite than in other elites in the Wyoming Valley.

39. For a discussion of the continuing importance of ethnicity and religion, see Timothy L. Smith, "Religion and Ethnicity in America," *American Historical Review* 83 (1978): 1155–85; Kathleen Neils Conzen, *Immigrant Milwaukee, 1836–1860: Accommodation and Community in a Frontier City* (Cambridge, Mass.: Harvard University Press, 1976); John Bodnar, *Immigration and Industrialization: Ethnicity in an American Mill Town* (Pittsburgh: University of Pittsburgh Press, 1977); Josef Barton, *Peasants and Strangers: Italians, Rumanians and Slovaks in an American City, 1890–1950* (Cambridge, Mass.: Harvard University Press, 1975).

40. For a general description of the economy of the Wyoming Valley, see Adolph, *Industrial Survey of the Wyoming Valley*.

41. For examples, see *Wilkes-Barre Record*, 8 January 1932, 11 November 1930, 6 February 1931, 23 August 1924, 22 January 1923, and 16 and 26 March 1932.

42. *Wilkes-Barre City Directory, 1922* (Wilkes-Barre: R. L. Polk & Co., 1922); *Wilkes-Barre City Directory, 1927* (Wilkes-Barre: R. L. Polk & Co., 1927); Harvey and Smith, *A History of Wilkes-Barre*, 5:363–64, and 6:642–43, 745.

43. Harvey and Smith, *A History of Wilkes-Barre*, 5:327, 333, and 6:397, 432–33, 508, 530, 533, 551, 554–55, 588, 592–93, 620–21, 624, 635, 679; *Eastern Pennsylvanians*, pp. 205, 239, 259, 324.

44. For examples of members of the Kingston elite who belonged to these groups in Wilkes-Barre, see Harvey and Smith, *A History of Wilkes-Barre*, 5:259, 320, and 6:454–55, 458, 574, 569, 588; *Eastern Pennsylvanians*, pp. 259, 317.

45. For examples of members of the Plymouth and Pittston elites who belonged to these Wilkes-Barre organizations, see *Eastern Pennsylvanians*, pp. 132, 233, 330, 359; Harvey and Smith, *A History of Wilkes-Barre*, 5:219, 286, 306, 308, 320, 359–60, 370, and 6:381, 415–16, 444, 451, 464, 525–26, 555–57. For examples in general, see *Wilkes-Barre Record*, 29 June 1928, 30 March 1930, 8 and 12 January 1932, 17 February 1932, and 2 and 23 March 1932.

46. In an earlier publication, I suggested that the growing ties with the metropolitan centers and their leadership groups may well have undermined the upper class by drawing its leaders (actually, I intended the succeeding generation, rather than those men and women in their prime during the 1920s) to New York City and Philadelphia. E. G. Hartmann, Professor Emeritus, Suffolk University, Boston, disagreed, arguing that the upper-class families died out rather than migrating out of the city. In an attempt to answer this question, I have been studying the evolution of leadership in the Wyoming Valley, 1930–1980. The situation is more complex than I anticipated. Families did die out. Members also migrated to New York City, Detroit, Wilmington, Los Angeles, Troy (N.Y.), and San Francisco. (These data are collected from the obituaries, as they list the places of residence of the relatives of the deceased.) I also discovered that, while many left, some were brought back to Wilkes-Barre to be buried in the Hollenback Cemetery. It appears that the combination of families dying out and out-migration depleted the ranks of the upper class. The Great Depression of the 1930s and the collapse of the coal industry also forced younger members of the upper class to leave in search of opportunity elsewhere. At the same time, the upper class began to suburbanize. Technology (i.e., automobiles), the new road system, and the development of residential areas outside the Wyoming Valley made this possible. Glen Summit (already a summer resort for the upper class), Dallas, Bear Creek, Trucksville, Lake Carey, and other areas drew the upper class out of Wilkes-Barre. The upper-class families also began to spend entire seasons outside the region. Pinehurst, N.C.; Breton Woods, New Hampshire; Florida; and other locations became part-time residences for the upper class. Announcements of departures, summer parties, and destinations appeared in the social section of the local newspapers. A possible sign that the upper class had begun to feel the effects of migration and mortality occurred on 1 June 1937, when Colonel Ernest G. Smith issued a public appeal in the *Wilkes-Barre Record* for new members to join the Wyoming Historical and Geological Society, whose numbers had shrunk during the previous years. I hope soon to have a clear picture of what was happening to the regional urban leadership groups. My thanks to Professor Hartmann; his wide knowledge of the history of the region, along with his extraordinary insight, stimulated my thinking and has led to my continuing research.

NOTES TO CHAPTER 5

1. Eliot Jones, *The Anthracite Coal Combinations in the United States with Some Accounts of the Early Developments of the Anthracite Industry* (Cambridge, Mass.: Harvard University Press, 1914), 607; W. W. Munsell, ed., *History of Schuylkill County, Pennsylvania* (New York: W. W. Munsell and Company, 1881), 32–33; Ralph Trego, *A Geography of Pennsylvania* (Philadelphia: Edward C. Biddle, 1843), 118–19, 342–43.

2. Robert Allison, "Early History of Coal Mining and Mining Machinery in Schuylkill County," *Publications of the Schuylkill County Historical Society* 4 (1914): 134–40; E. Digby Baltzell, *Philadelphia Gentlemen* (Chicago: Quadrangle Press, 1971), 104–5, 119–21; Frederick M. Binder, "Anthracite Enters the American Home," *Pennsylvania Magazine of History and Biography* 82 (1958): 83–89; Ele Bowen, *The Coal Regions of Pennsylvania, Being a General Geological, Historical and Statistical Review of the Anthracite Coal Districts* (Pottsville: Benjamin Bannan, 1848), 24–30; Alfred D. Chandler, Jr., "Anthracite Coal and the Beginnings of the Industrial Revolution in the United States," *Business History Review* 66 (1972): 141–81; Adolf W. Schalck and the Honorable D. C. Henning, eds., *History of Schuylkill County*, 2 vols. (Harrisburg: State Historical Association, 1907), 1:100–101, 103; Clifton Yearly, *Enterprise and Anthracite: Economics and Democracy in Schuylkill County, 1820–1875* (Baltimore: Johns Hopkins University Press, 1961), 25–28, 153–54; Trego, *Geography of Pennsylvania*, pp. 156–57.

3. Herbert C. Bell, ed., *History of Northumberland County* (Chicago: Brown, Runk and Company, 1891), 366–70, 374, 379; *Digest of Titles of Corporations Chartered by the Legislature of Pennsylvania between the Years 1700 and 1866, Inclusive* (Philadelphia: John Campbell Publisher and Bookseller, 1867); Jay V. Hare, *History of the Reading Which Appeared as a Serial in the Pelat and Philadelphia and Reading Railway Men Beginning May 1909–Ending February, 1914* (Philadelphia: John H. Strock, 1966), 91–93, 123–31, 240–43; *Laws of the General Assembly of the State of Pennsylvania, 1856,* C. 197, pp. 162–72; *Laws, 1858,* C. 205, pp. 170–71; *Laws, 1860,* C. 671, pp. 822–23; *Laws, 1866,* C. 1029, p. 1095, and C. 284, pp. 316–17; *Laws, 1869,* C. 709, p. 727; Munsell, *History of Schuylkill County, Pennsylvania,* 8–10, 33, 41–53, 56–58, 60–61, 91–92; Louis Polinak, *When Coal Was King* (Lebanon: Applied Arts Publishing, 1974), 16–17; Schalck and Henning, *History of Schuylkill County,* 1:100–101, 103; Yearly, *Enterprise and Anthracite,* pp. 159–62; *Miners' Journal,* Pottsville, Pennsylvania, 1 January 1857, 3 January 1857, and 26 November 1859. For a contemporary account of the early development of the coal industry in Northumberland County, see *Miners Journal,* 9 January 1858.

4. Edward J. Davies II, "The Urbanizing Region: Leadership and Urban Growth in the Anthracite Coal Regions, 1820–1885" (Ph.D. diss., University of Pittsburgh, 1977), p. 259.

5. Yearly, *Enterprise and Anthracite,* pp. 28, 30–32, 35, 38, 165–66.

6. Munsell, *History of Schuylkill County, Pennsylvania,* pp. 54–55; Peter Roberts, *The Anthracite Coal Industry* (New York: Macmillan Company, 1910), 117–19.

7. The slope had five chief disadvantages: (1) It was restricted to one vein. (2) Drawing and hoisting required tremendous strain on miners. (3) Coal, having been extracted, had to be hauled to the breaker. (4) Depth was limited. (5) Work had to

stop before miners could seek another vein. See Bell, *History of Northumberland County*, pp. 360–63; Roberts, *The Anthracite Coal Industry*, p. 17; Munsell, *History of Schuylkill County, Pennsylvania*, pp. 54–55; and Yearly, *Enterprise and Anthracite*, pp. 103, 107, 108–15, 118–19.

8. Yearly, *Enterprise and Anthracite*, pp. 108–15, 118–19.

9. Ibid., pp. 28, 30, 35, 38, 57–59, 60–62, 111, 113–15; Jones, *The Anthracite Combinations*, pp. 17–19, 20, 22.

10. Yearly, *Enterprise and Anthracite*, pp. 28, 30, 35, 38.

11. For sources of control and mining techniques from the 1850s onward, see chap. 6.

12. *Miners Journal*, 6 September 1856: R. G. Dun and Company Collection, All Counties Volume, Schuylkill County, vols. 172–75. Harvard University, Baker Library, Manuscript Division. See 172:79 (Haywood and Lee), and 258 (Benjamin Haywood); and *Pennsylvania Census Records, 1870, Schuylkill County, Manufacturing*, MicroPhoto Division, Bell and Howell, Worcester, Ohio (for example, see Middleport, Mahanoy City, Mahanoy Township, Schuylkill Township, East Norwegian Township, Blythe Township, Foster Township, Reilly Township, Rush Township). On the disadvantages of slope, see Yearly, *Enterprise and Anthracite*, pp. 116, 118–19; on technology, see Munsell, *History of Schuylkill County, Pennsylvania*, pp. 54–55.

13. Davies, "Urbanizing Region," p. 258; *Miners Journal*, 7 June 1873.

14. *Laws of the General Assembly of the State of Pennsylvania, 1857*, C. 618, pp. 579–80, and C. 683, pp. 645–46; *Laws, 1863*, C. 609, p. 647, C. 103, pp. 108–9, and C. 491, pp. 557–59; Yearly, *Enterprise and Anthracite*, pp. 135–38; R. G. Dun and Company Collection, 172:148 (Mount Carbon Railroad Company).

15. Hare, *History of the Reading*, pp. 240–43; *Laws of the General Assembly of the State of Pennsylvania, 1857*, C. 683, pp. 645–46; *Laws, 1863*, C. 609, p. 647; *Laws, 1864*, C. 103, pp. 108–9, and C. 491, pp. 557–59.

16. For a description of this political opposition, see Yearly, *Enterprise and Anthracite*, 68–72, 87–89, 75, 136, 148–50, 197–98; David Montgomery, *Beyond Equality: Labor and the Radical Republicans, 1862–1872* (New York: Vintage Books, 1967), 15.

17. J. H. Beers, *Schuylkill County, Pennsylvania*, 2 vols. (Chicago: J. H. Beers and Company, 1916), 1:1–2, 39–40, 83–84, 116–17, 120–24; *Boyd's City Directory of Pottsville Including Palo Alto, Mount Carbon and Mechanicsville, 1879–1880* (Pottsville: William H. Boyd and Company, 1881); Mrs. Ella Zerbey Elliot, *Old Schuylkill Tales* (Pottsville: Mrs. Ella Zerbey Elliot Newspapers, 1907), 207–8, 292–95; Munsell, *History of Schuylkill County, Pennsylvania*, pp. 207–8, 295–98, 303–4, 308–9, 377–79; *The Reading Railroad* (Philadelphia: Berk & McFetridge, Printers, 1898), 159–60; Charles Robeson, *The Manufactories and Manufacturers of Pennsylvania of the Nineteenth Century* (Philadelphia: Galaxy Publishing Company, 1875), 102–5, 207–8, 433–34; Samuel Wiley and Henry Ruoff, *Biographical and Portrait Cyclopedia of Schuylkill County, Pennsylvania* (Philadelphia: Rush, West & Company, 1893), 211–12, 216–18, 295–98, 349–50, 381–82, 444–49, 457–58, 486–88, 584–85, 625–26, 712–14; Yearly, *Enterprise and Anthracite*, pp. 66–67, 128–29; Joseph Henry Zerbey, *History of Pottsville and Schuylkill County, Pennsylvania*, 6 vols. (Pottsville: J. H. Zerbey Newspapers, 1935), 3:1168–69; R. G. Dun and Company Collection, 172:104 (Enoch McGinnis). See also Beers, *Schuylkill County*, 1:39–41; Schalck and Henning, *History of Schuylkill County*, 2:390–91; Wiley and Ruoff, *Biographical and Portrait Cyclopedia*, pp. 368–69; and *Manuscript Census Returns, Ninth Census of the United States*,

1870, Schuylkill County, Pennsylvania, National Archives Microfilm Series, M-593, Rolls 1447, 1448, 1449.

18. For examples, see Beers, *Schuylkill County,* 1:1–2; *Boyd's City Directory of Pottsville, 1879–1880;* Mrs. Ella Zerbey Elliot, *Blue Book of Schuylkill County* (Pottsville: Joseph A. Zerbey, Proprietor Publishers, 1916), 177–78; Elliot, *Old Schuylkill Tales,* pp. 258, 292–95; Munsell, *History of Schuylkill County, Pennsylvania,* pp. 305–7, 338, 383, R16, R17, R21, R55; *Pottsville Daily Republican,* 26 November 1884, 19 December 1884, 25 September 1885, and 12 December 1885; *Reading Railroad,* pp. 153–58, 163–64; Robeson, *Manufactories and Manufacturers,* pp. 103–4, 433–34; Wiley and Ruoff, *Biographical and Portrait Cyclopedia,* pp. 167, 339–40, 374–75, 381–82, 385–86, 457–58, 483–84, 486–88, 585–86, 625–27.

19. Wiley and Ruoff, *Biographical and Portrait Cyclopedia,* pp. 374–75.

20. Elliot, *Old Schuylkill Tales,* pp. 258, 292–95; Robeson, *Manufactories and Manufacturers,* pp. 433–34; Wiley and Ruoff, *Biographical and Portrait Cyclopedia,* pp. 486–88; *Miners Journal,* 6 June 1856; *Reading Railroad,* pp. 143–53; Munsell, *History of Schuylkill County, Pennsylvania,* pp. 305–7; Wiley and Ruoff, *Biographical and Portrait Cyclopedia,* pp. 234, 283, 486–88, 625–26, 744–45; *Weekly Miners Journal,* 19 February 1875; *Pottsville Daily Republican,* 22 July and 24 July 1885; R. G. Dun and Company Collection, 172:58, 84, 95, 133 (George Bright), 154 (William Donaldson & Son), 157 (J. J. O'Connor & Frank Patterson), 187 (Bright & Co.), 227 (Audenreid); 173:126 (Repplier & Moodie), 174:134 (Andrew Robertson); Herbert Bell, ed., *History of Northumberland County* (Chicago: Brown, Runk and Company, 1891), 892–94.

21. *Manuscript Census Returns, Ninth Census of the United States, 1870, Schuylkill County; Boyd's City Directory of Pottsville, Including Palo Alto, Mount Carbon and Mechanicsville, 1879–1880; Directory of Reading, Easton, Pottsville, Allentown and Lebanon, Together with a Business Directory and a Large List of Farmers of the Counties of Berks, Lebanon, Northampton and Schuylkill for 1860* (Philadelphia: William H. Boyd and Company, 1860); *Gospell's Directory of Reading, Allentown, Easton, Pottsville and Bethlehem, 1864–65* (Lancaster: James Gospell, Publisher, Printed by S. A. Wylie, 1864); *Boyd's Business Directory and Gazeteer of Reading, Harrisburg, Pottsville, Allentown, Norristown, Lebanon and Over Fifty Principal Towns of the Philadelphia and Reading Railroad and Its Branches, 1879–1880* (Pottsville: W. Harry Boyd, 1879).

22. For examples in addition to Donaldson, see Beers, *Schuylkill County,* 1:19–20, 25–27, 411–13; Elliot, *Blue Book,* pp. 177–78; Elliot, *Old Schuylkill Tales,* pp. 258, 292–95; Munsell, *History of Schuylkill County, Pennsylvania,* pp. 297–98, 303–4, 307–8, 311–19, 377–78; (hereafter HSSCO); Edwin O. Parry Papers, M110.3, M140.4, T. Prop. 3, 13 Coal 5, Historical Society of Schuylkill County, Pennsylvania; *Reports of the Inspectors of Coal Mines of the Anthracite Coal Regions for the Year 1870* (Harrisburg: Benjamin Singerly, State Printer, 1870), 107, 109–10, 112, 124–25, 142–43, 146–47, 156–57, 158, 164, 166, 177, 180–81, 183, 190, 210–11, 215; *Reading Railroad,* pp. 153–54; Robeson, *Manufactories and Manufacturers,* pp. 207–8, 443–44, 477–78; Wiley and Ruoff, *Biographical and Portrait Cyclopedia,* pp. 209–11, 217–18, 282, 349–50, 381–82, 486–88; Schalck and Henning, *History of Schuylkill County,* 2:36–37; Zerbey, *History of Pottsville and Schuylkill County,* 3:1168–69; and Yearly, *Enterprise and Anthracite,* pp. 49–51. For an example of a land company prohibited from mining coal, see R. G. Dun and Company Collection, 172:175 (Herscher & Co.).

23. *Miners Journal,* 10 January 1857, 6 February 1850; Munsell, *History of Schuylkill County, Pennsylvania,* pp. 307–8; Robeson, *Manufactories and Manufacturers,* pp. 477–78, Wiley and Ruoff, *Biographical and Portrait Cyclopedia,* pp. 458–62.

24. R. G. Dun and Company Collection, All Counties Volume: 350, 355 (Francis W. Hughes), 351, 355 (Charlemagne Tower), 351 (Christopher Loeser), 354 (Benjamin Cummings); 172:28 (Francis W. Hughes), 147 (James Wren & Bros.); *Miners Journal,* 19 September 1857; Leonard Hal Bridges, *Iron Millionaire: The Life of Charlemagne Tower* (Philadelphia: University of Pennsylvania Press, 1952).

25. Beers, *Schuylkill County,* 1:24–25; Munsell, *History of Schuylkill County, Pennsylvania,* pp. 304–6; Wiley and Ruoff, *Biographical and Portrait Cyclopedia,* pp. 219–20, 229–32.

26. Beers, *Schuylkill County,* 1:1–2, 24–27, 32–35, 43–44, 112–13, 116–17; *Boyd's City Directory of Pottsville Including Palo Alto, Mount Carbon and Mechanicsville, 1879–1880;* Samuel Daddow and Benjamin Bannon, *Coal, Iron and Oil, or The Practical American Miner* (Philadelphia: J. P. Lippincott and Company, 1866), 705–12, 762, 765, 769, 772–73, 776; Munsell, *History of Schuylkill County, Pennsylvania,* pp. 304–96; *Reading Railroad,* pp. 153–54, 155–57, 159–63; Wiley and Ruoff, *Biographical and Portrait Cyclopedia,* pp. 209–11, 219–20, 229–32, 296–98, 712–13, 744–45; Robeson, *Manufactories and Manufacturers,* pp. 102–4; Wiley and Ruoff, *Biographical and Portrait Cyclopedia,* pp. 584–85.

27. Bell, *History of Northumberland County,* pp. 374–84; Centennial Committee, *Mahanoy City, Schuylkill County, Pennsylvania, 1863–1963* (Mahanoy City: Centennial Committee, 1963), 59–71; Harry Rockman, *The Path of Progress: Shenandoah, Pennsylvania, Centennial, 1866–1966* (Reading: Reading Eagle Press, 1967), 10–30; Wiley and Ruoff, *Biographical and Portrait Cyclopedia,* pp. 163–65; Yearly, *Enterprise and Anthracite,* pp. 73–74.

28. Daddow and Bannon, *Coal, Iron and Oil,* pp. 760–66; Roberts, *Anthracite Coal Industry* (New York: Macmillan and Company, 1901), 50; Yearly, *Enterprise and Anthracite,* pp. 53–55, 73–75, 79, 82–84, 89–90, 128–34.

29. Daddow and Bannon, *Coal, Iron and Oil,* pp. 762–65, 769, 772, 773, 776; *Boyd's City Directory of Pottsville Including Palo Alto, Mount Carbon and Mechanicsville, 1867–1868* (Pottsville: W. H. Boyd and Company, 1868), 574–75; *Laws of the General Assembly of the State of Pennsylvania, 1857,* C. 618, pp. 579–80, C. 683, pp. 645–46; *Laws, 1863,* C. 609, p. 647; *Laws, 1864,* C. 108, pp. 108–9, C. 491, pp. 557–59; Munsell, *History of Schuylkill County, Pennsylvania,* pp. 295–96, 377–79; Wiley and Ruoff, *Biographical and Portrait Cyclopedia,* pp. 295–97. The extent of outside control before 1865 and 1870 is difficult to gauge. Not until 1865, when two Pottsville leaders published a fairly comprehensive study of the region, and 1870, when the state mining reports appeared, were any statistical data available for the region. Studies which cover the pre-1860 period suggest the strong presence of outside landlords who regularly drained off profits. Yet, none of these works provided a systematic comparative analysis of local vs. outside control. Apparently, the Pottsville operators and landowners did exercise substantial influence in the anthracite industry before the mid-1850s. My analysis is necessarily limited to 1864 and 1870. In 1870, the state began publishing mining reports on the anthracite coal regions. Before that year, only one source, published in 1864, recorded coal productions for the regions. Until the state reports appeared in 1870, no thorough listing of land ownership existed. After the early 1870s, the PRRCO and the PRC&ICO had purchased almost all the coal lands

in the region. The analysis is by no means exhaustive; it makes clear, however, that the Pottsville elite was not the dominating force in the anthracite industry. See Yearly, *Enterprise and Anthracite*; H. Benjamin Powell, "Coal, Philadelphia and the Schuylkill" (Ph.D. diss., Lehigh University, 1968); R. G. Dun and Company Collection, 172:44 (Lauberry Coal Co.), 128, 236 (Northized Coal Co.), 164 (Phoenix), 210 (Bear Ridge Coal Co.), 204 (Greenwood Coal Co.), 216 (Locust Coal Co.), 218 (Honey Brooke Coal Co.), 225 (Jno. Brock), 226 (Boston Coal Co.); 173:303 (Philadelphia Coal Co.); 174:245 (Locust Mountain Coal and Iron Co.), 328 (Girard Mammoth Coal Co.), 385 (New Philadelphia Mining Co.); *Weekly Miners Journal*, Pottsville, Pennsylvania, 14 November 1879; *Miners Journal*, 18 July 1855. The remaining production was controlled by operators from communities outside the region who were headquartered in places other than the metropolitan centers mentioned.

30. Munsell, *History of Schuylkill County, Pennsylvania*, pp. 295–96; Wiley and Ruoff, *Biographical and Portrait Cyclopedia*, pp. 295–97; Zerbey, *History of Pottsville and Schuylkill County*, 5:1168–69.

31. *First Annual Report of the Bureau of Statistics of Labor and Agriculture of Pennsylvania for the Years 1872–1873* (Harrisburg: Benjamin Singerly, 1874), 365; *Reports of the Inspectors of Coal Mines for the Year 1870*, pp. 106–235; see also Daddow and Bannon, *Coal, Iron and Oil*, pp. 705–7, 761–71.

32. Bell, *History of Northumberland County*, pp. 369–73; Jones, *The Anthracite Coal Combinations*, pp. 34–40; Munsell, *History of Schuylkill County, Pennsylvania*, pp. 56–58; Polinak, *When Coal Was King*, pp. 16–17; untitled papers on the railroads in Schuylkill County, Historical Society of Schuylkill County, Pottsville; Yearly, *Enterprise and Anthracite*, pp. 41, 176, 201–5, 209.

33. Yearly, *Enterprise and Anthracite*, pp. 75, 79, 82–84, 89–90.

34. Bell, *History of Northumberland County*, pp. 381–83; Centennial Committee, *Mahanoy City*, pp. 59–71; Jones, *The Anthracite Combination*, p. 41; Beers, *History of Schuylkill County*, 1:106–7; Munsell, *History of Schuylkill County, Pennsylvania*, pp. 60–62, 177, 183–85, 207–10, 222–23, 277–79; Rockman, *Path of Progress*, pp. 10–30; Roberts, *Anthracite Coal Industry*, pp. 18–19; Wiley and Ruoff, *Biographical and Portrait Cyclopedia*, pp. 163–65; Yearly, *Enterprise and Anthracite*, pp. 74–75, 79, 82–84, 89–90, 201–5, 209. For a detailed analysis, see Marvin Schlegel, *Ruler of the Reading: The Life of Franklin B. Gowen, 1836–1889* (Harrisburg: Pennsylvania Historical and Museum Commission, 1947).

35. Beers, *Schuylkill County*, 1:1–2, 25–27, 32–35, 43–44; Munsell, *History of Schuylkill County, Pennsylvania*, pp. R27, 303–4, 377–79; untitled papers on PRRCO, Historical Society of Schuylkill County; *Reading Railroad*, pp. 153–57, 159–60; Robeson, *Manufactories and Manufacturers*, pp. 103–4, 477–78; Schalck and Henning, *History of Schuylkill County*, 1:283–84; Wiley and Ruoff, *Biographical and Portrait Cyclopedia*, pp. 211–12, 349–50, 374–75, 457–58, 486–88, 584–85, 625–26; Yearly, *Enterprise and Anthracite*, pp. 128–29.

36. For examples of iron and steel companies, see R. G. Dun and Company Collection, 172:50 (Geo. W. Snyder), 79 (Haywood & Lee), 154, 293 (Charles Atkins); 173:232 (Schuylkill Steel Co.), 307 (Lee & Wren), 370, 408 (Pottsville Spike & Bolt Works); 436 (Pottsville Iron & Steel Co.), and the *Pottsville Daily Republican*, 17 November 1884. For other examples of coal-related companies, see R. G. Dun and Company Collection, 173:21 (Schuylkill County Lumber Co.); 174:236 (Pottsville

Cement & Pipe Co.), 273 (Miners' Supply Co.), 327 (Pennsylvania Diamond Drill Co.), 328 (Samuel Griscom & Co.).

37. Elliot, *Old Schuylkill Tales*, pp. 258, 292–95; Munsell, *History of Schuylkill County, Pennsylvania*, pp. 305–6, 308–9; Robeson, *Manufactories and Manufacturers*, p. 102–5, 207–8, 433–34; Wiley and Ruoff, *Biographical and Portrait Cyclopedia*, pp. 211–12, 349–50, 374–75, 457–58, 486–88, 584–85, 625–26; Yearly, *Enterprise and Anthracite*, pp. 128–29.

38. Bell, *History of Northumberland County*, p. 683; Elliot, *Old Schuylkill Tales*, pp. 258, 292–95; *Laws of the General Assembly of the State of Pennsylvania, 1872*, C. 1200, p. 1220; Munsell, *History of Schuylkill County, Pennsylvania*, pp. 308–11; untitled papers of the iron and steel industry, Historical Society of Schuylkill County; Robeson, *Manufactories and Manufacturers*, pp. 34–35, 102–5, 433–34, 493–94; Wiley and Ruoff, *Biographical and Portrait Cyclopedia*, pp. 211–12, 223–33, 234, 294–95, 328, 457–58, 486–88, 625–26; R. G. Dun and Company Collection, 172:40–41 (Robert Allison & Frank Bannon), 79 (Palo Alto Iron Works), 143 (Port Carbon Iron Co.); 173:319 (Schuylkill Iron Co.), 461 (Theodore Garreston & John E. Wynkoop); 174:498 (Grant Iron Works), 359 (Schuylkill Haven Iron Co).

39. *Laws of the General Assembly of the State of Pennsylvania, 1872*, C. 1200, p. 1220; Robeson, *Manufactories and Manufacturers*, pp. 102–3; Zerbey, *History of Pottsville and Schuylkill County*, 5:2091; Wiley and Ruoff, *Biographical and Portrait Cyclopedia*, p. 327. For examples of the financial stress of these companies, see R. G. Dun and Company Collection, 142:96 (George Pomeroy), 143 (Port Carbon Iron Company); 173:232 (Schuylkill Steel Co.), 307 (Lee & Wren), 319 (Schuylkill Iron Co.), 461 (Theodore Garreston & John Wynkoop; also see Norwegian Iron Co.); 174:236 (Pottsville Cement Pipe Co.), 485, 531 (George Snyder Iron & Steel Works), 498 (Grant Iron Works), 593 (Pottsville Spike & Bolt Works); 609 (Pennsylvania Diamond Drill Co.), and the *Pottsville Daily Republican*, 17 November 1884.

40. *Boyd's City Directory of Pottsville Including Palo Alto, Mount Carbon and Mechanicsville, 1867–1880*; Munsell, *History of Schuylkill County, Pennsylvania*, pp. 274–75; Zerbey, *History of Pottsville and Schuylkill County*, 1:82–84; National Archives, *Manuscript Census Returns, Eighth Census of the United States, 1860, Schuylkill County, Pennsylvania*, Microfilm Series M-563, Rolls 1179, 1180; National Archives, *Manuscript Census Returns, Ninth Census of the United States, 1870, Northumberland County, Pennsylvania*, Microfilm Series M-562, Roll 1348, and M-563, Roll 1385; R. G. Dun and Company Collection, 172:57, 183 (Jacob Huntzinger); 174:1, 257 (William and Jacob Huntzinger); Davies, "Urbanizing Region," p. 298, esp. Table VI-8 for specific citations.

41. Bell, *History of Northumberland County*, pp. 622–24; *Boyd's City Directory of Pottsville Including Palo Alto, Mount Carbon and Mechanicsville, 1867–1868*; *Laws of the General Assembly of the State of Pennsylvania, 1856*, C. 170, p. 156; Wiley and Ruoff, *Biographical and Portrait Cyclopedia*, pp. 163–65.

42. *Boyd's City Directory of Pottsville Including Palo Alto, Mount Carbon and Mechanicsville, 1879–1880*; Munsell, *History of Schuylkill County, Pennsylvania*, pp. 274–75; *Weekly Miners Journal*, 11 January 1878. The latter lists all the depositors and savers of the Miners Trust and Company Bank of Pottsville.

43. Munsell, *History of Schuylkill County, Pennsylvania*, pp. 275, 297–98, 312; *Boyd's City Directory of Pottsville, Including Palo Alto, Mount Carbon and Mechanicsville, 1879–1880*; Wiley and Ruoff, *Biographical and Portrait Cyclopedia*, pp. 160–61, 217–

18; Zerbey, *History of Pottsville and Schuylkill County,* 2:824–25; R. G. Dun and Company Collection, 174:398 (Pennsylvania National Bank); *Miners Journal,* 14 January 1871; *Weekly Miners Journal,* 15 January 1875, 16 February 1877, 9 March 1877, 18 April 1877, 11 January 1878.

44. Wiley and Ruoff, *Biographical and Portrait Cyclopedia,* pp. 160–61, 217–18, 183–86; *Weekly Miners Journal,* 22 January, 16 April, 9 August, 24 September 1875, 9 March, 16 February 1877, 11 January 1878; *Boyd's City Directory of Pottsville, Including Palo Alto, Mount Carbon and Mechanicsville, 1879–1880; Laws of the General Assembly of the State of Pennsylvania, 1870,* C. 971, p. 1051, and C. 1350, pp. 1359–60; Munsell, *History of Schuylkill County, Pennsylvania,* pp. 163–70; R. G. Dun and Company Collection, 172:221 (Pennsylvania Central Insurance Company); *Miners Journal,* 10 January 1857.

45. *Weekly Miners Journal,* 9, 16, and 30 March, 14 September, 2 and 6 November 1877; R. G. Dun and Company Collection, 172:57, 183 (Jacob Huntzinger); 173:311 (Safe Deposit Bank of Pottsville); 174:233 (Merchants Exchange Bank of Pottsville), 235 (Mountain City Bank), 236 (Pottsville Bank), 246 (Union Hall Association of Pottsville), 257 (William and Jacob Huntzinger), 398 (Pennsylvania National Bank).

46. *Boyd's City Directory of Pottsville Including Palo Alto, Mount Carbon and Mechanicsville, 1867–1868; Boyd's City Directory of Pottsville Including Palo Alto, Mount Carbon and Mechanicsville, 1879–1880; Laws of the General Assembly of the State of Pennsylvania, 1870,* C. 971, p. 1051, and C. 1350, pp. 1359–60; Munsell, *History of Schuylkill County, Pennsylvania,* pp. 163–70; Wiley and Ruoff, *Biographical and Portrait Cyclopedia,* pp. 183–86; R. G. Dun and Company Collection, 172:221 (Pennsylvania Central Insurance Company); 174:237 (Pottsville Life Insurance and Trust Company); *Weekly Miners Journal,* 16 April, 9 August, 24 September 1875.

47. Davies, "Urbanizing Region," p. 261; *Reading Railroad,* pp. 154–64.

48. Munsell, *History of Schuylkill County, Pennsylvania,* pp. 297–98; *Manuscript Census Returns, Ninth Census of the United States, 1870, Schuylkill County, Pennsylvania,* M-593, Roll 1447; Wiley and Ruoff, *Biographical and Portrait Cyclopedia,* pp. 217–18, 481–82.

49. Some prominent members of the elite and their relatives were Edward Patterson; Jacob Huntzinger; George, Benjamin, and Clifford Pomeroy; John M. Wetherill; John Price Wetherill; William Donaldson; John Shippen; Charlemagne Tower; George DeKeim; and George and James Wren. Among affected transient coal operators and merchants were William Kendrick, John McBarron, William Glammyre, C. M. Will, Daniel Dougherty, S. Bowman, and John C. Hughes. For those with assets between $10,000 and $29,000, Charles Logan, J. L. Loose, Jacob Kyle, Conrad Goslichell, Wolf Galland, P. P. Eisenbowen, Richard Hurst, Herman Kuhn, Abraham Mussil, Henry Vandusen (laborer), Henry Weber, and Edward Morrison were evaluated. In analyzing the third group, I checked also for persistence of relatives and included only persons whose families were entirely gone. See *Manuscript Census Returns, Ninth Census of the United States, 1870, Schuylkill County, Pennsylvania; Boyd's City Directory of Pottsville Including Palo Alto, Mount Carbon and Mechanicsville, 1879–1880; Directory of Reading, Easton, Pottsville for 1860; Gospells Directory, 1864–1865; Boyd's Central Pennsylvania Business Directory and Gazetteer of Reading, Harrisburg, Williamsport, Lancaster, Pottsville, Allentown, Norristown, Lebanon, Pottstown and Over Ninety of the Principal Towns in the Counties of Berks, Chester, Columbia, Dauphin, Lancaster, Lebanon, Lehigh, Lycoming, Northumberland, Montour, Schuylkill on the Line*

of the Philadelphia and Reading Railroad and Its Branches, Pennsylvania Schuylkill Valley Railroad, etc., 1890 (Reading, Penn.: W. H. Boyd, 1890), 355–86; R. G. Dun and Company Collection, 172:96 (George Pomeroy), 147 (James Wren & Brothers), 282 (John E. and Edward W. Wynkoop; John, bankrupt, persists; Edward is gone by 1879 or 1880); (Zaccur P. Boyer); 173:307 (Lee & Wren), 461 (Theodore Garreston & John E. Wynkoop); 174:498 (Grant Iron Works); All Counties Volume: 351, 355 (Charlemagne Tower).

50. Beers, Schuylkill County, 1:16–18; Laws of the General Assembly of the State of Pennsylvania, 1865, C. 802, p. 815; Munsell, History of Schuylkill County, Pennsylvania, pp. 281–83; Henry Poor, Poor's Manual of the Railroads of the United States, 1872–1873 (New York: H. V. and H. V. Poor, 1873), 420; Reading Railroad, pp. 159–60; Schalck and Henning, History of Schuylkill County, 1:123–24; Wiley and Ruoff, Biographical and Portrait Cyclopedia, pp. 281–83, 297–98, 740–42; Zerbey, History of Pottsville and Schuylkill County, 1:247–49, 256–62.

51. Zerbey, History of Pottsville and Schuylkill County, 1:247–49, 256–62.

NOTES TO CHAPTER 6

1. On overpopulation in southeastern Pennsylvania, see John Modell, "The Peopling of a Working Class Ward," Journal of Social History 5 (1971): 71–95. For descriptions of elites with similar characteristics, see Michael Katz, "The Entrepreneurial Class in a Canadian City in the Mid-Nineteenth Century," Journal of Social History 8 (1975): 1–29; and Clyde Griffen and Sally Griffen, Natives and Newcomers: The Ordering of Opportunity in Mid-Nineteenth-Century Poughkeepsie (Cambridge, Mass.: Harvard University Press, 1978), esp. chap. 4, "Men at the Top." On pre-1800 German migration, see Hans Fenske, "International Migration: Germany in the Eighteenth Century," Central European History 13 (1980): 332–47. For later migrations, see Klaus J. Bade, "German Emigration to the United States and Continental Immigration to Germany in the Late Nineteenth and Early Twentieth Centuries," Central European History 13 (1980): 348–77. For a description of the British cultures in America and in the coalfields, specifically, see Roland T. Berthoff, British Immigrants in Industrial America (Cambridge, Mass.: Harvard University Press, 1953), 1–11, 62–75, 127–42.

2. Reginald Rix, interview with author, Pottsville, Pennsylvania, 18 June 1974; Mr. Rix is a former director of the Historical Society of Schuylkill County. See also Mrs. Ella Zerbey Elliot, Old Schuylkill Tales (Pottsville: Mrs. Ella Zerbey Elliot, 1907), 213–30; Timothy L. Smith, "Religion and Ethnicity in America," American Historical Review 83 (1978): 1155–85.

3. History Compiled for First Methodist Episcopal Church, Pottsville, Pennsylvania on the Occasion of Its Centennial Anniversary by Pottsville Evening Republican and Pottsville Morning Paper (Pottsville: J. H. Zerbey Newspapers, 1932), 10; W. W. Munsell, ed., History of Schuylkill County, Pennsylvania (New York: W. W. Munsell and Company, 1881), 308–9; Charles Robeson, The Manufactories and Manufacturers of Pennsylvania of the Nineteenth Century (Philadelphia: Galaxy Publishing Company, 1875), 102–5; Samuel Wiley and Henry Ruoff, Biographical and Portrait Cyclopedia of Schuylkill

County, Pennsylvania (Philadelphia: Rush, West & Company, 1893), 211–12, 229–32, 278–79.

4. J. H. Beers, *Schuylkill County, Pennsylvania*, 2 vols. (Chicago: J. H. Beers and Company, 1916), 1:1–4, 11–12, 14–16, 17–18, 24–27, 37–43, 66–67, 83–84, 108–11, 116–17, 512; Munsell, *History of Schuylkill County, Pennsylvania*, pp. 308–9; Wiley and Ruoff, *Biographical and Portrait Cyclopedia*, pp. 744–45.

5. Adolph Schalck and the Honorable D. C. Henning, eds., *History of Schuylkill County*, 2 vols. (Harrisburg: State Historical Association, 1907), 1:275–76, 286–87.

6. Janice Weiss, "Educating for Clerical Work: The Nineteenth-Century Private Commercial School," *Journal of Social History* 13 (1979): 407–20.

7. Wiley and Ruoff, *Biographical and Portrait Cyclopedia*, pp. 283, 458–62, 486–90; Mrs. Ella Zerbey Elliot, *Blue Book of Schuylkill County* (Pottsville: Joseph A. Zerbey, Proprietor Publishers, 1916), 179–88; Robeson, *Manufactories and Manufacturers*, pp. 433–34; *Weekly Miners Journal* (Pottsville, Pennsylvania), 16 December 1885.

8. Beers, *Schuylkill County*, 1:37–39; Schalck and Henning, *History of Schuylkill County*, 2:354–55; Wiley and Ruoff, *Biographical and Portrait Cyclopedia*, pp. 318–19. For other examples, see Beers, *Schuylkill County*, 1:14–16, 209–11; Munsell, *History of Schuylkill County, Pennsylvania*, pp. 311a, 301–8; Wiley and Ruoff, *Biographical and Portrait Cyclopedia*, pp. 159–60, 281–83, 294–97, 318–19, 427–28, 278–79; Schalck and Henning, *History of Schuylkill County*, 2:296–97, 381–82.

9. Munsell, *History of Schuylkill County, Pennsylvania*, pp. 297–98, 307–8; Robeson, *Manufactories and Manufacturers*, pp. 433–34, 477–88; Wiley and Ruoff, *Biographical and Portrait Cyclopedia*, pp. 744–45.

10. Beers, *Schuylkill County*, 1:25–27; Munsell, *History of Schuylkill County, Pennsylvania*, pp. 297–98, 307–8; Robeson, *Manufactories and Manufacturers*, pp. 433–34, 477–78; Wiley and Ruoff, *Biographical and Portrait Cyclopedia*, pp. 209–11, 217–18, 283, 486–87, 749–50.

11. *Publications of the Schuylkill Historical Society*, nos. 1–5 (1907–1924). For a description of social organization among the working class, see Clifton Yearly, Jr., *Britons in American Labor* (Baltimore: Johns Hopkins University Press, 1957), 121–42. On the impact of ethnicity on British immigrants, see Berthoff, *British Immigrants*, pp. 165–84.

12. *Boyd's City Directory of Pottsville Including Palo Alto, Mount Carbon and Mechanicsville, 1867–1868* (Pottsville: William H. Boyd and Company, 1868); *Boyd's City Directory of Pottsville, Ashland and Mechanicsville, 1870–1871* (Pottsville: Wm. H. Boyd and Company, 1871); *Boyd's City Directory of Pottsville, Including Palo Alto, Mount Carbon and Mechanicsville, 1879–1880* (Pottsville: Wm. H. Boyd and Company, 1880); *Directory of Reading, Easton, Pottsville, Allentown and Lebanon, Together with a Business Directory and Large List of Farmers of the Counties of Berks, Lebanon, Northampton and Schuylkill for 1860* (Philadelphia: Wm. H. Boyd and Company, 1860). For a description of urban neighborhoods, see James Borchert, "Urban Neighborhood and Community: Informal Group Life, 1850–1970," *Journal of Interdisciplinary History* 11 (1981): 607–31.

13. In addition to city directories, see Pottsville Club Records, Historical Society of Schuylkill County (hereafter HSSCO), Pottsville, Pennsylvania; Elliot, *Old Schuylkill Tales*, pp. 258, 292–95; Wiley and Ruoff, *Biographical and Portrait Cyclopedia*, pp. 219–20, 486–88, 683–84.

14. *The Reading Railroad* (Philadelphia: Burk & McFetridge Printers, 1898), 155–57; Schalck and Henning, *History of Schuylkill County*, 2:242–43.

15. Munsell, *History of Schuylkill County, Pennsylvania*, pp. 283, 306; Schalck and Henning, *History of Schuylkill County*, 1:165.

16. Beers, *Schuylkill County*, 1:43–44.

17. Horace E. Hayden, Alfred Hand, and John W. Jordan, *Genealogical and Family History of the Wyoming and Lackawanna Valleys, Pennsylvania*, 2 vols. (New York: Lewis Publishing Company, 1906), 1:43–45, 85–88; Oscar J. Harvey and Ernest G. Smith, *A History of Wilkes-Barre, Luzerne County, Pennsylvania*, 6 vols. (Wilkes-Barre: Rader Publishing House, 1909–1930), 6:604–5.

18. Beers, *Schuylkill County*, 1:2–4, 24–35; Wiley and Ruoff, *Biographical and Portrait Cyclopedia*, 219–20, 484–86, 505–6.

19. Beers, *Schuylkill County*, 1:27–92; Munsell, *History of Schuylkill County, Pennsylvania*, pp. 302, 310–11.

20. Beers, *Schuylkill County*, 1:41–43; *Laws of the General Assembly of the State of Pennsylvania, 1845*, C. 275, p. 413; *Laws, 1851*, C. 775, p. 484; *Laws, 1854*, C. 747, p. 860; *Laws, 1870*, C. 149, pp. 162–63; Munsell, *History of Schuylkill County, Pennsylvania*, pp. 274–76, 297–98, 301, 311–19; Joseph H. Zerbey, *History of Pottsville and Schuylkill, Pennsylvania*, 6 vols. (Pottsville: J. H. Zerbey Newspapers, Inc., 1934–35), 1:284–85.

21. *Boyd's City Directory of Pottsville Including Palo Alto, Mount Carbon and Mechanicsville, 1879–1880*; Beers, *Schuylkill County*, 1:1–2, 32–35, 113–15; and 2:512; *History Compiled for Methodist Episcopal Church*, p. 10; *Laws of the General Assembly of the State of Pennsylvania, 1870*, C. 149, pp. 162–63; Schalck and Henning, *History of Schuylkill County*, 2:26–27, 126–27, 278–84, 501–2; Wiley and Ruoff, *Biographical and Portrait Cyclopedia*, pp. 211–12, 215–20, 222–23, 457–58, 584–85; Zerbey, *History of Pottsville and Schuylkill County*, 1:82–84, 247–49, 256–58, 264–65, and 2:749–50, 824–25.

22. Munsell, *History of Schuylkill County, Pennsylvania*, pp. 294–96; *Weekly Miners Journal*, 2 April 1875; *Pottsville Daily Republican*, 4 April 1885; *Weekly Miners Journal* (Pottsville, Pennsylvania), 6 September 1856, 10 January 1857; R. G. Dun and Company Collection, Harvard University, Baker Library, Manuscript Collection: All Counties Volume, Schuylkill County, vols. 172–175; All Counties Volume, Northumberland County, vols. 124–25, 172:108 (Charles Baber), 174:328 (Samuel Griscom & Company). For other examples of partnerships, see 172:256 (Potts and Vastine), 64 (Lippincott & Taylor), 173:126 (Repplier and Moodie), 461 (Theodore Garreston and John E. Wynkoop), 174:498 (Grant Iron Works). For partnerships involving family members, see 172:97 (Hiram Parker & Son), 147 (J. Wren & Brothers), 174:137 (Andrew Robertson). These were not included in calculating partnerships.

23. Munsell, *History of Schuylkill County, Pennsylvania*, pp. 304–6; Wiley and Ruoff, *Biographical and Portrait Cyclopedia*, pp. 24–25; R. G. Dun and Company Collection, 174:386 (Phillips and Sheafer).

24. Munsell, *History of Schuylkill County, Pennsylvania*, pp. 308–11, 309a; Wiley and Ruoff, *Biographical and Portrait Cyclopedia*, pp. 211–12, 326–27, 625–26, 712–13; Beers, *Schuylkill County*, 1:27–29; Schalck and Henning, *History of Schuylkill County*, 2:283–84; Robeson, *Manufactories and Manufacturers*, pp. 102–5; *History Compiled for Methodist Episcopal Church*, p. 10; R. G. Dun and Company Collection, 174:386 (Phillips and Sheafer).

25. R. G. Dun and Company Collection, 172:58, 84, 95, 133, 187 (George Bright), 64, 149 (George H. Potts).

26. Schalck and Henning, *History of Schuylkill County,* 2:73–74.

27. Beers, *Schuylkill County,* 1:25–27; Wiley and Ruoff, *Biographical and Portrait Cyclopedia,* pp. 209–11, 488–90, 449–50, 625–26; R. G. Dun and Company Collection, 172:147 (James Wren & Bros.), 248 (Benjamin Haywood); 173:307 (George Wren & Lee). For other examples, see R. G. Dun and Company Collection, 172:151, 412 (George Lauer), 175 (Tyson & Co.), 150, 154 (William Donaldson); All Counties Volume: 351, 355 (Charlemagne Tower).

28. Beers, *Schuylkill County,* 1:2–4, 113–15; *Weekly Miners Journal,* 11 March 1857; Wiley and Ruoff, *Biographical and Portrait Cyclopedia,* pp. 449–50, 215–16, 484–86; Munsell, *History of Schuylkill County, Pennsylvania,* pp. 301–2; Schalck and Henning, *History of Schuylkill County,* pp. 178–79.

29. Beers, *Schuylkill County,* 1:14–16; Munsell, *History of Schuylkill County, Pennsylvania,* pp. 119, 259, R45; Schalck and Henning, *History of Schuylkill County,* 2:381–82; Wiley and Ruoff, *Biographical and Portrait Cyclopedia,* pp. 259–60, 272–73, 505–6; *Weekly Miners Journal,* 2 April 1875 and 27 August 1880; R. G. Dun and Company, All Counties Volume: 350, 355 (Francis W. Hughes), 355 (Benjamin Bartholomew); 172:28 (Francis W. Hughes).

30. Anniversary and dinner invitations of the Fishing Party, 1860, 1883, 1884, HSSCO; "Pottsville, Pennsylvania" (leaflet), 1883, HSSCO; Miners Journal Book and Job Office, HSSCO; Pottsville Club Records, HSSCO; *Weekly Miners Journal,* 19 October 1877, 15 May 1882; *Pottsville Daily Republican,* 3 December 1884, 21 May 1885; Schalck and Henning, *History of Schuylkill County,* 1:26–27; *Reading Railroad,* pp. 155–57, 159–60, 286–87.

31. Munsell, *History of Schuylkill County, Pennsylvania,* pp. 303–4, 311–19; Wiley and Ruoff, *Biographical and Portrait Cyclopedia,* pp. 381–82, 744–45; Robeson, *Manufactories and Manufacturers,* pp. 103–4; *Weekly Miners Journal,* 15 May 1882, 19 May 1883, and 21 May 1875; Minute Book of the Famous Pottsville Party, HSSCO. The founding of the athletic association is described in the *Weekly Miners Journal.* See, for example, 20, 27 September 1878.

32. Munsell, *History of Schuylkill County, Pennsylvania,* pp. 75–78; Schalck and Henning, *History of Schuylkill County,* 1:273–74; Harold Aurand, *From the Molly Maguires to the United Mine Workers: The Social Ecology of an Industrial Union, 1869–1897* (Philadelphia: Temple University Press, 1971); Zerbey, *History of Pottsville,* 1:110–13, 277; *Weekly Miners Journal,* 28 June 1873, 19 October 1879, and 17 May 1878.

33. On the establishment of the National Guard, see Walter Millis, *Arms and Men: A Study of American Military History* (New Brunswick, N.J.: Rutgers University Press, 1956), 143–45; Munsell, *History of Schuylkill County, Pennsylvania,* pp. 304–6.

34. Munsell, *History of Schuylkill County, Pennsylvania,* pp. 307–8; Wiley and Ruoff, *Biographical and Portrait Cyclopedia,* pp. 259–60, 295–96, 458–62; Robeson, *Manufactories and Manufacturers,* pp. 477–78; *Miners Journal,* 6 February 1850, 18 July, 17 October, and 5 December 1857, 6 February 1858, and 31 May 1869; *Weekly Miners Journal,* 19 October 1878, 27 August 1880.

35. Elliot, *Old Schuylkill Tales,* pp. 258, 292–93; Robeson, *Manufactories and Manufacturers,* pp. 102–5, 433–34; Wiley and Ruoff, *Biographical and Portrait Cyclopedia,* pp. 211–12, 486–88, 740–44; *Weekly Miners Journal,* 13 July 1878; *Pottsville Daily*

Republican, 12, 16 December 1885. For other examples, see *Pottsville Daily Republican,* 29 December 1885 (Charles M. Atkins); *Weekly Miners Journal,* 28 March, 4 April 1879 (Henry Guiterman; he was a resident of Port Carbon but a close business ally of the Pottsville elite); and *Pottsville Daily Republican,* 11, 14 April 1886 (Charles E. Rosengarten).

36. Wiley and Ruoff, *Biographical and Portrait Cyclopedia,* pp. 215–16, 217–18, 222–23; Munsell, *History of Schuylkill County, Pennsylvania,* pp. 297–98; Beers, *Schuylkill County,* p. 1:180; Schalck and Henning, *History of Schuylkill County,* 2:400–401. See also Beers, *Schuylkill County,* 1:1–2, 44–45; Schalck and Henning, *History of Schuylkill County,* 1:26–27, 178–79; Munsell, *History of Schuylkill County, Pennsylvania,* pp. R30, 301.

37. Beers, *Schuylkill County,* 1:1–2, 4–8, 14–16, 37–39, 41–43, 64–67; Munsell, *History of Schuylkill County, Pennsylvania,* pp. 311–19, 311a; Schalck and Henning, *History of Schuylkill County,* 2:26–27, 242–43, 283–84, 296–97, 354–55, 381–83, 547–48, Wiley and Ruoff, *Biographical and Portrait Cyclopedia,* pp. 297–320, 740–42, 744–45.

38. Beers, *Schuylkill County,* 1:1–2, 24–25, 20–21, 50–51; 64–67, 110–11, 150–51; Munsell, *History of Schuylkill County, Pennsylvania,* R30, 303–4; Wiley and Ruoff, *Biographical and Portrait Cyclopedia,* pp. 215–17, 222–23, 229–32, 245–46, 274–75, 278–79, 298–300, 320–21, 374–75, 381–82, 449–50, 491–92, 457–58, 505–6, 584–85, 744–45, 749–50; Schalck and Henning, *History of Schuylkill County,* 2:26–27, 178–79, 242–23, 204–5, 283–84, 296–97, 334–35, 428–29; *Reading Railroad,* pp. 155–57, 159–60; *History Compiled for Methodist Episcopal Church,* pp. 26, 35; *Weekly Miners Journal,* 2 April 1875, 13 September 1875, 14 September 1885; *Pottsville Daily Republican,* 4, 7 April 1885 and 26 November 1884.

39. Beers, *Schuylkill County,* pp. 1:14, 110–11, 151; Munsell, *History of Schuylkill County, Pennsylvania,* pp. 311a–312; Schalck and Henning, *History of Schuylkill County,* 2:242–43, 334–35; *Reading Railroad,* pp. 155–57; Wiley and Ruoff, *Biographical and Portrait Cyclopedia,* pp. 274–75, 744–45; *Weekly Miners Journal,* 1 March 1878; R. G. Dun and Company Collection, 172:151, 412 (George Lauer).

NOTES TO CHAPTER 7

1. For information on population statistics, see Francis Walker, Superintendent, *A Compendium of the Ninth Census of the United States: 1870* (Washington, D.C.: Government Printing Office, 1872), 251–55; Francis Walker and Charles W. Seaton, Superintendents, *A Compendium of the Tenth Census: 1880* (Washington, D.C.: Government Printing Office, 1883), 298–302; U.S. Bureau of the Census, *Fifteenth Census of the United States, Population II* (Washington, D.C.: Government Printing Office, 1936), 692–99, 660–73, 734–39.

2. For discussions of leaders with similar origins, see Herbert Gutman, "The Reality of the Rags to Riches 'Myth': The Case of Paterson, New Jersey, Locomotive, Iron and Machinery Manufacturers, 1830–1880," in *Nineteenth-Century Cities,* ed. Stephan Thernstrom and Richard Sennett (New Haven, Conn.: Yale University Press, 1969), 98–124; Clyde Griffen and Sally Griffen, *Natives and Newcomers: The Ordering of Opportunity in Mid-Nineteenth-Century Poughkeepsie* (Cambridge, Mass.: Harvard Uni-

versity Press, 1978), chap. 4; Peter Decker, *Fortunes and Failures: White Collar Mobility in Nineteenth-Century San Francisco* (Cambridge, Mass.: Harvard University Press, 1978), chaps. 4 and 9; and Burton W. Folsom II, "Urban Networks: The Economic and Social Order of the Lackawanna and Lehigh Valleys during Early Industrialization, 1850–1880" (Ph.D. diss., University of Pittsburgh, 1976), chaps. on Scranton in the Lackawanna Valley.

3. Adolph Schalck and the Honorable D. C. Henning, eds., *History of Schuylkill County, Pennsylvania*, 2 vols. (Harrisburg: State Historical Association, 1907), 2:243–44; J. H. Beers, *Schuylkill County, Pennsylvania*, 2 vols. (Chicago: J. H. Beers and Co., 1916), 1:165–68; R. G. Dun and Company Collection, Harvard University, Baker Library, Manuscript Division. See All Counties Volume, Schuylkill and Northumberland Counties, vols. 124–26, 172–75. See 172:219 (Charles D. Kaier), 174:565, 634 (Charles D. Kaier). Also see *Book of Biographies: Biographical Sketches of Leading Citizens of the Seventeenth Congressional District, Pennsylvania* (Chicago: Biographical Publications Company, 1899), 518–19.

4. For discussions of the migrations from Ireland and Germany, see Klaus J. Bode, "German Emigration to the United States and Continental Immigration to Germany in the Late Nineteenth and Early Twentieth Centuries," *Central European History* 13 (1980): 332–47; and Lynn H. Lees and John Modell, "The Irish Countrymen Urbanized: A Comparative Perspective on the Famine Migration," *Journal of Urban History* 3 (1977): 391–409.

5. This information was drawn from the local histories for Schuylkill County and the biographical sketches of the individual leaders. For examples of church affiliations in Tamaqua, see Samuel Wiley and Henry Ruoff, *Biographical and Portrait Cyclopedia of Schuylkill County, Pennsylvania* (Philadelphia: Rush, West and Co., 1893), 404–7, 412–13; and W. W. Munsell, ed., *History of Schuylkill County, Pennsylvania* (New York: W. W. Munsell and Company, 1881), R37–R38. For examples of church affiliation in Ashland, see Wiley and Ruoff, *Biographical and Portrait Cyclopedia*, pp. R7–R8.

6. The information on these patterns of occupational mobility and educational experience were drawn from biographical sketches in the local histories for Schuylkill and Northumberland counties, described in the appendix.

7. Herbert C. Bell, ed., *History of Northumberland County, Pennsylvania* (Chicago: Brown, Runk & Co., 1891), 905–6; *Book of Biographies*, pp. 228–30; Wiley and Ruoff, *Biographical and Portrait Cyclopedia*, p. 267.

8. Schalck and Henning, *History of Schuylkill County*, 2:92–93, 440–41; Wiley and Ruoff, *Biographical and Portrait Cyclopedia*, pp. 257–58, 305–6, 319–20, 382–84, 705–6; Munsell, *History of Schuylkill County, Pennsylvania*, pp. 318, R11.

9. For some examples, see Munsell, *History of Schuylkill County, Pennsylvania*, p. 388; Wiley and Ruoff, *Biographical and Portrait Cyclopedia*, pp. 406–7; Bell, *History of Northumberland County*, pp. 869–70.

10. Bell, *History of Northumberland County*, pp. 904–5; *Book of Biographies*, pp. 263–65. For examples in Northumberland County, see Bell, *History of Northumberland County*, pp. 869–75, 891–92, 896–98, 905–6, 1014–15, 1017; *Book of Biographies*, pp. 228–30, 426–29, 480–82; for the northern rim, see Wiley and Ruoff, *Biographical and Portrait Cyclopedia*, pp. 244–45, 261–63, 269–74, 339–42, 625–27, 637–38; Munsell, *History of Schuylkill County, Pennsylvania*, pp. R19, R53, 383; Beers, *Schuylkill County*, 1:53–56, 165–68; and Schalck and Henning, *History of Schuylkill County*,

2:243–44. Southern Rim examples can be found in Wiley and Ruoff, *Biographical and Portrait Cyclopedia*, pp. 315–16, 327, 382–84, 389–90, 438–39, 454–55; Beers, *Schuylkill County*, pp. 1:136–37, 161–62, 204–5, 211–12; Munsell, *History of Schuylkill County, Pennsylvania*, pp. 51, 257, 268, 328; and Schalck and Henning, *History of Schuylkill County*, 2:442–43.

11. Bell, *History of Northumberland County*, pp. 896–98; Munsell, *History of Schuylkill County, Pennsylvania*, p. R29.

12. On Masonic Lodge No. 38 F&AM in Tamaqua and other social affiliations, see Munsell, *History of Schuylkill County, Pennsylvania*, pp. 328, R8; Schalck and Henning, *History of Schuylkill County*, 2:48–49, 71–72; Wiley and Ruoff, *Biographical and Portrait Cyclopedia*, pp. 228–29, 251–52, 257–58, 382–84.

13. For examples of outside-controlled coal companies that operated in the region, see R. G. Dun and Company Collection, 124:1 (Green Ridge Improvement Company, Coal Run Improvement Company, and Carbon Run Improvement Company), 94 (Shamokin and Bear Valley Coal Company), 172:164 (Phoenix Coal Company), 216 (Locust Dale Coal Company), 218 (Honey Brooke Coal Company), 220 (New Boston Coal Company), 173:303 (New Philadelphia Mining Company); *Weekly Miners Journal*, 14 November 1879 (Pond Creek Coal Company).

14. For examples, see Bell, *History of Northumberland County*, pp. 869–70, 875, 891, 907–8, 915–16; *Book of Biographies*, pp. 317–18, 426–29; Schalck and Henning, *History of Schuylkill County*, 2:315–16; Munsell, *History of Schuylkill County, Pennsylvania*, pp. 383, R56.

15. Munsell, *History of Schuylkill County, Pennsylvania*, p. R11.

16. For examples of the impact of the economic hard times on the coal-related industries, see R. G. Dun and Company Collection. For Port Carbon, see 172:128 (Tobias Winterstein), 173:319 (Schuylkill Iron Co.), 174:246 (Z. P. Boyer; resided in Pottsville). For Tremont, see 172:179 (Henry Heil); 173:179 (Henry Heil); 172:16, 20, 56, 77 (Carter and Allen), 173:208, 377 (Carter, Allen & Co.), 174:265, 569 (Tamaqua Rolling Mill Co.), 233, 235 (Shoener & Allen), 173:306 (Greenwood Rolling Mill Co.). For Ashland, see 172:140, 200, 215 (J. & M. Garner, Garner & Christian, Ashland Iron Co.); and for Mahanoy City, see 172:147 (J. Wren & Bros.), 173:307 (Lee & Wren), 174:491 (Grant Iron Works), 124:63 (Shamokin Iron Co.). For an example of markets, see R. G. Dun and Company Collection, 172:154, 293 (Charles Atkins), and 173:370 (Charles Atkins).

17. For southern rim occupational changes, N = 175; for southern rim geographic changes, N = 179. For northern rim occupational changes, N = 213; for northern rim geographic changes N = 218. For Northumberland County occupational changes, N = 253; for geographic changes in this county, N = 316.

18. Munsell, *History of Schuylkill County, Pennsylvania*, p. 383; R. G. Dun and Company Collection, 174:491 (Grant Iron Works).

19. Munsell, *History of Schuylkill County, Pennsylvania*, p. 233, R32; Wiley and Ruoff, *Biographical and Portrait Cyclopedia*, pp. 255–56, 341–42, 383, 672.

20. Munsell, *History of Schuylkill County, Pennsylvania*, pp. 51, 174, 328, R38, R55; Wiley and Ruoff, *Biographical and Portrait Cyclopedia*, pp. 226–27, 382–84, 439–40; Schalck and Henning, *History of Schuylkill County*, 2:468–71; Beers, *Schuylkill County*, 1:53–56, 93–94, 135–36; R. G. Dun and Company Collection, 174:569 (Tamaqua Manufacturing Company), 587 (Emmanuel Fry). For additional examples, see R. G.

Dun and Company Collection, 124:201 (Mount Carmel Savings Bank), 172:264 (First National Bank of Tremont), 267 (Ashland Savings Bank, Ashland Banking Company), 269 (Citizens Safe Deposit Bank of Mahanoy City), 294 (First National Bank of Minersville); 174:237 (Miners Banking Company of Shenandoah), 301 (Tamaqua Boot & Shoe Company); *Weekly Miners Journal*, 2 April 1875, 16 January 1877, 28 June 1878.

21. R. G. Dun and Company Collection, 124:49 (May, Audenreid & Company), 64 (William B. Douty & Co.), 78 (W. R. Kutzner & Co.), 92, 100 (S. R. Maganroth), 85, 15 (Valentine Fagley); 172:16, 20, 56 (Carter, Allen & Co.), 377 (Shoener & Allen), 120 (Bright & Co.); 173:208, 277 (Carter, Allen & Co.), 347 (Peter E. Buck); 174:223, 235 (Shoener & Allen), 313, 317 (S. M. Heaton & Co.), 574 (Carter, Allen & Co.), 175:85 (Peter E. Buck); Bell, *History of Northumberland County*, pp. 605, 860–62, 882, 885; Wiley and Ruoff, *Biographical and Portrait Cyclopedia*, pp. 240–41, 483–84, 637–38; *The Reading Railroad* (Philadelphia: Burk & McFetridge, Printers, 1898).

22. Beers, *Schuylkill County*, 1:165–68; *Book of Biographies*, pp. 480–82; Schalck and Henning, *History of Schuylkill County*, 1:243–44; R. G. Dun and Company Collection, 124:86 (S. A. Bergstresser).

23. Bell, *History of Northumberland County*, pp. 894–96; Wiley and Ruoff, *Biographical and Portrait Cyclopedia*, pp. 344–45.

24. *Manufacturing Manuscript Census, Seventh Census of the United States, 1850, Schuylkill County, Pennsylvania* (New Castle, Blythe and Reilly Townships, Shenandoah and Port Carbon), Bell and Howell, MicroPhoto Division, Worcester, Ohio; Wiley and Ruoff, *Biographical and Portrait Cyclopedia*, pp. 211–12, 486–88; Charles Robeson, *The Manufactories and Manufacturers of Pennsylvania of the Nineteenth Century* (Philadelphia: Galaxy Publishing Company, 1875), 104–5, 433–34; *Weekly Miners Journal*, 7 January 1874, 2 April 1875; *Pottsville Daily Republican*, 4 and 7 April 1885.

25. For a description of the mining activities of Pottsville entrepreneurs, see R. G. Dun and Company Collection, All Counties Volume: 350, 355 (Francis W. Hughes); 172:35, 38 (J. J. Conner; left Pottsville around 1870), 77 (P. D. Luther & Bro.), 60 (Milner & Haywood), 85 (Francis W. Hughes), 104 (Jno. Clayton & Enoch McGinnis), 157 (J. J. Conner & Frank Patterson), 232 (Jno. Lewis & Atkins), 236 (H. C. Russell); 173:461 (Theodore Garreston & John E. Wynkoop); 174:386 (Phillips & Sheafer); *Miners Journal*, 6 September 1856, 10 January 1857, 4 January 1868. For a description of the early industry, see William Lawton's series of articles in the *Weekly Miners Journal*, 7 June 1873.

26. R. G. Dun and Company Collection, 172:1, 107 (C. A. & A. M. Seltzer), 79 (Palo Alto Iron Works); 173:463 (Theodore Garreston & John E. Wynkoop); Beers, *Schuylkill County*, 2:110–12; Munsell, *History of Schuylkill County, Pennsylvania*, p. 308–9, 309a; Wiley and Ruoff, *Biographical and Portrait Cyclopedia*, pp. 211–12, 274–75, 453–58, 625–26; Schalck and Henning, *History of Schuylkill County*, 2:428–29; *Pennsylvania Census Records, 1880, Schuylkill County, Manufacturing* (Schuylkill Township), Bell and Howell, MicroPhoto Division, Worcester, Ohio; *Miners Journal*, 19 March 1859.

27. *Pennsylvania Census Records, 1870*, Tamaqua Borough; Wiley and Ruoff, *Biographical and Portrait Cyclopedia*, pp. 477–78; R. G. Dun and Company Collection,

172:20 (Charles, George and William Landefeldt), 439 (Orwigsburg Shoe Manufacturing Company); 174:464, 511, 546 (J. C. Bright & Co.).

28. R. G. Dun and Company Collection, 172:58, 84, 89, 120, 133 (George Bright & Co.), 150, 154 (William Donaldson & Son), 248 (Benjamin Haywood), 347 (Peter E. Buck); *Weekly Miners Journal*, 14 September, 2 November 1877.

29. R. G. Dun and Company Collection, 172:25 (William S. Moorehead), 45 (George Ricketts), 271 (Wadlinger), 232 (Lewis and Atkins), 246 (Schuylkill Iron Co.), 281 (E. A. Phillips & G. Moore); 173:347 (Peter E. Buck), 307 (Lee & Wren), 319 (Schuylkill Iron Co.); 174:491, 498 (Grant Iron Works), 580 (Daniel Focht); Munsell, *History of Schuylkill County, Pennsylvania*, p. 309a; Wiley and Ruoff, *Biographical and Portrait Cyclopedia*, pp. 625–26; *Weekly Miners Journal*, 14 September, 2 November 1877.

30. R. G. Dun and Company Collection, 174:284 (United Fire Association); *Weekly Miners Journal*, 30 March, 31 August, 14 September, and 2 November 1877.

31. R. G. Dun and Company Collection, 172:47 (Daniel Saylor & Sons); 173:439 (Orwigsburg Shoe Manufacturing Co.); 174:236 (Pottsville Bank), 246 (Union Hall Association of Pottsville), 465 (William B. Rudy); *Miners Journal*, 28 November 1857; *Weekly Miners Journal*, 18 January 1873, 15 January, 16 April, 9 August, 29 September 1875, 9 and 16 March 1877, and 6 February 1880.

32. R. G. Dun and Company Collection, 172:57, 157 (J. J. Connor & Frank Patterson), 120 (George Bright & Co.); 173:126 (Repplier & Moodie), 347 (Peter E. Buck); 174:301, 428 (Charles Meck & Daniel Nagle); 493 (Charles Barker); *Weekly Miners Journal*, 28 March, 4 April 1877; Wiley and Ruoff, *Biographical and Portrait Cyclopedia*, pp. 339–40; *Manufacturing Manuscript Census, 1850*, Blythe Township.

33. Munsell, *History of Schuylkill County, Pennsylvania*, pp. R10, R11, 344–45; *Weekly Miners Journal*, 5 September 1873, 17 May, 27 September 1878; *Miners Journal*, 5 December 1857, 6 February 1858, 31 May 1859.

34. Wiley and Ruoff, *Biographical and Portrait Cyclopedia*, pp. 385–86; *Boyd's City Directory of Pottsville, Including Palo Alto, Mount Carbon, and Mechanicsville, 1879–1880*; *Manuscript Census Returns, Ninth Census of the United States, 1870, Schuylkill County, Pennsylvania*, National Archives Microfilm Series, M-563, Rolls 1179, 1180. For other examples of kinship, see Munsell, *History of Schuylkill County, Pennsylvania*, p. R30; and Wiley and Ruoff, *Biographical and Portrait Cyclopedia*, pp. 222–23. See also Beers, *Schuylkill County*, 1:608, and Schalck and Henning, *History of Schuylkill County*, 2:271–72.

35. Beers, *Schuylkill County*, 1:27–29; Munsell, *History of Schuylkill County, Pennsylvania*, pp. 310–11. For another example of this pattern, see also Beers, *Schuylkill County*, 1:64–67; and Wiley and Ruoff, *Biographical and Portrait Cyclopedia*, pp. 298–302.

36. For examples, see Beers, *Schuylkill County*, 1:70–71; Munsell, *History of Schuylkill County, Pennsylvania*, pp. R10–R11, R21; Wiley and Ruoff, *Biographical and Portrait Cyclopedia*, pp. 226–27; Bell, *History of Northumberland County*, pp. 891–94, 926–27, 950–51; *Book of Biographies*, pp. 227–28, 397–98.

37. For mercantile ties, see R. G. Dun and Company Collection, 124:78 (W. R. Kutzner); 172:145 (Charles Meck), 64 (Lippincott and Taylor); 173:364 (Daniel Nagle); and 174:326 (H. Royer).

38. R. G. Dun and Company Collection, 172:28 (Francis W. Hughes); 173:208, 377 (Carter, Allen & Co.), 528 (Thomas H. Hutchinson); 174:722 (David J. Cleary); 175:240 (Kirshler & Fox), 293 (Kopitzsch Soap Co.); *Weekly Miners Journal,* 6 November 1877, 28 June 1878.

39. R. G. Dun and Company Collection, 172:108 (Charles Baber), 151, 412 (George Lauer), 175 (Tyson & Co.); 174:179 (Heber S. Thompson), 337 (James Muir), 392 (William H. Bright), 498 (People's Tea Company), 519 (William D. Baber), 586 (Morris Brothers); 175:91 (Patrick J. Ferguson).

40. For an early history of the mining industry and these ties, see the series of articles by William Lawton, a coal operator active in the 1830s, in *Miners Journal,* 7 June 1873. For an example of these early railroads, see R. G. Dun and Company Collection, 124:1 (Green Ridge Improvement Co., Coal Run Improvement Co., Carbon Run Improvement Co.), 94 (Shamokin & Bear Valley Coal Co.); 172:44 (Lauberry Coal Co.), 148 (Mount Carbon Railroad), 164 (Phoenix Coal Co.), 204 (Greenwood Coal Co.), 210 (Bear Ridge Coal Co.), 216 (Locust Dale Coal Co.), 218 (Honey Brooke Coal Co.), 225 (Locust Mountain Coal & Iron Co., Jonathan Brock), 226 (New Boston Coal Co.), 231 (Hickory Coal Co.); 173:303 (Philadelphia Coal Co.); 174:328 (Girard Mammoth Coal Co.), 385 (New Philadelphia Mining Co.), 476 (Bear Ridge Coal Co.); *Miners Journal,* 18 July 1855; *Weekly Miners Journal,* 14 November 1879.

41. R. G. Dun and Company Collection, 172:226 (L. C. Thompson), 246 (Schuylkill Iron Co.), 282, 288 (Theodore Garreston & John E. Wynkoop); 173:307 (Lee & Wren), 330 (L. C. Thompson), 461 (Theodore Garreston & John E. Wynkoop), 319 (Schuylkill Iron Co.); 174:235 (Mountain City Bank), 257 (William & Jacob Huntzinger), 359 (L. C. Thompson), 485, 531 (George Snyder Iron & Steel Works); 175:18 (L. C. Thompson); *Weekly Miners Journal,* 16 February, 16 and 30 March, 31 August, 14 September, 2 November 1877; *Pottsville Daily Republican,* 17 November 1884.

42. For examples, see R. G. Dun and Company Collection, 172:20 (Charles & George Huntzinger), 106 (Edward Yardley & Son), 120 (A. J. Medlar), 122 (William H. Sheafer), 123 (Rettig & Liebner), 204 (Charles H. Woltjen), 508 (Solomon Foster); 173:387 (J. Weissenger), 421 (Charles Kopitzsch), 436 (Pottsville Iron & Steel Co.), 425, 468 (Morris Rohrheimer), 174:254 (James Focht), 299 (George Shumway), 292 (George Baber), 346 (A. M. Halberstadt), 492, 672 (Jacob Ulmer), 645 (Charles A. Seltzer), 675 (Frank P. Bannon).

43. Munsell, *History of Schuylkill County, Pennsylvania,* pp. 330–31; Wiley and Ruoff, *Biographical and Portrait Cyclopedia,* pp. 163–77; untitled papers on the iron and steel industry, Historical Society of Schuylkill County, Pottsville, Pennsylvania (HSSCO hereafter); Joseph Henry Zerbey, *History of Pottsville and Schuylkill County,* 6 vols. (Pottsville: J. H. Zerbey Newspapers, 1935), 3:1168–69; Robeson, *Manufactories and Manufacturers,* pp. 34, 493–94. For examples of the impact of the depression and PRRCO intrusion, see R. G. Dun and Company Collection, 172:16, 20, 56 (Carter, Allen & Co.), 143 (Port Carbon Iron Works), 200 (Ashland Iron Co.); 173:208, 377 (Carter, Allen & Co.), 306 (Greenwood Rolling Mill Co.); 174:246 (Z. P. Boyer), 265 (Tamaqua Rolling Mill Co.), 233, 235, 377, 574 (Carter, Allen & Co.).

44. R. G. Dun and Company Collection, 172:128 (Tobias Winterstein), 179

(Henry Heil), 124 (Edward Shissler), 227 (Henry Heil), 264 (First National Bank of Tremont), 488 (William A. Gensmere); 173:246 (Z. P. Boyer), 301 (Edward Shissler), 346 (William G. Kear), 347 (Edward Hummel).

45. R. G. Dun and Company Collection, 124:78 (W. R. Kutzner & Co.), 63 (Shamokin Iron Works); 172:206 (William Bright & Co.); 174:237 (Miners Banking Co. of Shenandoah), 722 (David J. Cleary); *Weekly Miners Journal,* 16 January 1877, and 2 April, 23 July 1875, 28 June 1878.

46. Bell, *History of Northumberland County,* pp. 622–25, 659–61, 879–87; Wiley and Ruoff, *Biographical and Portrait Cyclopedia,* pp. 160–77; R. G. Dun and Company Collection, 174:237 (Miners Banking Co. of Shenandoah), 267 (Ashland Savings Bank); *Weekly Miners Journal,* 23 July 1877, 28 June 1878.

47. Examples of members of the elite and their relatives include Edward Patterson; Jacob Huntzinger; George, Benjamin, and Clifford Pomeroy; John M. Wetherill; John Price Wetherill; William Donaldson; John Shippen; Charlemagne Tower: George DeKeim; and George and James Wren. Transient coal operators and merchants included William Kendrick, John McBarron, William Glammyre, C. M. Well, Daniel Dougherty, S. Bowman, and John C. Hughes. Among those with assets of $10,000 to $29,000 were Charles Logan, J. L. Loose, Jacob Kizle, Conrad Goslichell, Wolf Galland, P. P. Eisenbowen, Richard Hurst, Herman Kuhn, Abraham Mussie, Henry Vandusen (laborer), Henry Weber, and Edward Morrison. In this last group, I checked also for persistence of relatives and included these persons only if family was entirely gone. See *Manuscript Census Returns, Ninth Census of the United States, 1870, Schuylkill County, Pennsylvania; Boyd's City Directory of Pottsville Including Palo Alto, Mount Carbon and Mechanicsville, 1879–1880; Directory of Reading, Easton, Pottsville . . . 1860; Gospell's Directory, 1864–65; Boyd's Central Pennsylvania Business Directory and Gazetteer of Reading, Harrisburg, Williamsport, Lancaster, Pottsville, Allentown, Norristown, Lebanon, Pottstown and Over Ninety of the Principal Towns in the Counties of Berks, Chester, Columbia, Dauphin, Lancaster, Lebanon, Lehigh, Lycoming, Northumberland, Montour, Schuylkill on the Line of the Philadelphia & Reading Railroad, Its Branches, Penna. Schuylkill Valley Railroad, etc., 1890* (Reading: W. H. Boyd, 1890); R. G. Dun and Company Collection, 172:13, 82 (H. L. Coke and Nicholas Seitzinger), 96 (George Pomeroy), 147 (James Wren & Brothers), 282 (John E. and Edward W. Wynkoop [John, bankrupt, persists, but Edward is gone by 1879 to 1880], Zaccur P. Boyer), 468 (Morris Rohrheimer), 173:307 (Lee & Wren), 461 (Theodore Garreston & John E. Wynkoop), 174:498 (Grant Iron Works); All Counties Vol.: 351, 355 (Charlemagne Tower).

48. Bureau of the Census, *Sixteenth Census of the United States, 1940, Volume I: Population* (Washington, D.C.: U.S. Government Printing Office, 1941), 921.

49. *Boyd's Shamokin (Pennsylvania) Directory 1930–1931* (Reading: W. H. Boyd Co., Publishers, 1930); Beers, *Schuylkill County,* vols. 1 and 2; Schalck and Henning, *History of Schuylkill County,* vol. 2; Pennsylvania Banking Commission, *Twenty-sixth Annual Report of the Commission of Banking* (Harrisburg: J. L. Kuhn, Printer to the Commonwealth, 1920), 180–85, 840–49; *Manuscript Census Returns, Twelfth Census of the United States, 1900, Schuylkill County, Northumberland County, Pennsylvania;* Archives of the Church of Jesus Christ of Latter-Day Saints, Microfilm, United States Section, Salt Lake City, Utah; *Boyd's Central Pennsylvania Business Directory and Gazetteer of Reading, Harrisburg, Williamsport, Lancaster, Pottsville, Allentown, Norristown, Lebanon, Pottstown and Over Ninety of the Principal Towns in the Counties of*

Berks, Chester, Columbia, Dauphin, Lancaster, Lebanon, Lehigh, Lycoming, Northumberland, Montour, Schuylkill on the Line of the Philadelphia & Reading Railroad, Its Branches, Penna. Schuylkill Valley Railroad, etc., 1890. See also the citation on finance in note 50. I also checked the R. G. Dun and Company records for bankruptcies and business failures. Examples of families who no longer have members in the urban elites of communities outside Pottsvile are Aucker, Becker, Bennett, Bird, Bittenbender, Booth, Boyd, Buck, Carey, Curnow, Derby, Douty, Dreher, Dunkelberger, Erieg, Eicke, Floyd, Fritsch, Fry, Fulton, Gaughan, Gensemere, Gilger, Glick, Gotshall, Graeber, Guss, Harvey, Heim, Hovan, Huber, John, Kase, King, Kutzner, Lawrence, Lieb, Llewellyn, Lyon, McEliece, McGinnis, McGinty, Mahon, Markle, Marr, May, Medler, Oram, Reed, Reilly, Reinhold, Rentz, Rhoads, Richardson, Russell, Schoener, Seiler, Shepp, Shipp, Shuster, Smith, Sollenberg, Spalding, Stager, Wagonseller, Watkins, Wiggan, Wilkinson, Wolf, Wren.

50. Zerbey, History of Pottsville and Schuylkill County, 1:65–69, 82–84, 110–13, 120–22, 141, 150–54, 277, 2:749–50, 746–48, 824–25, and 4:2090, 2098–99, 2106–7, 2197; Pottsville Daily Republican, 1920–22; Pottsville Club Membership Lists, HSSCO; "Minutes of the Famous Pottsville Party," HSSCO; Financing an Empire: History of Banking in Pennsylvania, 4 vols. (Philadelphia: S. J. Clarke's Publishing Co., 1928), 1:13–20, 154, 164, 200, 220–22, 240, 403; Pennsylvania Banking Commission, Twenty-sixth Annual Report of the Commission of Banking, pp. 840–42; Bell, History of Northumberland County; Boyd's City Directory of Pottsville and Surrounding Communities, 1930–1931 (Pottsville: W. H. Boyd and Company).

51. Boyd's City Directory of Pottsville, 1930–1931. Only males were traced for the elite, since family did not play the crucial role it had with the upper class in Wilkes-Barre. Examples of families who no longer had members in the elite (with few exceptions, these families no longer had male heirs in Pottsville) are Alstatt, Bannon, Bartholomew, Beatty, Bright, Campbell, Derr, Dobson, Dougherty, Evans, Fisher, Griscom, Haywood, Heffen, Hoover, Kopitzsch, Lauer, Loeser, Lord, Lucas, Mores, Moreton, Moorhead, Neuser, Newell, Nice, Noble, Parry, Patterson, Pomeroy, Pott, Potts, Price, Ramsey, Robertson, Seitzinger, Shepherd, Shippen, Sparks, Strouse, Stichter, Taylor, Tower, Weaver, Whitney, Wren, and Wynkoop. Examples of families whose members held positions of economic power in the 1920s are Atkins, Kaercher, Luther, Mortimer, Reilly, Ryon, Seltzer, Thompson, Ulmer, and Yuengling.

52. Boyd's City Directory of Pottsville, 1930–1931. R. G. Dun and Company Collection, 174:145 (Arnouse Light Co.), 170 (Keystone Boot & Shoe Co.), 262, 398 (Pottsville Boot & Shoe Manufacturing Co.), 402, 508 (Pottsville Printing & Publishing Co.); 175:364 (Tilt Silk Mill Co.), 260 (John William Hats & Caps), 279, 287, 395 (Standard Shirt Co.), 355 (Pottsville Steam Heat Co.).

Bibliography

SECONDARY SOURCES

Articles and Essays

Alcorn, Richard S. "Leadership and Stability in Mid-Nineteenth-Century America: A Case Study of an Illinois Town." *Journal of American History* 61 (1974): 685–702.

Bade, Klaus J. "German Emigration to the United States and Continental Immigration to Germany in the Late Nineteenth and Early Twentieth Centuries." *Central European History* 13 (1980): 348–77.

Baldwin, Robert. "Export Technology and Development: From Subsistence Level." *Economic Journal* 73 (1963): 80–92.

Barber, Bernard. "Family Status, Local Community Status and Social Stratification: Three Types of Social Ranking." *Pacific Sociological Review* 4 (1961): 463–69.

Barnes, J. A. "Class and Committees in a Norwegian Parish." *Human Relations: Studies toward the Integration of the Social Sciences* 7 (1954): 39–58.

———. "Networks and Political Process." In *Social Networks in Urban Situations: Analysis of Personal Relationships in Central African Towns*. Edited by J. Clyde Mitchell. Manchester: Manchester University Press, 1971.

Berry, Brian J. L. B. "Cities as Systems within Systems of Cities." In *Regional Development and Planning*, edited by John Friedman and William Alonso. Cambridge, Mass.: Harvard University Press, 1969.

Berthoff, Roland. "The Social Order of the Anthracite Region, 1825–1902." *Pennsylvania Magazine of History and Biography* 89 (1965): 261–91.

Binder, Frederick M. "Anthracite Enters the American Home." *Pennsylvania Magazine of History and Biography* 82 (1958): 83–99.

Blumin, Stuart. "The Historical Study of Vertical Mobility." *Historical Methods Newsletter* 1 (1968): 1–13.

————. "Mobility and Change in Antebellum Philadelphia." In *Nineteenth-Century Cities*, edited by Stephan Thernstrom and Richard Sennett. New Haven, Conn.: Yale University Press, 1969.

Borchert, James. "Urban Neighborhood and Community: Informal Group Life, 1850–1970." *Journal of Interdisciplinary History* 11 (1981): 607–31.

Borchert, John R. "American Metropolitan Evolution." *Geographic Review* 48 (1967): 302–32.

Boorstein, Daniel J. "The Businessman as City Booster." In *American Urban History: An Interpretive Reader with Commentaries*, edited by Alexander B. Callow, Jr., 2d ed. New York: Oxford University Press, 1973.

Bowden, Marty J. "Growth of the Central Districts in Large Cities." In *The New Urban History*, edited by Leo Schnore. Princeton, N.J.: Princeton University Press, 1975.

Chandler, Alfred D., Jr. "Anthracite Coal and the Beginnings of the Industrial Revolution in the United States." *Business History Review* 46 (1972): 141–81.

Chandler, Alfred D., Jr., and Galambos, Louis. "The Development of Large-Scale Economic Organizations in Modern America." In *Men and Organizations*, edited by Edwin J. Perkins. New York: G. P. Putnam's Sons, 1977.

Chudacoff, Howard. "A New Look at Ethnic Neighborhoods: Residential Dispersion and the Concept of Visibility in a Medium-Size City." *Journal of American History* 62 (1973): 76–93.

Conzen, Kathleen Neils. "Patterns of Residence in Early Milwaukee." In *The New Urban History*, edited by Leo Schnore. Princeton, N.J.: Princeton University Press, 1975.

Conzen, Michael P. "The Maturing Urban System in the United States, 1840–1910." *Annals, Association of American Geographers* 67 (1977): 88–108.

————. "A Transport Interpretation of the Growth of Urban Regions: An American Example." *Journal of Historical Geography* 1 (1975): 361–82.

Dahms, F. A. "The Evolution of Settlement Systems. A Canadian Example, 1851–1970." *Journal of Urban History* 7 (1981): 169–204.

Davies, Edward J., II. "Class and Power in the Anthracite Region: The Control of Political Leadership in Wilkes-Barre, Pennsylvania, 1845–1885." *Journal of Urban History* 9 (1983): 291–334.

Demerath, N. J. "Religion and Social Class in America." In *Sociology of Religion*, edited by Roland Robertson. Baltimore: Penguin Books, 1969.

Fanelli, A. A. "A Typology of Community Leadership Based on Influence and Interaction within Leadership Subsystems." *Social Forces* 34 (1956): 332–38.

Fenske, Hans. "International Migration: Germany in the Eighteenth Century." *Central European History* 13 (1980): 332–47.

Folsom, Burton W., II. "A Regional Analysis of Urban History: City Building in the Lackawanna Valley during Early Industrialization." *Working Papers from the Regional Economic History Research Center* 2 (1979): 71–100.

Galambos, Louis. "The Emerging Organizational Synthesis in American History." In *Men and Organizations*, edited by Edwin J. Perkins. New York: G. P. Putman's Sons, 1977.

Glazer, Walter S. "Participation and Power: Voluntary Associations and Functional Organization of Cincinnati in 1840." *Historical Methods Newsletter* 5 (1972): 150–68.

Goldhammer, H., and Shils, E. "Types of Power and Status." *American Journal of Sociology* 45 (1939): 171–82.

Gutman, Herbert. "The Reality of the Rags to Riches 'Myth.' " In *Nineteenth-Century Cities*, edited by Stephan Thernstrom and Richard Sennett. New Haven, Conn.: Yale University Press, 1969.

Hall, Peter D. "Marital Selection and Business in Massachusetts Merchant Families." In *The American Family in Social Historical Perspective*, edited by Michael Gordon. New York: St. Martin's Press, 1978.

Hall, VanBeck. "A Fond Farewell to Henry Adams: Ideas Relating Political History to Social Change during the Early National Period." In *The Human Dimension of Nation Making*, edited by James Ruby Martin. Madison: University of Wisconsin Press, 1976.

Harris, P. M. G. "The Social Origins of American Leaders: The Demographic Foundations." *Perspectives in American History* 3 (1969): 159–344.

Hays, Samuel P. "The New Organizational Society." In *Building the Organizational Society: Essays on Associational Activities in Modern America*, edited by Jerry Israel. New York: Free Press, 1972.

————. "New Possibilities for American Political History: The Social Analysis of Political Life." In *Sociology and History: Methods*, edited by Seymour Lipset and Richard Hofstadter. New York: Basic Books, 1968.

Hazeltine, Ralph. "Victor Piollet: Portrait of a Country Politician." *Pennsylvania History* 40 (1973): 1–18.

Hershberg, Theodore; Katz, Michael; Blumin, Stuart; Glasco, Laurence; and Griffen, Clyde. "Occupation and Ethnicity in Five Nineteenth-Century Cities: A Collaborative Inquiry." *Historical Methods Newsletter* 7 (1974): 174–216.

Hopkins, Richard. "Occupational and Geographic Mobility in Atlanta, 1870–1896." *Journal of Southern History* 34 (1968): 200–213.

Hurst, James W. "The Release of Energy." In *New Perspectives on American History*, edited by Stanley N. Katz and Stanley I. Kutler. 2 vols. Boston: Little, Brown and Company, 1968.

Jackson, Kenneth T. "Urban Deconcentration in the Nineteenth Century: A Statistical Inquiry." In *The New Urban History*, edited by Leo Schnore. Princeton, N.J.: Princeton University Press, 1975.

Jaher, Frederic Cople. "Businessmen and Gentlemen: Nathan and Thomas Gold Appleton—An Exploration in Intergenerational History." *Explorations in Entrepreneurial History* 4 (1966): 17–38.

————. "Nineteenth-Century Elites in Boston and New York." *Journal of Social History* 6 (1972): 30–72.

Jensen, Richard. "Quantitative Collective Biography: An Application to Metropolitan Elites." In *Quantification in American History: Theory and Research*, edited by Robert P. Swierenga. New York: Atheneum, 1970.

Katz, Michael. "The Entrepreneurial Class in a Canadian City in the Mid-Nineteenth Century." *Journal of Social History* 8 (1975): 1–29.

Kenyon, James B. "On the Relation between Central Function and Size of Place." *Annals of the Association of American Geographers* 57 (1967): 736–50.

Kutolowski, Kathleen Smith. "The Janus Face of New York's Local Parties: Genesee County, 1821–1827." *New York History* 59 (1978): 145–72.

Lampard, Eric. "American History and the Study of Urbanization." In *American Urban History*, edited by Alexander B. Callow, Jr. New York: Oxford University Press, 1969.

————. "The History of Cities in the Economically Advanced Areas." *Economic Development and Cultural Change* 3 (1955): 81–136.

————. "Urbanization and Social Change: On Broadening the Scope and Relevance of Urban History." In *The Historian and the City*, edited by Oscar Handlin and John Burchard. Cambridge, Mass.: M.I.T. Press, 1961.

Lees, Lynn H., and Modell, John. "The Irish Countrymen Urbanized: A Comparative Perspective on the Famine Migration." *Journal of Urban History* 3 (1977): 391–409.

Lubove, Roy. "Urbanization Process: An Approach to Historical Research." In *American Urban History*, edited by Alexander Callow. New York: Oxford University Press, 1969.

Lurie, Jonathan. "Lawyers, Judges and Legal Changes, 1852–1916: New York as a Test Case Study." *Working Papers from the Regional Economic History Research Center* 3 (1980): 31–57.

McKelvey, Blake. "The Emergence of Industrial Cities." In *American Urban History: An Interpretive Reader with Commentaries*, edited by Alexander B. Callow, Jr., 2d ed. New York: Oxford University Press, 1973.

Miller, D. C. "Industry and Community Power Structure." *American Sociological Review* 23 (1958): 9–15.

Miller, William. "American Historians and the Business Elite." *Journal of Economic History* 9 (1949): 184–208.

Modell, John. "The Peopling of a Working-Class Ward." *Journal of Social History* 5 (1971): 71–95.

Moltman, Guner. "American-German Return Migration in the Nineteenth and Early Twentieth Centuries." *Central European History* 13 (1980): 378–92.

Moore, Barrington. "Historical Note on the Doctors' Work Ethic." *Journal of Social History* 17 (1984): 547–52.

Morawska, Ewa. "The Internal Status Hierarchy in the East European Communities in Johnstown, PA, 1890's–1930's," *Journal of Social History* 16 (1982): 75-108.

Muller, Edward. "Regional Urbanization and the Selective Growth of Towns in North American Regions." *Journal of Historical Geography* 3 (1977): 22–39.

————. "Selective Urban Growth in the Middle Ohio Valley, 1800–1860." *Geographical Review* 66 (1976): 178–99.

Nash, Gary B. "The Philadelphia Bench and Bar, 1800–1861." *Comparative Studies in Society and History* 7 (1965): 203–20.

North, Douglas C. "Locational Theory and Regional Economic Growth." *Journal of Political Economy* 63 (1955): 243–58.

Olmstead, David. "Organizational Leadership and Social Structure in a Small City." *American Sociological Review* 90 (1954): 275–81.

Pellegrin, R. J., and Coates, C. H. "Absentee-Owned Corporations and Community Power Structure." *American Journal of Sociology* 61 (1956): 413–19.

Pessen, Edward. "The Egalitarian Myth and the American Social Reality: Wealth, Mobility and Equality in the 'Era of the Common Man.' " *American Historical Review* 76 (1971): 989–1034.

————. "The Lifestyle of the Antebellum Urban Elite." *Mid-America* 55 (1973): 163–83.

————. "Philip Hone Set: The Social World of the New York City Elite in the 'Age of Egalitarianism.' " *New York Historical Society Quarterly* 56 (1972): 285–308.

————. "The Social Configuration of the Antebellum City: An Historical and Theoretical Inquiry." *Journal of Urban History* 2 (1976): 267–306.

Pope, Liston. "Religion and Class Structure." *Annals of the American Academy of Political and Social Science* 265 (1949): 75–90.

Pred, Allan. "Manufacturing and the American Mercantile City, 1800–1840." *Annals of the American Association of Geographers* 56 (1966): 307–25.

Rosen, Lawrence, and Hall, Robert. "Mate Selection in the Upper Class." *Sociological Quarterly* 7 (1966): 157–96.

Rossi, Peter H. "Power and Community Structure." In *Political Sociology: Selected Essays*, edited by Lewis A. Croser. New York: Harper Torch, 1967.

Rothstein, Morton. "The Antebellum South as a Dual Economy: Tentative Hypothesis." *Agricultural History* 41 (1967): 373–82.

Rothstein, Morton; McSeveny, Samuel; Greven, Phillip; Zemsky, Roger; and Silbey, Joel. "Quantification and American History: An Assessment." In *The State of American History*, edited by Herbert Bass. Chicago: University of Chicago Press, 1970.

Rubin, Julius. "The Limits of Agricultural Progress in the Nineteenth-Century South." *Agricultural History* 49 (1975): 362–73.

————. "Urban Growth and Regional Development." In *The Growth of the Seaport Cities, 1790–1825*, edited by David T. Gilchrist. Charlottesville: University of Virginia Press, 1967.

Rutman, Darret B. "Community Study." *Historical Methods* 13 (1980): 29–41.

Schieber, Harry N. "Government and the Economy: Studies of the 'Commonwealth' Policy in Nineteenth-Century America." *Journal of Interdisciplinary History* 3 (1972): 135–54.

Schulze, Robert V. "The Bifurcation of Power in a City." In *Community Political Systems*, edited by Morris Janowitz. Glencoe, Ill.: Free Press, 1961.

Schumpeter, Joseph A. "The Creative Response in Economic History." *Journal of Economic History* 7 (1959): 149–59.

Sharpless, John B., and Warner, Sam B., Jr. "Urban History." *American Behavioral Scientist* 21 (1977): 221–44.

Singleton, Gregory. "Fundamentalism and Urbanization: A Quantitative Critique of Impressionistic Interpretations." In *The New Urban History*, edited by Leo Schnore. Princeton, N.J.: Princeton University Press, 1975.

Skinner, G. William. "Cities and the Hierarchy of Local Systems." In *The City in Late Imperial China*, edited by G. William Skinner. Stanford, Calif.: Stanford University Press, 1976.

———. "Marketing and Social Structure in Rural China, Part I." *Journal of Asian Studies* 24 (1964): 3–43.

———. "Mobility Strategies in Late Imperial China: A Regional System Analysis." In *Regional Analysis*, edited by Carol Smith. 2 vols. New York: Academic Press, 1976.

Smith, Daniel Scott. "Cyclical, Secular and Structural Change in American Elite Composition." *Perspectives in American History* 4 (1970): 351–74.

Smith, Timothy L. "Religion and Ethnicity in America." *American Historical Review* 83 (1978): 1115–85.

Smolensky, Eugene, and Ratajczak, David. "The Conception of Cities." *Explorations in Entrepreneurial History* 2 (1965): 90–131.

Sotow, James. "The Small City Industrialist, 1900–1950: A Case Study of Norristown, Pennsylvania." *Business History Review* 32 (1958): 102–15.

Stafford, Howard A. J. "The Functional Bases of Small Towns." *Economic Geography* 39 (1963): 165–75.

Still, Bayrd. "Patterns of Mid-Nineteenth-Century Urbanization in the Middle West." In *American Urban History*, edited by Alexander B. Callow, Jr. 2d ed. New York: Oxford University Press, 1973.

Sylla, Richard. "Federal Policy, Banking Market Structure and Capital Mobilization in the United States, 1863–1913." *Journal of Economic History* 29 (1969): 657–86.

———. "Forgotten Men of Money: Private Bankers in Early U.S. History." *Journal of Economic History* 36 (1976): 173–88.

Thernstrom, Stephan, and Knights, Peter. "Men in Motion: Some Data and Speculations about Urban Population in Nineteenth-Century America." *Journal of Interdisciplinary History* 1 (1970): 7–35.

Thompson, Wilbur. "Urban Economic Growth and Development in a National System of Cities." In *The Study of Urbanization*, edited by Philip M. Hauser and Leo F. Schnore. New York: John Wiley & Sons, 1965.

Tiebout, Charles. "Exports and Regional Economic Growth." *Journal of Political Economy* 64 (1965): 160–69.

Tobey, Ronald. "How Urbane Is the Urbanite? An Historical Model of the Urban Hierarchy and Social Motivation of the Service Classes." *Historical Methods Newsletter* 7 (1974): 259–75.

Turner, Ralph H. "Sponsored and Contested Mobility and the School System." *American Sociological Review* 25 (1960): 350–62.

Wade, Richard. "Urban Life in Western America, 1790–1830." In *American Urban History,* edited by Alexander B. Callow, Jr. 2d ed. New York: Oxford University Press, 1973.

Walton, John. "The Vertical Axis of Community Organization and the Structure of Power." In *The Search for Community Power,* edited by Willis D. Hawley and Frederick M. Wirt. Englewood Cliffs, N.J.: Prentice Hall, 1968.

Weiss, Janice. "Educating for Clerical Work: The Nineteenth Century Private Commercial Schools." *Journal of Social History* 12 (1979): 407–20.

Williamson, Jeffrey. "Antebellum Urbanization in the American Northeast." *Journal of Economic History* 25 (1965): 592–608.

Williamson, Jeffrey, and Swanson, J. A. "The Growth of Cities in the American Northeast, 1820–1920." Supplement to *Explorations in Entrepreneurial History* 4 (1966): 3–101.

Books

Alger, Horatio, Jr. *Ragged Dick and Mark, The Match Boy.* New York: Collier Books, 1977.

Aurand, Harold. *From the Molly Maguires to the United Mine Workers.* Philadelphia: Temple University Press, 1971.

Baldwin, Robert. *Economic Development and Growth.* 2d ed. New York: John Wiley & Sons, 1972.

Baltzell, E. Digby. *Philadelphia Gentlemen.* Chicago: Quadrangle Books, 1971.

———. *The Protestant Establishment.* New York: Vintage Books, 1966.

Barber, Bernard. *Social Stratification: A Comparative Analysis of Structure and Process.* New York: Oxford University Press, 1957.

Barton, Josef. *Peasants and Strangers: Italians, Rumanians and Slovaks in an American City, 1890–1950.* Cambridge, Mass.: Harvard University Press, 1975.

Belcher, Wyatt W. *The Economic Rivalry between St. Louis and Chicago, 1850–1880.* New York: Columbia University Press, 1947.

Berry, Brian J. L. B. *Geography of Market Centers and Retail Distribution.* Englewood Cliffs, N.J.: Prentice-Hall, 1967.

Berthoff, Roland T. *British Immigrants in Industrial America, 1790–1950.* Cambridge, Mass.: Harvard University Press, 1953.

———. *An Unsettled People: Social Order and Disorder in American History.* New York: Harper & Row, 1971.

Blouin, Francis. *The Boston Region, 1810–1850: A Study in Urbanization.* Ann Arbor, Mich.: UMI Research, 1980.

Blumin, Stuart. *The Urban Threshold: Growth and Change in a Nineteenth-Century American Community.* Chicago: University of Chicago Press, 1976.

Bogen, Julius I. *The Anthracite Railroads: A Study in American Enterprise.* New York: Ronald Press, 1927.

Bott, Elizabeth. *Family and Social Network.* New York: Free Press, 1971.

Bridenbaugh, Carl. *Cities in Revolt: Urban Life in America, 1743–1776.* New York: Alfred A. Knopf, 1955.

Bridges, Leonard Hal. *Iron Millionaire: The Life of Charlemagne Tower.* Philadelphia: University of Pennsylvania Press, 1952.

Brown, A. Theodore. *Frontier Community: A History of Kansas City to 1870.* Columbia: University of Missouri Press, 1964.

Calhoun, Daniel H. *The American Civil Engineer: Origins and Conflict.* Cambridge, Mass.: M.I.T. Press, 1960.

Calvert, Monte. *The Mechanical Engineer in America, 1830–1910: Professional Cultures in Conflict.* Baltimore: Johns Hopkins Press, 1967.

Chudacoff, Howard. *Mobile Americans: Residential and Social Mobility in Omaha, 1880–1920.* New York: Oxford University Press, 1972.

Clark, Victor S. *History of Manufacturers in the United States.* New York: McGraw-Hill Books, 1929.

Cole, Arthur C. *Business Enterprise in Its Social Setting.* Cambridge, Mass.: Harvard University Press, 1959.

Conzen, Kathleen Neils. *Immigrant Milwaukee, 1836–1860: Accommodation and Community in a Frontier City.* Cambridge: Harvard University Press, 1976.

Cook, Edward M., Jr. *Fathers of the Towns: Leadership and Community in Eighteenth-Century New England.* Baltimore: Johns Hopkins University Press, 1976.

Dahl, Robert. *Who Governs? Democracy and Power in an American City.* New Haven, Conn.: Yale University Press, 1971.

Decker, Peter. *Fortunes and Failures: White-Collar Mobility in Nineteenth-Century San Francisco.* Cambridge, Mass.: Harvard University Press, 1978.

Doherty, Robert. *Society and Power: Five New England Towns, 1800–1860.* Amherst: University of Massachusetts Press, 1977.

Dyos, H. J., ed. *The Study of Urban History.* New York: St. Martin's Press, 1963.

Eavenson, Harold N. *The First Century and a Quarter of American Coal Industry.* Baltimore: Waverly Press, 1942.

Farber, Bernard. *Guardians of Virtue: Salem Families in 1800.* New York: Basic Books, 1972.

———. *Kinship and Class: A Midwestern City.* New York: Basic Books, 1971.

Folsom, Burton W. II. *Urban Capitalists: Entrepreneurs and City Growth in Pennsylvania's Lackawanna and Lehigh Regions, 1800–1920.* Baltimore: Johns Hopkins University Press, 1981.

Freeman, Linton O. *Patterns of Local Community Leadership.* New York: Bobbs-Merrill Co., 1958.

Glabb, Charles, and Brown, A. Theodore. *A History of Urban America.* New York: Macmillan Publishing Co., Inc., 1967.

Goldfield, David R. *Urban Growth in the Age of Sectionalism: Virginia, 1847–1861.* Baton Rouge, La.: Louisiana State University Press, 1966.

Gordon, Milton. *Assimilation in American Life.* New York: Oxford University Press, 1964.

Green, George D. *Finance and Economic Development in the Old South: Louisiana Banking, 1804–1861.* Stanford, Calif.: Stanford University Press, 1972.

Griffen, Clyde, and Griffen, Sally. *Natives and Newcomers: The Ordering of Opportunity in Mid-Nineteenth-Century Poughkeepsie.* Cambridge, Mass.: Harvard University Press, 1978.

Hall, VanBeck. *Politics without Parties: Massachusetts, 1780–1791.* Pittsburgh: University of Pittsburgh Press, 1972.

Hanlon, Edward F. *The Wyoming Valley, An American Portrait.* Woodland, Calif.: Windsor Publications, 1983.

Hare, Jay V. *History of the Reading, Which Appeared as a Serial in the Pilat and Philadelphia and Reading Railway Men, Beginning May 1909—Ending February 1914.* Philadelphia: John H. Strock, 1966.

Hartz, Louis. *Economic Policy and Democratic Thought: Pennsylvania, 1776–1860.* Cambridge, Mass.: Harvard University Press, 1948.

Heilbrun, James. *Urban Economics and Public Policy.* New York: St. Martin's Press, 1974.

Highman, John. *Strangers in the Land: Patterns of American Nativism, 1860–1925.* New York: Atheneum, 1967.

Hoffecker, Carol. *Wilmington, Delaware: Portrait of an Industrial City.* Charlottesville: University of Virginia Press, 1974.

Horowitz, Morton J. *The Transformation of American Law, 1760–1860.* Cambridge, Mass.: Harvard University Press, 1977.

Hunter, Floyd. *Community Power Structure: A Study of Decision Makers.* Chapel Hill: University of North Carolina Press, 1953.

Hurst, James W. *Law and the Social Order in the United States.* Ithaca, N.Y.: Cornell University Press, 1977.

Ingham, John. *The Iron Barons: A Social Analysis of an American Urban Elite, 1874–1965.* Westport, Conn.: Greenwood Press, 1978.

Jaher, Frederic Cople. *The Urban Establishment: Upper Strata in Boston, New York, Charleston, Chicago and Los Angeles.* Chicago: University of Illinois Press, 1982.

James, John A. *Money and Capital Markets in Postbellum America.* Princeton, N.J.: Princeton University Press, 1978.

Jones, Chester Lloyd. *The Economic History of the Anthracite Tidewater Canals.* Philadelphia: John C. Winston Company, 1908.

Jones, Eliot. *The Anthracite Coal Combinations in the United States with Some Accounts of the Early Development of the Anthracite Industry.* Cambridge, Mass.: Harvard University Press, 1914.

Katz, Michael B. *The People of Hamilton, Canada West: Family and Class in a Mid-Nineteenth Century City.* Cambridge, Mass.: Harvard University Press, 1975.

Knights, Peter. *Plain People of Boston, 1830–1860: A Study in City Growth.* New York: Oxford University Press, 1971.

Lemon, James. *The Best Poor Man's Country.* New York: W. W. Norton & Company, 1976.

Lindstrom, Diane. *Economic Development in the Philadelphia Region, 1810–1850.* New York: Columbia University Press, 1978.

McKelvey, Blake. *Rochester, The Flower City: 1854–1890.* Cambridge, Mass.: Harvard University Press, 1949.

McLachan, James. *American Boarding Schools: A Historical Study.* New York: Charles Scribner's Sons, 1970.

Mandelbaum, Seymour. *Boss Tweed's New York.* New York: John Wiley & Sons, 1965.

Miller, Roberta B. *City and Hinterland: A Case Study of Urban Growth and Regional Development.* Westport, Conn.: Greenwood Press, 1979.

Miller, Zane. *Boss Cox's Cincinnati.* New York: Oxford University Press, 1968.

Millis, Walter. *Arms and Men: A Study of American Military History.* New Brunswick, N.J.: Rutgers University Press, 1956.

Mills, C. Wright. *The Power Elite.* New York: Oxford University Press, 1956.

Montgomery, David. *Beyond Equality: Labor and the Radical Republicans, 1862–1872.* New York: Vintage Books, 1967.

Morrill, Richard. *The Spatial Organization of Society.* Belmont, Calif.: Wadsworth Publishing Company, 1966.

Polinak, Louis. *When Coal Was King.* Lebanon, Penn.: Applied Arts Publishers, 1974.

Polsby, Nelson. *Community and Political Theory.* New Haven, Conn.: Yale University Press, 1967.

Powell, H. Benjamin. *Philadelphia's First Fuel Crisis.* University Park, Penn.: Pennsylvania State University Press, 1978.

Pred, Alan. *The Spatial Dynamics of U.S. Urban Industrial Growth, 1800–1914: Interpretive and Theoretical Essays.* Cambridge, Mass.: M.I.T. Press, 1966.

———. *Urban Growth and the Circulation of Information: The United States System of Cities, 1790–1840.* Cambridge, Mass.: Harvard University Press, 1973.

Presthus, Robert. *Men at the Top: A Study in Community Power.* New York: Oxford University Press, 1964.

Ridgeway, Whitman. *Community Leadership in Maryland, 1790–1840.* Chapel Hill: University of North Carolina Press, 1979.

Rubin, Julius. *Canal or Railroad? Imitation in Response to the Erie Canal in Philadelphia, Baltimore and Boston.* Philadelphia: American Philosophical Society, 1961.

Schieber, Harry N. *Ohio Canal Era: A Case Study of the Government and the Economy, 1820–1861.* Athens, Ohio: Ohio State University Press, 1969.

Schlegel, Marvin. *Ruler of the Reading: The Life of Franklin B. Gowen, 1836–1889*. Harrisburg: Pennsylvania Historical and Museum Commission, 1969.

Schnore, Leo F., ed. *The New Urban History*. Princeton, N.J.: Princeton University Press, 1975.

Shank, William H., P. E. *The Amazing Pennsylvania Canals*. York, Penn.: American Canal & Transportation Center, 1973.

Stein, Maurice R. *The Eclipse of Community: An Interpretation of American Studies*. New York: Harper & Row, 1960.

Still, Bayrd. *Milwaukee: The History of a City*. Madison: State Historical Society of Wisconsin, 1948.

Sullivan, William. *The Industrial Worker in Pennsylvania, 1800–1840*. Harrisburg: Pennsylvania Historical and Museum Commission, 1955.

Taylor, George R. *The Transportation Revolution, 1815–1860*. New York: Holt, Rinehart and Winston, 1951.

Thernstrom, Stephan. *Poverty and Progress*. New York: Atheneum, 1970.

———. *The Uncommon Bostonians: Poverty and Progress in the American Metropolis, 1880–1970*. Cambridge, Mass.: Harvard University Press, 1973.

Timberlake, Richard H., Jr. *Money, Banking and Central Banking*. New York: Harper & Row, 1965.

Vidich, Arthur, and Bensman, Joseph. *Small Town in Mass Society: Class, Power and Religion in a Rural Community*. Rev. ed. Princeton, N.J.: Princeton University Press, 1968.

Wade, Richard D. *The Urban Frontier*. Chicago: University of Chicago Press, 1964.

Ward, David. *Cities and Immigrants: A Geography of Change in Nineteenth-Century America*. New York: Oxford University Press, 1971.

Warner, Sam B., Jr. *Streetcar Suburbs: The Process of Urban Growth in Boston, 1870–1900*. Cambridge, Mass.: Harvard University Press, 1962.

Warner, W. Lloyd. *Yankee City*. Abridged ed. New Haven, Conn.: Yale University Press, 1967.

———, ed. *The Emergent American Society*. New Haven: Yale University Press, 1967.

Warner, W. Lloyd, and Lunt, Paul D. *The Social Life of the Modern American Community*. New Haven: Yale University Press, 1941.

Warren, Roland. *The Community in America*. 3d ed. Chicago: Rand McNally, 1978.

Weber, Michael. *Social Change in an Industrial Town*. University Park: Pennsylvania State University Press, 1976.

Wiebe, Robert H. *The Search for Order, 1877–1920*. New York: Hill and Wang, 1967.

Yearly, Clifton K., Jr. *Britons in American Labor*. Baltimore: Johns Hopkins Press, 1957.

———. *Enterprise and Anthracite: Economics and Democracy in Schuylkill County, 1820–1875*. Baltimore: Johns Hopkins Press, 1961.

Unpublished Material

Davies, Edward J., II. "The Urbanizing Region: Leadership and Urban Growth in the Anthracite Regions, 1830–1885." Ph.D. diss., University of Pittsburgh, 1977.

————. "Wilkes-Barre, 1870–1920: The Evolution of Urban Leadership during Industrialization." Unpublished, 1972.

Folsom, Burton W., II. "Urban Networks: The Economic and Social Order of the Lackawanna and Lehigh Valleys during Early Industrialization, 1850–1880." Ph.D. diss., University of Pittsburgh, 1976.

Patton, Spyridon G. "Some Impacts of the Reading Railroad on the Industrialization of Reading, Pa.: 1838–1910." Ph.D. diss., University of Pittsburgh, 1979.

Powell, H. Benjamin. "Coal, Philadelphia and the Schuylkill." Ph.D. diss., Lehigh University, 1968.

————. "Pioneering the Anthracite Industry: The Case of the Smith Coal Company." Unpublished manuscript. History Department, Bloomsburg State College, Bloomsburg, Pennsylvania. Photocopy.

Reid, Robert. "The Professionalization of Public School Teachers: The Chicago Experience." Ph.D. diss., Northwestern University, 1968.

Rubin, Julius. "City and Region in the Economic Growth of the American North and South before the Civil War." Mimeograph. University of Pittsburgh, 1965.

Silag, William. "City, Town and Countryside: Northwest Iowa and the Ecology of Urbanization, 1854–1900." Ph.D. diss., University of Iowa, 1979.

LOCAL HISTORIES AND BIOGRAPHICAL COLLECTIONS

Adolph, H. T. *Industrial Survey of the Wyoming Valley, 1930.* Wilkes-Barre, Pennsylvania: Lockwood Greene Engineers, Inc., 1930.

Allison, Robert. "Early History of Coal Mining and Mining Machinery in Schuylkill County." *Publications of the Schuylkill County Historical Society* 4 (1914): 134-40.

Battle, J. H., ed. *History of Columbia and Montour Counties, Pennsylvania.* Chicago: Brown, Runk and Company, 1887.

Beers, J. H. *Schuylkill County, Pennsylvania.* 2 vols. Chicago: J. H. Beers and Company, 1916.

Bell, Herbert, ed. *History of Northumberland County.* Chicago: Brown, Runk and Company, 1891.

The Biographical Encyclopedia of Pennsylvania of the Nineteenth Century. Philadelphia: Galaxy Publishing Company, 1874.

Bird, S. John. "Early Shamokin." *The Northumberland County Historical Society* 16 (1934): 145–69.

Book of Biographies: Biographical Sketches of Leading Citizens of the Seventeenth

Congressional District, Pennsylvania. Chicago: Biographical Publications Company, 1899.

Bradsby, H. C., ed. *History of Bradford County, Pennsylvania, with Biographical Selections.* Chicago: S. B. Nelson and Company, Publishers, 1891.

———. *History of Luzerne County, Pennsylvania, with Biographical Selections.* 2 vols. Chicago: S. B. Nelson and Company, 1893.

Brewster, William. *History of the Certified Township of Kingston, Pennsylvania, 1769–1927.* Wilkes-Barre: School District of the Borough of Kingston, 1930.

Centennial Anniversary, Orwigsburg, Pennsylvania, 1813–1913. Pottsville, Penn.: Seiders Printers, 1914.

Centennial Committee. *Mahanoy City, Schuylkill County, Pennsylvania, 1863–1963: A History.* Mahanoy City: Centennial Committee, 1963.

Chambers, George, Esq. *Historical Sketch of Pottsville, Schuylkill County, Pa.* Pottsville: Standard Publishing Company, Printer, 1876.

Commemorative Biographical Record of Northeastern Pennsylvania. Chicago: J. H. Beers Co., 1900.

Eastern Pennsylvanians. Philadelphia: Eastern Pennsylvania Biographical Association, 1928.

Edwards, Richard, ed. *Industries of Pennsylvania: Reading, Pottsville, Ashland, Shenandoah, Minersville, Birdsboro, Schuylkill Haven, Mahanoy City.* Philadelphia: Published by author, 1881.

Elliot, Mrs. Ella Zerbey. *Blue Book of Schuylkill County.* Pottsville: Joseph A. Zerbey, Proprietor Publishers, 1916.

———. *Old Schuylkill Tales.* Pottsville: Mrs. Ella Zerbey Elliot, 1907.

French, Samuel L. *Reminiscences of Plymouth, Luzerne County, Pennsylvania.* Plymouth: n.p., 1915.

Genealogical and Biographical Annals of Northumberland County, Pennsylvania. Chicago: J. L. Floyd & Co., 1911.

———. *The Harvey Book.* Wilkes-Barre: E. B. Yordy and Company, Printer, 1899.

Harvey, Oscar J. *A History of Lodge 61.* Wilkes-Barre: Yardley, 1897.

———. *A History of the Miners' National Bank of Wilkes-Barre, Pennsylvania.* Wilkes-Barre: Board of Directors of the Miners' National Bank, 1918.

Harvey, Oscar J., and Smith, Ernest G. *A History of Wilkes-Barre, Luzerne County, Pennsylvania.* 6 vols. Wilkes-Barre: Rader Publishing House, 1909–1930.

Hayden, H. C.; Hand, Alfred; and Jordan, J. W. *Genealogical and Family History of the Wyoming and Lackawanna Valleys.* 2 vols. New York: Lewis Publishing Company, 1906.

Historical and Biographical Annals of Columbia and Montour Counties, Pennsylvania. 2 vols. Chicago: J. H. Beers, 1915.

History Compiled for the First Methodist Episcopal Church, Pottsville, Pennsylvania on the Occasion of Its Centennial Anniversary by Pottsville Evening Republican and Pottsville Morning Paper. Pottsville: Zerbey Newspapers, 1932.

History of Bradford County, Pennsylvania. Philadelphia: L. H. Everts and Company, 1878.

Johnson, Frederick C., comp. *The Historical Record of Wilkes-Barre.* 16 vols. Wilkes-Barre: Wilkes-Barre Record, 1909.

Jordan, John W., ed. *Encyclopedia of Pennsylvania: Biography.* 32 vols. New York: Lewis Historical Publishing Company, 1914–1967.

Kulp, George B. *Families of the Wyoming Valley.* 3 vols. Wilkes-Barre: Wyoming Historical and Geological Society, 1885.

Miller, Rev. Jonathan W. *History of Frackville, Schuylkill County, Pennsylvania.* Frackville: Miners Journal, 1904.

Miner, Charles. *History of Wyoming in a Series of Letters to His Son, John Miner.* Philadelphia: J. Crissy, 1845.

Munsell, W. W., and Company. *A History of Luzerne, Lackawanna and Wyoming Counties, with Illustrations and Biographical Sketches of Some of Their Prominent Men and Pioneers.* New York: W. W. Munsell and Company, 1880.

————, ed. *History of Schuylkill County, Pennsylvania.* New York: W. W. Munsell and Company, 1881.

"Obituaries/Necrology." Proceedings and Collections of the Wyoming Historical and Geological Society. 20 vols. Wilkes-Barre: Wyoming Historical and Geological Society, 1886–1938.

The 175th Anniversary, Schuylkill Haven. Schuylkill Haven, Penn.: Civic Club of Schuylkill Haven, 1925.

Pearce, Stewart. *Annals of Luzerne County.* 2d ed. Philadelphia: J. B. Lippincott and Company, 1866.

Plumb, H. B. *History of Hanover Township Including Nanticoke, Ashley and Sugar Notch and Also a History of Wyoming Valley.* Wilkes-Barre: R. Baller, 1885.

Principal Cities and Towns on the Bloomsburg Division of the Delaware, Lackawanna and Western Railroad. Wilkes-Barre: J. A. Miller and Company, 1889.

Publications of the Historical Society of Schuylkill County. Vols. 1–5. Pottsville: Publisher varies, 1907–1924.

Raddin, George. *The Wilderness and the City: The Story of a Parish.* Wilkes-Barre: St. Stephen's Episcopal Church, 1968.

"Reports." *Proceedings and Collections of the Wyoming Historical and Geological Society* 22 (1938): xii–xv.

Robeson, Charles. *The Manufactories and Manufacturers of Pennsylvania of the Nineteenth Century.* Philadelphia: Galaxy Publishing Company, 1875.

Rockman, Harry. *The Path of Progress: Shenandoah, Pennsylvania Centennial, 1866–1966.* Reading, Penn.: Reading Eagle Press, 1967.

Rupp, Daniel. *History of Northampton, Lehigh, Monroe and Schuylkill Counties.* Harrisburg: Hill Lancaster, Hickock and Cantini, 1845.

Schalck, Adolf W., and Henning, Honorable D. C., eds. *History of Schuylkill County, Pennsylvania.* 2 vols. Harrisburg: State Historical Association, 1907.

Smith, S. R. *Leaders in Thought and Action: An Appreciation.* Wilkes-Barre: S. R. Smith, 1910.

———. *The Wyoming Valley in 1892.* Wilkes-Barre: Scranton Republican, 1892.
———. *The Wyoming Valley in the Nineteenth Century.* Wilkes-Barre: Wilkes-Barre Leader, Printer, 1894.
Stocker, Rhamanthus M. *Centennial History of Susquehanna County, Pennsylvania.* Philadelphia: R. J. Peck and Company, 1887.
Stoddard, Dwight J. *Prominent Men in Scranton and the Vicinity and Wilkes-Barre and the Vicinity.* Scranton, Penn.: Press of the Tribune Publishing Company, 1906.
Sutherland, J. H. *The City of Wilkes-Barre and Vicinity and Their Resources.* Wilkes-Barre: The Wilkes-Barre Leader Publishing House, 1897.
Wiley, Samuel, and Ruoff, Henry. *Biographical and Portrait Cyclopedia of Schuylkill County, Pennsylvania.* Philadelphia: Rush, West & Company, 1893.
Wilkes-Barre: The Diamond City, Its History, Its Industries, 1769–1906. Wilkes-Barre: Rader Publishing House, 1906.
Wilkes-Barre: The Progressive City, 1889. Wilkes-Barre: Enterprise Review, 1890.
Williams, Blair T. *The Michael Shoemaker Book.* Scranton, Penn.: International Textbook Press, 1924.
Wright, Hendrick R. *Historical Sketches of Plymouth, Luzerne County, Pennsylvania.* Philadelphia: T. B. Paterson and Brothers, 1873.
Zerbey, Joseph Henry. *History of Pottsville and Schuylkill County, Pennsylvania.* Pottsville: J. H. Zerbey Newspapers, 1934–1935.

CONTEMPORARY PUBLICATIONS

Annual Reports of the Board of Trade to the Mining Associations of Schuylkill County. Pottsville: n.p., 1833–1875.
"Benjamin Bannan's Annual Compilation of Statistics of the Anthracite Coal Trade." *Miners Journal.* Pottsville: Miners Journal, 1842–1875.
Bowen, Ele. *The Coal Regions of Pennsylvania, Being a General Geological, Historical and Statistical Review of the Anthracite Coal Districts.* Pottsville: Benjamin Bannan, 1848.
———. *The Pictorial Sketch-Book of Pennsylvania.* Philadelphia: W. White Smith, Publisher, 1854.
Daddow, Samuel, and Bannan, Benjamin. *Coal, Iron and Oil or the Practical American Miner.* Philadelphia: J. P. Lippincott and Company, 1866.
Financing an Empire: History of Banking in Pennsylvania. 4 vols. Philadelphia: S. J. Clarke's Publishing Co., 1928.
McGraw Electric Railway Manual, 1912. New York: McGraw Publishing Company, 1913.
Moody, John, ed. *Moody's Manual of Railroad and Corporate Securities.* New York: Poor's Publishing Company, 1918, 1922.
Pennsylvania State Gazetteer and Business Directory. Philadelphia: R. L. Polk and Company, 1833–1884.

Poor, Henry. *Poor's Manual of the Railroads of the United States, 1872–1873*. New York: H. V. and H. W. Poor, 1873.

Poor's and Moody's Manual Consolidated 1923 Industrials Section, vol. 11, K–Z. New York: Poor's Publishing Company, 1923.

Poor's Manual or Register of Directors and Corporation Securities. New York: Poor's Publishing Co., 1922.

Poor's Manual or Register of Public Utilities. New York: Poor's Publishing Company, 1922.

The Reading Railroad. Philadelphia: Burk & McFetridge Printers, 1898.

Report of the President and Managers of the Philadelphia and Reading Railroad Co. to the Stockholders, January, 1877. Philadelphia: Press of Helfenstein, Lewis & Greene, 1877.

Roberts, Peter. *Anthracite Coal Communities*. New York: Macmillan Company, 1904.

———. *Anthracite Coal Industry*. New York: Macmillan Company, 1907.

———. "The Slavs in Anthracite Coal Communities." *Charities and the Commons* (1904): 210–30.

Roberts, William F. *The Everhart Coal Company*. Boston: J. E. Farwell Company, 1864.

The Story of Anthracite. New York: Hudson Coal Company, 1932.

Swank, James. *The History of the Manufacture of Iron in All Ages*. Philadelphia: American Iron and Steel Association, 1892.

———. *Statistical Abstract: A Collection of Statistics Relating to the Iron and Steel Industries of the United States Which is Added . . . the Production and Prices of Anthracite Coal in the United States*. Philadelphia: n.p., 1888.

Taylor, George. *Effects of Incorporated Coal Companies upon the Anthracite Coal Trade of Pennsylvania*. Pottsville: Benjamin Bannan, 1831.

Trego, Charles B. *A Geography of Pennsylvania*. Philadelphia: Edward C. Biddle, 1843.

Virtue, George O. "Anthracite Laborers." *Bulletin of the Bureau of Labor* (1897): 758–75.

Warne, Frank J. "Organized Labor in the Anthracite Coal Fields." *Outlook*, 1902, pp. 4–10.

———. *The Slav Invasion and the Mine Workers*. Philadelphia: J. B. Lippincott, 1904.

Wetherill, J. Price. "An Outline of Anthracite Coal Mining in Schuylkill County, Pennsylvania." *Transactions of the American Institute of Mining Engineers* 5 (1876): 402–22.

GOVERNMENT RECORDS

State and Federal

Pennsylvania. Auditor General. *Annual Reports of the Auditor General of the State of Pennsylvania and of the Tabulations and Declarations from Reports of Railroad and Canal Companies for the Year 1867.* Harrisburg: Singerly and Myers, 1868.

———. *Report of the Auditor General on the Finances of the Commonwealth of Pennsylvania, November 30, 1877.* Harrisburg: Lane S. Hart, 1878.

———. *Report of the Auditor General on the Finances of the Commonwealth of Pennsylvania, 1880.* Harrisburg: Lane S. Hart, State Printer, 1881.

Pennsylvania. Banking Commission. *Pennsylvania Banking Commission Annual Reports, 1874–1904.* Harrisburg: J. L. Kuhn, Printer to the Commonwealth, 1875–1905.

———. *Twenty-Fourth Annual Report of the Commission of Banking.* Harrisburg: J. L. Kuhn, Printer to the Commonwealth, 1918.

Pennsylvania. Board of Commissioners. *Second Geological Survey of Pennsylvania, 1883: Report on the Mining Methods and Appliances Used in the Anthracite Fields,* by H. M. Chance. Harrisburg: 1883.

Pennsylvania. Bureau of Mines. *Reports of the Inspectors of Coal Mines of the Anthracite Coal Regions of Pennsylvania for the Year 1870.* Harrisburg: B. Singerly, State Printer, 1871.

———. *Reports of the Inspectors of Mines of the Anthracite Coal Regions of Pennsylvania, 1880.* Harrisburg: Lane S. Hart, 1881.

Pennsylvania. Bureau of Statistics. *First Annual Report of the Bureau of Statistics of Labor and Agriculture of Pennsylvania for the Years 1872–1873.* Harrisburg: Benjamin Singerly, 1874.

Pennsylvania. Bureau of Statistics and Information. *Report on Productive Industries, Railways, Taxes and Assessments, Waterways and Miscellaneous Statistics of the Commonwealth of Pennsylvania for the Year 1920.* Harrisburg: J. L. Kuhn, Printer, 1921.

Pennsylvania. Department of Labor and Industry. *Second Industrial Directory of Pennsylvania, 1916,* by John Price Jackson, Commissioner. Harrisburg: Wm. Stanley Ray, State Printer, 1916.

Pennsylvania. Department of Mines. *Report of the Department of Mines of Penna.* Harrisburg: J. L. Kuhn, 1919–1920.

Pennsylvania. Legislature. *A Digest of Titles of Corporations Chartered by the Legislature of Pennsylvania Between the Years 1700 and 1866 Inclusive.* Philadelphia: John Campbell Publisher and Bookseller, 1867.

———. *Laws of the General Assembly of the State of Pennsylvania, 1838–1890.* Harrisburg: Publisher varies, 1838–1890.

Pennsylvania. Secretary of Internal Affairs. *Annual Report of the Secretary of Internal Affairs of the Commonwealth of Pennsylvania, Part III: Industrial Statistics, 1872–1873.* Harrisburg: Benjamin Singerly, 1874.

———. *Annual Report of the Secretary of Internal Affairs of the Commonwealth of Pennsylvania, Part III: Industrial Statistics, 1875–1876.* Vol. 4. Harrisburg: B. F. Myers, 1877.

———. *Annual Report of the Secretary of Internal Affairs of the Commonwealth of*

Pennsylvania, Part III: Industrial Statistics, 1878–1879. Vol. 7. Harrisburg: Lane S. Hart, State Printer, 1880.

Pennsylvania. Secretary of Internal Affairs. *Annual Report of the Secretary of Internal Affairs of the Commonwealth of Pennsylvania, Part III: Industrial Statistics, 1878–1880.* Vol. 7. Harrisburg: Lane S. Hart, State Printer, 1881.

————. *Annual Report of the Secretary of Internal Affairs of the Commonwealth of Pennsylvania, Part III: Industrial Statistics, 1881–1882.* Vol. 10. Harrisburg: Lane S. Hart, State Printer and Binder, 1883.

————. *Annual Report of the Secretary of Internal Affairs of the Commonwealth of Pennsylvania, Part III: Industrial Statistics, 1885.* Vol. 8. Harrisburg: E. K. Meyers, State Printer, 1886.

————. *Annual Report of the Secretary of Internal Affairs of the Commonweatlh of Pennsylvania, Part III: Industrial Statistics, 1890–1891.* Vol. 9. Harrisburg: Benjamin Singerly, 1891.

————. *Fourth Industrial Directory of the Commonwealth of Pennsylvania.* Harrisburg: J. L. Kuhn, Printer, 1923.

United States. U.S. Bureau of the Census. *Financial Statistics of Cities Having a Population of over 30,000.* Washington: Goverment Printing Office, 1919.

————. *Fourteenth Census of the United States, Population II.* Washington: U.S. Government Printing Office, 1920.

————. *Fifteenth Census of the United States, Population II.* Washington: Government Printing Office, 1936.

————. *Sixteenth Census of the United States, 1940, Volume T, Population.* Washington: U.S. Government Printing Office, 1941.

United States. U.S. Census Office. *A Compendium of the Ninth Census of the United States, 1870,* by Francis Walker, Superintendent. Washington: Government Printing Office, 1872.

United States. U.S. Census Office. *A Compendium of the Tenth Census: 1880,* by Francis Walker and Charles W. Seaton, Superintendents. Washington: Government Printing Office, 1883.

————. *Ninth Census of Manufacturing: The Statistics of Wealth and Industry of the United States.* Washington: Government Printing Office, 1872.

————. *Population of the United States in 1860,* by Joseph C. G. Kennedy, Superintendent. Washington: Government Printing Office, 1864.

————. *Report on the Manufacturers of the United States at the Tenth Census, 1880.* Washington: Government Printing Office, 1883.

————. *Report on Mineral Industries, 1890,* by Robert Porter, Superintendent. Washington: Government Printing Office, 1892.

————. *Report on the Mining Industries of the United States.* Washington: Government Printing Office, 1886.

————. *Report on the Population of the United States at the Eleventh Census, 1890,* by Robert Porter and Carrol Wright, Superintendents. Washington: Government Printing Office, 1895.

————. *Report on the Social Statistics of Cities.* Edited by George E. Waring, Jr. 2 vols. Washington: Government Printing Office, 1886–87.

————. *Seventh Census of the United States: 1850,* by J. D. B. DeBow, Superintendent of the United States Census. Washington: Robert Armstrong, Public Printer, 1853.

————. *The Statistics of the Population of the United States.* Vol. 1. Washington: Government Printing Office, 1890.

NEWSPAPERS AND ALMANACS

Luzerne Union (Wilkes-Barre, Pennsylvania), 1853–1870.
Miners Journal (Pottsville, Pennsylvania), 1853–1872.
Pottsville (Pennsylvania) *Daily Republican,* 1884–1890.
Republican Farmer and Democratic Journal (Wilkes-Barre, Pennsylvania), 1845–1852.
Weekly Miners' Journal, Pottsville, 1873–1885.
————. Supplement, January to April 1875.
Wilkes-Barre (Pennsylvania) Times Leader, 1919–1978.
Wilkes-Barre (Pennsylvania) Record, 1881, 1885, 1919, 1970.
Wilkes-Barre Record Almanac, 1913. Wilkes-Barre: Wilkes-Barre Record, 1914.
Wilkes-Barre Record Almanac, 1918. Wilkes-Barre: Wilkes-Barre Record, 1919.
Wilkes-Barre Record Almanac, 1920. Wilkes-Barre: Wilkes-Barre Record, 1921.
Wilkes-Barre Record Almanac, 1921. Wilkes-Barre: Wilkes-Barre Record, 1922.
Wilkes-Barre Record Almanac, 1922. Wilkes-Barre: Wilkes-Barre Record, 1923.
Wilkes-Barre Record Almanac, 1923. Wilkes-Barre: Wilkes-Barre Record, 1924.
Wilkes-Barre Record Almanac, 1924. Wilkes-Barre: Wilkes-Barre Record, 1925.
Wilkes-Barre Record Almanac, 1925. Wilkes-Barre: Wilkes-Barre Record, 1926.
Wilkes-Barre Record Almanac, 1926. Wilkes-Barre: Wilkes-Barre Record, 1927.
Wilkes-Barre Record Almanac, 1927. Wilkes-Barre: Wilkes-Barre Record, 1928.
Wilkes-Barre Record Almanac, 1928. Wilkes-Barre: Wilkes-Barre Record, 1929.
Wilkes-Barre Record Almanac, 1929. Wilkes-Barre: Wilkes-Barre Record, 1930.
Wilkes-Barre Record Almanac, 1930. Wilkes-Barre: Wilkes-Barre Record, 1931.
Wilkes-Barre Record Almanac, 1931. Wilkes-Barre: Wilkes-Barre Record, 1932.
Wilkes-Barre Record Almanac, 1932. Wilkes-Barre: Wilkes-Barre Record, 1933.

CITY DIRECTORIES

Boyd's Business Directory and Gazetteer of Reading, Harrisburg, Pottsville, Allentown, Norristown, Lebanon and Over Fifty Principal Towns of the Philadelphia and Reading Railroad and Its Branches, 1879–1880. Pottsville: W. Harry Boyd, 1879.

Boyd's Central Pennsylvania Business Directory and Gazetteer of Reading, Harrisburg, Williamsport, Lancaster, Pottsville, Allentown, Norristown, Lebanon, Pottstown and Over Ninety of the Principal Towns in the Counties of Berks, Chester, Columbia, Dauphin, Lancaster, Lebanon, Lehigh, Lycoming, Northumberland, Montour, Schuylkill on the Line of the Philadelphia and Reading Railroad, Its Branches, Pennsylvania Schuylkill Valley Railroad, etc., 1890. Reading: W. H. Boyd, 1890.

Boyd's City Directory of Pottsville and Surrounding Communities, 1924–1926. Pottsville: W. H. Boyd's Company, 1927.

Boyd's City Directory of Pottsville and Surrounding Communities, 1930–1931. Pottsville: W. H. Boyd's Company, 1931.

Boyd's City Directory of Pottsville, Ashland and Mechanicsville, 1870–1871. Pottsville: William H. Boyd and Company, 1871.

Boyd's City Directory of Pottsville, Ashland and Tamaqua, 1883–1884. Pottsville: William H. Boyd and Company, 1884.

Boyd's City Directory of Pottsville, Including Palo Alto, Mount Carbon and Mechanicsville, 1867–1868. Pottsville: William H. Boyd and Company, 1868.

Boyd's City Directory of Pottsville, Including Palo Alto, Mount Carbon and Mechanicsville, 1879–1880. Pottsville: W. H. Boyd and Company, 1880.

Boyd's City Directory for Wilkes-Barre, Hazleton, Scranton and Surrounding Communities, 1873. Wilkes-Barre: William H. Boyd, 1873.

Boyd's Shamokin (Pennsylvania) Directory 1930–1931. Reading: W. H. Boyd Co., Publishers, 1930.

Boyd's City Directory of Wilkes-Barre, Hazleton, Scranton and Surrounding Communities, 1871–1872. Wilkes-Barre: Andrew Boyd and W. Harry Boyd.

Boyd's Wilkes-Barre City Directory, 1880–1882, Containing the Names of the Citizens together with a Business Directory of Ashley, Carbondale, Hazleton, Kingston, Pittston, Plymouth, Scranton and White Haven. Wilkes-Barre: Boyd's Cousins, 1880.

Business Directory of Luzerne County. Wilkes-Barre: American Directory and Publishing Company, 1894.

Directory of Pittston and West Pittston, Pleasant Valley, Hughestown, Exeter and Their Suburbs, 1888. Pittston: T. P. Robinson, 1888.

Directory of Reading, Easton, Pottsville, Allentown and Lebanon, Together with a Business Directory and a Large List of Farmers of the Counties of Berks, Lebanon, Northampton and Schuylkill for 1860. Philadelphia: William H. Boyd and Company, 1860.

Gospell's Directory of Reading, Allentown, Easton, Pottsville and Bethlehem, 1864–1865. Lancaster: James Gospell, Publisher, Printed by S. A. Wylie, 1864.

Polk's Pittston Directory, 1923–1924. Pittston: R. L. Polk & Co., 1924.

Wilkes-Barre City Directory, 1922. Wilkes-Barre: R. L. Polk & Co., 1922.

Wilkes-Barre City Directory, 1927. Wilkes-Barre: R. L. Polk & Co., 1927.

Wilkes-Barre, Pittston Directory for 1879–80 Containing the Names of the Inhabitants of Wilkes-Barre, Pittston and a Business Directory of Ashley, Kingston, Nanticoke, Parsons, Plains, Plymouth and Wyoming, 1879. Wilkes-Barre: Lant & Company, 1879.

INTERVIEWS

Hazeltine, Ralph. Interviews with author. Wilkes-Barre, Pennsylvania, 20 March 1972, 25 August 1976, 20 October 1972. Mr. Hazeltine formerly directed the Wyoming Historical and Geological Society.

Rix, Reginald. Interview with author. Pottsville, Pennsylvania, 18 June 1974. Mr. Rix formerly directed the Historical Society of Schuylkill County.

MANUSCRIPTS: PUBLIC AND PRIVATE

Private

Anniversary Dinner Invitation of the Pottsville Fishing Club, 1833 and 1885. Historical Society of Schuylkill County, Pottsville, Pennsylvania.

Death Register. First Presbyterian Church, Wilkes-Barre, Pennsylvania.

Death Register. Forty-Fort Cemetery, Forty-Fort, Pennsylvania.

Death Register. Hollenback Cemetery, Wilkes-Barre, Pennsylvania.

Death Register. Register of Wills Office, Luzerne County Courthouse, Wilkes-Barre, Pennsylvania.

Death Register. St. Stephen's Episcopal Church, Wilkes-Barre, Pennsylvania.

Estate Inventories, 1919–1967. Register of Wills. Luzerne County Courthouse, Luzerne County, Wilkes-Barre, Pennsylvania.

Hollenback, George. Papers. Wyoming Historical and Geological Society, Wilkes-Barre, Pennsylvania.

Journal of the Dundee Coal Company. Wyoming Historical and Geological Society, Wilkes-Barre, Pennsylvania.

Lehigh-Wilkes-Barre Coal Company. Papers. Wyoming Historical and Geological Society, Wilkes-Barre, Pennsylvania.

Map Collection. Wyoming Historical and Geological Society, Wilkes-Barre, Pennsylvania.

Miner Papers. Wyoming Historical and Geological Society, Wilkes-Barre, Pennsylvania.

Miners Journal. Pottsville, Schuylkill County, Pennsylvania. Marriages, Deaths, Burials, Obituaries, 1829–1865. Microfilm Archives of the Church of Jesus Christ of Latter-Day Saints, American Section, Salt Lake City, Utah.

Minute Book of the Famous Pottsville Party. Historical Society of Schuylkill County, Pottsville, Pennsylvania.

Minutes of the Sessions of the Presbyterian Church. First Presbyterian Church of Pottsville, 1834–1927. 2 vols. Philadelphia: Presbyterian Book of Publications. Microfilm Archives of the Church of Jesus Christ of Latter-Day Saints, American Section, Salt Lake City, Utah.

Minutes of the Sessions of the Presbyterian Church. First Presbyterian Church of Port Carbon, 1834–1927. 2 vols. Philadelphia: Presbyterian Book of Publications. Microfilm Archives of the Church of Jesus Christ of Latter-Day Saints, Salt Lake City, Utah.

Pamphlet 1883 from the Miners Journal Book and Job Office. Historical Society of Schuylkill County, Pottsville, Pennsylvania.

Parry, Edwin O. Papers. Historical Society of Schuylkill County, Pottsville, Pennsylvania.

"People of Importance." Historical Society of Schuylkill County, Pottsville, Pennsylvania.

Phillips, Edward. "History of the Wyoming Valley." 10 vols. Wyoming Historical and Geological Society, Wilkes-Barre, Pennsylvania.

Pottsville Club Records. Historical Society of Schuylkill County, Pottsville, Pennsylvania.

R. G. Dun and Company Collection, 1845–1894. Manuscript Division, Baker Library, Harvard University, All Counties Volumes, Schuylkill, Northumberland, Luzerne, Volumes 91–100, 172–176, 124–126.

Untitled Manuscript Papers on the Anthracite Industry. Historical Society of Schuylkill County, Pottsville, Pennsylvania.

Untitled Papers on the Iron and Steel Industry. Historical Society of Schuylkill County, Pottsville, Pennsylvania.

Untitled Papers on Philadelphia and Reading Railroad Company. Historical Society of Schuylkill County, Pottsville, Pennsylvania.

Untitled Papers on the Railroads in Schuylkill County. Historical Society of Schuylkill County, Pottsville, Pennsylvania.

Westmoreland Club. Westmoreland Club, 59 South Franklin Street, Wilkes-Barre, Pennsylvania, 1984.

Westmoreland Club Records, 1896–1927. Wyoming Historical and Geological Society, Wilkes-Barre, Pennsylvania.

Wilkes-Barre City Tax Records, 1910–1950. Wilkes College Special Collections, Wilkes-Barre, Pennsylvania.

Wilkes-Barre Street Railway Collection, 1865–1927. Wilkes College Library, Wilkes-Barre, Pennsylvania.

Will and Probate Records. Will Books A–K, 1790–1885. Luzerne County Courthouse, Wilkes-Barre, Pennsylvania.

Will Books, 1886–1913. 12 vols. Register and Recorder, Northumberland County Courthouse, Sunbury, Pennsylvania. Microfilm Archives of the Church of Jesus Christ of Latter-Day Saints, American Section, Salt Lake City, Utah.

Woodward, Stanley. Correspondence. Triton House Company, 1849–1851. Wyoming Historical and Geological Society, Wilkes-Barre, Pennsylvania.

Wright, George R. Diaries, 1874–1930. Wyoming Historical and Geological Society, Wilkes-Barre, Pennsylvania.

Wyoming Athenaeum Records. 2 vols. Wyoming Historical and Geological Society, Wilkes-Barre, Pennsylvania.

Public

Manuscript Census Returns, Seventh Census of the United States, 1850.

Bradford County, Columbia County, Wyoming County, Luzerne County, Pennsylvania. National Archives Microfilm Series, M-432, Rolls 757, 769, 793, 794, 838.

Schuylkill County, Pennsylvania. National Archives Microfilm Series, M-432, Rolls 826, 827.

Manuscript Census Returns, Eighth Census of the United States, 1860.

Bradford County, Columbia County, Wyoming County, Luzerne County, Pennsylvania. National Archives Microfilm Series, M-650, Rolls 1133, 1135; and M-653, Rolls 1079, 1197.

Schuylkill County, Pennsylvania. National Archives Microfilm Series, M-653, Rolls 1179, 1180.

Manuscript Census Returns, Ninth Census of the United States, 1870.

Bradford County, Columbia County, Wyoming County, Luzerne County, Pennsylvania. National Archives Microfilm Series, M-593, Rolls 1329, 1365, 1366, 1367.

Schuylkill County, Pennsylvania. National Archives Microfilm Series, M-593, Rolls 1447, 1448, 1449.

Northumberland County, Pennsylvania. National Archives Microfilm Series, M-562, Roll 1384; and M-563, Roll 1385.

Manuscript Census Returns, Twelfth Census of the United States, 1900, Schuylkill County and Northumberland County, Pennsylvania. Microfilm Archives of the Church of Jesus Christ of Latter-Day Saints, United States Section, Salt Lake City, Utah.

Pennsylvania Census Records, 1850, 1860, 1870, 1880.

Luzerne, Northumberland, and Schuylkill Counties, Manufacturing. MicroPhoto Division, Bell and Howell, Wooster, Ohio.

Index

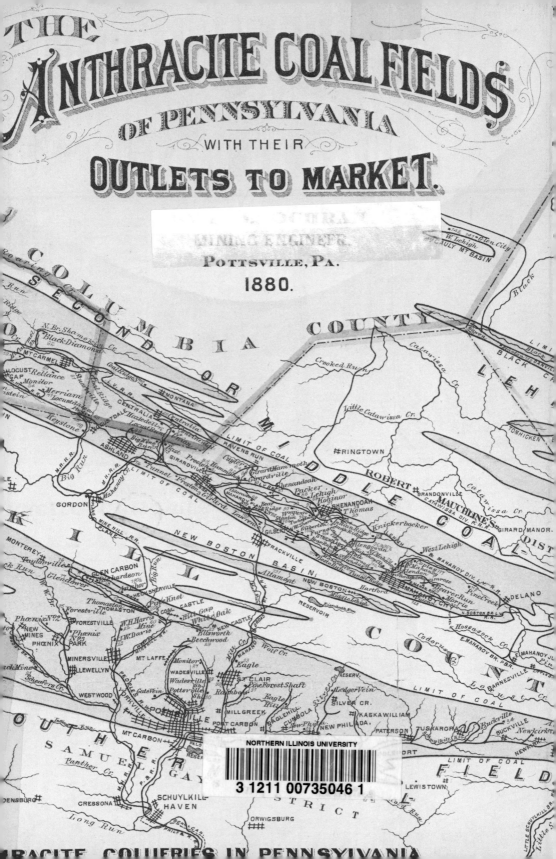

THE ANTHRACITE COAL FIELDS
OF PENNSYLVANIA
WITH THEIR
OUTLETS TO MARKET.

MINING ENGINEER.

POTTSVILLE, PA.

1880.